# ECONOMICS WORKBOOK

## Sixth Edition

## Peter Smith

Senior Lecturer in Economics
University of Southampton

## David Begg

Professor of Economics
Birkbeck College
University of London

**The McGraw-Hill Companies**

**London** • New York • Burr Ridge, IL • St Louis • San Francisco • Auckland •
Bogotá • Caracas • Lisbon • Madrid • Mexico • Milan • Montreal • New Delhi •
Panama • Paris • San Juan • São Paulo • Singapore • Sydney • Tokyo • Toronto

Published by

McGraw-Hill Publishing Company Europe
Shoppenhangers Road, Maidenhead, Berkshire, SL6 2QL, England
Telephone 01628 502500    Facsimile 01628 770224

---

*For Ashley and Eliot*

**British Library Cataloguing in Publication Data**

A catalogue record for this book is available from the British Library.

1 2 3 4 5 CUP 5 4 3 2 1 0

Printed and bound in Great Britain by Latimer Trend & Company Limited, Plymouth

ISBN 0 07 709614 2

# ECONOMICS WORKBOOK

## Sixth Edition

WITHDRAWN

# Contents

# Preface

Economics is not an armchair subject. The sixth edition of *ECONOMICS* by David Begg, Stanley Fischer and Rudiger Dornbusch provides a vibrant and comprehensive introduction to the principles of economics, but you will only confirm your insight of the subject by approaching it in an active way, by thinking about economic issues and by working through practical illustrations. *ECONOMICS WORKBOOK* provides a series of exercises and triggers for your thought that will supplement and guide your study of what we believe to be the most fascinating and challenging subject that you could choose to study.

The opening section of each chapter echoes the **Learning Outcomes** that head each corresponding chapter in *ECONOMICS* (the 'main text').

**IN THIS CHAPTER** highlights the key ideas and pieces of analysis introduced.

**Important Concepts and Technical Terms** provides a valuable check-list of key definitions, helping you to think carefully about important ideas and pieces of economic jargon. Many of the definitions echo the wording of the main text.

The **Exercises** put economics into action in a variety of carefully designed formats, whenever possible using 'real-world' data and allowing you to carry out economic analysis of many day-to-day issues.

Ready revision is facilitated by the **True/False** section, which includes commentary on many common fallacies of economic life.

**Economics in the News** uses up-to-date topical extracts from the media to show how economics can be applied to events happening around us in the real world.

**Questions for Thought** provides topics for further discussion – whether on your own or with your fellow-students. Some of the exercises in this section extend the concepts of the chapter and introduce new ideas and applications.

A vital part of *ECONOMICS WORKBOOK* is the **Answers and Comments** section, with its emphasis on clear explanations of answers, especially in areas where students often encounter difficulty. In many cases, you may find it helpful to tackle the questions step by step with the commentary, which is designed as a learning experience. Where appropriate the answers will refer you to relevant sections in the main text. You will notice that frequent reference in the Answers is made to the magazine *Economic Review* (which is edited by Peter Smith). More information about this will be found on the world-wide web at http://www.soton.ac.uk/~peters/er.

# 1 Economics and the Economy

## Learning Outcomes

- To show that economics is the study of how society resolves the problem of scarcity
- To consider different mechanisms through which society decides what, how and for whom to produce
- To discuss strengths and weaknesses of using the market to allocate and distribute scarce resources
- To develop the concept of opportunity cost
- To distinguish positive and normative economics
- To illustrate the different simplifications made in microeconomics and macroeconomics

**IN THIS CHAPTER** ... you will meet some fundamental concepts in economics, and get some glimpses of the way ahead. Much of economic analysis is driven by the existence of *scarcity* and the investigation of three questions that face any society – *what* goods and services to produce, *how* these goods and services are to be produced, and *for whom*. The decisions associated with these questions are taken in different ways in different societies. In a *market economy*, prices play a key role in guiding the way in which resources are allocated; in a *command economy*, central direction dictates the answers to the three questions. In reality, examples of neither extreme exist, and economic issues are determined by the interaction of private and governmental decisions within a so-called *mixed economy*. In this chapter, you will find out about these ideas, and will also encounter the notion of *opportunity cost* and the *production possibility frontier*. When a society allocates its resources efficiently, it will produce at a point on the production possibility frontier, but there may be circumstances in which resources are not fully utilised, leaving the society at a point *within* the frontier. The distinctions between *positive* and *normative* statements, and between *microeconomics* and *macroeconomics* will also be introduced. The difference between 'micro' and 'macro' is mainly one of focus: the way of thinking and modes of analysis have much in common, and you should try to avoid thinking of them as separate subjects. None the less, it is convenient to tackle them one at a time.

## Important Concepts and Technical Terms

Match each lettered concept with the appropriate numbered phrase:

| | | |
|---|---|---|
| *(a)* Scarce resource | *(e)* Positive economics | *(i)* Macroeconomics |
| *(b)* Law of diminishing returns | *(f)* Microeconomics | *(j)* Mixed economy |
| *(c)* Gross domestic product | *(g)* Production possibility frontier | *(k)* Normative economics |
| *(d)* Distribution of income | *(h)* Opportunity cost | *(l)* Command economy |

1  The branch of economics offering a detailed treatment of individual decisions about particular commodities.
2  Economic statements offering prescriptions or recommendations based on personal value judgements.
3  An economy in which the government and private sector interact in solving economic problems.
4  The way in which income (in a country or in the world) is divided between different groups or individuals.
5  The quantity of other goods that must be sacrificed in order to obtain another unit of a particular good.
6  A resource for which the demand at a zero price would exceed the available supply.
7  The branch of economics emphasizing the interactions in the economy as a whole.
8  The value of all goods and services produced in the economy in a given period such as a year.
9  A curve which shows, for each level of the output of one good, the maximum amount of the other good that can be produced.
10  The situation in which, as more workers are employed in an industry, each additional worker adds less to total industry output than the previous additional worker added.
11  A society where the government makes all decisions about production and consumption.
12  Economic statements dealing with objective or scientific explanations of the working of the economy.

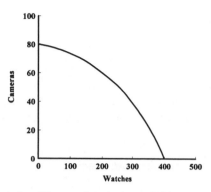

**Figure 1-1   The production possibility frontier**

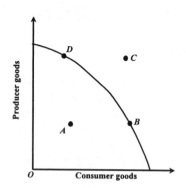

**Figure 1-2   Production possibility frontier for an economy**

## Exercises

1   A tribe living on a tropical island includes five workers whose time is devoted either to gathering coconuts or to collecting turtle eggs. Regardless of how many other workers are engaged in the same occupation, a worker may gather either 20 coconuts or 10 turtle eggs in a day.
   *(a)* Draw the production possibility frontier for coconuts and turtle eggs.
   *(b)* Suppose that a new climbing technique is invented making the harvesting of coconuts easier. Each worker can now gather 28 coconuts in a day. Draw the new production possibility frontier.

2   Figure 1-1 shows a society's production possibility frontier for cameras and watches.
   *(a)* Identify each of the following combinations of the two goods as either efficient, inefficient, or unattainable:
       *(i)*   60 cameras and 200 watches.
       *(ii)*  60 watches and 80 cameras.
       *(iii)* 300 watches and 35 cameras.
       *(iv)*  300 watches and 40 cameras.
       *(v)*   58 cameras and 250 watches.
   *(b)* Suppose the society is producing 300 watches and 40 cameras, but wishes to produce an additional 20 cameras. How much output of watches must be sacrificed to enable these cameras to be made?
   *(c)* How much output of watches would need to be given up for a further 20 cameras (80 in all) to be produced?
   *(d)* Explain the difference in the shape of the frontier in Figure 1-1 as compared with the ones you drew in exercise 1.

3   Figure 1-2 illustrates a production possibility frontier for an economy.
   Associate each of the points *(A, B, C, D)* marked on Figure 1-2 with one of the following statements:
   *(a)* A combination of goods which cannot be produced by the society given its current availability of resources and state of technology.
   *(b)* The combination of goods produced by an economy with full employment which wishes to devote its resources mainly to the production of investment goods.
   *(c)* A combination of goods produced by an economy in recession.
   *(d)* The combination of goods produced by an economy with full employment which wishes to devote its resources mainly to the production of goods for consumption.

4   Which of the following statements are *normative,* and which are *positive?*
   *(a)* The price of oil more than tripled between 1973 and 1974.
   *(b)* In the late 1990s, the poor countries of the world received less than their fair share of world income.
   *(c)* The world distribution of income is too unjust, with poor countries having 35 per cent of the world's population, but receiving only 2 per cent of world income.
   *(d)* Since the 1970s, inflation has fallen in most Western economies, but the unemployment rate has increased.
   *(e)* The UK government ought to introduce policies to reduce the unemployment rate.

*(f)* Smoking is antisocial and should be discouraged.
*(g)* The imposition of higher taxes on tobacco will discourage smoking.
*(h)* The economy of the USA is closer to a free market system than that of Cuba.

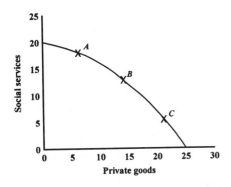

**Figure 1-3    Society's choice between social services and private goods**

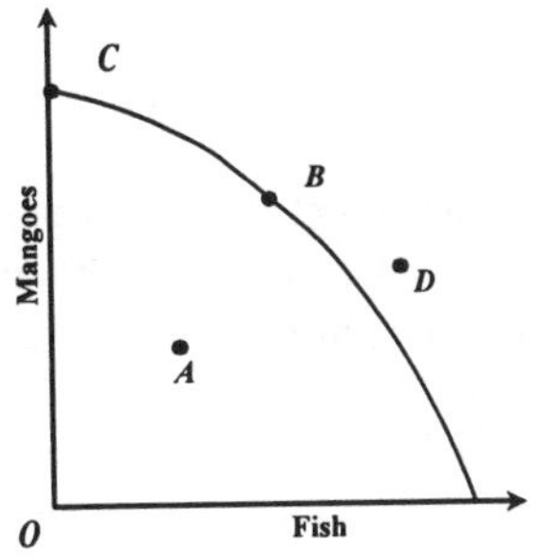

**Figure 1-4    Fish or mangoes?**

5    Which of the following statements are the concern of microeconomics and which of macroeconomics?
   *(a)* Along with other Western economies, the UK faced a sharp rise in unemployment in the early 1980s.
   *(b)* The imposition of higher taxes on tobacco will discourage smoking.
   *(c)* Unemployment among building labourers rose sharply in the early 1980s.
   *(d)* An increase in a society's aggregate income is likely to be reflected in higher consumer spending.
   *(e)* A worker who has received a pay rise is likely to buy more luxury goods.
   *(f)* A firm will invest in a machine if the expected rate of return is sufficiently high.
   *(g)* High interest rates in an economy may be expected to discourage aggregate investment.
   *(h)* The level of gross domestic product in the UK is higher this year than in 1991.

6    Figure 1-3 shows society's choice between social services and private goods, in the form of a production possibility frontier. The three points *A*, *B*, and *C* represent economies in which the government plays a more or less active role. Match each of the points with the most appropriate of the following descriptions of hypothetical economies:
   *(a)* An economy in which the government intervenes as little as possible, providing only the minimum necessary amounts of essential services.
   *(b)* An economy in which the government takes a great deal of responsibility, taxing at a high level and providing considerable social services.
   *(c)* An economy in which the government provides more than the minimum necessary amounts of social services, but leaves room for a buoyant private sector.

7    A jungle tribe catches fish and gathers mangoes. The tribe's production possibility frontier for these two goods is shown in Figure 1-4. Which of the following bundles of the goods can be reached with present resources?
   *(a)* Only *A*.
   *(b)* Only *B*.
   *(c)* Only *A* and *B*.
   *(d)* Only *A*, *B*, and *C*.
   *(e)* Only *D*.

8   Which of the following statements would *not* be true for a pure 'command economy'?
   *(a)* Firms choose how much labour to employ.
   *(b)* The distribution of income is government controlled.
   *(c)* The government decides what should be produced.
   *(d)* Production techniques are not determined by firms.
   *(e)* A government planning office decides what will be produced, how it will be produced, and for whom it will be produced.

## True/False

1   Economics is about human behaviour, so cannot be a science.
2   The oil price shocks of 1973–74 and 1979–80 had no effect on what was produced in the UK.
3   An expansion of an economy's capacity to produce would be reflected in an 'outwards' movement of the production possibility frontier.
4   An economy in which there is unemployment is not producing on the production possibility frontier.
5   Adam Smith argued that individuals pursuing their self-interest would be led 'as by an invisible hand' to do things that are in the interests of society as a whole.
6   China is an example of a command economy in which private markets play no part.
7   The government should subsidize the health bills of the aged.
8   Gross domestic product is the value of all goods produced in the economy during a period.
9   Many propositions in positive economics would command widespread agreement among professional economists.

## ECONOMICS IN THE NEWS

### A bridge too far?
*(adapted from the Financial Times, 24 May 1997)*

Back in the 1980s the Scottish Office had a dream: to get 500,000 vehicles a year over the sea to Skye by a privately financed road bridge rather than via the ferries which plied the stormy beauty of the Kyle of Lochalsh route.

It organized a design competition, sought private finance and by 1995 had 'clearly achieved' its primary objective, the National Audit Office said this week.

Yet the most remarkable point to emerge from the NAO's first full study of a PFI project is that the most critical question of all about any private finance deal – is it genuinely good value to the public purse? – is one the Audit Office has found itself unable to answer.

The reason is that the Scottish Office failed to compare the new crossing with the realistic alternative: sticking with the ferries. Comparing the PFI bridge with a publicly funded one would not provide the answer, because it was clear that without a privately financed bridge, there would have been no bridge at all – certainly well into the next century, if ever.

In future, the NAO concluded, departments should compare their proposed PFI deals to the real alternatives, not a theoretical publicly funded option.

The NAO's report shows that the £24m bridge will in total cost users and taxpayers £39m – plus the loss of £1m a year in operating surplus generated by the nationalized ferries which it replaced.

There have, however, been clear benefits. Save for some lorries, tolls are lower in real terms than the previous ferry fares. Journey times are shorter. Congestion has been reduced. Reliability in bad weather is far better. And when Skye Bridge has collected its £23.6m in discounted revenues – in some 14 to 18 years' time on present trends – tolling will cease.

The NAO found, however, that because the Scottish Office failed to compare building the bridge to running the ferries and continuing to improve them and their berthing facilities as the need arose, while offsetting those costs against the operating surplus that Caledonian MacBrayne made on the route – it is not possible to say whether the bridge is good value or not.

1    Identify the benefits expected from this new bridge.
2    What are the key elements of costs?
3    In what sense is opportunity cost important for this sort of decision, in which the benefits and costs must be weighed against each other?

## Questions for Thought

1    We have seen that economics is concerned with three fundamental questions: *what* is produced, *how* it is produced, and *for whom* it is produced. For each of the following economic events, think about which of the three fundamental questions are of relevance:
   (a)  The discovery of substantial reserves of natural gas in a readily accessible site.
   (b)  A change in the structure of income tax, such that income is redistributed from 'rich' to 'poor'.
   (c)  The privatization of a major industry.
   (d)  The invention of the microcomputer.
   (e)  An increase in the price of imported goods.
2    An economy can choose between producing goods to be consumed now and producing *investment goods* which have an effect on the future productive capacity of the economy. Figure 1-5 illustrates the production possibility frontier between the two sorts of goods.
   (a)  For this economy, what can we say about the position of the frontier in subsequent periods?
   (b)  How is your answer to (a) affected by the particular choice point selected in a given period?
3    Table 1-1 presents data on the sectoral structure of national output in four countries. Examine the changing structure of production in each of the countries in Table 1-1. What stage of industrialization has each country reached?

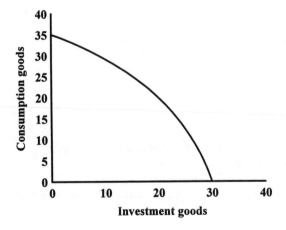

**Figure 1-5    The choice between consumption and investment goods**

**Table 1-1    The structure of production**
(Distribution of GDP (%))

| Country | | Agriculture | Industry | Services |
|---|---|---|---|---|
| A | 1965 | 52 | 13 | 35 |
|   | 1997 | 44 | 17 | 39 |
| B | 1965 | 51 | 13 | 36 |
|   | 1997 | 16 | 42 | 41 |
| C | 1965 | 38 | 25 | 37 |
|   | 1997 | 6 | 43 | 51 |
| D | 1965 | 10 | 44 | 46 |
|   | 1997 | 2 | 38 | 60 |

Source: *World Development Report 1998/99.*

# 2   The Tools of Economic Analysis

## Learning Outcomes

- To explain why theories are deliberate simplifications of reality
- To distinguish time-series and cross-section data
- To show how to construct index numbers
- To distinguish nominal and real variables
- To explain how to build a simple theoretical model
- To show how to plot data and interpret scatter diagrams
- To examine how 'other things equal' allows important influences to be ignored temporarily but not forgotten

**IN THIS CHAPTER ...** you will be introduced to the kinds of data that economists use, and to some of the tools that help us to make sense of them. Economists cannot set up laboratory experiments to test economic theories, but must rely on observing the real world. Economists express their theories in the form of *models* and use *data* about the world to evaluate them. Many of the data used by economists take the form of *time-series*, which are observations on economic variables at different points in time. *Cross-section* data are observations across individual firms or households at a single moment in time. Economists use a variety of tools to help in the analysis of data. *Index numbers* and graphical presentation are especially useful. It is also important to be able to adjust data for the effects of changing prices, given that so many economic variables are inevitably measured in money terms. *Econometrics* brings together economics, mathematics and statistics to assist in this sifting of evidence.

## Important Concepts and Technical Terms

Match each lettered concept with the appropriate numbered phrase:

| | | |
|---|---|---|
| (a) Growth rate | (f) Real price | (k) Cross-section |
| (b) Index number | (g) Time series | (l) Econometrics |
| (c) Model | (h) Positive relationship | (m) Negative relationship |
| (d) Nominal variable | (i) Retail price index | (n) Real variable |
| (e) Purchasing power of money | (j) Other things equal | |

1   A sequence of measurements of a variable at different points in time.
2   A situation in which higher values of one variable are associated with lower values of another variable.
3   The price of a commodity relative to the general price level for goods.
4   A simplifying assumption which enables the economist to focus on key economic relationships.
5   A deliberate simplification of reality based on a series of simplifying assumptions from which it may be deduced how people will behave.
6   An index of the prices of goods purchased by a typical household.
7   A variable measured in money terms at current prices.
8   The percentage change in a variable per period (typically per year).
9   Measurements of an economic variable at a point in time for different individuals or groups of individuals.
10   An index of the quantity of goods that can be bought for £1.
11   A way of expressing data relative to a given base value.
12   A situation in which higher values of one variable are associated with higher values of another variable.
13   A variable measured at constant prices, or after adjustment has been made for inflation.
14   The branch of economics devoted to measuring relationships using economic data.

# Exercises

1   Which of the following data sets would be *time series* and which would relate to a *cross-section?*
    (a) Consumers' expenditure on durable goods, annually 1990–99.
    (b) Households' expenditure on housing in urban areas in 1999.
    (c) Monthly price index for potatoes for 1999.
    (d) Gross domestic product of the UK for each quarter of 1999.
    (e) Average weekly earnings for a sample of 350 individuals first interviewed in 1990 and re-interviewed in 1993, 1996 and 1999.
    (f) Unemployment categorized by area, 14 October 1999.

2   Table 2-1 presents information about agricultural employment in six European countries in the two years 1970 and 1990.
    (a) From observation of the figures (i.e. without reaching for your calculator), comment on the trend in agricultural employment in the six countries. In which countries was the trend *most* and *least* strong?
    (b) For each country, calculate an index for 1990, using 1970 as a base.
    (c) Reassess your response to part (a). Did you correctly identify the countries in which the trend was most and least strong?

3   On average, about 11 per cent of expenditure by households is on alcohol and tobacco; the remaining 89 per cent is on 'other goods and services'. (These proportions are 'close to' those used in construction of the UK retail price index, as are other data in this exercise.) Price indices for these goods are given in Table 2-2.
    (a) Construct an aggregate price index for the economy based on weights of 0.11 for alcohol and tobacco and 0.89 for other goods and services.
    (b) Using this aggregate price index, calculate the annual rate of inflation for the years 1995–98.
    (c) Although this gives a general view of inflation in the economy, individuals may view inflation differently if their pattern of expenditure differs from that of society at large. Calculate the rate of inflation for an individual whose expenditure pattern conforms to the norm except for the fact that she is a non-smoking teetotaller.
    (d) Draw two charts, one showing the three price indices, the second showing your two calculated inflation series.

**Table 2-1    Agricultural employment in six European countries (thousands)**

| Country | 1970 | 1990 | (1970 = 100) |
|---|---|---|---|
| Belgium | 177 | 100 | |
| Denmark | 266 | 147 | |
| Greece | 1279 | 900 | |
| France | 2751 | 1325 | |
| Italy | 3878 | 1895 | |
| UK | 787 | 569 | |

Source: *OECD Labour Force Statistics 1970–90,* Paris, 1992.

**Table 2-2    Price indices, 1994–98 (1987 = 100)**

| | 1994 | 1995 | 1996 | 1997 | 1998 |
|---|---|---|---|---|---|
| Price index, alcohol and tobacco | 161.6 | 169.4 | 176.4 | 184.2 | 193.9 |
| Price index, other goods and services | 141.9 | 146.6 | 149.8 | 154.2 | 159.1 |
| Aggregate price index | | | | | |
| Inflation | | | | | |
| Inflation for non-smoking teetotaller | | | | | |

**Table 2-3    Imports and income, UK, 1990–96 (Constant 1995 prices, in £ million)**

| Year | Imports of goods and services | Real personal disposable income |
|------|------|------|
| 1992 | 178 879 | 461 964 |
| 1993 | 184 607 | 475 850 |
| 1994 | 194 551 | 481 924 |
| 1995 | 205 221 | 494 574 |
| 1996 | 223 961 | 505 392 |
| 1997 | 245 047 | 525 721 |
| 1998 | 265 691 | 525 797 |

Source: *Monthly Digest of Statistics.*

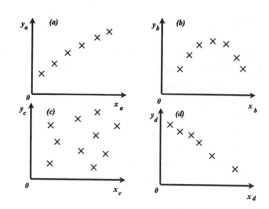

**Figure 2-1    Patterns of association**

**4**    *(a)* Using the data of Table 2-3, draw a scatter diagram with real imports on the vertical axis and real income on the horizontal axis.

*(b)* Does your diagram suggest a *positive* or a *negative* association between these variables?

*(c)* Does this conform to your economic intuition concerning imports and income?

*(d)* Can you think of variables likely to be covered by the 'other things equal' clause for this relationship?

**5**    Figure 2-1 shows scatter diagrams for different types of association between variables. Match each with the most appropriate description from the following:

*(i)* A negative linear relationship.

*(ii)* A positive linear relationship.

*(iii)* A nonlinear relationship.

*(iv)* No apparent pattern of relationship.

To which of these would you *not* attempt to fit a straight line?

**6**    The retail price index for clothing and footwear in 1994–98 based on 13 January 1987 = 100 took values as follows:

| 1994 | 1995 | 1996 | 1997 | 1998 |
|------|------|------|------|------|
| 120.4 | 120.6 | 119.7 | 120.6 | 119.9 |

*(Source: Labour Market Trends, December 1999)*

*(a)* What additional information would you require to gauge whether the *real* price of clothing was rising or falling in this period?

*(b)* Use the data you calculated as the aggregate price index in question 3 to calculate a real price index for clothing and footwear.

*(c)* Comment upon the meaning of your results.

**7**    Consider the following simple economic model, which relates to the demand for chocolate bars:

Quantity of chocolate bars demanded = $f$ {price of chocolate bars; consumer incomes}

*(a)* Using only words, explain this statement.

*(b)* Assuming consumer incomes to be held constant, would you expect the quantity demanded and the price of chocolate bars to be positively or negatively associated?

*(c)* Assuming the price of chocolate bars to be held constant, what sort of association would you expect to observe between the quantity of chocolate bars demanded and the level of consumer incomes?

*(d)* Do you consider this model to be complete, or are there other economic variables that you would have included?

**Table 2-4    Household expenditure on food, UK 1997 (in £ million)**

|  | Quarter 1 | Quarter 2 | Quarter 3 | Quarter 4 |
|---|---|---|---|---|
| At current prices | 12 929 | 13 193 | 13 109 | 14 029 |
| At constant 1995 prices | 12 552 | 12 949 | 12 747 | 13 520 |

Source: *Economic Trends Annual Supplement.*

**Figure 2-2    UK savings ratio 1963–98**
Source: *Economic Trends Annual Supplement and Monthly Digest Statistics.*

8    The following information relates to components of a retail price index for 1999:

| Item | Weight | Price index (1985 = 100) |
|---|---|---|
| Food, catering and alcohol | 3 | 170 |
| Housing, fuel and light | 2 | 186 |
| Other goods and services | 5 | 173 |

What is the value of the aggregate price index?
*(a)* 172.0
*(b)* 173.0
*(c)* 174.7
*(d)* 176.3
*(e)* 178.0

9    Using the data in Table 2.4:
*(a)* Calculate total real expenditure on food in 1997.
*(b)* Calculate total money expenditure on food in 1997.
*(c)* Calculate for each quarter the ratio of current price to constant price expenditure and multiply by 100. How might you interpret the results?

10    Figure 2-2 shows UK households' savings as a percentage of disposable income since 1963. Describe the general trend of the series and comment on the pattern displayed over time.

## True/False

1    Economics cannot claim to be a science since it is incapable of controlled laboratory experiments.
2    We may accumulate evidence in support of an economic theory, but we can never prove beyond doubt that it is 'true'.
3    Charts are a useful way of highlighting the important features of a data series.
4    When we observe a strong association between two variables we know that one depends causally upon the other.
5    Cross-section data are more often used in microeconomics because they deal with individuals.
6    Invoking 'other things equal' enables us to ignore the complicated parts of an economic model.
7    Economic models deal with straight-line relationships between variables.
8    If you look hard enough at the facts, you will inevitably discover the correct theory.
9    Index numbers are an invaluable device if we wish to compare two variables measured in different units.
10    A positive economic relationship is one that supports our model.
11    Inflation is measured by the price level.
12    Real wage rates are calculated by adjusting nominal wage rates for changes in the cost of living.

## ECONOMICS IN THE NEWS

### High street prices hard hit
*(Adapted from the Financial Times, 15 December 1999)*

The underlying rate of inflation was unchanged at 2.2 per cent in November, according to official figures. But prices on the high street are being hit hard, with clothing and footwear showing the biggest fall in more than 45 years. It was the eighth successive month that the rate has been below the government's target of 2.5 per cent. The headline rate – which includes mortgage interest payments – rose slightly to 1.4 per cent from 1.2 per cent in October. The retail prices index stood at 166.7 in November.

Prices in many sectors are falling, reflecting what retailers report as tough trading conditions and sluggish growth in sales volumes. Car prices as measured by the Office for National Statistics – which collects used-car prices as a guide to the new and used markets – fell by 1.5 per cent in the month to November, and have fallen by 6 per cent over the year – the biggest fall since records began in 1988. Prices in clothing and footwear have been showing steady year-on-year declines since June 1998. Although the average price of computers rose by 1.7 per cent in the month – an increase blamed on rising prices of computer chips following disruption to supply caused by earthquakes in Korea and Taiwan – the average price of audio-visual equipment has fallen by 16 per cent over the year.

Prices of CDs and tapes have fallen by 9 per cent over the year – perhaps reflecting the threat of competition from online retailers, as well as some aggressive price-cutting campaigns by supermarket chains. Books, another area where online retailing has been expanding fast, seem less affected – the price index for books and newspapers rose by 3 per cent on the year. But overall, retailers are downbeat about the prospects for raising prices. They say experience of falling prices has created an expectation among consumers that prices will continue to drop, and this is keeping demand low.

In the run-up to Christmas, trading has been slow as shoppers wait for the pre-Christmas sales. 'A price-cutting agenda has been created to which all retailers must respond,' said Alastair Eperon, a director of Boots. 'To varying degrees, all retailers are responding.'

Prices of services, on the other hand, are still generally rising quite strongly. The measure of house prices used in the retail prices index rose by 10 per cent over the year. The index measure of car insurance premiums, which includes vehicle taxes, has risen by 13 per cent, and personal services such as haircuts also increased by 6 per cent. Despite warnings of a price war, the price of package holidays abroad was up by 6 per cent over the past year.

1    Should a relatively low inflation rate be seen as beneficial or disadvantageous to the economy?
2    How does the simple model of demand presented in Section 2-5 of the main text help us to interpret the commodity price changes discussed in the passage?

## Questions for Thought

1    Which of the following represents the weighted index number of prices for year $Y$ based on the information in Table 2-5?
   *(a)*  94.6
   *(b)*  105.7
   *(c)*  113.3
   *(d)*  131.0
   *(e)*  Cannot be determined from the above, because one needs to know the total expenditure on each item
2    Devise a simple economic model to analyse the demand for school lunches.
3    What sorts of graphical techniques might you use to illustrate the data presented in Table 1-1 in the previous chapter of this Workbook?
4    How might economic analysis help us to explain family size?

Table 2-5    Components of a price index

| Commodity | Price in base year | Price in year Y | Weights |
|---|---|---|---|
| 1 | 10p | 12p | 2 |
| 2 | 100p | 80p | 5 |
| 3 | 50p | 70p | 3 |
|   |   |   | 10 |

# 3    Demand, Supply, and the Market

## Learning Outcomes

- To show how a market reconciles demand and supply through price adjustment
- To explain what is meant by equilibrium price and equilibrium quantity
- To discuss the principal factors that shift demand and supply curves
- To distinguish free markets and markets in which price controls operate
- To explain how the operation of markets provides one answer to what, how, and for whom goods and services are produced

**IN THIS CHAPTER ...** you will meet one of the most important concepts in all of economics – the *market* – together with the associated ideas of *demand* and *supply*. In so doing, you will see how we begin to tackle the key questions of how society decides what, how, and for whom to produce. We define the *demand* for a good as the amount of that good which buyers are prepared to purchase at each conceivable price, holding other influences on demand constant. We expect the *quantity demanded* to be higher when price is relatively low. The *demand curve* illustrates this graphically; its position depends upon the factors held constant by assumption. The sellers of a good will make decisions about how much to supply based on the selling price, the price of inputs and the technology used in production. We define the *supply* of a good as the amount that suppliers are prepared to sell at each potential price, other things being equal. We would expect the *quantity supplied* to be positively related to the selling price. The *supply curve* is a graphical illustration of this relationship. When price is at such a level that buyers demand just the quantities that sellers supply, then the market is said to be in *equilibrium*. You will encounter *normal* and *inferior* goods, plus the economist's idea of *substitutes* and *complements,* and learn to distinguish between movements *of* and *along* demand and supply curves.

## Important Concepts and Technical Terms

Match each lettered concept with the appropriate numbered phrase

| | | |
|---|---|---|
| (a) Market | (e) Comparative-static analysis | (i) Free market |
| (b) Equilibrium price | (f) Market price | (j) Excess demand |
| (c) Normal good | (g) Demand | (k) Supply |
| (d) Excess supply | (h) Inferior good | (l) Price controls |

1  The price at which the quantity supplied equals the quantity demanded.
2  A good for which demand falls when incomes rise.
3  The price prevailing in a market.
4  The study of the effect (on equilibrium price and quantity) of a change in one of the 'other things equal' factors.
5  A set of arrangements by which buyers and sellers are in contact to exchange goods and services.
6  Government rules or laws that forbid the adjustment of prices to clear markets.
7  A good for which demand increases when incomes rise.
8  The situation in which quantity supplied exceeds quantity demanded at a particular price.
9  The quantity of a good that sellers wish to sell at each conceivable price.
10  The situation in which quantity demanded exceeds quantity supplied at a particular price.
11  A market in which price is determined purely by the forces of supply and demand.
12  The quantity of a good that buyers wish to purchase at each conceivable price.

**Table 3-1    Demand and supply of baked beans**

| Price (pence) | Quantity demanded (million tins/year) | Quantity supplied (million tins/year) |
|---|---|---|
| 8 | 70 | 10 |
| 16 | 60 | 30 |
| 24 | 50 | 50 |
| 32 | 40 | 70 |
| 40 | 30 | 90 |

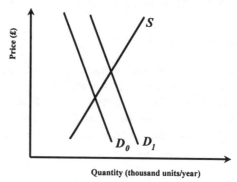

**Figure 3-1    The demand for pens**

## Exercises

1   Suppose that the data of Table 3-1 represent the market demand and supply schedules for baked beans over a range of prices.

*(a)* Plot on a single diagram the demand curve and supply curve, remembering to label the axes carefully.

*(b)* What would be the excess demand or supply if price were set at 8p?

*(c)* What would be the excess demand or supply if price were set at 32p?

*(d)* Find the equilibrium price and quantity.

*(e)* Suppose that, following an increase in consumers' incomes, the demand for baked beans rises by 15 million tins/year at each price level. Find the new equilibrium price and quantity.

2   The distinction between shifts of the demand and supply curves and movements along them is an important one. Place ticks in the appropriate columns of Table 3-2 to show the effects of changes in the 'other things equal' categories detailed in the first column. (Two ticks are required for each item.)

**Table 3-2    Movements of and along a curve**

| Change in 'other things equal' category | Shift of demand curve | Movement along demand curve | Shift of supply curve | Movement along supply curve |
|---|---|---|---|---|
| Change in price of competing good | | | | |
| Introduction of new technique of production | | | | |
| A craze for the good | | | | |
| A change in incomes | | | | |
| A change in the price of a material input | | | | |

*[Please note that in questions 3–8 more than one answer is possible.]*

3   In Figure 3.1 the demand curve for pens has moved from $D_0$ to $D_1$. Which of the following could have brought about the move?

*(a)* A fall in the price of a substitute for pens.

*(b)* A fall in the price of a complement to pens.

*(c)* A fall in the price of a raw material used to produce pens.

*(d)* A decrease in consumers' incomes (assume that a pen is an inferior good).

*(e)* A decrease in the rate of value added tax.

*(f)* A decrease in consumers' incomes (assume that a pen is a normal good).

*(g)* An advertising campaign for pens.

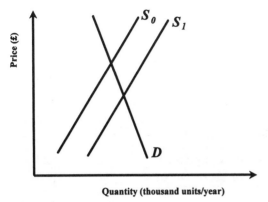

Figure 3-2    The supply of tents

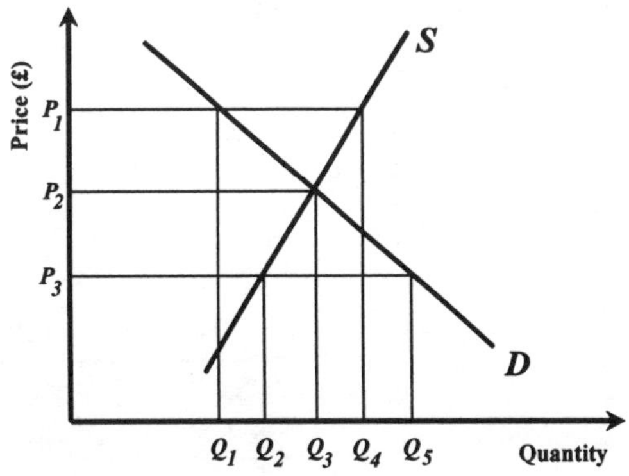

Figure 3-3    The market for eggs

4    Which of the following would probably lead to a shift in the demand curve for cameras?
     (a)  A decrease in the price of cameras.
     (b)  An increase in real incomes.
     (c)  A decrease in the price of film.

5    In Figure 3-2 the supply curve for tents has moved from $S_0$ to $S_1$. Which of the following could have brought about this move?
     (a)  The introduction of a new improved method of producing tents.
     (b)  A fall in the price of a complement to tents.
     (c)  An increase in the wage rate paid to tent workers.
     (d)  An increase in consumers' incomes (assume that a tent is a normal good).
     (e)  A fall in the price of a tent component.

6    Which of these goods would you expect to be 'normal' goods, and which 'inferior'?
     (a)  Colour television.
     (b)  Coffee.
     (c)  Rice.
     (d)  Monochrome television.
     (e)  Bus journey.

7    Which of these goods might be regarded as 'substitutes' for strawberries, and which 'complements'?
     (a)  Raspberries.
     (b)  Fresh cream.
     (c)  Petrol.
     (d)  Ice cream.
     (e)  Roast beef.
     (f)  Bus journey.
     (g)  Lap-top computer.

8    Suppose that Figure 3-3 depicts the market for eggs, and that the government decides to safeguard egg production by guaranteeing producers a minimum price for eggs. Thus, if eggs are left unsold to households, the government promises to buy up the surplus at the set price.
     (a)  What would be the equilibrium price and quantity in the absence of intervention?
     (b)  What would be the market price if the government were to guarantee a price of $P_1$?
     (c)  What would be the quantity demanded by households at this market price?
     (d)  How many eggs would need to be purchased by the government at this price?
     (e)  What would be the market price if the government were to guarantee a price of $P_3$?
     (f)  What would be the quantity demanded by households at this market price?
     (g)  How many eggs would need to be purchased by the government at this price?

9    Which of the following could cause a rise in house prices?
   *(a)* A decline in house building.
   *(b)* An increase in lending by building societies.
   *(c)* A rise in mortgage interest rates.
   *(d)* An increase in the willingness of local authorities to sell council houses to tenants.

10   Suppose that the data of Table 3-3 represent the (linear) market demand and supply schedules for commodity $X$ over a range of prices.

Table 3-3    Demand and supply of good $X$

| Price (pence) | Quantity demanded (units/year) | Quantity supplied (units/year) |
|---|---|---|
| 15 | 50 | 35 |
| 16 | 48 | 38 |
| 17 | 46 | 41 |
| 18 | 44 | 44 |
| 19 | 42 | 47 |
| 20 | 40 | 50 |
| 21 | 38 | 53 |
| 22 | 36 | 56 |

*(a)* Plot the demand curve and supply curve.
*(b)* Find the equilibrium price and quantity. Suppose that a tax of 5p per unit is imposed on firms supplying this commodity. Thus, if a firm charges 20p per unit to buyers, the government takes 5p, and the firm receives 15p.
*(c)* Draw the supply curve after the tax is imposed – i.e. the relation between quantity supplied and the price paid by consumers.
*(d)* Find the equilibrium price and quantity.

## True/False

1    A change in the price of a good will cause a shift in its demand curve.
2    An increase in consumers' incomes will cause an expansion in the demand for all goods.
3    A poor potato harvest will result in higher prices for chips, other things being equal.
4    The price charged for a good is the equilibrium price.
5    An inferior good is one that has been badly produced.
6    Mad cow disease led to an increase in the price of pork.
7    If the demand for a good rises following an increase in consumers' incomes (other things being equal), that good is known as 'normal'.
8    The imposition of a minimum legal wage will lead to an increase in employment.
9    In everyday parlance, two goods $X$ and $Y$ are known as complements if an increase in the price of X, other things being equal, leads to a fall in demand for good $Y$.
10   The imposition of a £1 per unit tax on a good will lead to a £1 increase in the price of the good.
11   When the Pope gave permission for Catholics to eat meat on Fridays, the equilibrium price and quantity of fish fell.

# ECONOMICS IN THE NEWS

## Lack of rain threatens peanut prices
*(adapted from the Financial Times, 1 May 1997)*

Crunch it, spread it, grind it or merely chew it – the peanut is one of the world's favourite snack foods and an important source of protein. But unless there is a wet summer in the US, peanut lovers could face much higher retail prices later this year, because of a serious drought in Argentina, one of the world's leading producers.

Argentina's early peanut harvest is now under way and is proving a big disappointment. With about a quarter of the harvest now dug out of the ground, it is clear that the almost complete absence of rain in Argentina between mid-January and March has seriously damaged the crop. Instead of the anticipated minimum of 1500 kg a hectare, farmers are garnering 1000 kg or less. Prices have soared as a result, from about $700 a tonne in January to more than $900 a tonne.

In the last three years, Argentina has begun to challenge China and India for the position of the world's second biggest producer of peanuts, after the US. Moreover, Argentina's peanuts are rated as being of high quality, superior to India's. In addition, as much of China's output is for domestic consumption, the Argentine crop has become an important influence of prices.

Mr Peter Morgan, a director of Barrow, Lane and Ballard, the London-based trader of edible nuts, said that US farmers would probably increase their plantings as a result of Argentina's shortfall, and that as a consequence prices may fall later in the year.

1   Sketch a demand and supply diagram, and plot the short-run effects of the failure of the harvest in Argentina.
2   How does this help to explain the response of US farmers to the change in the market?
3   Three weeks after the above passage appeared, the *Financial Times* reported that China's peanut exports were expected to fall by more than one-third, '...as failed harvests last year and shrinking peanut acreage has severely cut national output'. What effects would you expect to follow from this?

## Questions for Thought

1   Sketch a diagram showing the demand and supply curves for a commodity. Suppose that the price of the commodity is set at a level which is above the market clearing price. How will producers and consumers perceive this market situation? How are they likely to react? How would your analysis differ if the market price were to be set below the equilibrium level?
2   How would you expect the market for coffee to react to a sudden reduction in supply, perhaps caused by a poor harvest? Would you expect the revenue received by coffee-growers to fall or rise as a result?
3   Discuss some of the ways in which a change in the demand or supply conditions in a market may spill over and affect conditions in another market. Provide some examples of such spillover effects.
4   Suppose you are trying to observe the demand curve for a commodity. When you collect price and quantity data for a sequence of years, you find that they suggest a *positive* relationship. What line of reasoning and additional information would you need to use in order to make an interpretation of the data?

# 4    Government in the Mixed Economy

**Learning Outcomes**

- To study different forms of government intervention in a market economy, and explain why they are needed
- To show what determines the incidence of a tax
- To distinguish transfer payments and government spending on the purchase of goods and services
- To analyse why public goods, externalities, monopoly power and informational problems can give rise to market failure
- To consider why intervention may also reflect a wish to redistribute or a view about what citizens ought to consume
- To examine how government policy choices may themselves be modelled
- To introduce the principal-agent problem and some of its applications

**IN THIS CHAPTER ...** you will explore three important questions about the role of the government in the economy. We look at what economic activities are carried out by governments. We explore the rationales offered by economic theory to justify such activities. Finally, we consider how government decisions are taken. In exploring this topic, you will explore some of the features that distinguish *socialist* and *capitalist* economies. In mixed economies, the government acts also as a direct participant in the market by buying and selling goods and services, and may act to redistribute income. Governments raise funds to finance these expenditures by *taxation* and by *borrowing*. Governments have also intervened to counteract the *business cycle*. The fundamental economic justification for intervention is in cases of market failure. As you study this chapter, you will also encounter concepts of *public goods, externalities* and the *free-rider* problem.

## Important Concepts and Technical Terms

Match each lettered concept with the appropriate numbered phrase:

| | | |
|---|---|---|
| (a) Public good | (e) Budget deficit | (i) Transfer payments |
| (b) Regulation | (f) Externality | (j) Capitalist economy |
| (c) Private good | (g) Free-rider | (k) Paradox of voting |
| (d) Socialist economy | (h) Principal-agent problem | (l) Merit good |

1  Payments for which no current direct economic service is provided in return.
2  An economy in which the legal framework outlaws the private ownership of businesses.
3  A situation in which government expenditure exceeds government revenue such that borrowing is undertaken, and government debt increases.
4  An economy in which businesses are owned by individuals and operated for private profit.
5  A good that even if it is consumed by one person, is still available for consumption by others.
6  Rules imposed by governments to control the operation of markets.
7  A good that society thinks people should consume or receive, no matter what their incomes are.
8  Exists when the production or consumption of a good directly affects businesses or consumers not involved in buying and selling it but when those spillover effects are not fully reflected in market prices.
9  A good that, if consumed by one person, cannot be consumed by another.
10  Someone who gets to consume a good that is costly to produce without paying for it.
11  An argument demonstrating that majority voting does not necessarily permit consistent decision-making.
12  A situation in which the delegation of decision-making causes a conflict of interests between principal and agent.

# Exercises

1   Figure 4-1 shows UK general government revenue and expenditure as a percentage of gross domestic product (GDP at market prices) for the period 1965–97.

   *(a)* In which years was the government *not* operating with a budget deficit?

   *(b)* Government debt fell in the UK as a percentage of national income between 1980 and 1989 (see main text, Table 4-3). Can you explain this by studying Figure 4-1? If not, what additional factors do you think might be important?

   *(c)* Mrs Thatcher was first elected in 1979 and pursued a 'disengagement' strategy. However, you can see in Figure 4-1 that government expenditure did not begin to fall relative to GDP until about 1983. Why might it be difficult for a government to find ways of reducing its level of involvement in the economy?

   *(d)* See if you can find data on the level of activity of the government in the UK economy for a more recent year. How has the situation developed since 1997?

2   This exercise echoes and extends some analysis first introduced in Chapter 3 (exercise 10). Figure 4-2 shows the market for a good before and after the imposition of a unit tax on the sales of the good.

   *(a)* Which supply curve represents the 'with-tax' market?

   *(b)* Which area represents the revenue received by the government from this tax?

   *(c)* Identify the area representing the incidence of the tax on
       (i)  buyers of the good.
       (ii) sellers of the good.

   *(d)* Given your answer to *(c)*, which group bears the main burden of the tax? How would you expect your answer to differ if the demand curve were relatively elastic and the supply curve relatively inelastic?

3   Which of the following are *not* examples of transfer payments?

   *(a)* Unemployment benefit.
   *(b)* Payment of the council tax.
   *(c)* Old-age pension.
   *(d)* Supplementary benefit.
   *(e)* Nurses' pay.

4   The general argument in favour of government intervention in the economy is in cases of *market failure.* Which of the following might, in principle, offer scope for governments to improve the allocation of resources?

   *(a)* The economy is caught in the downswing of the business cycle.
   *(b)* The need for provision of national defence.
   *(c)* A firm discharges toxic waste into the sea close to a tourist beach area.
   *(d)* The establishment of health and safety regulations.
   *(e)* The merger of two large companies in an industry creates a new firm having potential monopoly power.
   *(f)* The need to protect weaker (poorer) members of society.

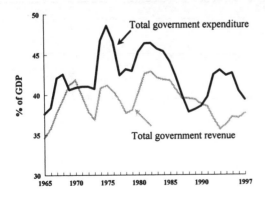

Figure 4-1    UK government revenue and
              expenditure

Source: *Economic Trends Annual Supplement, Economic Trends.*

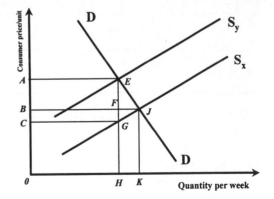

Figure 4-2    A commodity tax

5    Which of the following is nearest to being a 'pure' public good?
   (a)  Defence.
   (b)  Education.
   (c)  Water supply.
   (d)  Health services.
   (e)  Postal services.

6    Which of the following are merit goods?
   (a)  Any good that cannot be provided by private enterprise because non-payers cannot be excluded from enjoying its benefits.
   (b)  Any good that is made available to consumers on merit.
   (c)  Any good that the government believes consumers will buy too little of if it is provided by private enterprise at market prices.
   (d)  Any good provided free of charge to consumers by the government.
   (e)  Any good where the private benefits of consuming the good exceed its social benefits.
   (f)  Any good that society thinks people should receive regardless of income.

7    Suppose that a new motorway is planned which will have the effect of relieving traffic congestion on an important route between London and the coast. The building of the road will also have environmental consequences. In the following list (which is not intended to be exhaustive), identify which benefits and costs will be reflected in market prices.
   (a)  Savings in time expected to result from faster travel.
   (b)  Destruction of an area of great natural beauty.
   (c)  Costs of policing the construction work, resulting from public demonstrations against the destruction of an area of great natural beauty.
   (d)  Improvements in health resulting from lower pollution levels.
   (e)  Wage costs incurred during construction work on the motorway.
   (f)  Cost of building materials used in construction of the motorway.
   (g)  Reduction in congestion and pollution in villages and towns located on the existing road.

8    Table 4-1 shows the ranking of 5 possible outcomes by 5 voters.
   (a)  How many voters would vote for outcome A as against B?
   (b)  How many would vote for B as against C?
   (c)  For C as against D?
   (d)  For D as against C?
   (e)  And for E as against A?
   (f)  Comment on the significance of this sequence of results for decision-making.
   (g)  What sort of voters' preferences could allow this problem to be evaded?

Table 4-1    Each voter's ranking of outcomes A, B, C, D, and E

| Voter | A | B | C | D | E |
|-------|---|---|---|---|---|
| 1 | 1 | 3 | 5 | 2 | 4 |
| 2 | 3 | 5 | 2 | 4 | 1 |
| 3 | 5 | 2 | 4 | 1 | 3 |
| 4 | 2 | 4 | 1 | 3 | 5 |
| 5 | 4 | 1 | 3 | 5 | 2 |

9    Which of the following would be classified as public goods?
   (a)  Lighthouses.
   (b)  International football matches.
   (c)  Council houses.
   (d)  The telephone service.
   (e)  Flood control.
   (f)  The London Underground.
   (g)  Street lighting.
   (h)  Police force.

## True/False

1  A socialist economy is one in which the private ownership of property is prohibited by law.
2  A capitalist economy is one in which the free market is given free rein.
3  The experience of the transition economies of Eastern Europe was one of instant success, thus illustrating the superiority of the free market.
4  In the year 2000, government spending relative to national income in the UK was the lowest among the industrial market economies.
5  In the late 1980s, government debt relative to national income in the UK was low compared to most industrial market economies.
6  When demand for a commodity is highly elastic, the main burden of a sales tax will fall on the consumer.
7  Transfer payments are a means by which governments influence for whom goods and services are produced.
8  The function of government intervention is less to tell people what they ought to like than to allow them better to achieve what they already like.
9  The paradox of voting states that even when people disagree, majority voting produces consistent decision making.
10  The median voter result implies that extreme outcomes will be avoided.

## ECONOMICS IN THE NEWS

### Seattle weathers fiscal damage from loss of car-tax revenue
*(Adapted from The Seattle Times, Washington, 16 November 1999)*
A plan before the Seattle City Council this week includes nearly $4.5 million in new spending, including money for a skateboard park, self-cleaning public toilets, farmers' markets, the Seattle Chinese Garden and noise meters for police. It also includes a sizeable 'rainy day' account, bigger than even Mayor Paul Schell originally proposed.

City officials aren't exactly whistling 'We're in the money.' But higher-than-expected income this year from property, sales and businesses taxes has nearly made a wash of the $20.4 million the city stands to lose in the Motor Vehicle Excise Tax, replaced under I-695 by a $30 flat fee. This could hit Seattle's $2 billion annual budget hard. Pressure could mount on Seattle to make up for cuts in service provided by King County and the state. The city also has borrowed a lot of money recently, mostly for the new Civic Centre, and the repayments will stretch resources especially hard for the next few years. The City Council is considering some cuts to this year's update of the two-year budget, but mostly in places the public won't notice. The city still will have more than $3 million to support neighborhood art and improvement projects.

In large part, the plan the council will vote on Monday takes the sting out of the budget cuts unveiled by the mayor the day after voters approved I-695. The council essentially reversed about half of the cuts, substituted some of its own and then turned up another $3 million, mostly from rosier projections on real-estate sales taxes this year and from shifting the costs of streetlight operations to City Light three months sooner than originally anticipated. Gone from the plan as of Monday are $1.5 million in across-the-board cuts to department budgets, including police, and a plan to eliminate $200,000 in bonuses for city managers. The council is set to restore the $300,000 trim the mayor proposed to a new rainy-day account. It is also looking at adding back the $100,000 for a skateboard park near Seattle Centre that Schell had cut. The money would have mostly come from a program to repave streets. The council plans to put $432,000 back, enough to leverage another $864,000 in state and federal grants to fix potholes.

1  In the passage, a range of expenditures undertaken by the Seattle City Council is identified. Which of these items relate to public goods, to merit goods, and which might be neither?
2  Which of the items would encourage you to vote for your own Councillors?

## Questions for Thought

1  Consider the various ways in which governments intervene in economic activity. Provide examples of government actions which influence the three central economic questions introduced in Chapter 1: *what* goods and services are produced, *how* these goods and services are produced, and *for whom* they are produced.
2  Assess the likely effectiveness of imposing high taxes on tobacco.
3  To what extent can the public provision of a health service be justified by arguments about market failure?

# 5   The Effect of Price and Income on Demand Quantities

## Learning Outcomes

- **To develop the concepts of own-price and cross-price elasticity of demand**
- **To analyse how (own) price elasticity relates to the revenue effect of a price change**
- **To show why bad harvests can help farmers**
- **To explain the fallacy of composition**
- **To relate cross-price elasticity to the concepts of complements and substitutes**
- **To define the income elasticity of demand, and relate it to inferior, normal and luxury goods**

**IN THIS CHAPTER ...** you will begin to look more closely at the notions of market equilibrium that were introduced in Chapter 3, with the focus on *demand*. For a supplier of a product, an important issue is that of how consumers will respond to a change in the product price. This can be measured by the *own-price elasticity of demand,* which reflects the degree of sensitivity of demand to a change in price. For conventional downward-sloping demand curves, the price elasticity of demand is negative. When the percentage change in quantity demanded is greater than the percentage change in price, then demand is said to be *elastic*, whereas it is *inelastic* when the elasticity is between 0 and –1. The size of the elasticity depends crucially upon the availability of substitutes for the good: if there are no ready substitutes for a good, its demand will tend to be inelastic. The *cross-price elasticity of demand* measures the responsiveness of demand for a good to changes in the prices of another good. The *income elasticity* measures sensitivity to a change in consumer incomes. A *normal good* has a positive income elasticity; for an *inferior good* it is negative. When we draw a demand curve, we focus on the relationship between the demand for a good and its price, holding 'other things equal', where this includes the prices of other goods and consumer incomes. The position of the demand curve is determined by these factors. Knowledge of income and cross-price elasticities tells us how the demand curve will shift as either incomes or other prices change.

## Important Concepts and Technical Terms

Match each lettered concept with the appropriate numbered phrase:

| | | | | | |
|---|---|---|---|---|---|
| *(a)* | Cross-price elasticity of demand | *(f)* | Substitutes | *(k)* | Inferior good |
| *(b)* | Inelastic demand | *(g)* | Unit elastic demand | *(l)* | Complements |
| *(c)* | Long run | *(h)* | Short run | *(m)* | Luxury good |
| *(d)* | Normal good | *(i)* | Income elasticity of demand | *(n)* | Own-price elasticity of demand |
| *(e)* | Necessity | *(j)* | Elastic demand | | |

1   The percentage change in quantity demanded divided by the corresponding percentage change in income.
2   The quantity demanded is insensitive to price changes: elasticity is between 0 and –1.
3   A good with a positive income elasticity of demand.
4   A good with a negative income elasticity of demand.
5   A measure of the responsiveness of demand for a good to a change in the price of another good.
6   A good having an income elasticity of demand less than 1.
7   The percentage change in the quantity of a good demanded divided by the corresponding change in its price.
8   Two goods for which a rise in the price of one is generally associated with an increase in demand for the other.
9   A good having an income elasticity of demand greater than 1.
10   The quantity demanded is highly responsive to price changes: elasticity is more negative than –1.
11   Expenditure is unchanged when price falls: elasticity is equal to –1.
12   The period necessary for complete adjustment to a price change.
13   Two goods for which an increase in the price of one is generally associated with a fall in demand for the other.
14   The period during which consumers are still in the process of adjusting to a price change.

# Exercises

**Table 5-1    The demand for rice popsicles**

| Price per packet (£) | Quantity demanded (thousands) | Total spending (revenue) (£ thousands) | Own-price elasticity of demand |
|---|---|---|---|
| 2.10 | 10 | | |
| 1.80 | 20 | | |
| 1.50 | 30 | | |
| 1.20 | 40 | | |
| 0.90 | 50 | | |
| 0.60 | 60 | | |
| 0.30 | 70 | | |

**Table 5-2    Cross-price and own-price elasticities of demand in Mythuania**

| Percentage change in quantity demanded of: | In response to a 1% change in price of | | |
|---|---|---|---|
| | Food | Wine | Beer |
| Food | −0.25 | 0.06 | 0.01 |
| Wine | −0.13 | −1.20 | 0.27 |
| Beer | 0.07 | 0.41 | −0.85 |

1   Table 5-1 presents the quantity of rice popsicles demanded at various alternative prices:
   *(a)* Draw the demand curve on graph paper, plotting price on the vertical and quantity on the horizontal axis.
   *(b)* Suppose price were £1.20. What would be the change in quantity demanded if price were to be reduced by 30 pence? Would your answer be different if you started at any other price?
   *(c)* Calculate total spending on rice popsicles at each price shown.
   *(d)* Calculate the own-price elasticity of demand for prices between 60p and £2.10.
   *(e)* Draw a graph showing total revenue against sales. Plot revenue on the vertical axis and quantity demanded on the horizontal.
   *(f)* At what price is revenue at its greatest?
   *(g)* At what price is the demand elasticity equal to −1?
   *(h)* Within what ranges of prices is demand
      *(i)* elastic?
      *(ii)* inelastic?

2   Answer the following questions using the estimated elasticities presented in Table 5-2.
   *(a)* Comment on the own-price demand elasticities of the three goods, identifying for which goods demand is elastic and for which it is inelastic.
   *(b)* What is the effect of a change in the price of food on the consumption of wine and of beer? What does this suggest about the relationship between food and the other commodities?
   *(c)* Figure 5-1 shows the demand curve for wine *(D_w)*. Sketch in the effect on the demand curve of an increase in the price of:
      *(i)* food.
      *(ii)* beer.

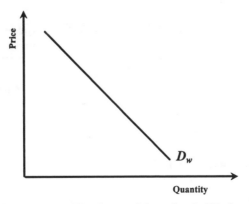

**Figure 5-1    The demand for wine in Mythuania**

3    Table 5-3 presents the total spending and income of a household in two years.
     (a)  Calculate the budget shares in each year for each good.
     (b)  Calculate the income elasticity of demand for each good.
     (c)  Classify each of the goods as either 'normal' or 'inferior'.
     (d)  Classify each of the goods as either a 'luxury' or a 'necessity'.

**Table 5-3    Total spending and income of a household**

|  | *Income Year 1* £100 | *Income Year 2* £200 | *Budget share (year 1)* | *Budget share (year 2)* | *Income elasticity of demand* | *Normal (No) or inferior (I) good* | *Luxury (L) or Necessity (Ne)* |
|---|---|---|---|---|---|---|---|
| Good A | £30 | £50 | | | | | |
| Good B | £30 | £70 | | | | | |
| Good C | £25 | £20 | | | | | |
| Good D | £15 | £60 | | | | | |

4    Which of the demand curves *DD* and *dd* in Figure 5-2 would you expect to represent the long-run demand for electricity? Explain your answer.

5    Sketch the effect of a *fall* in income upon the demand curve for each of the goods whose income elasticities are given in Table 5-4.

6    Which of the following would an economist describe as inferior or normal goods?
     (a)  A good with income elasticity of –0.1.
     (b)  A good with cross-price elasticity of +0.3.
     (c)  A good with own-price elasticity of –1.1.
     (d)  A good with income elasticity of +0.9.
     (e)  A good with own-price elasticity of –0.2.
     How would you interpret an own-price elasticity of +0.3?

7    Flora Teak likes a nice cup of tea but is equally content to accept a cup of coffee. She takes two teaspoons of sugar in coffee, but none in tea. What signs would you expect to observe for her cross-price elasticities between the three commodities?

8    Suppose that butter and margarine have a cross-price elasticity of demand of 2 and that the price of butter rises from 80p per 250g to 90p per 250g. What would be the percentage change in the demand for margarine?

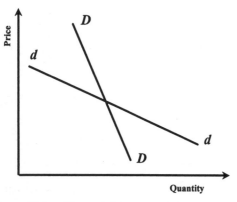

**Figure 5-2    Short- and long-run demand curves for electricity**

**Table 5-4    Income elasticity of demand for three goods**

| Good X | 1.7 |
|---|---|
| Good Y | –0.8 |
| Good Z | 0 |

**Table 5-5    Income and bacon**

| Real income (£ p.a.) | Quantity of bacon (kg/month) |
|---|---|
| 4000 | 2.0 |
| 6000 | 3.0 |
| 8000 | 3.5 |
| 10000 | 4.0 |
| 12000 | 4.3 |
| 14000 | 4.4 |
| 16000 | 4.5 |

**Table 5-6    Income elasticities**

| Good | Income elasticity of demand |
|---|---|
| Milples | 0.46 |
| Nohoes | −1.73 |
| Bechans | 2.31 |
| Zegroes | 0.00 |

9   For which of the following commodities would you expect demand to be *elastic* and which *inelastic?*
   *(a)* Bread.
   *(b)* Theatre tickets.
   *(c)* Foreign holidays.
   *(d)* Fuel and light.
   *(e)* Catering.
   *(f)* Dairy produce.
   *(g)* Clothing.

10  A household's income and consumption pattern were observed at various points in time. Table 5-5 shows income and quantities of bacon purchased.
   *(a)* Construct a scatter diagram showing bacon consumption on the vertical axis and income on the horizontal.
   *(b)* Does your diagram show a positive or a negative relationship between these variables?
   *(c)* Does this suggest that bacon is a normal or an inferior good?
   *(d)* What might your diagram look like for an inferior good?

11  An economy is prospering; the real incomes of its citizens are expected to grow at a rapid rate during the next five years. Four of the commodities produced in the economy have income elasticities as shown in Table 5-6. Assess the prospects for the four industries.

## True/False

1   Price elasticities measure the response of quantity demanded to changes in the relative price of goods.
2   The own-price elasticity of demand is constant throughout the length of a straight-line demand curve.
3   Price cuts will increase total spending on a good if demand is inelastic.
4   Total revenue is maximized when the demand elasticity is equal to −1.
5   Broadly defined commodity groups such as food are likely to have more elastic demand than narrowly defined commodities such as rump steak.
6   The budget share of a normal good will always rise following an increase in income.
7   If two goods are substitutes, the cross-price elasticity of demand is likely to be negative.
8   A general inflation will have substantial effects on the pattern of demand.
9   A poor harvest may be disastrous for farmers by reducing the revenue received from sale of their produce.
10  What is true for the individual is not necessarily true for everyone together, and what is true for everyone together does not necessarily hold for the individual.
11  Higher levels of consumer income must be good news for producers.
12  For price changes, we say that demand is more elastic in the long run than in the short run. The same arguments suggest that income elasticities of demand should be higher once consumers have had time to adjust to the increase in their incomes. The reason economists emphasize the long-run/short-run distinction for price elasticity, but not for income elasticity of demand, is that changes in income are usually small.

## ECONOMICS IN THE NEWS

### The decline of the FA Cup

*(Based on an article by Stefan Szymanski in Economic Review, Volume 17(4), April 2000)*

The decision of Manchester United not to participate in the FA Cup in the year 2000 caused considerable controversy. Instead of defending the trophy that they won in 1999, they chose to enter the new World Club Cup. One reason for their decision could have been political pressure, but it may also have been financial self-interest. Not only were the broadcast rights to the World Club Cup substantial, but Manchester United may also have calculated that the FA Cup is a competition of declining interest to its fans.

The decline of the FA Cup is not apparent from looking at Cup match attendance figures on their own. All forms of football in England have enjoyed increased popularity in recent years. Football has become, for the time being at least, fashionable. Thus even the FA Cup has attracted increasing attendance. However, relative to the other main form of football competition, the League championships of the four English divisions, interest in the FA Cup has fallen. Twenty years ago, a typical FA fixture attracted an average attendance some 50 per cent higher than an equivalent League fixture. Since the late 1970s, this percentage has fallen steadily, until in 1998, League matches actually attracted higher attendances.

Although real incomes grew steadily between 1949 and 1985, attendance at football matches declined. This was a period during which there was considerable discomfort – and even danger – from attendance at football matches. However, from the mid-1980s football clubs went through a transformation in their image, investing in facilities and improving conditions at grounds. The trend in attendance since the mid-1980s has been upwards. As people have got richer, there have been increases in both attendance at football matches and in ticket prices (which have risen much faster than the annual rate of inflation).

But why should the improvement have affected League matches more than the FA Cup? Notice that uncertainty of outcome is a very important factor in determining the attractiveness of a sporting event. A match or a championship in which the eventual winner is known with a very high probability is much less attractive than a situation where anybody can win. The upward shift in the demand curve for football matches has led to higher attendance and higher prices, but not to an increase in supply of football clubs. Instead, the result has been to accentuate the gap between the rich and poor clubs. This in turn has led to a reduction in the frequency of 'giantkilling' events, and hence the relative decline in interest in competitions such as the FA Cup.

1   Would you regard attendance at football matches as a normal or an inferior good? Would your answer be valid for the whole period from 1949 to date? If not, why might the nature of the good have changed?
2   Do you accept the argument advanced in the final paragraph of the passage? If it is indeed valid, what could be done to arrest the decline of the FA Cup?

## Questions for Thought

1   The prices of some goods are seen to be more volatile than others. Why might the price elasticity of demand be an important influence on fluctuations in the prices of different products?
2   Explain why each of the following factors may influence the own-price elasticity of demand for a commodity.
    *(a)* Consumer preferences: that is, whether consumers regard the commodity as a luxury or a necessity.
    *(b)* The narrowness of definition of the commodity.
    *(c)* The length of period under consideration.
    *(d)* The availability of substitutes for the commodity.
3   The coffee market is subject to volatility caused by weather conditions in key supplying countries like Brazil. What *other* factors are likely to influence this market?
4   Imagine that you are responsible for running a bus company, and you have access to the following information about the elasticities of demand for coach travel:
    *(a)* Income elasticity –0.4.
    *(b)* Own-price elasticity –1.2.
    *(c)* Cross-elasticity with respect to rail fares +2.1.
    How might this information be of use to you in circumstances when your company is running a service which is currently making a loss?

# 6    The Theory of Consumer Choice

## Learning Outcomes

- To explain how a budget constraint is derived from consumer income and market prices
- To define consumer tastes, diminishing marginal utility and a diminishing marginal rate of substitution
- To show how to represent tastes as indifference curves
- To use indifference curves and budget lines to show what a consumer will do in order to maximize utility
- To analyse the effect of giving a consumer more income
- To explain income and substitution effects, and use them to analyse the effect of a price change
- To relate the market demand curve to individual demand curves

**IN THIS CHAPTER ...** you will be introduced to analysis that shows how decisions made by individual potential buyers of a good can be brought together to form the demand curve. In choosing what commodities to buy, individual consumers do not have complete freedom of choice. We assume that they will try to gain as much satisfaction as possible, but will be constrained by their income and by the prices that must be paid for the goods. Given these, decisions will be determined by personal preferences. Our model must formalize these four elements: motivation, income, prices, and preferences. The *budget constraint* separates the affordable from the unattainable. Consumer preferences may be represented by *indifference curves*, showing the consumption bundles yielding equal *utility*. The slope of an indifference curve is the *marginal rate of substitution* of one good for another – the quantity of one good which the individual must sacrifice in order to increase the quantity of the other good by one unit while maintaining the total level of utility. An individual will maximize utility where an indifference curve is tangent to the budget line. At this unique choice point. the slope of the indifference curve (the marginal rate of substitution) is equal to the slope of the budget line (the ratio of the relative prices of the goods). By varying the price of a good and observing the effect upon consumption of that good, we can construct an individual's demand curve for the good. An individual's reaction to a price change can be thought of as the combination of the *substitution effect* and the *real income effect*. It is important to see the link between individual decisions about demand and the market demand curve for a good. If individuals take demand decisions in isolation from those taken by other consumers, then market demand is obtained by horizontal addition of the individual demand curves.

## Important Concepts and Technical Terms

Match each lettered concept with the appropriate numbered phrase:

| | | |
|---|---|---|
| (a) Utility | (f) Individual demand curve | (j) Market demand curve |
| (b) Income expansion path | (g) Marginal rate of substitution | (k) Complementarity |
| (c) Budget constraint | (h) Utility maximization | (l) Giffen good |
| (d) Indifference curve | (i) Income effect | |
| (e) Substitution effect | | |

1   A curve showing how the chosen bundle of goods varies with consumer income levels.
2   The sum of the demand curves of all individuals in that market.
3   The quantity of one good that the consumer must sacrifice to increase the quantity of the other good by one unit without changing total utility.
4   A situation where goods are necessarily consumed jointly.
5   An inferior good where the income effect outweighs the substitution effect, causing the demand curve to slope upwards to the right.
6   That part of a consumer's response to a price change arising from the change in his or her purchasing power.
7   That part of a consumer's response to a price change arising from the change in relative prices.
8   A curve showing all the consumption bundles that yield the same utility to the consumer.
9   The assumption that the consumer chooses the affordable bundle that yields the most satisfaction.
10  The set of different consumption bundles that the consumer can afford, given income and prices.
11  The satisfaction a consumer derives from a particular bundle of goods.
12  A curve showing the amount demanded by a consumer at each price.

## Exercises

1  Ashley, a student living at home, has a weekly allowance of £60, which he spends on two goods: food and entertainment. Draw Ashley's budget line for each of the following situations, using the vertical axis for food and the horizontal axis for entertainment:
   (a)  The price of food $(P_f)$ is £1.50 per unit: the price of entertainment $(P_e)$ is £1.50 per unit.
   (b)  $P_f$ is £1.50p; $P_e$ is £2.
   (c)  $P_f$ is £2; $P_e$ is £1.50.
   (d)  $P_f$ is £1; $P_e e$ is £1.
   (e)  $P_f$ is £1.50; $P_e e$ is £1.50, but Ashley's allowance is increased to £75 per week.
   Comment on the budget lines of (d) and (e) compared with (a).

2  Table 6-1 summarizes part of Ashley's preferences for food (F) and entertainment (E), by showing various combinations of the two goods between which he is indifferent. Each of the three sets of bundles represents a different utility level.

Table 6-1    Ashley's preferences for food and entertainment

| Utility set 1: IC1 | | Utility set 2: IC2 | | Utility set 3: IC3 | |
|---|---|---|---|---|---|
| E | F | E | F | E | F |
| 2 | 40 | 10 | 40 | 12 | 45 |
| 4 | 34 | 12 | 35 | 14 | 39 |
| 8 | 26 | 14 | 30 | 16 | 34 |
| 12 | 21 | 17 | 25 | 18 | 30 |
| 17 | 16 | 20 | 20 | 21 | 25 |
| 22 | 12 | 25 | 16 | 27 | 20 |
| 30 | 8 | 30 | 13 | 37 | 15 |
| 40 | 5 | 38 | 10 | 44 | 13 |
| 50 | 4 | 50 | 8 | 50 | 12 |

   (a)  Use the information from the table to sketch three indifference curves, plotting food on the vertical axis and entertainment on the horizontal axis.
   (b)  Which of the three indifference curves represents the highest level of utility?
   (c)  Which of the three indifference curves represents the lowest level of utility?
   (d)  Consider the following bundles of goods:
       A:  50(E), 8(F)
       B:  45(E), 4(F)
       C:  12(E), 45(F)
       D:  25(E), 16(F)
       E:  21(E), 11(F).
   Rank the five bundles in descending order of satisfaction.
   (e)  Can the information in this exercise be used to find Ashley's optimal choice point?
   (f)  Superimpose on your graph the budget line from part (a) of exercise 1. Can you now find the consumption bundle that maximizes Ashley's utility?

3  Which of the following statements is *not* valid? A utility-maximizing consumer chooses to be at a point at a tangent between his budget line and an indifference curve because:
   (a)  this is the highest indifference curve that can be attained.
   (b)  at any point to the left of the budget line some income would be unused.
   (c)  all combinations of goods that lie to the right of his budget line are unreachable, given money income.
   (d)  this point represents the most favourable relative prices.
   (e)  at any other point on the budget line he will gain less utility.

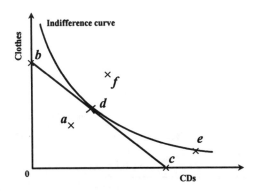

Figure 6-1    Barbara's choice between CDs and clothes

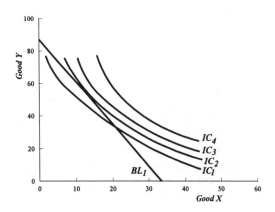

Figure 6-2    Christopher's preferences between goods $X$ and $Y$

4    Barbara is choosing how to allocate her spending between CDs and clothes. Figure 6-1 shows her budget line and an indifference curve. Match each lettered point on the diagram with the appropriate numbered phrase:
   (1)   The point at which Barbara maximizes her utility.
   (2)   The point at which Barbara buys only CDs and no clothes.
   (3)   A consumption bundle which would not exhaust Barbara's budget for these goods.
   (4)   A point yielding the same satisfaction as at $d$ but which Barbara cannot afford.
   (5)   The point at which Barbara buys only clothes, and no CDs.
   (6)   A consumption bundle preferred to point $d$ but which Barbara cannot afford.

5    Christopher is choosing between two goods $X$ and $Y$. Figure 6-2 shows some of his indifference curves between these goods. $BL_1$ represents his budget line, given his income and the prices of the goods.
   (a)   Suppose that Christopher's tastes and the prices of $X$ and $Y$ remain constant, but his income varies. Plot the income expansion path.
   (b)   Classify the two goods as being either 'normal' or 'inferior'.
   (c)   What form would the income expansion path take if both $X$ and $Y$ were normal goods?
   (d)   Is it possible to draw an income expansion path to depict the case where both $X$ and $Y$ are inferior goods?

6    Christopher is still choosing between goods $X$ and $Y$. Figure 6-3 is the same as Figure 6-2. Suppose that Christopher's tastes, income, and the price of good $Y$ remain fixed, but the price of good X varies.
   (a)   Show on the diagram the way in which Christopher's demand for X varies as the price of X varies.
   (b)   Is it possible to derive Christopher's demand curve for $X$ from this analysis?
   (c)   Comment on the cross-price effect – that is, the way in which the demand for good $Y$ changes as the price of $X$ changes.

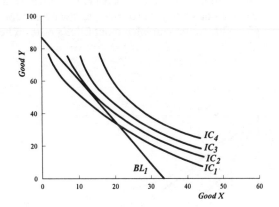

Figure 6-3    Christopher's preferences between goods $X$ and $Y$

7    A consumer begins at point *P* in Figure 6-4 with the budget line as depicted. Which of the following could have transpired if the consumer later chooses to be at *Q*?
  (a) A change in tastes.
  (b) A small increase in the price of *X* and a larger percentage decrease in the price of *Y*.
  (c) An increase in the price of *X* and a smaller percentage increase in the price of *Y*.
  (d) A fall in real income.
  (e) Equal percentage increases in money income and both prices.

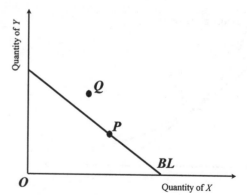

Figure 6-4  A change in a consumer's choice point

8    Figure 6-5 shows how Debbie reacts to a fall in the price of beefburgers, in her choice between beefburgers and pork chops.
    *AB* represents the original budget line and *OX₁* the quantity of beefburgers bought by Debbie. After the price fall, the budget line moves to *AC*, and Debbie now consumes *OX₂* beefburgers.
  (a) Illustrate the real income and substitution effects involved in Debbie's reaction to the price fall. (*Hint* You will need to be careful, because the discussion of this topic in the main text (Section 6-3) is in terms of a price *increase*. A price fall must be treated a little differently.)
  (b) Does your analysis reveal beefburgers to be a normal or an inferior good?
  (c) Do the income and substitution effects reinforce each other or work in opposite directions?
  (d) Under what circumstances would the opposite be the case?

9    In reality, we cannot observe indifference curves. However, we can observe prices and income, and in some situations we can make inferences about consumer preferences. Suppose we observe Eliot in two different circumstances. He is choosing between goods *X* and *Y* and has constant money income, but faces different prices in two situations. His budget lines are shown in Figure 6-6.
    *AB* is his initial budget line and *CD* the new one after an increase in the price of *X* and a fall in the price of *Y*. His initial choice point was at *E*. All questions relate to his subsequent choice.
  (a) If Eliot's tastes do *not* change, is it possible that he would choose to be at point *F*? Explain your answer.
  (b) If Eliot's tastes do not change, is it possible that he would choose to be at point *G*? Explain your answer.
  (c) If Eliot's tastes do not change, in what section of the budget line *CD* would you expect his choice to lie?
  (d) What would you infer about Eliot's tastes if he *does* choose point G?

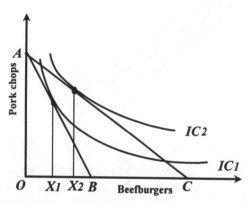

Figure 6-5    Debbie's choice between beefburgers and pork chops

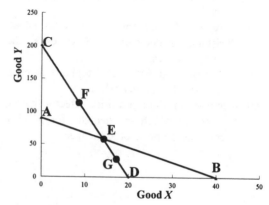

Figure 6-6    Eliot's preferences

10  *Please notice that this exercise is based on material in the Appendix to Chapter 6 in the main text and assumes that utility can be measured.*

Frank reads magazines and listens to cassettes. Table 6-2 shows the utility he derives from consuming different quantities of the two commodities, given consumption of other goods. The price of magazines is £1.50 and the price of cassettes is £7.50. Suppose that Frank has a fixed budget of £30 to spend on these goods, and is currently buying 2 cassettes and 10 magazines. The issue to consider is whether he is maximizing his utility for a given expenditure.

(a)  How much utility does Frank receive from his current combination of goods?
(b)  Calculate the *marginal* utility that Frank derives from magazines and cassettes.
(c)  Sketch Frank's marginal utility schedule for cassettes.
(d)  Can we yet pronounce on whether Frank is maximizing utility?
(e)  What is Frank's utility if he spends his entire budget on cassettes?
(f)  Calculate the ratios of marginal utility to price for each of the commodities.
(g)  What combination of the two commodities maximizes Frank's utility given his budget?

**Table 6-2    Frank's utility from magazines and cassettes**

| | Magazines | | | Cassettes | | |
|---|---|---|---|---|---|---|
| | (1) | (2) | (3) | (4) | (5) | (6) |
| Number consumed | Utility (utils) | Marginal utility | $\frac{MU_m}{P_m}$ | Utility (utils) | Marginal utility | $\frac{MU_c}{P_c}$ |
| 1 | 60 | | | 360 | | |
| 2 | 111 | | | 630 | | |
| 3 | 156 | | | 810 | | |
| 4 | 196 | | | 945 | | |
| 5 | 232 | | | 1050 | | |
| 6 | 265 | | | 1140 | | |
| 7 | 295 | | | 1215 | | |
| 8 | 322 | | | 1275 | | |
| 9 | 347 | | | 1320 | | |
| 10 | 371 | | | 1350 | | |

## True/False

1  Indifference curves always slope downwards to the right if the consumer prefers more to less.
2  Indifference curves never intersect if the consumer has consistent preferences.
3  The slope of the budget line depends only upon the relative prices of the two goods.
4  The budget constraint shows the maximum affordable quantity of one good given the quantity of the other good that is being purchased.
5  An individual maximizes utility where his budget line cuts an indifference curve.
6  A change in money income alters the slope and position of the budget line.
7  All Giffen goods are inferior goods.
8  All inferior goods are Giffen goods.
9  The income expansion path slopes upwards to the right if both goods are normal goods.
10  The substitution effect of an increase in the price of a good unambiguously reduces the quantity demanded of that good.
11  If following an increase in the price of $X$, the substitution effect is exactly balanced by the income effect, then $X$ is neither a normal nor an inferior good.
12  The theory of consumer choice demonstrates that consumers prefer to receive transfers in kind rather than transfers in cash.

## ECONOMICS IN THE NEWS

### Tigers fill up their tanks
*(Adapted from the Financial Times, 10 June 1997)*

One thing unites Bangkok, Jakarta and Kuala Lumpur more than their skyscrapers or ambitions to count among the 21st century's industrial power-houses. All three cities suffer from horrendous traffic.

Yet the governments of Thailand, Indonesia and Malaysia would all like to see many more cars on the road in their race to industrialize. The world's car-makers would love to help them: for motor manufacturers, south-east Asia holds much the same promise as South America or Eastern Europe, the industry's two other boom regions. The reason for such enthusiasm is that vibrant growth in south-east Asia has boosted private incomes.

Greater wealth has spurred greater car ownership. Thailand and Indonesia hold great potential because of their large size and populations. Although Malaysia is a minnow in population, its higher incomes offer more immediate returns. Demand for cars should rise in all three countries because of ambitious road-building programmes.

In Malaysia, taxes and tariffs almost quadruple the price of an imported car. Even models assembled locally from foreign kits face levies of up to 112 per cent. In Indonesia, mark-ups can more than triple the price of a fully built-up import and double the cost of a locally assembled vehicle. Both countries use such methods to nurture 'national' brands.

1    What factors does the passage suggest are the key determinants of the demand for cars?
2    Why should governments want to encourage higher car ownership if roads are inadequate to cope with increased traffic?

## Questions for Thought

1    The market demand curve has been portrayed as the horizontal sum of the individual demand curves, under the assumption that individual preferences are independent. However, suppose this assumption is not valid; for instance, it might be that consumers will demand more of a good if they think that 'everyone is buying it' – or they may demand more if they think it is exclusive because few can afford it. How would these interdependencies affect the relationship between the individual and market demand curves?

2    So far, we have always assumed that indifference curves are downward-sloping: this follows from the assumptions we made about consumer preferences. For instance, we assumed that there is always a diminishing marginal rate of substitution between the goods and that more is always better. If an individual has preferences which do not fit these rules, then the indifference curves can turn out to have quite a different pattern. In Figure 6-7 are some indifference curves reflecting different assumptions about preferences.

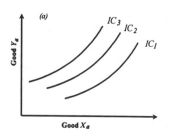
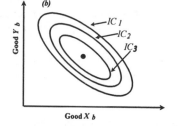
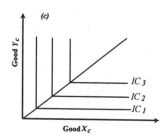

**Figure 6-7    Unconventional preferences**

In each case, utility increases from *IC1* to *IC2* to *IC3*. For each set of indifference curves, explain the nature of consumer preferences and suggest examples of pairs of commodities which might illustrate these preferences.

**3**  Will an increase in the hourly wage rate induce an individual worker to work longer or shorter hours? On the face of it, this seems an alien concept in the context of this chapter. However, an individual has preferences about other things than goods – for instance, between income and leisure (that is, hours not working). We can thus draw indifference curves between income (on the vertical axis) and hours of leisure (on the horizontal axis). If the individual gives up an hour of leisure, he receives an income, dependent upon the wage rate; so we can draw a budget line whose slope depends upon the wage rate. The higher the wage rate, the steeper the budget line. Use this framework to think about the question posed.

**4**  Felicity gains utility from listening to CDs and from watching videos. If she wishes to maximize her utility, which of the following conditions must be met?

*(a)*  The marginal utility from CDs must be equated with the marginal utility from videos.

*(b)*  She must receive the same total utility from each of the two commodities.

*(c)*  The price of CDs multiplied by the marginal utility obtained from CDs must be equal to the product of price and marginal utility of videos.

*(d)*  The ratio of the marginal utility of CDs to the price of CDs must be equated to the ratio of marginal utility of videos to the price of videos.

*(e)*  The ratio of the total utility of CDs to the price of CDs must be equated to the ratio of total utility of videos to the price of videos.

# 7 Business Organization and Behaviour

## Learning Outcomes

- To explain the different legal forms in which a business can be owned and run
- To define revenue, cost, profit, and cash flow
- To construct balance sheets, both for flows within a year and for net wealth at a point in time
- To distinguish economic and accounting definitions of cost
- To discuss the assumption that a firm's output level is chosen to maximize profits
- To relate this output choice to marginal cost and marginal revenue

**IN THIS CHAPTER ...** you will look at how the *supply* of a commodity is decided, and at who takes decisions about how much should be produced, and the price at which it should be sold. *Firms* are organized in a variety of ways. Most numerous are *sole traders*, individuals running small businesses on their own account. Larger concerns may become *partnerships*, in which the business is jointly owned by two or more people. Finally, there are *companies*, in which ownership is distributed among the shareholders. We shall refer to all such organizations as *firms*. The viability of a firm depends upon both *profitability* and *cash flow*. *Profit* is defined as the excess of revenues over costs, where costs include *opportunity cost*. This reflects the notion that the true, or economic, cost of using a resource is the amount forgone by not using that resource in its best alternative use. In order to analyse decisions taken by firms, it is necessary to make an assumption about what firms are trying to achieve. Much mainstream economic analysis assumes that firms aim to *maximize profits*, although in practice this aim may be tempered by other objectives, especially where there is separation of ownership from control. This may give rise to the *principal-agent* problem. Total cost will normally increase as output rises: more labour must be hired, more inputs used, and so on, although some (fixed) costs may be incurred regardless of the output level. Total revenue will also vary at different levels of output, and the maximization of profits depends upon how both total costs and total revenue vary. Profits are maximized where *marginal cost* equals *marginal revenue*.

## Important Concepts and Technical Terms
Match each lettered concept with the appropriate numbered phrase:

| | | |
|---|---|---|
| (a) Total revenue | (f) Opportunity cost | (k) Inventories |
| (b) Assets | (g) Accounting cost | (l) Dividends |
| (c) Profits | (h) Liabilities | (m) Supernormal profits |
| (d) Total cost | (i) Depreciation | (n) Hostile takeover |
| (e) Marginal cost | (j) Marginal revenue | (o) Principal-agent problem |

1  That part of profits that the firm does not wish to re-invest and is thus paid to shareholders.
2  The profit over and above the return which the owners could have earned by lending their money elsewhere at the market rate of interest.
3  Goods held in stock by the firm for future sales.
4  A situation in which a company is bought out although uninvited by existing managers.
5  The increase in total revenue when output is increased by 1 unit.
6  The loss in value resulting from the use of machinery during the period.
7  The increase in total cost when output is increased by 1 unit.
8  What the firm owns.
9  All expenses of production including both fixed costs and those costs which vary with the level of output (and including opportunity cost).
10  What the firm owes.
11  The receipts of a business from sale of its output, equal to total expenditure by consumers on the firm's product.
12  The excess of total revenue over total cost.
13  The actual payments made by a firm in a period.
14  A situation which arises from conflict of interest between owners and managers.
15  The amount lost by not using a resource in its best alternative use.

## Exercises

1   Set out below are descriptions of four hypothetical firms. Identify each as being either a sole trader, a partnership, or a company.

*(a)* Count & Balance is a firm of chartered accountants. The five qualified accountants who work for the firm share the profits between them and are jointly responsible for any losses, as the firm does not have limited liability.

*(b)* Will Mendit & Son is a small family business. Will does electrical repair work while his son helps with the paperwork and assists with some repairs; they each take their share of the earnings. If the firm were to go bankrupt, Will would have to sell his car, and his son his motorbike.

*(c)* D. Harbinger Limited supplies communication equipment to the military. Profits are distributed among the shareholders, who have limited liability. The original founder of the firm has now retired, leaving management in the hands of the board of directors.

*(d)* Connie Fection runs a sweet shop, living in a flat over the premises with her daughter, who is paid to work the till on four afternoons a week. Connie does not have limited liability and in case of difficulty would have to sell her possessions.

2   The following items represent the expenditures and receipts of Lex Pretend & Sons Limited during 1999. Prepare the income statement for the firm and calculate profits before and after tax on the assumption that the firm is liable only for corporation tax of 30 per cent on its profits.

*(a)* Rent £25 000.

*(b)* Proceeds from sale of 5 000 units of good $X$ at £40 each.

*(c)* Travel expenses £19 000.

*(d)* Stationery and other office expenses £15 000.

*(e)* Wages £335 000.

*(f)* Telephone £8 000.

*(g)* Proceeds from sale of 4 000 units of good $Y$ at £75 each.

*(h)* Advertising £28 000.

3   Fiona Trimble is a sole trader operating in the textile industry. During the past year, revenue received amounted to £55 000 and she incurred direct costs of £27 000. Fiona had £25 000 of financial capital tied up in the business during the whole year. Had she chosen to work for the large company round the corner, she could have earned £21 000. Calculate the following items (you will need to know that the going market rate of interest was 10 per cent):

*(a)* Accounting cost.

*(b)* Accounting profit.

*(c)* Opportunity cost of Fiona's time.

*(d)* Opportunity cost of financial capital.

*(e)* Total economic cost.

*(f)* Economic profit (supernormal)

4   The following items comprise the assets and liabilities of GSC Limited (the Great Spon Company) as at 31 March 2000. Incorporate them into a balance sheet for the firm and calculate the net worth of the company. Note that the company has been in operation for just one year, and that buildings and other physical capital are assumed to depreciate at the rate of 20 per cent per annum.

*(a)* Wages payable £25 000.

*(b)* Inventories held £80 000.

*(c)* Bank loan payable £50 000.

*(d)* Buildings, original value £300 000.

*(e)* Cash in hand £30 000.

*(f)* Accounts receivable £55 000.

*(g)* Accounts payable £40 000.

*(h)* Mortgage £180 000.

*(i)* Salaries due to be paid £30 000.

*(j)* Physical capital other than buildings, original value £250 000.

**Table 7-1    Costs and revenue for a firm**

| Total Production (units/week) | Price received (£) | Total costs |
|---|---|---|
| 1 | 25 | 10 |
| 2 | 23 | 23 |
| 3 | 20 | 38 |
| 4 | 18 | 55 |
| 5 | 15 | 75 |
| 6 | 12½ | 98 |

**Table 7-2    Marginal revenue, marginal costs for a firm**

| Total production (units/week) | Marginal revenue (£) | Marginal cost (£) |
|---|---|---|
| 0 | | |
| | 72 | 17 |
| 1 | | |
| | 56 | 15 |
| 2 | | |
| | 40 | 25 |
| 3 | | |
| | 24 | 40 |
| 4 | | |
| | 8 | 60 |
| 5 | | |

5   Table 7-1 contains data which represent the cost and revenue situation of a firm.
   *(a)* Calculate marginal cost as output rises.
   *(b)* Calculate marginal revenue as output rises.
   *(Hint:* You will need first to calculate total revenue.)
   *(c)* At what level of output would profits be maximized?
   *(d)* Calculate profit at each level of output.

6   Mr Smith owns a small factory. Every Thursday one of his lorry drivers spends the morning driving Mrs Jones round the shops. The lorry driver is, of course, paid his normal wage and Mrs Jones gives him an extra £5. Which of the following identifies the opportunity cost to Mr Smith of the lorry driver's chauffeuring?
   *(a)* The £5 plus the wage he would normally earn.
   *(b)* The work he would have done if not taken away.
   *(c)* The wage he would normally earn.
   *(d)* The £5 Mrs Jones pays him.

7   Table 7-2 summarizes marginal revenue and marginal cost for a firm.
   *(a)* Plot marginal revenue and marginal cost schedules, associating each marginal value with the midpoint of the quantity interval (i.e. place the marginal cost of the first unit midway between 0 and 1, etc.).
   *(b)* At what (approximate) level of output would the firm choose to operate if it wanted to maximize profits?
   *(c)* At what (approximate) level of output would the firm choose to operate if it wanted to maximize *revenue?* *(Hint* You will need to extend your MR line a little.)
   *(d)* If marginal cost were to increase by £30 at each level of output at what point would profits be maximized?
   *(e)* Given the original level of marginal cost, at what level of output would the firm maximize profits if marginal revenue were to increase by £34 at each level of output?

8   Which of the following might describe the motivation for a firm in setting output and (where appropriate) price?
   *(a)* The wish to maximize profits.
   *(b)* The wish to maximize sales.
   *(c)* The wish to obtain as large a market share as possible.
   *(d)* The wish to obtain enough profit to keep the shareholders content.
   *(e)* The wish to see the firm grow as quickly as possible.
   Which of these do you consider to be most important?

## True/False

1  Small traders are the most numerous form of business organization in the UK, but companies are, on average, the most profitable.
2  The balance sheet of a firm summarizes information concerning the flow of receipts and expenditures during a given year.
3  To avoid the possibility of having to sell their possessions, shareholders should be careful to buy shares in thriving firms.
4  Firms that show an accounting profit must be thriving.
5  Opportunity cost plus accounting cost equals economic cost.
6  The net worth of a firm as revealed by the balance sheet does not necessarily reflect the true worth, which should take notice of 'goodwill' factors.
7  Firms maximize profits by selling as much output as they can.
8  When a firm's demand curve slopes down, marginal revenue will fall as output rises.
9  Long-term profitability is all that matters; cash flow is unimportant.
10  Any firm wanting to maximize profits will minimize cost for any given level of output.
11  A fall in marginal revenue will cause profits to be maximized at a lower output level.
12  Inventories are produced by mad scientists.
13  When the firm's demand curve slopes down, marginal revenue must be less than the price for which the last unit is sold.
14  More than 90 per cent of UK corporate investment is financed from retained profits.

## ECONOMICS IN THE NEWS

### BA tries to lure travellers
*(Adapted from The Independent, 5 January 2000)*

Up to 2000 people are to be given the chance to fly around the world for £140 as part of British Airways' latest promotion, launched on the same day as the latest cut-price airline. January is a sluggish month for travel and BA is to deliver vouchers with offers of cheap flights and bonuses to 23 million households.

The promotion also includes 1000 flights to New York on Concorde for £100 plus taxes, and money-off vouchers to cities in Europe and the Far East. A spokeswoman said the promotion was to encourage travel in the first month of the new millennium – but it was perhaps no coincidence that KLM yesterday launched its pay-as-you-go service.

Buzz, launched by the British subsidiary of KLM Royal Dutch Airlines, will fly to seven destinations from Stansted. There will be at least three flights a day to Berlin, Dusseldorf, Frankfurt, Lyons, Milan, Paris and Vienna. Travellers can book by phone or over the Internet before buying 'add-on' services such as drinks and meals. Prices are expected to be 25 per cent less than full ticket prices for similar routes. A spokesman said: 'We are treating people as individuals and saying they can buy . . . meals and drinks if they feel like it and it's not already included in the cost of the ticket.'

The airline is following in the steps of BA's no-frills subsidiary Go, and its rivals easyJet and Ryanair.

A BA spokeswoman denied the promotion had been deliberately launched on the same day as Buzz. 'We . . . had no idea they were launching today. This year, because it is the millennium, we have decided to do an extra-big promotion but we are not in competition with any low-cost airlines.'

Of the 23 million vouchers, 21 million are standard offers allowing travellers to choose. They range from £100 off a flight to the Far East, £25 off tickets to North America and £150 off Middle East flights.

The other 2 million vouchers have a variety of promotions, including extra money off and the so-called 'gold' offers of round-the-world tickets and flights on Concorde as well as upgrades on seats.

1  Are the cost-cutting tactics and special offer deals described in the passage consistent with profit maximization?
2  To what extent are BA's actions constrained or stimulated by the need to respond to the actions of rival firms? Are the airline companies unusual in this respect?

## Questions for Thought

1    Why might marginal cost be falling at low levels of output? What might cause marginal cost to rise?
2    What do you consider to be the opportunity cost that you are incurring by thinking about this question?
3    Suppose that you own shares in a computer software company, but do not become directly involved in the running of the company as your activities as a rock star keep you fully occupied. Your hope is that the firm will maximize profits, although you know that this is a tough and competitive market. In thinking about the following questions, you may find it helpful to read them in conjunction with the commentary provided.
   *(a)*  Are the managers of the company likely to share your enthusiasm for profit maximization?
   *(b)*  Is it possible for you to impose profit maximization, and to monitor the actions of the managers?
   *(c)*  Would the threat of a hostile takeover be a help or a hindrance in this?
   *(d)*  How might the threat of a hostile takeover affect the long-term position of the firm?
   *(e)*  What steps might you take to safeguard your interests?

# 8 Developing the Theory of Supply: Costs and Production

## Learning Outcomes

- To explain the production function and its relation to the avoidance of waste
- To define technology and a technique of production
- To show how a firm's choice of production technique is affected by prices of the inputs that it purchases
- To distinguish total, average, and marginal cost, both in the long run and in the short run
- To consider different returns to scale and their relation to the shape of average cost curves
- To distinguish fixed and variable factors in the short run, and explain the law of diminishing returns
- To derive a firm's chosen output level, in the short run and in the long run, including temporary shutdown and permanent exit

**IN THIS CHAPTER ...** you will look more carefully at how an individual firm decides how much to produce in order to maximize profits. As a key part of this, you will need to explore the way in which costs vary with the level of production. Important in this concept are the choice of technique and technology, and the existence of *economies of scale*. The *law of diminishing returns* will be explained. You will also see how the relative prices of the inputs that a firm purchases turn out to be an important influence on the choice of technique. You will encounter the notion of the *production function* and see how economists distinguish between the *short* and *long run*. These issues come together to enable us to identify the firm's choice of output level in the short run and in the long run. The *minimum efficient scale* is also introduced, which will be of significance when we come to investigate market structure in a later chapter.

## Important Concepts and Technical Terms

Match each lettered concept with the appropriate numbered phrase:

| | | |
|---|---|---|
| (a) Production function | (g) Economies of (increasing returns to) scale | (l) Long-run total cost |
| (b) Fixed costs | | (m) Minimum efficient scale |
| (c) Constant returns to scale | (h) Long run | (n) Diseconomies of (decreasing returns to) scale |
| (d) Long-run average cost | (i) Variable costs | |
| (e) Law of diminishing returns | (j) Long-run marginal cost | |
| (f) Short-run marginal cost | (k) Short run | |

1  The specification of the maximum output that can be produced from any given amount of inputs.
2  The total cost of producing a given output level when the firm is able to adjust all inputs optimally.
3  The period long enough for the firm to adjust all its inputs to a change in conditions.
4  The output level at which further economies of scale become unimportant for the individual firm and the average cost curve first becomes horizontal.
5  The situation in which long-run average costs increase as output rises.
6  The increase in short-run total costs (and in short-run variable costs) as output is increased by one unit.
7  The cost per unit of producing a given output level when the firm is able to adjust all inputs optimally.
8  Costs that change as output changes.
9  The situation where, beyond some level of the variable input, further increases in the variable input lead to a steadily decreasing marginal product of that input.
10  The increase in long-run total costs if output is permanently raised by one unit.
11  Costs that do not vary with output levels.
12  The situation when long-run average costs are constant as output rises.
13  The situation when long-run average costs decrease as output rises.
14  The period in which the firm can make only partial adjustment of its inputs to a change in conditions.

## Exercises

**Table 8-1     Production techniques for toffee**

**Table 8-2     Output and long-run total cost**

| Output | Technique A L | Technique A K | Technique B L | Technique B K | Technique C L | Technique C K |
|---|---|---|---|---|---|---|
| 1 | 9 | 2 | 6 | 4 | 4 | 6 |
| 2 | 19 | 3 | 10 | 8 | 8 | 10 |
| 3 | 29 | 4 | 14 | 12 | 12 | 14 |
| 4 | 41 | 5 | 18 | 16 | 16 | 19 |
| 5 | 59 | 6 | 24 | 22 | 20 | 25 |
| 6 | 85 | 7 | 33 | 29 | 24 | 32 |
| 7 | 120 | 8 | 45 | 38 | 29 | 40 |

Note: *L* denotes labour; *K* denotes capital.
All measured in units per week.

| Output (units/week) | Total cost (£) | Long-run average cost | Long-run marginal cost |
|---|---|---|---|
| 0 | 0 | | |
| 1 | 32 | | |
| 2 | 48 | | |
| 3 | 82 | | |
| 4 | 140 | | |
| 5 | 228 | | |
| 6 | 352 | | |

1   A firm making toffees has a choice between three production techniques, each using different combinations of labour input and capital input, as shown in Table 8-1. Suppose labour costs £200 per unit/week and capital input costs £400 per unit/week.
  (a)  Calculate total cost for each level of output.
  (b)  For each level of output, state which production technique should be adopted by the firm.
  (c)  Suppose that the price of labour input increases to £300 per unit/week, but the price of capital remains constant. In what way would you expect the firm's choice of technique to be affected by this change in relative prices?
  (d)  With the new labour cost, state which production technique should be adopted for each output level and calculate total cost.

2   A firm faces long-run total cost conditions as given in Table 8-2.
  (a)  Calculate long-run average cost and long-run marginal cost.
  (b)  Plot long-run average cost and long-run marginal cost curves.
  (*Hint*  Remember to plot *LMC* at points half-way between the corresponding output levels.)
  (c)  At what output level is long-run average cost at a minimum?
  (d)  At what output level does long-run marginal cost equal long-run average cost?

3   Look at the diagram you drew in exercise 2.
  (a)  Within what range of output does this firm experience economies of scale (increasing returns to scale)?
  (b)  Within what range of output does the firm experience diseconomies of scale (decreasing returns to scale)?
  (c)  What is the minimum efficient scale for this firm?
  (d)  Suppose that you could measure returns to scale at a particular point on the LAC curve: what would characterize the point where LAC is at a minimum?

4   Which of the following statements describes the law of diminishing returns? Suppose in each case that labour is a variable factor, but capital is fixed. As more labour is used:
  (a)  Total output will fall because the extra units of labour will be of poorer quality than those previously employed.
  (b)  The relative shortage of capital will eventually cause increases in total product to become progressively smaller.
  (c)  The cost of the product will eventually be forced up because the wage rate will rise as labour becomes more scarce.
  (d)  After a while fewer units of labour will be needed in order to produce more output.
  (e)  The marginal revenue obtained from each additional unit produced will decline.

**Table 8-3    Short-run costs of production**

| Output (units/week) | Short-run average variable cost (SAVC) |
|---|---|
| 1 | 17 |
| 2 | 15 |
| 3 | 14 |
| 4 | 15 |
| 5 | 19 |
| 6 | 29 |

**Table 8-4    Output and labour input**

| Labour input (workers/week) | Output (goods/week) | Marginal product of labour | Average product of labour |
|---|---|---|---|
| 0 | 0 | | |
| 1 | 35 | | |
| 2 | 80 | | |
| 3 | 122 | | |
| 4 | 156 | | |
| 5 | 177 | | |
| 6 | 180 | | |

5    Which of the following conditions is (are) necessary before the law of diminishing returns to a factor can be said to operate.
   (a) Other factors are held constant.
   (b) The state of technical knowledge does not change.
   (c) All units of the variable factor are homogeneous.

6    A firm faces fixed costs of £45 and short-run average variable costs as shown in Table 8-3.
   (a) From the figures in Table 8-3, calculate short-run average fixed cost, short-run average total cost, short-run total cost, and short-run marginal cost.
   (b) Plot *SAVC*, *SATC* and *SAMC*; check that *SMC* goes through the minimum points of the other two curves.
   (c) If the firm were to increase production from 5 to 6 units/week, the short-run marginal cost would be high. Explain why this should be so, being sure to describe the role played by the marginal product of labour.

7    In the short run, a firm can vary labour input flexibly but cannot change the level of capital input. Table 8-4 shows how output changes as only labour input is varied.
   (a) Calculate the marginal product of labour *(MPL)* and the average product of labour *(APL)*.
   (b) Plot *MPL* and *APL*.
   (c) At *approximately* what level of labour input do diminishing returns set in?
   (d) At *approximately* what level of labour input does MPL cut APL?
   (e) How would you expect the *MPL* curve to be affected by a change in the level of capital input?

8    Which of the following statements about the short-run marginal cost curve are *not* true?
   (a) Marginal cost equals average cost when average cost is at a minimum.
   (b) When average cost is falling, marginal cost will be below average cost.
   (c) Marginal cost is greater than average cost when the number of units produced is greater than the optimum technical output.
   (d) Marginal cost will be rising under conditions of diminishing returns.
   (e) Marginal cost is unaffected by changes in factor prices.
   (f) Marginal cost depends in part upon fixed costs.

9    Each of the four separate short-run average total cost curves in Figure 8-1 overleaf represents a different scale of operation of a firm.
   (a) On the basis of Figure 8-1, what would be the most efficient level of output for the firm to produce?
   (b) If the firm were to expand its scale of operation beyond this point what would be the nature of the returns to scale?
   (c) Which of the four scales of operation would be appropriate if the firm wished to produce OA output?
   (d) If the firm then wanted to expand to produce *OB* output, what would be the chosen scale of operation in the short run and in the long run?
   (e) Sketch in the long-run average cost curve for the firm.

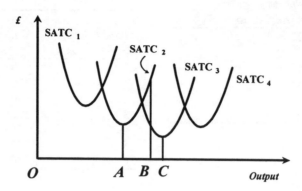

**Figure 8-1    Short-run average cost**

10   A firm has selected the output level at which it wishes to produce. Having checked the marginal condition, the firm is now considering the average condition as it applies in the short run and the long run. Cost conditions are such that *LAC* is £12; *SATC* is £17 (made up of *SAVC* £11 and *SAFC* £6). In Table 8-5, tick the appropriate short- and long-run decisions for the firm at each stated market price.

| | Short-run decision | | | Long-run decision | | |
|---|---|---|---|---|---|---|
| Price (£) | Produce at a profit | Produce at a loss | Close down | Produce at a profit | Produce at a loss | Close down |
| 18 | | | | | | |
| 5 | | | | | | |
| 7 | | | | | | |
| 13 | | | | | | |
| 11.50 | | | | | | |

## True/False

1   Capital and labour are the only two factors of production which the firm needs to consider when making its output decision.

2   The typical U-shape often assumed for the long-run average cost curve is valid only for a firm facing economies of scale at low levels of output, changing to diseconomies as output expands.

3   Specialization (the division of labour) can lead to economies of scale.

4   Small firms are always less efficient than large ones.

5   Firms who make losses are lame ducks who should be closed down at once.

6   A firm will close down in the short run if price is less than average revenue.

7   The long-run supply decision is determined by finding the level of output at which long-run marginal cost is equal to marginal revenue.

8   Holding labour constant while increasing capital input will lead to diminishing returns.

9   *LAC* is falling when *LMC* is less than *LAC* and rising when *LMC* is greater than *LAC; LAC* is at a minimum at the output level at which *LAC* and *LMC* cross.

10   Empirical evidence suggests that if there were more than one refrigerator manufacturer in the UK, it would be impossible for every firm in that industry to be producing at minimum efficient scale.

11  The decision whether to continue to produce should be taken regardless of how much money has been devoted to the project in the past.

12  The long-run average cost curve passes through the lowest point of each short-run average cost curve.

## ECONOMICS IN THE NEWS

### A policy of reducing costs
*(Adapted from the Financial Times, 24 January 1997)*

Royal & Sun Alliance, the composite insurer which sprang forth from the £6bn merger of two rivals last July, has been keeping a low profile while it grapples with the task of integration and achieving targeted savings of £175m by 1998. It would be an understatement to say a merger of this scale is fraught with complications, especially when the central plank of this particular deal is the loss of 5000 jobs, 80 per cent of which are in the UK. Analysts say it is looking increasingly likely that the published targets for cost savings will be exceeded as economies of scale not included in earlier forecasts add extra benefits.

For example, Royal & Sun Alliance is thought to have negotiated a 10 to 15 per cent reduction in the cost of its reinsurance. The group had anticipated taking on more risk, but secured the same cover for less cost. Other economies of scale, like the cost of developing information technology, have not yet been quantified, but are expected to trim expenses by several million pounds a year.

The reason for this obsession with cutting costs is rooted in the state of the insurance market, especially in the UK, where the onslaught from direct writers over the past 10 years has had a big impact on the market share of the composites.

Banks have also begun to make inroads by using their branch networks and strong branding to sell personal insurance, while low barriers to entry in commercial lines have allowed foreign competitors to establish a strong position. Of equal importance to cutting costs is the group's long-term strategy, and management has said even less about this.

All of the UK-based composites are small compared with European and US counterparts. These companies have responded to the demands of big commercial clients seeking global coverage by using a strong capital base to finance expansion overseas. If Royal & Sun wants to be a truly global insurer, then it will need a bigger presence in all the main overseas markets.

1  Identify the key aspects of the insurance market that make economies of scale possible for Royal & Sun Alliance.

2  How are these changes likely to affect the degree of competitiveness in the insurance market?

## Questions for Thought

1  Explain why in some industries large firms are able to produce at lower average cost than small firms. Name some industries with this characteristic. In what sorts of activity might the reverse be true, and why?

2  Is it possible for an industry to experience economies of scale and diminishing returns to labour simultaneously?

3  It has been suggested that in practice firms do not know all the details of the various cost curves that we have discussed. If this is so, how relevant is all this analysis?

4  Think about how you would expect economies of scale to have changed in recent years in each of the following activities. What effects might these changes have on the way that these markets might be expected to operate?

*(a)* Telecommunications.
*(b)* Banking.
*(c)* Motor vehicles.
*(d)* Textiles.
*(e)* Opticians.
*(f)* Water supply.

# 9  Perfect Competition and Monopoly: The Limiting Cases of Market Structure

## Learning Outcomes

- To understand the concepts of perfect competition and pure monopoly
- To show why a perfectly competitive firm chooses the output at which price equals marginal cost
- To relate entry and exit to the level of profits of existing firms
- To derive industry supply curves from the marginal cost curves of perfectly competitive firms
- To master comparative static analysis of shifts in demand or supply
- To analyse a market in which international trade takes place
- To explain why a monopolist chooses output to equate marginal cost and marginal revenue
- To compare a monopolist's output with that of a perfectly competitive industry
- To show how the ability to price discriminate affects a monopolist's output and profits

**IN THIS CHAPTER ...** you will begin to explore the important topic of *market structure,* which greatly influences the determination of an industry's price and output. Two benchmark, but extreme forms of market structure are *monopoly* and *perfect competition.* In a perfectly competitive market, there are many buyers and sellers of a good, none of whom believe that they can have any influence on market price. Consequently, each firm is a *price-taker* – each must accept the going market price. Do you remember that we included opportunity cost in the costs faced by a firm? This now becomes crucial. If firms make profits *above* costs, then this will be an inducement for more firms to enter the market, which will then move towards long-run equilibrium. In pure monopoly, there is only one seller of a good, who thus faces the (downward-sloping) market demand curve. Unlike the firm under perfect competition, the monopoly has some control over price as well as output. A comparison of perfect competition and monopoly markets suggests that the monopolist will produce lower output at a higher price. However, the existence of *barriers to entry* is crucial if the monopolist is to maintain its market position.

## Important Concepts and Technical Terms

Match each lettered concept with the appropriate numbered phrase:

| | | | | | |
|---|---|---|---|---|---|
| (a) | Perfectly competitive market | (e) | Law of One Price | (i) | Supernormal profits |
| (b) | Industry supply curve | (f) | Monopoly | (j) | Firm's supply curve |
| (c) | Natural monopoly | (g) | Marginal firm | (k) | Monopsony |
| (d) | Shutdown price | (h) | Normal profit | (l) | Free entry or exit |

1  A market in which both buyers and sellers believe that their own buying or selling decisions have no effect on the market price.
2  The curve showing the quantity that the firm wants to produce at each price.
3  The least efficient firm in a perfectly competitive industry, just making normal profits.
4  A market structure in which there is only one buyer or potential buyer of the good in that industry.
5  A situation in which firms can leave or join an industry without hindrance.
6  A market structure in which there is only one seller or potential seller of the good in that industry.
7  A situation in which the price of a given commodity would be the same all over the world if there were no obstacles to trade and no transport costs.
8  An industry in which the firm faces such substantial economies of scale that long-run average cost falls over the entire range of output, making it difficult for more than one firm to operate.
9  The price below which the firm reduces its losses by choosing not to produce at all.
10  That level of profits which just pays the opportunity cost of the owners' money and time.
11  An excess of total revenue over total cost.
12  The curve showing the total quantity that firms in (or potentially in) an industry want to supply at each price.

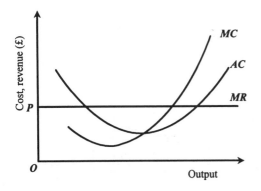

Figure 9-1    A firm under perfect competition

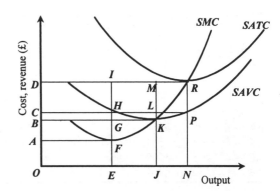

Figure 9-2    Short-run cost curves for a perfectly competitive firm

## Exercises

1   A firm operating in a perfectly competitive industry faces the cost curves shown in Figure 9-l. *OP* is the going market price.
   (a)  Mark on the diagram the profit-maximizing level of output.
   (b)  Mark on the diagram the area representing the profits made by the firm at this level of price and output.
   (c)  If you were told that this industry was in equilibrium, would you judge it to be a short-run or a long-run equilibrium? Justify your answer.
   (d)  How would you expect the firm to be affected by a decrease in the market demand for the commodity produced by this industry?

2   Figure 9-2 shows the short-run cost curves for a perfectly competitive firm.
   (a)  What is the shutdown price for the firm?
   (b)  At what price would the firm just make normal profits?
   (c)  What area would represent total fixed cost at this price?
   (d)  Within what range of prices would the firm choose to operate at a loss in the short run?
   (e)  Identify the firm's short-run supply curve.
   (f)  Within what range of prices would the firm he able to make short-run supernormal profits?

3   A monopolist faces the cost and revenue conditions shown in Figure 9-3.
   (a)  Mark on the diagram the profit-maximizing level of output.
   (b)  Mark on the diagram the price at which the monopolist would choose to sell this output.
   (c)  Identify the area representing the level of monopoly profits at this price and output.
   (d)  How would you expect the monopolist to be affected by a decrease in the market demand for the commodity?

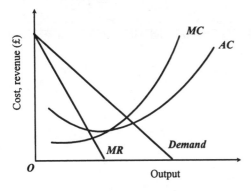

Figure 9-3    A monopolist's cost and revenue conditions

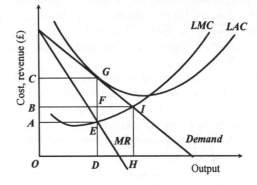

Figure 9-4    The long-run position of a monopolist

### Table 9-1    A monopolist's demand curve

| Demand ('000s/week) | Price (£) | Total revenue | Marginal revenue |
|---|---|---|---|
| 0 | 40 | | |
| 1 | 35 | | |
| 2 | 30 | | |
| 3 | 25 | | |
| 4 | 20 | | |
| 5 | 15 | | |
| 6 | 10 | | |
| 7 | 5 | | |

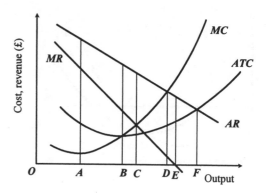

Figure 9-5    Cost and revenue for a firm

4    Figure 9-4 on the previous page shows the long-run cost and revenue situation facing a monopolist.
   (a)    What is the profit-maximizing level of output?
   (b)    At what price would the monopolist choose to sell the good?
   (c)    What level of supernormal profits would be made in this situation?
   (d)    How much output (and at what price) would the monopolist produce if forced to set price equal to marginal cost?

5    Table 9-1 represents the demand curve faced by a monopolist.
   (a)    Calculate total revenue and marginal revenue.
   (b)    Plot average revenue and marginal revenue.
   (c)    On a separate graph, plot total revenue.
   (d)    At what level of demand is total revenue at a maximum.
   (e)    At what level of demand is marginal revenue equal to zero?
   (f)    At what level of demand is there unit own-price elasticity of demand?

6    Figure 9-5 shows a firm's cost and revenue position. At which output level would the firm be
   (a)    maximizing profits?
   (b)    maximizing total revenue?
   (c)    producing the technically optimum output?
   (d)    making only normal profits?

7    Under which of the following conditions will a profit-maximizing, perfectly competitive firm close down in the short run?
   (a)    Price is less than marginal cost.
   (b)    Average revenue is less than average cost.
   (c)    Average fixed cost is greater than price.
   (d)    Average revenue is less than average variable cost.
   (e)    Total cost is greater than total revenue.

8    Which of the following situations characterize a perfectly competitive market, and which relate to a monopoly (or to both)? Assume that firms are aiming to maximize profits.
   (a)    Price exceeds marginal cost.
   (b)    Price equals marginal revenue.
   (c)    Marginal revenue equals marginal cost.
   (d)    Abnormal profit is zero in long-run equilibrium.
   (e)    New firms are excluded from the market.
   (f)    A firm chooses its price-output combination.
   (g)    There are no barriers to entry.
   (h)    Average revenue exceeds marginal revenue.
   (i)    Price equals marginal cost.

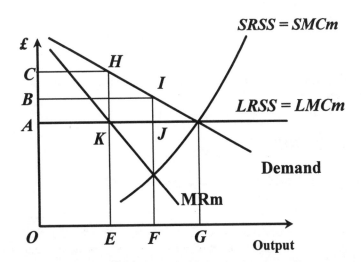

**Figure 9-6    The monopolization of a perfectly competitive industry**

9   Which of the following corresponds most closely to the economists' notion of 'normal profit'?
   (a)   The level of profits a firm makes by setting *MC=MR*.
   (b)   The level of profits made by the typical firm in the industry.
   (c)   The level of profits a firm would tend to make under normal conditions of trade.
   (d)   The level of profits needed to persuade a firm to stay in its current line of business.
   (e)   The rate of profits that ensures a comfortable standard of living for the entrepreneur.

10  A perfectly competitive industry is taken over by a monopolist who intends to run it as a multi-plant concern. Consequently, the long-run supply curve of the competitive industry *(LRSS)* becomes the monopolist's long-run marginal cost curve *(LMCm)*; in the short run the *SRSS* curve becomes the monopolist's *SMCm*. The position is shown in Figure 9-6.
   (a)   What was the equilibrium price and industry output under perfect competition?
   (b)   At what price and output would the monopolist choose to operate in the short run?
   (c)   At what price and output would the monopolist maximize profits in the long run?
   (d)   What would be the size of these long-run profits?

## True/False

1   Price is equal to marginal revenue for a firm under perfect competition.
2   The short-run supply curve for a perfectly competitive firm is flatter than the long-run supply curve.
3   A firm making economic profits is said to be making normal profits.
4   An industry in which long-run average costs fall throughout the relevant range of output is ideally suited for a perfectly competitive market.
5   The supply curve of an industry is obtained by a horizontal aggregation of the quantities supplied by firms in the industry at each price.
6   A monopolist will always produce on the inelastic part of the demand curve.

7   Other things being equal, an increase in variable costs will cause a monopolist to increase output and reduce price.

8   A monopolist makes supernormal profits because it is more efficient than a competitive industry.

9   Total revenue is maximized when average revenue is at a maximum.

10  A monopolist may increase total profits by charging different prices in different markets.

11  A perfectly competitive firm will be selling at a price equal to marginal cost, but a monopolist can set a price above marginal cost.

12  Very small firms typically do little research and development, whereas many larger firms have excellent research departments.

## ECONOMICS IN THE NEWS

### EUROSTAR lowest prices ever

*(Adapted from the Daily Telegraph, 16 November 1999)*

EUROSTAR introduced its lowest fares yesterday in an effort to stimulate demand, as the company admitted that it is likely to continue making losses until well into the next century. On the fifth anniversary of the first direct trains from London to Paris and Brussels, the operator revealed that passenger volumes were growing so slowly that it had asked Railtrack for a reduction in its line usage charges. For the next four weeks, day returns of £45 will be available on Saturdays and Sundays, and the offer will then be extended to all days of the week, including bank holidays, until Jan 16. Seats in first-class will cost £75. A fare of £29 return is being brought in for the next six months, aimed at the weekend 'night clubber' market. This will be available on trains leaving Waterloo after 4pm on Saturday, and returning from Paris or Brussels before 10am the next day.

Regular ticket prices are at an historic low, with the cheapest standard day return at £79, compared with £95 when Eurostar launched in 1994. The company hopes that such discounts will fill seats and enable losses to fall to £75 million for the current financial year. However, it would now be 'extremely tough' to meet forecasts of moving into profit by 2005. Gordon Bye, managing director, said trading had proved far more difficult than the company had envisaged when it came into being as part of British Rail. It was then forecast that annual passenger numbers would by now have reached 12 million, almost double the 6.6 million currently expected. The low-fare air market had not been foreseen, but was making massive inroads into Eurostar's share of the short-haul leisure break market. Mr Bye said the company had found particular difficulty in increasing demand among Continental passengers.

1   Although there is only one Channel Tunnel, it is clear that Eurostar faces competition. From whom? How does this affect Eurostar's decisions on price?

2   Identify the ways in which Eurostar is seeking to discriminate in its pricing policy. What characteristic of consumers enables the firm to act in this way?

## Questions for Thought

1   We have seen that a monopolist wishing to maximize profits will tend to restrict output and increase price. Can you think of circumstances in which a monopolist might choose not to take full advantage of these potential profits?

2   Explain why it is said that the firm under perfect competition operates at the technically optimum point of production in the long run. Can any conclusions be drawn about the efficient allocation of resources in the industry?

**3**  The monopoly producer of a commodity supplies two separate markets. The commodity is one that cannot be resold – in other words, it is not possible for a consumer to buy in market 2 and resell in market 1. Figure 9-7 shows the demand and marginal revenue curves in the two markets and in the combined market. Notice that the *MR* curve for the combined market has a 'jump' in it at the point where price falls sufficiently for the monopolist to make sales in market 2.

This question extends the analysis of Section 9-9 in the main text: you may wish to tackle it slowly, with the help of the comments provided in the 'Answers and Comments' section. Throughout the analysis, the monopolist's output level is decided by reference to marginal cost and revenue in the *combined* market. You can draw lines across to the submarket diagrams to find *MR* and *AR*.

*(a)*   What level of output will the monopolist produce to maximize profits?

*(b)*   If the monopolist sets a common price to all customers, what would that price be?

*(c)*   How much will the monopolist sell in each of the two submarkets?

*(d)*   At this selling price, what is marginal revenue in each of the two markets?

*(e)*   If the monopolist now finds that price discrimination is possible, how could profits be increased?
        *(Hint:* Your answer to part *(d)* is important here.)

*(f)*   With price discrimination, what prices would the monopolist set in each market, and how much would be sold?

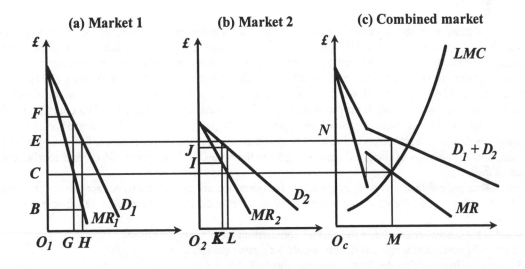

**Figure 9-7    A discriminating monopolist**

**4**  This question extends the discussion of Figure 9-6 (exercise 10), in which we were looking at the case of a perfectly competitive industry being taken over by a monopolist.  We saw that under perfect competition, equilibrium would be *at* output *OG*, price *OA*, whereas the profit-maximizing monopolist would restrict output in the short run to *OF* and raise price to *OB*, and in the long run move to *OE, OC*. We will consider the two long-run equilibrium positions.  An amended version of Figure 9-6 appears as Figure 9-8.

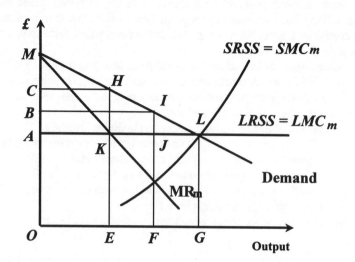

**Figure 9-8    The monopolization of a perfectly competitive industry revisited**

However. first think a bit about the demand curve. What does a point on the demand curve really represent? At a point such as *I,* consumers are jointly prepared to pay a price *OB* for *OF* output. In a sense, *OB* is the consumers' valuation of a marginal unit of the good. Indeed, on this argument we might describe the demand curve as representing the 'marginal social benefit' function. Notice that at the higher price *OC* there are still consumers prepared to purchase *OE* units of the good. When the price is only *OB,* those consumers pay less at the margin than they would have been prepared to pay for at least some of the units. We could argue that this implies that they receive a 'surplus' above what they actually pay at point *I.* This is sometimes known as the *consumer surplus*; it is represented in Figure 9-6 by the area under the demand curve. For example, at point *I,* consumers' total valuation of the good they consume is the area *OMIF*; they pay *OBIF,* and receive consumer surplus of *BMI.*

This was a long preamble to a very short question! However, the concept of consumer surplus will reappear later in the book, and it is good for you to be prepared. Three short questions to see whether this discussion has made sense to you:

*(a)*  What is the consumer surplus at the perfect competition long-run equilibrium?

*(b)*  What is the consumer surplus at the monopoly long-run equilibrium?

*(c)*  So what has happened to the 'lost' consumer surplus?

# 10  Market Structure and Imperfect Competition

## Learning Outcomes

- To define imperfect competition, oligopoly, and monopolistic competition
- To show how differences in cost and demand lead to different market structures
- To analyse the tangency equilibrium in monopolistic competition
- To consider the tension between collusion and competition within a cartel
- To analyse games, and define the concepts of commitment and credibility
- To explain why there is little market power in a contestable market
- To define innocent entry barriers and analyse how strategic entry barriers can be created

**IN THIS CHAPTER ...** you will encounter forms of *imperfect competition:* in particular, *monopolistic competition* and *oligopoly*. It is especially important to be able to analyse oligopoly because of its prevalence in the real world. The *kinked demand curve* model is one famous oligopoly model, and more recently, *game theory* has been developed to analyse this market structure. Firms are seen as players in a game, choosing their moves according to perceptions about the likely moves of other players (firms). Tensions are inherent in a cartel: firms gain by collusion, but the incentive for an individual firm to cheat is ever-present.

## Important Concepts and Technical Terms

Match each lettered concept with the appropriate numbered phrase:

| | | |
|---|---|---|
| (a) Oligopoly | (f) Product differentiation | (k) Kinked demand curve |
| (b) Imperfect competition | (g) Pre-commitment | (l) Prisoners' dilemma |
| (c) Contestable market | (h) Monopolistic competition | (m) Innocent entry barrier |
| (d) Credible threat | (i) Predatory pricing | (n) Nash equilibrium |
| (e) Dominant strategy | (j) Game theory | |

1  A market structure in which firms recognize that their demand curves slope downwards and that output price will depend on the quantity of goods produced and sold.
2  An industry with only a few producers, each recognizing that its own price depends not merely on its own output but also on the actions of its important competitors in the industry.
3  A tactic adopted by existing firms when faced by a new entrant, involving deliberately increasing output and forcing down the price, causing all firms to make losses.
4  The analysis of the principles behind intelligent interdependent decision-making.
5  The demand curve perceived by an oligopolist who believes that competitors will respond to a decrease in his price but not to an increase.
6  An industry having many sellers producing products that are close substitutes for one another, and in which each firm has only a limited ability to affect its output price.
7  Actual or perceived differences in a good compared with its substitutes, designed to affect potential buyers.
8  A situation in which a player's best strategy is independent of that adopted by other players.
9  An arrangement entered into voluntarily which restricts one's future options.
10  A game between two players, each of whom has a dominant strategy.
11  A barrier to entry not deliberately erected by firms.
12  The threat of a punishment strategy which, after the fact, a firm would find it optimal to carry out.
13  A situation where each player chooses the best strategy, given the strategies followed by the other players.
14  A market characterized by free entry and free exit.

## Exercises

1  For each of the situations listed below, select the market form in the list which offers the best description.

*Market forms*    A         Perfect competition
                  B         Monopoly
                  C         Oligopoly
                  D         Monopolistic competition
                  E         Monopsony

(a) A fairly large number of firms, each supplying branded footwear at very similar prices.
(b) A sole supplier of telecommunication services.
(c) A large number of farmers supplying carrots at identical prices.
(d) A few giant firms supplying the whole of the market for car tyres.
(e) A single buyer of coal-cutting equipment.
(f) A sole supplier of rail transport.

2  Table 10-1 presents some hypothetical concentration ratios and information about scale economies in a number of industries.

(a) Which industry is most likely to be operated as a monopoly?
(b) Which industry(ies) would you expect to find operating under conditions of perfect competition?
(c) In which industry(ies) would conditions be conducive to oligopoly?
(d) In which industry(ies) would oligopoly be unlikely to arise? Explain your answer.

3  Which of the following characteristics are typical of an industry operating under monopolistic competition in long-run equilibrium? (Note: there may be more than one valid response.)

(a) Individual firms in the industry make only small monopoly profits.
(b) Individual firms in the industry would be keen to sell more output at the existing market price.
(c) There is product differentiation.
(d) Each firm faces a downward-sloping demand curve.
(e) Firms operate below full capacity output.
(f) Firms maximize profits where marginal cost equals marginal revenue.
(g) There is collusion among firms in the industry.
(h) The profits accruing to firms are just sufficient to cover the opportunity cost of capital employed.

4  Figure 10-1 shows a profit-maximizing firm in monopolistic competition.

(a) How much output will be produced by the firm?
(b) At what price will the output be sold?
(c) Will the firm make supernormal profits in this situation? If so, identify their extent.
(d) Would you consider this to be a long-run or short-run equilibrium for the firm?
(e) Explain your answer to (d) and describe how the situation might differ in the 'other run'.

**Table 10-1    Concentration and scale economies in Hypothetica**

| Industry | Three-firm concentration ratio (CR) | Number of plants at min. efficient scale allowed by market size (NP) |
|---|---|---|
| A | 100 | 1 |
| B | 11 | 221 |
| C | 81 | 3 |
| D | 49 | 5 |
| E | 21 | 195 |

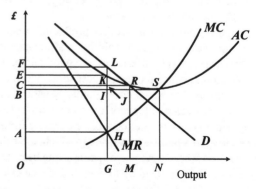

**Figure 10-1  A firm in monopolistic competition**

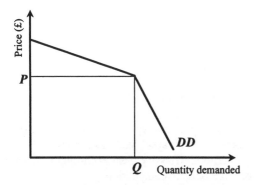

**Figure 10-2   A firm's perceived demand curve**

|  | Profits | Firm Y chooses: | | | |
|--|---------|-----------------|--|--|--|
|  |  | Low output | | High output | |
|  |  | X | Y | X | Y |
| Firm X chooses: | Low output | 15 | 15 | 2 | 20 |
|  | High output | 20 | 2 | 8 | 8 |

**Figure 10-3   The Prisoners' Dilemma game**

5   In an oligopolistic market, which of the following conditions tend to favour collusion and which are more likely to encourage non-cooperation?

| Influence | Encourages collusion | Favours non-cooperation |
|-----------|----------------------|-------------------------|
|  | *(Tick one column)* | |
| Barriers to entry | | |
| Product is non-standard | | |
| Demand and costs are stable | | |
| Collusion is legal | | |
| Secrecy about price and output | | |
| Collusion is illegal | | |
| Easy communication of price and output | | |
| Standard product | | |

6   Figure 10-2 shows the demand curve *(DD)* for the output of an individual firm, as perceived by that firm. The firm is currently producing the amount *OQ* at a price *OP*. Assess the likely validity of each of the following inferences that may be drawn concerning conditions in the industry of which this firm is a part:
   *(a)* The firm may be slow to change price, even if faced by a change in cost conditions.
   *(b)* The firm is a discriminating monopolist, charging different prices in two separated markets.
   *(c)* The industry is a non-cooperative oligopoly in which the individual firm must take into consideration the likely behaviour of the few rival firms.
   *(d)* The firm faces production difficulties at levels of output above *OQ* as a result of labour shortages.

7   Suppose that there are two firms (X and Y) operating in a market, each of which can choose to produce either 'high' or 'low' output. Figure 10-3 summarizes the range of possible outcomes of the firms' decisions in a single time period. Imagine that you are taking the decisions for firm X.
   *(a)* If firm Y produces 'low', what level of output would maximize your profit in this time period?
   *(b)* If you (X) produce 'high', what level of output would maximize profits for firm Y?
   *(c)* If firm Y produces 'high', what level of output would maximize your profit in this time period?
   *(d)* Under what circumstances would you decide to produce 'low'?
   *(e)* Suppose you enter into an agreement with firm Y that you both will produce 'low': what measures could you adopt to ensure that Y keeps to the agreement?
   *(f)* What measures could you adopt to convince Y that you will keep to the agreement?
   *(g)* Suppose that the profit combinations are the same as in Figure 10-3 except that if both firms produce 'high' each firm makes a loss of 8. Does this affect the analysis?

8  Which of the following entry barriers are 'innocent', and which are strategic?
   (a) Exploiting the benefits of large-scale production.
   (b) Undertaking a research and development (R&D) project to develop new techniques and products.
   (c) Holding a patent on a particular product.
   (d) Producing a range of similar products under different brand-names.
   (e) Extensive multi-media advertising.
   (f) Installing more machinery than is required for normal (or current) levels of production.
   (g) Holding an absolute cost advantage.
9  A crucial characteristic of a monopoly is the existence of barriers to entry. One type of such barrier is patent protection. Suppose the monopolist's patent on a good expires. How is the market likely to adjust?
10 Think about some of the firms that operate in your own neighbourhood. Classify them according to market structure – i.e. as perfect competition, monopoly, oligopoly, or monopolistic competition.

## True/False

1  The firm under imperfect competition has some influence over price, evidenced by the downward-sloping demand curve for its product.
2  A key aspect of an oligopolistic market is that firms cannot act independently of each other.
3  An industry where diseconomies of scale set in at a low level of output is likely to be a monopoly.
4  A firm in long-run equilibrium under monopolistic competition produces at an output below the technically optimum point of production.
5  A feature of the kinked oligopoly demand curve model is that price may be stable when costs for a single firm change, but may change rapidly when the whole industry is faced with a change in cost conditions.
6  Firms under oligopoly face kinked demand curves.
7  A player holding a dominant strategy always wins.
8  Cartels may be made workable if their members are prepared to enter into binding pre-commitments.
9  A cartel member's announcement of intent to adopt a punishment strategy will maintain a cartel.
10 A monopolist always maximizes profits by setting marginal cost equal to marginal revenue.
11 Free exit from a market implies that there are no sunk or irrecoverable costs.
12 Fixed costs may artificially increase scale economies and help to deter entry by firms new to the industry.

## ECONOMICS IN THE NEWS

### A warning for web debutants
(Adapted from The Financial Times, 23 December 1999)

As the founder of E*Trade, one of the hottest companies on the internet, Bill Porter could be a role model for entrepreneurs hoping to make it big in e-commerce. The online investing service is one of the few Internet companies that has made money. Yet rather than acting as cheerleader to web start-ups, Mr Porter's message is one of caution for the would-be billionaires. 'I wouldn't want to be getting into the Internet business today,' says Mr Porter, shaking his head. 'It takes only one to two people in a garage to establish a site. There are so many ideas, so many garages, so many companies to finance. The market is flooded. Some will be winners, but most will not.'

'You have to go for the niche businesses now,' says Mr Porter of the situation in the US. 'I wouldn't want to try to put up a general auction site or a book seller today. The door has closed a bit.'

Along with the competition from other Internet businesses, a further challenge for start-ups comes from big bricks-and-mortar companies, which are beginning to vie for e-commerce space as well. 'Big companies are finally starting to notice the big potential of e-commerce,' says Mr Porter. 'The major players are catching on; they are getting wiser and wiser about how to use the Internet, and that raises the cost of entry for others. It's all about market share and brand name.' Word-of-mouth and media buzz is no longer enough to create a big brand. Instead, corporations are spending vast amounts of money on advertising in traditional venues. E*Trade was this year's biggest advertising spender during the US World Series baseball games on television. Few start-ups can match the hundreds of millions of dollars traditional companies can spend on branding.

These kinds of barriers have not stopped Internet start-ups from proliferating. Yet it means that the most successful ones will probably be niche players: companies such as Boatscape.com, which sells used boats over the web. 'There are a multitude of these sites,' says Mr Porter. 'They might be very successful at what they do and are providing a great service for society. But chances are they're not going to rise up and challenge Amazon.'

1   What barriers to entry might firms introduce to protect themselves against entry from new entrants operating on the Internet?
2   What sort of market structure do you think most closely typifies the markets described in the passage?

## Questions for Thought

1   Exercise 8 listed various sorts of entry barriers. Can you think of examples of British industries in which they appear to be operative?
2   Figure 10-4 shows the trading conditions for a two-firm cartel. Panels *(a)* and *(b)* show respectively the conditions facing the two firms A and B; panel *(c)* shows the combined cartel position. *D=ARc* in panel *(c)* shows the market demand curve, and *MRc* is the associated marginal revenue curve. Notice that firm A has a cost advantage over firm B.
    *(a)* If the two firms collude to maximize profits in the combined market, what joint output level will they choose?
    *(b)* At what price will the cartel sell the good?
    *(c)* If each firm accepts the cartel *MR* level, how much output will each produce?
    *(d)* Identify profit levels in each of the firms.
    *(e)* Suppose that firm B imagined that it was a price-taker at the price set by the cartel. What would be its perceived profit-maximizing output level?
    *(f)* If firm B were to set output at this level, what would be the effect on market price?

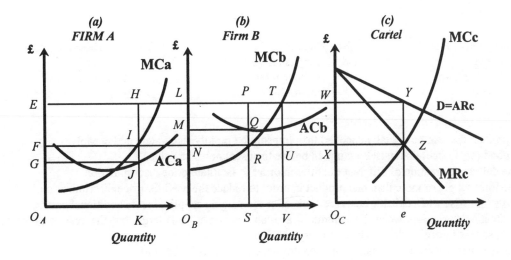

**Figure 10-4    A two-firm cartel**

3   For many years the only information that tobacco manufacturers were allowed to include in their advertising was that smoking is harmful. Why should they bother?
4   If oligopoly is so common in the real world, and perfect competition is so rare, why do we bother with the theory of perfect competition?

# 11   The Information Economy

## Learning Outcomes

- To analyse the significance of the key attributes of information products: experience, overload, network externalities and switching costs
- To identify the special cost characteristics of an e-product: high fixed costs of production but almost zero marginal cost of distribution
- To explain that this cost structure fosters monopolies that will want to price discriminate
- To analyse explicit price discrimination and versioning; and the use of bundling to reduce the need for price discrimination
- To discuss how specialization in complementary activities gives rise to a role for strategic alliances
- To consider the role of the standard in a network, and the nature of competition between networks to set national or international standards

**IN THIS CHAPTER ...** you will use the economic analysis that you have learned so far to explore the *information economy*. Information or e-products have attributes that seem to set them apart, involving *experience, overload, switching costs* and *network externalities*. These attributes have important implications for the way that they are viewed by consumers, and treated by producers. The production of information products is characterized by high fixed costs but very low marginal costs, inclining such markets towards monopoly and encouraging firms to seek for ways of introducing *price discrimination*, for example through *versioning*. The use of *bundling* and the importance of establishing *standards* will also be explored.

## Important Concepts and Technical Terms

Match each lettered concept with the appropriate numbered phrase:

| | | | | | |
|---|---|---|---|---|---|
| *(a)* | Switching cost | *(e)* | Bundling | *(i)* | Price discrimination |
| *(b)* | e-product | *(f)* | Experience good | *(j)* | 2-part tariff |
| *(c)* | Network externality | *(g)* | Niche market | *(k)* | Strategic alliance |
| *(d)* | Standard | *(h)* | Versioning | *(l)* | Information overload |

1   A product that can be digitally encoded then transmitted rapidly, accurately and cheaply.
2   A good (or service) that must be sampled before the user knows its value.
3   The deliberate creation of different qualities in order to facilitate price discrimination.
4   The joint supply of more than one product in order to reduce the need for price discrimination.
5   Costs that arise when existing costs are sunk, so that changing supplier incurs additional costs.
6   A situation that arises when the volume of available information is large, but the cost of processing it is high, so that screening devices become very valuable.
7   The technical specification that is common throughout a particular network.
8   A situation that arises when an additional network member conveys benefits to those already on the network.
9   A pricing arrangement in which an annual charge is levied to cover fixed costs, together with a small price per unit related to marginal costs.
10   A blend of co-operation and competition in which a group of suppliers provide a range of products that partly complement one another.
11   A situation in which a supplier is able to charge different prices to different customers for the same product.
12   A market based on the specialist preferences of a group of consumers.

## Exercises

1   Which of the following goods or services may be classified as information products?
    *(a)* Music.
    *(b)* Pencil.
    *(c)* Today's issue of *The Guardian.*
    *(d)* A dictionary.
    *(e)* Refrigerator.
    *(f)* Computer.
    *(g)* Web page.
    *(h)* A football match.

2   You receive an email from a company offering a tutoring service for economics students. For £100 per month, you can have access to a web site that provides advice on aspects of economic theory.
    *(a)* Would you subscribe?
    *(b)* Given that this is an experience good, and you would probably not subscribe without some assurance that the product will be useful you, which of the following might make you more likely to respond favourably to the invitation to subscribe?
        *(i)* The web site is run by one of the top university economics departments in the UK.
        *(ii)* The firm is offering a free preview of part of the web site – the section on game theory.
        *(iii)* You are familiar with the firm, having used one of its other web sites in the past.
        *(iv)* The firm offers you a week's free trial of the whole site.
        *(v)* You have an end of semester examination next week.

3   The delivery of an information product entails the following sorts of costs:
    A          Production costs
    B          Reproduction costs
    C          Distribution costs
    (a) Classify each of these cost items as a fixed or variable cost.
    (b) Evaluate the likely relative magnitude of these items.
    (c) What do your answers imply for returns to scale?

4   Figure 11-1 shows the market for a good which has network externalities associated with it. $D_1$ represents the initial demand curve, and $P_1$ is the initial price being charged.
    *(a)* What is the initial equilibrium quantity demanded?
    Suppose the firm reduces price from $P_1$ to $P_2$:
    *(b)* What is the new equilibrium quantity demanded in the short run?
    *(c)* What effect might this have on the attractiveness of the network?
    *(d)* Which is the new (short-run) demand curve and equilibrium quantity demanded?
    *(e)* Sketch in the long-run demand curve (i.e. the demand curve recognising the existence of the network externality).

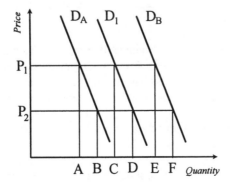

**Figure 11-1    Demand with a network externality**

5    Which of the following products are subject to versioning?
    *(a)*  Books.
    *(b)*  Railways.
    *(c)*  Sausages.
    *(d)*  Computer software.
    *(e)*  Air travel.

6    Which of the following are important characteristics of an information product – and why do they matter?
    *(a)*  You cannot know its value until you have it.
    *(b)*  Once you have it, you don't need it again.
    *(c)*  More of it may reduce utility.
    *(d)*  Once you have chosen a particular product you may be stuck with it.
    *(e)*  The more other people who have it, the more useful it is to you.

7    You have developed some specialist computer software that will offer an improved service for potential clients who currently use *Package X*, which is produced by a rival company, Comp.or. To set up an account for a typical new customer will cost you £30, but will entail hassle to the customer that she values at £65.
    *(a)*  What are the total switching costs?
    *(b)*  If the present value of the expected future stream of profit from a customer is £90, do you proceed with the new product?
    *(c)*  Would your decision be different if the expected profit stream is £200?
    *(d)*  What steps might you take to attract customers in this situation?
    *(e)*  What action might Comp.or take to protect its own market position?

8    Table 11-1 sets out the willingness to pay for two goods of three supermarket customers.

**Table 11-1    Willingness to pay (£)**

|          | *Pizza* | *Treacle tart* |
| -------- | ------- | -------------- |
| Anna     | 3       | 0              |
| Bob      | 0       | 3              |
| Caroline | 2       | 2              |

    *(a)*  What would the supermarket's revenue be if it set prices of £3 for pizza and for treacle tart?
    *(b)*  What would the supermarket's revenue be if it set prices of £2 for pizza and for treacle tart?
    *(c)*  What would revenue be if it set prices at £3 for pizza, £3 for treacle tart, but with the option of buying both for £4?
    *(d)*  How could the supermarket find out how to reach the pricing strategy expressed in *(c)*?

9    Could a market for an information product be perfectly competitive? What alternative markets structures are likely, and why?

## True/False

1    Revenues from e-commerce are forecast to rise almost five-fold in Western Europe between 1999 and 2002.
2    It took Yahoo! only 5 years to overtake General Motors in terms of its market capitalization.
3    The problem with information is that once you have it, you do not need to buy it.
4    Search engines are among the most popular web sites because they help users to cope with information overload.
5    The fixed costs of learning a new word processor or other software packages are high, so there is a strong incentive to stick with what you know.
6    The more people that join a network, the more people will want to join it.
7    The typical cost structure of an information product leads us to expect that a perfectly competitive market will develop.
8    The production of 'student' and 'professional' versions of computer software packages is an attempt by the producers to introduce a form of price discrimination.
9    Bundling beats uniform pricing across users, but is usually less effective than perfect price discrimination.

10  Strategic alliances are good for the consumer.
11  European firms lagged behind their American counterparts in developing a standard for mobile telephony.
12  The information revolution has required a revolution in economic analysis in order to understand what is happening.

## ECONOMICS IN THE NEWS

### 1 Web offers new departure for low-cost airlines
*(Adapted from The Financial Times, 7 January 2000)*

The battle of Europe's low-cost airlines is hotting up with the web at its centre. KLM joins the daft name brigade with the launch of its subsidiary Buzz to rival British Airways' Go and the independent easyJet. All offer discounts if you book online – but how easy is it?

Buzz and Go have nice simple sites. Go has the edge: its design is cleaner, and it has separate pages for specialist information, while Buzz makes you trawl through a mass of detail before getting to the booking bit. Go deals with its more complex pricing structure by showing you the lowest price (with the greatest restrictions), but then allowing you to trade up. easyJet's site has more problems – probably because it has been around long enough to become over-complex. I had several error messages, and many pages are too long. The Special Offers Page is unhelpful, listing dozens of offers without prices before sending you to locate the relevant booking area by yourself. The site switches between languages, depending on the departure airport but does not translate – a good way of stressing the airline's Europeanness but a bit confusing (and why are the gift prices only in sterling?). What is needed next is a comparison site that will tell me which airlines give the best deals. It's got to be there soon if it isn't already.

A reader suggested I have a look at car rental sites. Most, he says, are 'astonishingly bad'. He is right – doubly so as they are aimed at business travellers spoilt by the slick offerings of hotel groups and airlines. I looked at four sites, and found that they all need proper usability studies and better attention to detail to get up to scratch. I suspect that if one of them got its act together, the others would soon be forced to follow.

Londoners who spent millennium night stuck on the Underground should look at Tubehell – a site that feeds on the despair of the system's users. Its excellent design features a tube train with horns, and it has plenty of jokey features, including an interactive Commuter Happiness Index. The discussion forum lets travellers vent their spleen, while TubeNation asks for profiles (including favourite food, film, etc.), that other members can look up. It is the business model behind Tubehell that is intriguing – it has the makings of a powerful online community of young, mainly affluent, Londoners. As it explains in its 'buy' section, it hopes to negotiate discounts for members with traders near a particular station, based on the number of locals who have signed up. 'The more that register, the better the deal.' It's an idea that deserves to work – whether it does or not will depend largely on the skill of the company's management.

1   Suppose you represented one of the firms mentioned in this review of web sites. What sort of action might you consider in response?
2   Assess the importance of network externalities in the strategy adopted by Tubehell.
3   Given that you will be answering these questions at a later date, you might like to browse the web to view some of the sites mentioned. Are they still there? Is there evidence that they have improved things?

## 2 Christmas post killed internet book boom
*(Adapted from The Guardian, 8 January 2000)*

Book sales via the internet put on a huge spurt before Christmas – but were then killed almost stone dead by the uncertain British postal service. A bonanza which gave net book firms a faster rate of sales than high street book retailers ended abruptly on December 11, when customers realized they could no longer be sure of getting presents through the post in time. After that, electronic sales collapsed to a level lower than normal while ordinary bookshop trade surged ahead.

The sales pattern emerges from the first market research to compare the two sectors of the book trade in their peak pre-Christmas season, when they do more than a quarter of their annual business. Net companies have until now been highly secretive about sales figures. The pre-Christmas slump demonstrates that the infant electronic bookshops – which are deeply feared by their conventional rivals – have disadvantages as well as strengths. Figures from the trade research organization BookTrack show that in the eight-week run-up to Christmas, conventional shops sold 30.8m books. This compared with sales of only an estimated 490,000 for the five internet warehouses – a final Christmas market share of 1.6%.

BookTrack says high street shops should be pleased 'that in the four most crucial weeks of the year it will be possible for them to compete effectively with the virtual world'. Nevertheless the net firms, all less than two years old, will view their temporary pre-December surge as a heartening pointer to future expansion. BookTrack's study suggests that it boosted their normal sales by more than a third and gave them a temporary market share of about 4%. Their overall yearly market share is estimated to have doubled to 3% since 1998.

Next Christmas the battle will intensify. Net companies are expected to try to extend their November surge by opening Christmas marketing campaigns in October. Meanwhile two high street chains WH Smith and Waterstone's, have begun talks about hitting back by installing net terminals linked to their own web sites in high street stores.

The BookTrack analysis reveals that the internet sector is desperately weak in two lucrative book categories, food and drink books and books for children. Children's books accounted for only 4% of internet sales, compared with 15% in high street shops. For food and drink, the figures were 6% and 10%. However, net sites are notably strong on medical, management, computer software and economics books, and on cut-price student set books. The net companies, which draw on all 1.5m books in print in the UK, also do well on 'backlist' titles published in the early 1990s or the 1980s. Only 56% of the titles they sold in 1999 were published that year, compared with 76% for high street stores.

The study is based on sales figures since late November from four of the five top UK internet booksellers, which asked not to be named. It does not include the market leader, Amazon.co.uk, but BookTrack is certain that its sales followed the pattern.

1    What characteristics of books make them especially suitable for sale via the internet?
2    Why might internet sales display such a different pattern in terms of the categories of books sold? How would you expect this to change in the future?

## Questions for Thought

1    The internet was originally developed by academics in different universities and countries wanting to exchange information freely. What does economics have to say about the market equilibrium here? To put it another way, should access to the internet remain free?
2    Why should firms like Microsoft and Intel choose to form a strategic alliance rather than undergoing a full merger?
3    Microsoft became embroiled in a lengthy and costly battle with the US Justice Department over the bundling of its Internet Explorer, which was competing with the well-established Netscape Navigator. Netscape argued that Microsoft was being predatory in pricing the Internet Explorer at zero, whereas Microsoft countered by saying that Internet Explorer was part of a larger integrated package. Use the concepts introduced in this chapter to come to your own view of Microsoft's strategy.

# 12 The Analysis of Factor Markets: Labour

## Learning Outcomes

- To analyse the firm's demand for factors in the long run and in the short run
- To define marginal value product, marginal revenue product, and marginal cost of a factor, and relate these to the structure of input and output markets
- To derive the industry demand for labour from that of individual firms in the industry
- To discuss labour supply decisions, both for labour force participation and for hours of work
- To distinguish transfer earnings and economic rent
- To analyse labour market equilibrium and discuss processes that prevent labour markets clearing continuously
- To explain how minimum wages affect employment
- To define isoquants and examine their role in the choice of production technique

**IN THIS CHAPTER ...** you will explore a number of important questions. Why are some occupations paid more than others? Why do some individuals in the same occupation earn more than others? Why are different production techniques adopted in different countries in the same industry? How may unemployment arise? This will require consideration of both the demand and the supply of labour. The demand for labour is a *derived demand*: a firm demands labour not for its own sake, but for the output produced, so decisions about the demand for labour are closely bound up with the firm's output decision. The *supply* of labour can be analysed using the theory of consumer choice, in which we envisage individuals as choosing between work (income) and leisure. Having investigated these topics, you will then analyse whether an equilibrium will be reached between the demand for and the supply of labour – and whether wages will be sufficiently flexible to enable this to happen. If for any reason the wage rate in a labour market is higher than is necessary for equilibrium, then the result will be *involuntary unemployment*.

## Important Concepts and Technical Terms

Match each lettered concept with the appropriate numbered phrase:

| | | | | | |
|---|---|---|---|---|---|
| (a) | Insider-outsider distinctions | (e) | Poverty trap | (i) | Equalizing wage differential |
| (b) | Efficiency wage theory | (f) | Minimum wage | (j) | Transfer earnings |
| (c) | Economic rent | (g) | Participation rate | (k) | Marginal cost of labour |
| (d) | Derived demand | (h) | Involuntary unemployment | (l) | Labour mobility |

1  The demand for a factor of production – not for its own sake, but for the output produced by the factor.
2  A condition that may result in effective barriers to entering employment in existing firms.
3  The monetary compensation for differential non-monetary characteristics of the same job in different industries, so that workers with a particular skill have no incentive to move between industries.
4  The cost of an additional unit of labour
5  A legal constraint imposed on firms establishing the lowest wage payable to workers.
6  The minimum payments required to induce a factor to work in a particular job.
7  The ability of workers to leave low-paying jobs and join other industries where rates of pay are higher.
8  A condition that occurs when workers are prepared to work at the going wage rate but cannot find jobs.
9  The extra payment a factor receives over and above that required to induce the factor to supply its services in that use.
10  The percentage of a given group of the population of working age who decide to enter the labour force.
11  A theory which argues that firms may pay existing workers a wage which on average exceeds the wage for which workers as a whole are prepared to work.
12  A situation in which unskilled workers are offered such a low wage that they lose out by working.

## Exercises

### Table 12-1 Output and labour input, etc.

| Labour input (workers/ week) | Output (goods/ week) | Marginal physical product of labour (MPL) | Price (£) | Total revenue | Marginal revenue per unit output | Marginal value product of labour | Marginal revenue product of labour |
|---|---|---|---|---|---|---|---|
| 0 | 0 | | | | | | |
| | | 35 | | | | | |
| 1 | 35 | | 12 | | | | |
| | | 45 | | | | | |
| 2 | 80 | | 10 | | | | |
| | | 42 | | | | | |
| 3 | 122 | | 8 | | | | |
| | | 34 | | | | | |
| 4 | 156 | | 6 | | | | |
| | | 21 | | | | | |
| 5 | 177 | | 4 | | | | |
| | | 3 | | | | | |
| 6 | 180 | | 2 | | | | |

1   Table 12-1 reproduces some information used (and calculated) in exercise 7 of Chapter 8: we are now in a position to carry the analysis further.
   A new column in the table shows the price which must be charged by the firm to sell the output produced. The firm is a 'wage-taker', and must pay £280 per unit of labour input however much labour is hired. The only other costs to the firm is capital, for which the firm incurs a fixed cost of £200.
   (a)  Calculate the marginal value product of labour (MVPL).
   (b)  Calculate the marginal revenue product of labour (MRPL).
   (c)  Plot MVPL and MRPL curves.
   (d)  At what level of labour input will profits be maximized in the short run?
   (e)  Calculate the level of short-run profits.

2   Figure 12-1 opposite shows marginal cost, marginal product of labour curves, and the wage rate for a firm. Identify the profit-maximizing level of output for each of the following firms:
   (a)  A perfectly competitive firm facing a perfectly competitive situation in the labour market.
   (b)  A firm having no influence on the price of its output but acting as a monopsonist in the labour market.
   (c)  A firm facing a downward-sloping demand curve for its product and acting as a monopsonist in the labour market.
   (d)  A firm facing downward-sloping demand for its product but a perfectly competitive labour market.
   (e)  What is the effect of monopoly and monopsony power on the firm's labour demand?

3   Figure 12-2 opposite shows George's indifference curves between income and leisure.
   Suppose that George faces no fixed costs of working and receives £50 unearned income whether or not he chooses to work.
   (a)  Add to the diagram his budget line if he can work at the rate of £5 per hour.
   (b)  How many hours will George choose to work?
   (c)  Suppose the wage rate increases to £7.50: show how this affects the budget line.
   (d)  How many hours will George now choose to work?
   (e)  Does George regard leisure as a normal or an inferior good?

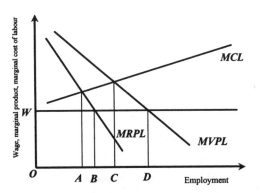

Figure 12-1  Monopoly and monopsony power

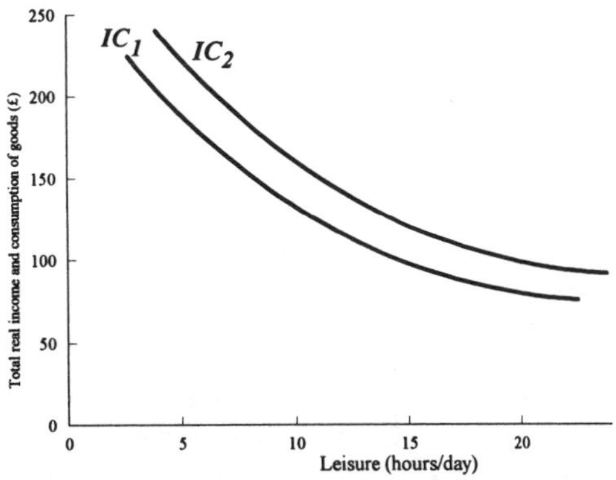

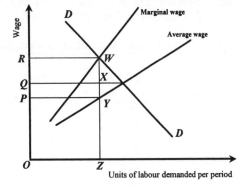

Figure 12-2  George's supply of labour

4    An industry's demand for clerical workers is shown in Figure 12-3, together with its supply curve.
  (a)  Initially the industry demand curve is $DL$ and it faces the supply curve $SL$. What is the equilibrium wage and employment level?
  (b)  Suppose the industry faces a decline in the demand for its output: what would be the new equilibrium wage and employment level? Explain your answer.
  (c)  Beginning again at $DL$, $SL$, the industry now finds that an increase in the demand for clerical workers in another industry has affected their wages elsewhere. How would the equilibrium wage and employment level be affected for this industry?
  (d)  From $DL$, $SL$ the industry demand for labour moves to $D'L$, but the clerical workers' trade union resists a wage cut, maintaining the wage rate at its original level. Identify the nature and extent of the disequilibrium.

5    Figure 12-4 represents a monopsonistic labour market in which employees are not organized into a union.
  (a)  What is the wage rate that will be paid by the employer?
  (b)  What is the employer's wage bill?
  (c)  What is the surplus that accrues to the employer?
  (d)  What would the wage have been if the employer had not been a monopsonist, but was a 'wage-taker' in the labour market?

6    Figure 12-5 overleaf illustrates the demand and supply situation in a particular labour market. Suppose the market to be in equilibrium:
  (a)  Which area represents the amount of transfer earnings?
  (b)  Identify the amount of economic rent.
  (c)  How would the relative size of economic rent and transfer earnings differ if the supply of labour were more inelastic?

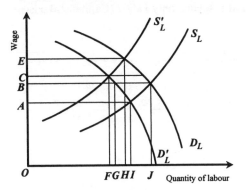

Figure 12-3  Equilibrium in an industry labour market

Figure 12-4  A monopsonistic labour market

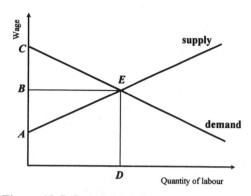

**Figure 12-5  Supply and demand in a labour market**

**Figure 12-6   An individual's labour supply**

7    Figure 12-6 shows the amount of labour supplied by an individual at different wage rates. Which of the following statements concerning the reaction to a move from $W_1$ to $W_2$ is not valid?
(a)   The individual's employer fails to induce an increase in hours worked by this move.
(b)   The firm substitutes capital for labour.
(c)   The employer could have induced the same amount of hours worked by offering a wage rate $W_x$.
(d)   The individual demands more leisure.
(e)   In the choice between income and leisure, the 'income effect' dominates the 'substitution effect'.

8    A firm is seeking the cost-minimizing method of producing a good. Various combinations of labour and capital can be used to produce a particular level of output, as shown in Table 12-2.
(a)   Draw the isoquants for these three levels of output.
(b)   Draw the isocost line showing the combinations of capital and labour input which the firm could purchase for £1000 if capital costs £20 per unit and labour costs £2 per unit.
(c)   What is the maximum amount of output which the firm could produce in these conditions? How much capital and labour is used in producing this output?
(d)   Draw the isocost line if the firm still spends £1000, but the cost of labour increases to £3 per unit.
(e)   What is the maximum output which could now be produced? How much capital and labour would now be used?
(f)   Calculate the percentage change in the use of capital and labour in (e) compared with (c). Is this what you would expect to happen?
(g)   How much output could be produced by the firm if it spends only £800? (Capital still costs £20 per unit, and labour £3 per unit.)

**Table 12-2   Production techniques available to a firm**

| To produce | | | | | |
|---|---|---|---|---|---|
| *10 units of output* | | *20 units of output* | | *30 units of output* | |
| *Capital* | *Labour* | *Capital* | *Labour* | *Capital* | *Labour* |
| 35 | 80 | 42 | 100 | 45 | 170 |
| 28 | 100 | 30 | 150 | 35 | 210 |
| 20 | 134 | 25 | 170 | 30 | 230 |
| 16 | 160 | 20 | 200 | 27 | 245 |
| 13 | 200 | 16 | 240 | 21 | 295 |
| 10 | 248 | 12 | 300 | 18 | 350 |
| 7 | 300 | 10 | 350 | 16 | 400 |
| 5 | 350 | 8 | 400 | 14 | 450 |

9    Which of the following may cause involuntary unemployment?
   *(a)*    Minimum wage legislation intended to protect the lower-paid.
   *(b)*    The payment of higher-than-average wage rates by employers wishing to discourage quits.
   *(c)*    Economies of scale.
   *(d)*    Entry barriers confronting outsiders being implemented by insiders.
   *(e)*    Action taken by a strong trade union to increase rates of pay for its members.
10   Examine theories which have been advanced to explain inflexibility in a labour market. Which of these do you find plausible in the current UK situation?

## True/False

1    The labour market ensures that a helicopter pilot is paid the same money wage in whatever industry he or she is employed.
2    Following an increase in labour cost, a firm will employ more capital input.
3    For a firm operating under perfect competition in both output and labour markets, profits are maximized by employing labour up to the point where the marginal value product of labour equals the money wage rate.
4    For a firm operating under perfect competition in both output and labour markets, profits are maximized by employing labour up to the point where the marginal physical product of labour equals the real wage rate.
5    A firm with monopsony power is not a price-taker in its input markets.
6    For a firm with a downward-sloping demand curve, the marginal revenue product of labour is greater than the marginal value product of labour.
7    For a competitive industry, the industry labour demand curve is the horizontal aggregation of the firms' MVPL curves.
8    An individual's labour supply curve is always upward-sloping – a higher real wage induces the individual to work longer hours.
9    The participation rate is higher for unmarried than for married women.
10   Labour mobility provides a crucial link between industry labour markets.
11   Economic rent reflects differences in individuals' supply decisions, not in their productivity.
12   Involuntary unemployment arises from inflexibility in the labour market.

## ECONOMICS IN THE NEWS

### Meaner than need be: do not freeze the minimum wage
*(Adapted from The Guardian 7 January 2000)*

Apart from the millennium bug, the other disaster that did not happen was a pay explosion following the introduction of the minimum wage. Remember all those heavy warnings that the introduction of a £3.60 hourly minimum wage would open the floodgates and lead to wage inflation? Well, it did not happen. A report by the Low Pay Commission to the government has concluded that, though it is too early for a definitive judgement, the 'knock on' effects of a higher minimum wage on other workers appear to have been minimal.

The minimum wage has been a great success in giving some 2m people - 8% of workers - new basic pay rights. It has confounded the Tories who said it would destroy jobs: the number of jobs in all the sectors most affected has increased. It has demolished the barmy army of Thatcherite economists who said Britain's only hope of survival in the globalized economy was to lower wages to match the third world. Why were they wrong? Because nearly all these lowest paid jobs are in the service sectors - catering, security, cleaning and caring. People will always need their hair cut, their offices cleaned and old people cared for whatever the cost: it is not work that can be snatched away to a factory in Indonesia or a call centre in Pakistan. There has been virtually no evidence of employers going out of business. The Low Pay Commission concludes that if some do, then better managed companies paying better wages quite rightly take their place. Larger companies welcomed the minimum wage because it stopped cowboys undercutting them with cheap bad services paid for in starvation wages. The Low Pay Unit, lobbying for the poorest workers, conclude that nearly 2m workers have received an average 20% rise, though along with the home workers' lobby they are still concerned about enforcement. Only yesterday the DTI was busily pumping out good news about the £12,000 they had managed to get in back wages for a group of Thai workers in Scotland paid only 96p an hour.

With so much favourable opinion behind it, you would have thought the government would have moved swiftly to probe whether the minimum could be raised to nearer £4 an hour without triggering inflation. Instead, according to leaked reports, ministers are thinking of freezing it for a year from April at its present level, thereby ensuring a cut in real terms. They should think again. A freeze would hit the living standards of the poorest workers, while all around them are getting increases (not least in the City, where it promises to be another bumper year). Future administrations, Labour or Conservative, could use it as a precedent to do the same. It would also go against the spirit of the commission's step-by-step approach to raising the minimum wage, which led it to recommend an increase to £3.70 later this year (which the government did not agree to).

There are two other reasons for raising the minimum wage now. First, if it is going to lead to lost jobs, then this is a good (or less bad) time for this to happen, when unemployment is still dropping and labour shortages may soon be appearing which could absorb displaced workers. Second, it is an almost obscene time to permit a fall in the real value of the minimum wage when the treasury is running into an unexpectedly large budget surplus. If we cannot look after poorer workers in these circumstances, when can we ever hope to do so?

1  Based on economic analysis, how would the imposition of a minimum wage be expected to affect a labour market?
2  Do the main arguments about the minimum wage concern equity or efficiency?
3  Has the UK minimum wage kept pace with inflation since the passage was written in early 2000? Do you support this policy, and why?

## Questions for Thought

1  In an earlier chapter, we saw that a firm operating under perfect competition would maximize profits in the short run by producing at the point where $SMC=MR$. Now it transpires that the firm should employ labour up to the point where $W=MVPL$. Can you reconcile these two methods?

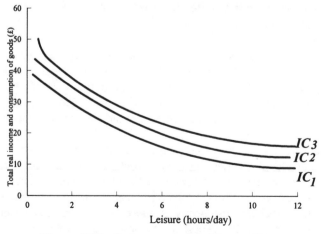

**Figure 12-7    Labour supply with overtime**

2    Figure 12-7 on the previous page shows Helen's indifference curves between income and leisure. Helen receives £10 per day unearned income only if she does not work. She never chooses to work more than 12 hours per day, so the diagram focuses on only the relevant 12 hours.

   (a)    Mark on the diagram the point where Helen would be if she chooses not to work.

   (b)    Add to the diagram Helen's budget line if she can work at £2.50 per hour.

   (c)    Assuming Helen has complete flexibility on hours of work, how many hours will she choose to work at that rate of pay?

   (d)    Amend the budget line to conform to a situation in which Helen earns 'treble time' for hours worked in excess of 8 hours a day.

   (e)    How many hours will Helen now choose to work?

3    Figure 12-8 shows a production function for a good: *1X, 2X, 3X*, etc., are isoquants showing the various combinations of capital and labour that can be used to produce different levels of output of the good: *C0, C1, C2*, etc., are isocost lines, whose slope represents the current relative prices of capital and labour.

   (a)    Which isocost line represents the least-cost method of producing 3 units of output *(3X)*?

   (b)    Suppose that in the short run, the amount of capital input available is fixed at K*. Consider how labour input must change if output is increased from 2X to 3X and then to 4X. What does this suggest for the return to labour?

   (c)    Given the technology embedded in the isoquants, the path *ABCDE* shows least-cost ways of producing different output levels under the assumptions that both capital and labour inputs can be varied and that relative factor prices remain unchanged. What do these points imply for the shape of the long-run average cost curve?

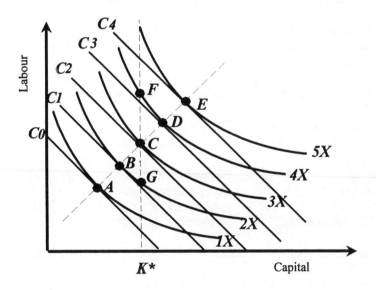

**Figure 12-8    Isoquants**

# 13 Human Capital, Discrimination, and Trade Unions

## Learning Outcomes

- **To show how workers differ, and explore consequences of these differences**
- **To analyse how investment in human capital allows workers to be more productive and earn more**
- **To explain how signalling may identify innate differences in workers, allowing the more skilled to be allocated to more demanding and more valuable jobs**
- **To study different forms of direct and indirect discrimination, both in the labour market and before people become workers**
- **To examine the role of trade unions, both in restricting labour supply to force up the wage and in coordinating helpful changes that enhance productivity and the value of workers**

**IN THIS CHAPTER ...** you will investigate some important aspects of labour markets in more depth. Workers differ in many characteristics: gender, race, age, experience, training, trade union membership, or innate ability. To explore *discrimination* in a labour market, we must sift these. Some are outside the control of the individual. Others, such as education and training, are not. Education affects the level of income and the pattern of earning across a worker's lifetime. Training may be seen as being an investment in *human capital*, undertaken for the benefits expected from higher future earnings, despite the costs incurred. Balancing these items entails *cost-benefit analysis*. Demand and supply analysis is crucial. An increase in demand for educated workers in the short run will lead to an increase in the *wage differential*. In the long run, this may affect supply of educated workers, through an increase in demand for education. The distinction between general and firm-specific skills may affect labour mobility. We also examine whether education adds directly to productivity, or whether it acts as a *signalling* device. Average weekly earnings for women are about two-thirds of earnings for men. However, the difference partly reflects differences in employment patterns between men and women, and may also reflect earlier education choices made by women. Access to education may also be significant when we consider racial discrimination. Trade union members also tend to enjoy higher earnings than other workers. The extent to which this reflects the use of monopoly power by the unions depends in part upon the elasticity of demand for labour; higher earnings may also reflect productivity agreements between unions and employers.

## Important Concepts and Technical Terms
Match each lettered concept with the appropriate numbered phrase:

| | | | | | |
|---|---|---|---|---|---|
| (a) | Human capital | (e) | Signalling | (h) | General human capital |
| (b) | Cost-benefit analysis | (f) | Compensating wage | (i) | Discrimination |
| (c) | Trade union | | differentials | (j) | Closed shop |
| (d) | Firm-specific human capital | (g) | Age-earnings profile | | |

1  A procedure for making long-run decisions by comparing the present value of the costs with the present value of the benefits.

2  The stock of expertise accumulated by a worker, valued for its income-earning potential in the future.

3  A situation in which a group of workers is treated differently from other groups because of the personal characteristics of that group, regardless of qualifications.

4  Differences in wage rates reflecting non-monetary aspects of working conditions.

5  An agreement that all a firm's workers will be members of a trade union.

6  The skills which a worker acquires that can be transferred to work for another firm.

7  The theory that educational qualifications indicate a worker's worth even when not directly relevant to his or her productivity.

8  The skills which a worker acquires that cannot be transferred to work for another firm.

9  A schedule showing how the earnings of a worker or group of workers vary with age.

10  A worker organization designed to affect pay and working conditions.

## Exercises

1   Ian, a teenager, is considering whether or not to undertake further education. Having studied A level Economics, he decides to apply cost-benefit analysis to evaluate his decision. After applying appropriate discount rates, he arrives at the following valuations (the units are notional):

|  | Present value |
|---|---|
| Books, fees | 3000 |
| Benefits (non-monetary) of student life | 2500 |
| Income forgone (net) | 7000 |
| Additional future expected income due to qualification | 9000 |

(a)  Given these valuations, would Ian decide upon further education?
(b)  How would Ian's calculations be affected if he were not confident of passing his examinations at the end of his course?
(c)  Ian's friend Joanne shares Ian's views about the economic value of education, but is much less keen on the idea of university life. How would her calculations differ?
(d)  Keith subscribes to the 'eat, drink, and be merry, for tomorrow we die' philosophy, and is keen to enjoy life in the present. How would his calculations differ from Ian's?

2   Below are figures showing how pre-tax earnings vary with age for three groups of male workers in full-time employment in the economy of Hypothetica. Average gross weekly earnings are measured in Hypothetical dollars.

| Group | A | B | C |
|---|---|---|---|
| Age: | | | |
| 20–29 | 236 | 180 | 200 |
| 30–39 | 310 | 200 | 250 |
| 40–49 | 370 | 195 | 280 |
| 50–64 | 425 | 185 | 235 |

(a)  Plot the age-earnings profile for each group of workers.
(b)  The distinguishing characteristic of each group is the level of highest educational attainment. Using your knowledge of similar groups in the UK, associate each of the following with the appropriate age-earnings profile:
   (i)     Workers with GCE A levels or their equivalent.
   (ii)    Workers with no formal qualifications.
   (iii)   Workers with a university degree or equivalent.

3   In the economy of Elsewhere, the following observations are made. Which of them would provide strong evidence of discrimination?
(a)  Women earn less than men.
(b)  Female trainee accountants earn less than male trainee accountants.
(c)  Black workers earn less than white workers.
(d)  Black machine tool fitters earn less than white machine tool fitters.

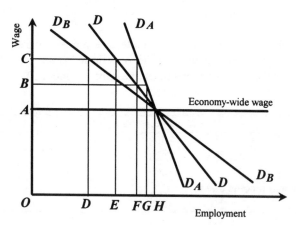

**Figure 13-1   Unions, wages, and employment**

**4**   Figure 13-1 shows the position in a labour market. *OA* represents the economy-wide wage rate. *DD* is the initial demand curve for labour.
(a)  Identify the initial equilibrium for the industry.
(b)  Suppose a trade union restricts the supply of labour to *OE*. What is the equilibrium wage in the industry?
(c)  In the long run, this industry faces increased competition from overseas suppliers, who face lower labour costs. Which of the demand curves in the diagram might represent the industry's new (derived) demand for labour?
(d)  What is the new equilibrium for the industry?
(e)  What wage rate would the union need to accept to maintain employment at OE?

**5**   Data on wages, salaries, and earnings all seem to indicate that in the labour force as a whole, men tend to receive higher pay than women. Which of the following may contribute to this overall earnings differential?
(a)  Female workers are more likely to work part-time.
(b)  Men work in different industries and occupations.
(c)  Companies promote women more slowly, and offer them less training.
(d)  Women choose different subjects at school.
(e)  Fewer women choose to undertake higher education.
(f)  Women are biologically different from men.
(g)  Employers discriminate against women.

**6**   In some professions, it is necessary to undertake several years of training in order to qualify for entry. However, the returns to such training are perceived to be high in terms of future earnings potential.
(a)  What is the opportunity cost of undertaking professional training?
(b)  How is this likely to be seen relative to the potential returns?
(c)  If the manufacturing sector of the economy is in relative decline, and the economy is also in recession, how will this affect the demand for professional training?
(d)  Examine the long-term prospects for earnings in the professions.

**7**   Explain how each of the following situations may influence the bargaining position of a trade union in negotiating with employers.
(a)  There is excess demand for labour.
(b)  There is a 'closed shop'.
(c)  The marginal revenue product of labour is less than the wage rate.
(d)  Unemployment is at an historically high level.
(e)  The demand for labour is highly inelastic.
(f)  The union faces a monopsony buyer of labour.

8    Table 13-1 shows estimated private and social rates of return to education at different levels in various parts of the world.

**Table 13-1 Estimated rates of return to education**

| Country group | Social return | | Private return | |
|---|---|---|---|---|
| | Secondary | Higher | Secondary | Higher |
| Africa | 17 | 13 | 26 | 32 |
| Asia | 15 | 13 | 15 | 18 |
| Latin America | 18 | 16 | 23 | 23 |
| Industrial | 11 | 9 | 12 | 12 |

Source: George Psacharopoulos, 'Education and development: a review', *World Bank Research Observer*, Vol. 3(1), 1988.

(a)  How do these rates of return compare with those of other types of investment?
(b)  Why should the rate of return be so much higher for some parts of the world?
(c)  At what level of education are private returns maximized?
(d)  At what level of education are social returns maximized?
(e)  How is this seeming conflict likely to be resolved?
(f)  Will all groups in society perceive these returns in the same way?

## True/False

1    The human capital approach assumes that wage differentials reflect differences in the productivity of different workers.
2    Workers in firms receiving general training will be offered high but shallow age-earnings profiles.
3    Reading Classics at university does nothing to improve productivity; it is more profitable to leave school and go straight into industry.
4    Free schooling between 16 and 18 means that children from poor families can stay on in education as easily as children from wealthy families.
5    The perceived return from higher education is less for women than for men, so fewer women than men decide to invest in higher education.
6    Black workers earn less than white workers; therefore employers are racist.
7    Differences in the occupational structure of the employment of men and women do not suffice to explain differences in earnings.
8    By 1980, more than two-thirds of the civilian labour force in the UK belonged to trade unions.
9    Since many low-paid workers belong to a trade union, this proves that unions have little effect on improving pay and conditions for their members.
10    The largest rise in wages would be achieved by restricting labour supply in the industry where the demand for labour is most inelastic.
11    The UK is the most strike-prone economy in the world.

## ECONOMICS IN THE NEWS

### 1    University degrees bring 'substantial returns'
*(Adapted from the Financial Times, 21 May 1997)*

People who complete a university degree can expect 'substantial' financial returns, according to a report published yesterday by the Institute for Fiscal Studies. Over a 40-year working life, the graduate can expect to receive about £80,000 more than someone who opts out of higher education.

In the report, based on a survey of nearly 3,000 people in their early 30s, men with first degrees are shown to have wages about 127 per cent higher than male non-graduates, even allowing for factors such as differing academic ability and family background. The payback is even more striking for women. On average, women graduates earn 36 per cent more than female non-graduates.

While women graduates earn nearly 25 per cent less than male graduates, the wage differential between men and women without degrees is more than 40 per cent. A typical hourly wage for a male non-graduate with at least one A level was about £10.18 in 1995. By contrast, a male graduate was paid £11.62. For women, the non-graduate was earning £6.61, while the graduate was earning £9.71.

Mr Richard Blundell, one of the report's authors, said that over a year, graduates could expect the equivalent of a £1500–£2000 bonus as a result of their degree. The report says that 'if today's graduates will be able to secure similar returns, then it may be deemed feasible to expect future graduates to contribute a larger share of the costs of higher education themselves'.

1    Did the theoretical discussion of this chapter lead you to expect this level of returns from a university education?
2    To what extent does the report suggest that a degree may help to narrow the gender earnings gap?
3    Would you expect the subject of study to have an additional effect on relative earnings? In what way?

## 2   Do unions still matter?
*(Adapted from Stephanie Flanders column in the Financial Times, 26 May 1997)*

It was all smiles at number 10 last week as John Monks, TUC general secretary, went to meet the newly elected Prime Minister, Tony Blair. All smiles, but no beer and sandwiches. New Labour has vowed there will be no special treatment for union leaders, and they look as if they mean it. All of which leaves a question for the unions: if they cannot hope for a favoured seat at the table in a Labour government, and they can no longer act as the last defence of workers in Tory Britain, what *can* they do?

One answer would be that they can do what they have always done, the world over: get higher wages and benefits for their members. Union membership in the UK had risen to about 50 per cent of the workforce by 1979. At that time, researchers calculated that the average wage gap between union and non-union workers was about 10 per cent, the same as it had been in 1970, when unions had not yet been marked as the 'enemy within'.

In the US, where union members accounted for slightly less than 30 per cent of the workforce, the premium fluctuated around the 15 per cent mark between 1967 and 1979. By most reckonings union plants paid the price for this premium in terms of lower employment growth and profitability relative to other workplaces.

Cut to the mid-1990s, and union membership in the UK is down to 32 per cent of workers. In the US, only 15 per cent of the labour force, and a mere 10 per cent of employees in the private sector were members of a union in 1995. Yet recent research by David Blanchflower suggests that the union wage premium in either country has hardly budged. Other things being equal, he calculates that union members in the UK still earned 12.5 per cent more than non-union workers in 1994. Stripping out the effects of the economic cycle, the union wage premium has averaged 10.7 per cent since 1983.

1    In the final paragraph of this passage, reference is made to 'other things being equal'. What factors would need to be taken into account in this context?
2    Why should we expect the wage premium to be affected by the overall performance of the economy?
3    Do unions still matter?

## Questions for Thought

1    Would society find it worth while to invest in a higher education system if degree training provides only a signalling device and has no effect on the productivity of workers?
2    If strikes benefit neither employers nor employees, why do they ever happen?
3    A firm that has been operating without trade unions becomes unionized. Is it necessarily the case that employment in that firm will fall?

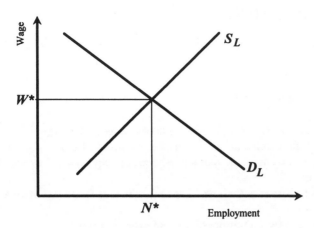

**Figure 13-2    Equilibrium in a labour market**

4    We have shown equilibrium in a labour market in Figure 13-2.
It has been argued that a trade union may attempt to gain higher wages for its members by restricting employment. How might the union select the desired wage/employment combination? (*Hint:* Try to think of the trade union as a monopoly seller of labour, and look back to the analysis of monopoly in Chapter 9 to see how it could be applied in this case.)

5    Suppose there is a significant structural change in an economy, away from manufacturing activity and towards services. What effect would you expect this to have on the gender balance of the labour force and the level of unemployment?

# 14 Capital and Land: Completing the Analysis of Factor Markets

## Learning Outcomes

- To study the markets for inputs of capital and land, and to analyse how incomes of factors are therefore determined
- To define and study the functional and personal distributions of income
- To distinguish flows over time and stocks measured at a point in time
- To conduct simultaneous analysis of the market for renting capital services and the market for buying new capital assets
- To explain the concept of present values, which collapse future flows into their equivalent stock value today
- To consider the difference between nominal and real interest rates
- To analyse how saving and investment, or thrift and the productivity of new capital formation, determine the equilibrium real interest rate
- To show how land is allocated between competing uses

**IN THIS CHAPTER ...** you will consider the other important factors of production – capital and land. *Capital* is taken to refer to physical capital – the stock of produced goods used in the production of other goods, including machinery, buildings, and vehicles. *Land* is a factor of production provided by nature. Capital and land together comprise the *tangible wealth* of an economy. Tangible wealth per worker has increased in the UK in recent years, suggesting that the economy is becoming more capital-intensive. You will need to distinguish between *stocks* and *flows* and between asset prices and rental payments. The *asset price* of a capital good requires careful interpretation. The purchase of a capital asset entitles the buyer to the future stream of services produced by that asset. At the time of purchase, it is the *present value* of that future stream of services which is relevant. We may regard the interest rate as the opportunity cost of the money used to buy the asset.

## Important Concepts and Technical Terms

Match each lettered concept with the appropriate numbered phrase:

| | | | | | |
|---|---|---|---|---|---|
| (a) | Land | (f) | Wage:rental ratio | (k) | Real rate of interest |
| (b) | Personal income distribution | (g) | Required rental | (l) | Present value |
| (c) | Physical capital | (h) | Nominal rate of interest | (m) | Opportunity cost of capital |
| (d) | Capital:labour ratio | (i) | Saving | (n) | Functional income |
| (e) | Asset price | (j) | Financial capital | | distribution |

1  The stock of produced goods that contribute to the production of other goods and services.
2  The factor of production that nature supplies.
3  The value today of a sum of money due at some time in the future.
4  The difference between current income and current consumption.
5  The rate of return available on funds in their best alternative use: may be represented by the real interest rate.
6  Shows the division of national income between the different factors of production.
7  The return on a loan measured as the increase in goods that can be purchased, not as the increase in the money value of the loan fund.
8  A measure of relative factor prices: the price of labour relative to the price of capital.
9  Shows how national income is divided between different individuals, regardless of the factor services from which these individuals earn their income.
10  Describes the relative importance of inputs of capital and labour in the production process.
11  The sum for which a capital asset can be purchased outright.
12  The return on a loan measured in money terms.
13  Assets such as money or bank deposits which may be used to buy factors of production.
14  The rental rate that just allows the owner of capital to cover the opportunity cost of owning it.

# Exercises

1   Identify each of the following as being either a 'stock' or a 'flow':
   (a) Vans owned by Rent-a-Van Limited.
   (b) Land available for planting wheat.
   (c) Use of truck for delivery.
   (d) Railway lines.
   (e) TV programme as viewed by consumer.
   (f) Use of office space.

2   A 10 per cent government bond with a nominal value of £100 sells on the stock exchange for £62.50.
   (a) What is the prevailing rate of interest?
   (b) What would the rate of interest be if the price of the bond were £75?
   (c) If the rate of interest fell to 8 per cent, for what price would you expect the bond to sell?

3   Lucy has £100 to save or spend. If she loans out the money she will receive £112 in a year's time. Inflation is proceeding at 14 per cent per annum.
   (a) What is the nominal rate of interest which Lucy faces?
   (b) What is the real rate of interest?
   (c) Financially, would Lucy be advised to save or spend?
   (d) How would your answer be affected if the inflation rate were 10 per cent, with the nominal interest rate at the same level?

4   A machine is expected to be productive for three years, bringing earnings of £2000 in each year and being worth £6000 as scrap at the end of the third year. Using present value calculations, what would be the 'break-even' price for the machine if
   (a) the interest rate is 8 per cent?
   (b) the interest rate is 10 per cent?
   (c) the interest rate is 8 per cent and it is realized that no account has been taken of inflation which is expected to be 7 per cent per annum?

5   An economy has two sectors: agriculture and industry. Figure 14-1 shows their demand schedules for land DA1 and DI respectively). SS represents the total fixed supply of land.
   (a) Identify the equilibrium rental rate, and each sector's demand for land.
   Suppose that the government is concerned about the level of food imported into the economy and decides to encourage domestic food production by subsidizing agricultural land. This has the effect of shifting the demand curve for agricultural land to DA2.
   (b) How will land be allocated between agriculture and industry in the short run?
   (c) What will be the rental rates in the two sectors in the short run?
   (d) What will be the equilibrium position in the long run?

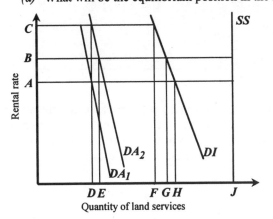

**Figure 14-1   Allocating land between alternative uses**

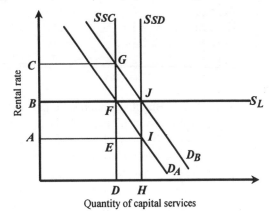

**Figure 14-2   Capital adjustment**

6   A firm is considering the purchase of a piece of capital equipment, to be funded by a bank loan. (For simplicity, assume that both capital good and loan last for ever.) The cost of the equipment is £25000 and the interest on the bank loan is fixed at 10 per cent per annum. Maintenance and depreciation amount to 12 per cent of the cost of the machine each year. Inflation is occurring at an annual rate of 8 per cent.
    *(a)* What is the required rental on the capital equipment?
    *(b)* What would be the required rental if inflation increased to 10 per cent per annum?

7   Figure 14-2 on previous page shows the demand for capital services, and short- and long-run supply curves. Suppose that workers in the industry agree to accept a wage cut.
    *(a)* Identify the initial equilibrium position before the wage cut is implemented.
    *(b)* What does the rental rate here represent – i.e. how is it determined?
    *(c)* Identify the short-run position after the wage cut.
    *(d)* Can this position be sustained? If not, why not?
    *(e)* What is the long-run equilibrium position?
    *(f)* How do we normally describe the adjustment process that has taken place between *(c)* and *(e)*?

8   Which of the following statements could validly be applied to the UK?
    (a)  There has been little change in the shares of factors of production in pre-tax earnings in recent decades.
    (b)  Labour receives the greatest portion of national income.
    (c)  Wealth is less equally distributed than income.
    (d)  Capital stock grew much more rapidly than the labour force between 1981 and 1996.
    (e)  Inequality in the distribution of wealth contributes to inequality in the distribution of income.

9   Table 14-1 shows information concerning the distribution of 'original' and 'disposable' household income in the UK in 1997/98. Original income represents income before account is taken of any taxes, benefits, etc. Disposable income adds in transfer payments and deducts direct tax payments Complete columns (5) and (6) of the Table to show amounts of income accruing to the bottom 20, 40, 60, etc., per cent of households.
    Economists sometimes try to illustrate such data on distribution using 'Lorenz curves'. Construct a diagram plotting the figures from column (4) on the horizontal axis and those from column (5) on the vertical axis. Joining the points gives a *Lorenz curve*. The closer the curve to a straight line joining (0,0) to (100,100), the more even the distribution. Draw a second Lorenz curve using the figures in column (6): the difference between the two should give an impression of the redistributive effect of UK taxation and benefits.

**Table 14-1    UK income distribution**

| (1) Proportion of households (%) | (2) Original income | (3) Disposable income | (4) Cumulative households | (5) Cumulative Original income | (6) Percentages Disposable income |
|---|---|---|---|---|---|
| Bottom 20 | 2 | 8 | 20 | | |
| Next 20 | 7 | 12 | 40 | | |
| Next 20 | 15 | 16 | 60 | | |
| Next 20 | 25 | 23 | 80 | | |
| Top 20 | 51 | 42 | 100 | | |

Source: *Economic Trends.*

In 1995 in Brazil, the poorest 20 per cent of the population received 2.5 per cent of income, the next 20 per cent received 5.7 per cent, the next 20 per cent, 9.9 per cent, the next 20 per cent, 17.7 per cent, and the richest 20 per cent received 64.2 per cent of total income. Construct a Lorenz curve showing this distribution and compare it with that for the UK. (Data are taken from the *World Development Report 1998/99*.)

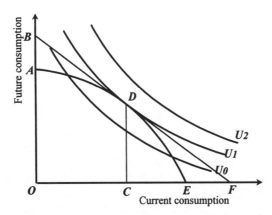

**Figure 14-3   Current and future consumption**

10  Figure 14-3 shows an economy in equilibrium, with the single consumer choosing between current and future consumption.
   (a) Identify the equilibrium point.
   (b) How much is saved at this point?
   (c) If all current resources were invested in new capital goods, what would be the maximum attainable future consumption level?
   (d) How would you measure the rate of return on investment?
   (e) What determines the slope of the price line?

11  Back in Chapter 6, we saw that a consumer's reaction to a price change can be analysed in terms of real income and substitution effects. Explain how the same sort of decomposition can be used to analyse the effect of savings of a change in the interest rate. What would you expect to be the net effect on savings of an increase in the interest rate?

12  Consider a movement of a production possibility frontier between current and future consumption. Which of the following factors would cause the new frontier to have a steeper slope at each output of current consumption? (Note: more than one answer may be valid.)
   (a) An increase in thriftiness of members of society.
   (b) An increase in the productivity of new capital equipment.
   (c) A fall in the rate of interest.
   (d) A rise in the rate of interest.
   (e) An increase in investment.
   (f) A technological break-through improving efficiency in production.

## True/False

1  Tangible wealth includes land, machinery, factory buildings, vehicles, and government bonds.
2  Since people cannot be bought and sold, there can be no asset price for labour.
3  The present value of a capital asset is the sum of future rental payments that asset will provide.
4  Inflation makes nominal interest rates go up. This must reduce the present value of future income.
5  The real interest rate can be negative.
6  The flow of capital services can be varied in the long run but is rigidly fixed in the short run.
7  Differences in rental rates can lead to the transfer of capital between industries or even nations.
8  Equilibrium in the market for land demands that rents be equal in all sectors.
9  The main feature distinguishing between the three factors of production (land, capital, and labour) is the speed of adjustment of their supply.
10  In the long run the supply of labour is less elastic than the supply of capital.
11  Labour's share in UK national income increased markedly between 1981–89 and 1998.
12  The distribution of wealth is even more unequal than that of income.

## ECONOMICS IN THE NEWS

### Blair pledges to tackle inequality
*(Adapted from The Financial Times 17 December 1999)*

The Prime Minister pledged yesterday to tackle a Britain divided into the 'haves and have nots' – just as a study showed that income inequality is again rising in the UK. The increase threatens the government's plans to eliminate child poverty and produce a fairer society, according to work by the Institute for Fiscal Studies.

After a period in the early to mid-1990s when the recession saw the rise in inequality flatten and even fall slightly, it is now increasing again, the study shows. While the first three Budgets from Gordon Brown have redistributed cash to the less well-off, the scale has been modest, Jayne Taylor, a senior research economist at IFS, said. 'If inequality is going to go on rising, as I suspect will happen, that is likely to more than offset the redistribution that the government has undertaken so far.'

Between 1979 and 1991, the richest groups saw their income grow substantially, while the poorest groups saw hardly any change in real terms. The rich pulled away from the middle and the middle did better than the bottom, producing a growth in inequality on an unprecedented scale, the IFS paper shows. The recession in the early 1990s halted that. But over 1996 and 1997 the gap started to widen. This was due to various factors, chiefly a greater disparity in wages between top and bottom, but also more income from occupational pensions, investments and savings, which are most often held by the better-off.

There has also been a marked growth in self-employment, which tends to have an even wider spread of income than that of wages. More builders, plumbers and hairdressers have become self-employed at the bottom end, while fee income for self-employed professionals and consultants at the top has increased sharply.

Tony Blair, the prime minister, said the issues of social exclusion, unemployment, child poverty and homelessness were now 'at the heart of government' after years of neglect under the Tories. Britain, he said, 'is still divided into haves and have nots' and the government still had a long way to go.

1    How might you try to measure the gap between rich and poor?
2    What would you regard as the key policies for narrowing the inequalities between rich and poor?

## Questions for Thought

1    Distinguish between economic rent and transfer earnings. With reference to examples, explain what determines the economic rent received by factors of production.
2    Examine the extent to which it is helpful to treat energy as a fourth factor of production.

# 15  Coping with Risk in Economic Life

## Learning Outcomes

- To distinguish risk aversion, risk neutrality, and risk loving
- To show why diminishing marginal utility leads to risk aversion
- To explain how insurance reduces risk through risk pooling, and reduces the cost of bearing risk through risk spreading
- To analyse how inside information about one's own opportunities or characteristics gives rise to moral hazard and adverse selection
- To show that the return on an asset is not just the cash flow in dividends or interest but also capital gains (losses) while the asset is held
- To consider how positive, zero, or negative correlation of asset returns affects the possibility of risk pooling through diversification
- To discuss an efficient asset market
- To define spot and forward markets, and explain how hedging can shift the burden of risk on to someone prepared to bear it at a smaller price

**IN THIS CHAPTER ...** you will take an economist's eye view of *uncertainty* and *risk*. Two characteristics of risk are especially important: the most likely outcome of an action, and the range and variability of the possible outcomes. An assumption often made by economists when considering risk is that individuals face diminishing marginal utility of wealth. During this chapter, you will meet the concepts of risk-pooling, moral hazard and adverse selection. In choosing how to hold their wealth, individuals face a choice between risk and return. Forward markets allow agents to contract to buy or sell commodities at a date in the future at a price agreed now, but reflecting the expected price at the future date.

## Important Concepts and Technical Terms

Match each lettered concept with the appropriate numbered phrase:

*(a)* Risk-pooling
*(b)* Risk-neutral
*(c)* Beta
*(d)* Speculative bubble
*(e)* Hedgers
*(f)* Moral hazard
*(g)* Spot price
*(h)* Adverse selection
*(i)* Risk-averse
*(j)* Forward market
*(k)* Risk-sharing
*(l)* Theory of efficient markets
*(m)* Risk-lover
*(n)* Speculators

1  A measurement of the extent to which a share's return moves with the return on the whole stock market.
2  The reduction of uncertainty about the average outcome by spreading the risk across many individuals who independently face that risk.
3  A view of a market as a sensitive processor of information, quickly responding to new information to adjust prices correctly.
4  A person who will accept a bet even when a strict calculation reveals that the odds are unfavourable.
5  A trader in a forward market who expects to earn profits by taking risks.
6  The spreading of risk among insurance companies, thus reducing the stake of each individual company.
7  A situation where the act of insuring increases the likelihood of the occurrence of the event against which insurance is taken out.
8  A market in contracts made today for delivery of goods at a specified future date at a price agreed today.
9  A person who ignores the dispersion of possible outcomes, but is concerned with the average outcome.
10  A market in which everyone believes the price will rise tomorrow, even if the price has already risen a lot.
11  Traders who use a forward market to reduce their risk by making contracts about future transactions.
12  The price for immediate delivery of a commodity.
13  A person who will refuse a fair gamble, requiring sufficiently favourable odds that the probable monetary profit outweighs the risk.
14  The situation faced by insurance companies in which the people wishing to insure against a particular outcome are also those most likely to require a payoff.

## Exercises

1  Maureen, Nora, and Olga are each offered the opportunity of buying a sketch, allegedly by a famous artist, for £500. If genuine, the value of the sketch would be £1000; if phoney it would be totally worthless. There is a 50–50 chance of each alternative. Maureen rejects the idea outright, Nora jumps at the chance, and Olga flips a coin to decide.
   *(a)* Characterize each attitude to risk.
   *(b)* Would you buy the sketch?
   *(c)* What does this imply about your own attitude to risk?
   *(d)* Would your attitude differ if you had recently won £1 million on the pools?

2  In which of the following circumstances are risks being pooled?
   *(a)* Insurance for David Beckham's legs (or some other top footballer of your choice).
   *(b)* Car insurance.
   *(c)* Insurance for contents of a freezer.
   *(d)* Insurance against an accident at a nuclear power station.
   *(e)* Medical insurance for a holiday abroad.

3  Which of the following situations illustrate moral hazard, and which adverse selection?
   *(a)* Paula never locks her car, knowing it is adequately insured.
   *(b)* Having taken our life insurance in favour of his family, Quentin continues to smoke heavily.
   *(c)* Rosemary takes out life insurance, knowing that her heavy smoking has given her terminal lung cancer.
   *(d)* Having insured against rain, Simon makes advance payments to cricket stars for his Easter single-wicket competition.
   *(e)* Tessa takes out extra health insurance shortly before going on a skiing holiday.

4  Suppose you wish to invest £200 in shares. Two industries, chemicals and computers, have shares on offer at £100 each. The return expected from the two industries are independent. In each case, there is a 50 per cent chance that returns will be good (£12) and a 50 per cent chance that returns will be poor (£6).
   *(a)* If you buy only chemicals shares, and times are good, what return will you earn?
   *(b)* If you buy only computers shares, and times are bad, what return will you earn?
   *(c)* If you put all your funds in one industry, what is your average expected return?
   *(d)* If you put all your funds in one industry, what is the chance of a poor return?
   *(e)* What is your average return if you diversify?
   *(f)* If you diversify, what is the chance of a poor return (i.e. the same level as part *(b)*)?

5  Match each lettered definition with the numbered term (suppose that contracts are established for one year hence and that today's date is 1 July 2000):
   *(a)* The price of gold on 1 July 2000 for delivery and payment on 1 July 2000.
   *(b)* The price in the forward market on 1 July 2000 at which gold is being traded for delivery and payment on 1 July 2001.
   *(c)* Today's best guess about what the spot price will be on 1 July 2001.
   *(d)* The price of gold being traded in the spot market on 1 July 2000.
   *(e)* The differences between the expected future spot price and the current forward price.

   (1)  Risk premium.
   (2)  Future spot price.
   (3)  Today's spot price.
   (4)  Forward price.
   (5)  Expected future spot price.

6   Which of the following offers the best chance of a better-than-average return in the stock market?
   (a)  Careful reading of the financial press.
   (b)  Sticking a pin into the financial pages of the newspaper.
   (c)  Employing a financial adviser.
   (d)  Computer analysis of past share price movements.
   (e)  Being the first agent to react to news.
7   Which of the following statements is/are correct?
   (a)  A share with beta = 1 moves independently of the rest of the market.
   (b)  A share with a high beta moves with the market, but more sluggishly.
   (c)  A share with a negative beta decreases the riskiness of a portfolio.
   (d)  A share with a negative beta increases the riskiness of a portfolio.
   (e)  Most shares have a beta close to 1.
8   Which of the following statements concerning unit trusts is/are true?
   (a)  They allow small savers to diversify their risks.
   (b)  They normally give a fixed rate of interest and re-invest surpluses so as to give unit trust holders capital appreciation.
   (c)  Their price remains constant so that unit trust holders can never lose their savings in monetary terms.
   (d)  They are especially attractive to risk-lovers.

## True/False

1   A risk-lover is indifferent to risk.
2   The principle of diminishing marginal utility of wealth makes most people risk-averse.
3   Insurance companies often do not insure against acts of God because these risks cannot be pooled.
4   In purely economic terms, life insurance premia should be lower for women than for men because women live longer than men on average.
5   Treasury bills are more risky than company shares.
6   A risk-averse financial investor prefers higher average return on a portfolio but dislikes higher risk.
7   Diversification means not putting all your eggs in one basket.
8   Diversification fails when share returns are negatively correlated.
9   In equilibrium, low beta shares will have below average prices.
10  Speculative bubbles are less likely the larger the share of the total return that comes in the form of dividends rather than capital gains.
11  A forward market in cars would help to stabilize prices.
12  A trader buying forward in the hope of a higher future spot price is hedging.

## ECONOMICS IN THE NEWS

### Hotspots for the financial tourist
*(Adapted from the Independent on Sunday 9 January 2000 )*

First-time investors tend to opt for 'safe' UK funds. But after a while safe becomes boring, so what's the next step when you are ready for something more exciting? Europe is touted as the hot region to invest in this year, just as Japan was last year. European funds may not have produced stellar returns in recent months but they have made steady progress, a trend which is set to continue. 'There is a wide range of economies at different stages of development, which gives skilful fund managers a great deal to run at,' says Craig Wetton of Bath-based financial advisers Chartwell. 'For instance, the Baltic states and Sweden have both been showing very positive returns in recent months.'
   If you are keen to diversify your portfolio, Europe is not the only region you should consider. A geographical spread of funds reduces risk as the damage done by an economic downturn or stock market crash in one region is limited. And if you aren't in a particular market, you won't enjoy the gains in the good times. Some markets will be riskier than those you have previously been exposed to, so it is important to treat them as long-term projects

and only invest money that you can afford to lose. If you are in this position, higher- risk funds offer greater potential for dramatic growth.

So where should you look? To ignore North America would be to discount more than half the global economy in terms of market capitalisation. Yet British investors have been fighting shy of American investment in recent years: just over 5 per cent of unit trust money is invested in pure US funds (though multi-country funds will also have a big chunk in the US market). British caution over the US is a reflection of repeated predictions of market crashes – yet the Dow Jones on the whole continues to climb steadily upwards. 'Paradoxically,' says Ian Chimes of Credit Suisse Asset Management, 'British investors are much happier about the Far East. This means they pass up the likes of Microsoft and Coca-Cola in favour of Indonesian rubber plantation holdings.'

An alternative to regional diversification is to look at sectors. The most obvious at the moment are technology and, in particular, the internet. There are several impressive technology trusts around, but most are heavily skewed towards US stocks. Framlington's NetNet fund, which invests in internet-linked firms, is also US-oriented. Not only will this give you some exposure to the American stock market, it will provide an inroad into a sector where the US is well ahead of everyone else.

1    What determines whether an investor looks for excitement or safety in a portfolio?
2    On the basis of the information in the passage, in which regions or sectors would you choose to invest?
3    Did you choose a balanced mix of regions and sectors, or did you decide to put all your eggs into one basket? What does this say about your attitude towards risk?

## Questions for Thought

1    Explain why the occurrence of large positive or negative returns on shares in particular years was probably unanticipated.
2    Discuss whether the stock market most resembles a casino or an efficient market. What sort of evidence helps your decision?
3    Regardless of how you believe the stock market does work, which is the more desirable method if we are concerned that funds are appropriately allocated between firms?
4    Discuss whether moral hazard or adverse selection might influence the markets for insurance against unemployment or bad health in a situation where there is no state provision of such insurance.

# 16 Introduction to Welfare Economics

## Learning Outcomes

- To explain the role of value judgements in welfare economics
- To define horizontal equity and vertical equity
- To consider the concept of Pareto efficiency and show how the Invisible Hand might make free competitive markets efficient
- To analyse why distortions lead to pure waste that reduce efficiency
- To develop the second-best argument that, when some distortions cannot be eliminated, it may not be efficient to eliminate other distortions
- To explain why externalities lead to inefficiency, and examine when property rights can set up the implicit market to solve the problem
- To discuss the market failures that give rise to pollution and congestion
- To view other inefficiencies in risk, safety, and quality as further examples of missing markets, and explain why such markets fail to exist

**IN THIS CHAPTER ...** you will tackle some contentious issues. Welfare economics is a branch of economics which attempts to assess how an economy is working. You will meet two key issues: allocative efficiency and equity. The *efficiency* of the allocation of resources may be assessed by the Pareto criterion. A key issue is whether the free market allows an economy to attain a Pareto-efficient allocation of resources without the need for intervention. It could be suggested that the free market should be allowed to take the economy to an efficient resource allocation and that the government should intervene only if redistribution proves to be necessary. However, there are circumstances in which the free market may fail to operate effectively, perhaps because of market failure. This chapter focuses on the existence of *externalities* and the absence of some markets. The granting of property rights may allow the 'internalization' of externalities, by making explicit who should compensate whom and forcing the implicit market into existence.

## Important Concepts and Technical Terms

Match each lettered concept with the appropriate numbered phrase:

| | | |
|---|---|---|
| (a) Horizontal equity | (e) Second-best | (i) Externality |
| (b) Resource allocation | (f) Free-rider problem | (j) Pareto-efficient |
| (c) Property rights | (g) Market failure | (k) Vertical equity |
| (d) Welfare economics | (h) Allocative efficiency | (l) Distortion |

1  The branch of economics dealing with normative issues, its purpose being not to describe how the economy works but to assess how well it works.
2  The identical treatment of identical people.
3  A list or complete description of who does what and who gets what.
4  Circumstances in which equilibrium in free unregulated markets will fail to achieve an efficient allocation.
5  The different treatment of different people in order to reduce the consequences of these innate differences.
6  A situation causing society's marginal cost of producing a good to diverge from society's marginal benefit from consuming that good.
7  A situation in which an individual has no incentive to pay for a good which is costly to produce, as he or she can consume it anyway.
8  A theory by which the government may increase the overall efficiency of the whole economy by introducing new distortions to offset distortions that already exist.
9  A situation when an economy is getting the most out of its scarce resources and not squandering them.
10  A situation arising whenever an individual's production or consumption decision directly affects the production or consumption of others, other than through market prices.
11  An allocation of resources such that, given consumer tastes, resources, and technology, it is impossible to move to another allocation which would make some people better off and nobody worse off.
12  The legal right to compensation for infringement of vested rights.

## Exercises

1   Suppose that Ursula and Vince judge their utility in terms of the goods they receive. Figure 16-1 shows a number of alternative allocations of goods between the two of them.

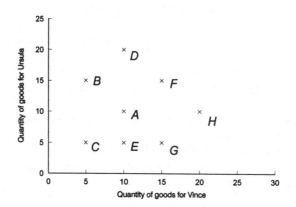

**Figure 16-1 Allocation of goods between Ursula and Vince**

In the following questions, the Pareto criterion should be used to assess alternative allocations:
*(a)* Which allocations are superior to A?
*(b)* Which allocations are inferior to A?
*(c)* Are there any allocations which you have not mentioned in your answers to *(a)* and *(b)*? If so, explain why you have not been able to judge them either superior or inferior to A. Is society indifferent between such points?
Suppose that the quantity of goods available is 20:
*(d)* Which allocations are inefficient?
*(e)* Which allocations are efficient?
*(f)* Which allocations are infeasible?

2   Suppose that an economy has many producers and consumers, but only two goods, food and books. Both markets are unregulated and perfectly competitive. The equilibrium price of food is £20 and that of books is £10. Labour is the variable factor of production, and workers gain equal job satisfaction from working in each of the two sectors. The economy is in equilibrium.
*(a)* How much additional utility (in money value) did consumers obtain from the last book produced?
*(b)* How many books would consumers exchange for one unit of food if their utility were to remain constant?
*(c)* What was the marginal cost of the last book and last unit of food produced? Justify your answer.
*(d)* What can be said about relative wage rates in the two sectors?
*(e)* What is the ratio of the marginal physical product of labour in production of books to that in production of food?
*(f)* How many additional books could be produced if one less unit of food is produced?
*(g)* Bearing in mind your answers to parts *(b)* and *(f)*, what can be said about the allocation of resources in this economy?

3   Part *(a)* of Figure 16-2 shows the demand curve for books *(DD)* in the economy of exercise 2. *SS* shows the supply curve for books.
*(a)* Identify equilibrium price and quantity.
*(b)* Suppose the authorities impose a tax on books: identify the tax-inclusive supply curve and the new equilibrium consumer price and quantity. What is the amount of the tax?
*(c)* At this equilibrium, what is the marginal social cost of books? What is the marginal consumer benefit?

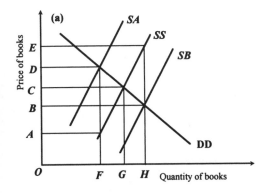

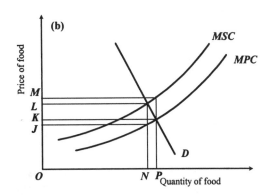

**Figure 16-2    A commodity tax and the second best**

Given that the books tax is imposed as in part *(b)*, now consider the market for food, shown in panel *(b)* of Figure 16-2. *D* represents the demand curve, *MPC* the marginal private cost of food, and *MSC* the marginal social cost of producing food.

*(d)* Identify equilibrium price and quantity in market for food.

*(e)* Does this equilibrium ensure a satisfactory resource allocation? Explain your answer.

*(f)* Explain the divergence between *MPC* and *MSC*.

*(g)* Given that the tax on books must remain, what is the preferred output of the food industry? How could the authorities bring about this production level?

4   Which of the following would be indicative of market failure? (Note: more than one response may be appropriate.)

*(a)* Traffic congestion.

*(b)* The existence of a collusive oligopoly.

*(c)* The absence of a forward market for cars.

*(d)* The presence of a market in which marginal social benefit exceeds marginal private benefit.

*(e)* A situation in which a firm is free to pollute the atmosphere around its factory (a residential area) without cost.

5   A dog-owner daily allows his dog to foul the pavement. In what sense is this an externality? In the absence of a realistic charge to dog-owners, would you expect there to be too many or too few dogs for social efficiency? Should the authorities tackle this problem by raising the dog licence fee or by restricting the number of licences issued – or should they leave things as they are?

6   Two neighbouring factories in a remote rural area operate independently. One is a branch of a company *(XYZ plc)* which has incurred the cost of improving and maintaining the main road linking the two factories with the motorway. The other factory makes no contribution towards the road, but shares its advantages. Figure 16-3 overleaf illustrates the position facing *XYZ plc*, which is assumed (for simplicity) to be a price-taker in this market, with demand curve horizontal at *DD*. *MPC* represents the marginal private cost faced by *XYZ plc*.

*(a)* At what point will the firm produce?

*(b)* Taking account of the externality of the road, identify the marginal social cost curve *(MSCX* or *MSCY)*. Explain your answer.

*(c)* What would be the socially efficient point of production? Why?

*(d)* What is the social cost of producing at *(a)* rather than at *(c)*?

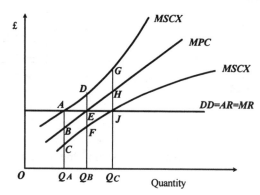

**Figure 16-3    The effect of a production externality**

7    A factory emits smoke during the production process which imposes an external diseconomy upon the environment. The following data describe the situation:

| Output (units) | Marginal private cost (£) | Marginal revenue (£) | Marginal social cost of air pollution (£) |
|---|---|---|---|
| 1 | 12 | 24 | 4 |
| 2 | 12 | 22 | 6 |
| 3 | 12 | 20 | 8 |
| 4 | 12 | 18 | 10 |
| 5 | 12 | 16 | 12 |
| 6 | 12 | 14 | 14 |
| 7 | 12 | 12 | 16 |
| 8 | 12 | 10 | 18 |

Initially, the firm maximizes profits without regard to the social cost of air pollution. If, subsequently, the authorities levy pollution tax on the firm equal to the marginal social cost, which of the following describes what happens to output?
*(a)* Falls by 4 units.
*(b)* Falls by 2 units.
*(c)* Falls by 1 unit.
*(d)* Remains constant.
*(e)* Rises by 1 unit.

8    Which of the following describes a situation in which resource allocation may be said to be efficient?
*(a)* Production processes use as little energy as possible.
*(b)* No one can be made better off without someone else being made worse off.
*(c)* There is no need to trade with other countries.
*(d)* The balance of payments is in surplus.
*(e)* The production of one commodity cannot be increased without reducing the production of another commodity.
*(f)* All private companies within the economy are producing at an equilibrium level of output in order to maximize profits.
*(g)* Gross national income grows at a planned percentage rate every year.

9    A local government councillor said: 'The authority is short of revenue and the roads into the town centre are congested; therefore, we should double car parking charges.'

If this is the aim of the policy, which of the following assumptions is/are implicitly being made?

*(a)* The elasticity of demand for car parking in the town centre is less than unity.

*(b)* The social costs of driving to the town centre outweigh the social benefits.

*(c)* The local authority has no substantial competition in the provision of car parking facilities in the town centre.

10 Explain the sense in which some pollution might be socially desirable.

(*Hint:* You may find it helpful to draw a diagram to show the effects of pollution in a market. For example, imagine that you live in a flat overlooking the sea, but that offshore there is an oil refinery. This means that you have to spend extra time cleaning the floor, and must wash your clothes more frequently. The oil refinery is imposing costs on to you and your neighbours (i.e. society) that it does not have to pay for. Draw a diagram to show the firm's production decision, and then compare this with the optimal position for society as a whole. The question is whether the optimum position requires zero pollution?)

## True/False

1 Welfare economics deals with normative issues.

2 An allocation of resources in which it is impossible to make any one individual better off without making somebody else worse off is Pareto-efficient.

3 If every market in the economy but one is a perfectly competitive free market, the resulting equilibrium throughout the economy will be Pareto-efficient.

4 If a distortion is unavoidable in a particular sector, the best action for the government to take is to ensure that the other sectors are distortion-free.

5 Under imperfect competition, marginal revenue is different from average revenue: this causes market failure.

6 The formal establishment of property rights can help to achieve the socially efficient allocation by internalizing externalities.

7 River pollution represents a situation where private cost exceeds social cost.

8 Private cost exceeds social cost whenever a firm fails to make a profit.

9 Pollution still exists; therefore past pollution control has been ineffective.

10 An important problem which inhibits the development of forward and contingent markets is the provision of information.

11 Human life is beyond economic calculation and must be given absolute priority, whatever the cost.

12 Estimates for the implicit social marginal benefit from saving life in the UK range from £50 to £20 million.

## ECONOMICS IN THE NEWS

### Singapore begins electronic road pricing
*(Adapted from Associated Press, 1 April 1998)*

Commuters on their way to work on Wednesday on one of Singapore's main highways will be participating in the world's most sophisticated electronic road pricing system. Cars using the East Coast Parkway to reach the centre city during morning rush hour will hear an electronic gadget on their dashboards beep and see the device deduct a toll from their stored value cash card. If that doesn't happen, they'll have to pay a fine of S$70 (US$43.50).

The evidence will be collected by a computerized robotic eye in a gantry that spans the highway. It takes a picture of the driver and the car, records the time of day and the exact violation. Whether the cash card was placed incorrectly or a fuse is blown in the dashboard device, the transport authorities will know. 'The ... system is able to differentiate between a violation and a technical fault,' said Land Transport Authority spokesman Zainul Abidin Ibrahim. There will be no grace period. Motorists have been bombarded with messages through the media for months to install the devices, get them checked and purchase their stored value cards.

The Land Transport Authority estimates that 55 per cent of Singapore's 680,000 cars have the devices. But because the system 'is the first of its kind in the world,' it is being phased in, one highway at a time, 'so that teething problems can be sorted out and motorists have time to familiarize themselves with the system,' Zainul said. Simpler systems, based on prepurchased data cards or chips, are operated on New York and New Jersey roads in the United States, and on toll roads leading into Oslo, the capital of Norway.

The Singapore system not only takes photographs and records all the data of the event, but also checks every car in every lane, and adjusts the price deducted depending on the time of day. Singaporeans, used to a lot of government control in a republic where one party has been in power since 1965, are not so much worried about privacy as the extra charges they will have to pay to use the highways.

In line with the government's determination to keep Singapore from developing the traffic jams and smog of other Asian cities – such as Jakarta and Bangkok – driving around this 648-square-kilometer (259-square-mile) island probably is more expensive than anywhere else in the world. Road taxes, insurance and car ownership permits auctioned for tens of thousands of dollars each month are all intended to keep down the number of cars on the road, authorities say. But callers to radio talk shows and newspaper letter writers suggest a widespread feeling that the new electronic highway toll like the other measures – is simply to generate more government revenue.

Taxi passengers will pay an extra 70c and private vehicle owners an extra S$2 each time they use the monitored highway between 8 and 9 a.m. The price is halved if the commuter travels a half-hour earlier or later. In September, the system will be extended to two other main highways. Eventually, the central business district will also be monitored electronically, eliminating the last of the 117 private police officers who have for years checked road use visually, noting down license plates of cars without the proper permits as they whiz by.

1  Explain the economic reasoning underlying the use of electronic road pricing.
2  Do you regard as being more important to control car ownership or car usage?
3  Singapore is a small city-state, with a land area not much larger than the Isle of Wight. Does this suggest that a road-pricing scheme is more likely to be effective than in a country like the UK? Why?

## Questions for Thought

1  The nuclear accident at Chernobyl created widespread radioactive pollution. Discuss how you would assess the costs and benefits of nuclear energy.
2  Discuss how the granting of property rights could help to internalize externalities suffered by people living near football grounds or having noisy neighbours.

# 17 Taxes and Government Spending

## Learning Outcomes

- To discuss types of government spending and the different motives for them
- To show why pure public goods cannot be provided by a market
- To distinguish average and marginal tax rates; and direct and indirect taxes
- To analyse tax incidence, and relate the size of a tax distortion to the elasticities of supply and demand of the commodity being taxed
- To show how taxes can compensate for externalities
- To explain what is meant by supply-side economics
- To develop the Laffer curve, and analyse why there is a limit on the maximum revenue that can be raised by any tax
- To discuss how mobility of people, capital, and products across political jurisdictions may limit economic sovereignty

**IN THIS CHAPTER ...** you will look more carefully at the role of government in a modern market economy. In the UK in the early 1980s, total government expenditure amounted to more than 40 per cent of national income, much of it going on health, defence, education, and transfer payments. The distinction between spending on goods and services and on transfers is an important one: if the government spends on goods and services, it pre-empts scarce resources which cannot then be used in the private sector. Transfer payments do not pre-empt, but redistribute income between groups in society. Such payments accounted for an increasing proportion of government spending as the rate of unemployment rose. As well as considering such issues involving government expenditure, you will also look at the economics of taxation as the chapter progresses.

## Important Concepts and Technical Terms

Match each lettered concept with the appropriate numbered phrase:

| | | |
|---|---|---|
| (a) Council tax | (f) Merit good | (k) Benefits principle |
| (b) Progressive tax structure | (g) Laffer curve | (l) Deadweight tax burden |
| (c) Corporation tax | (h) Direct tax | (m) Wealth tax |
| (d) Indirect tax | (i) Marginal tax rate | (n) Regressive tax structure |
| (e) Incidence of a tax | (j) Tiebout model | |

1  A tax structure in which the average tax rate rises with an individual's income level.
2  The waste caused by a distortionary tax leading to a misallocation of resources.
3  A description of the relationship between tax rates and tax revenue.
4  A tax on asset holdings or transfers rather than the income from asset holding: examples in the UK are rates and capital transfer tax.
5  A tax structure in which the average tax rate falls as income level rises.
6  The principle underlying a tax structure in which people who receive more than their share of public spending pay more than their share of tax revenues.
7  The percentage taken by the government of the last pound that an individual earns.
8  A tax levied on expenditure on goods and services.
9  An important model of local government, sometimes called the model of the 'invisible foot'.
10  A tax with a mixture of property, income and household tax components.
11  Tax paid by UK companies based on their taxable profits after allowance for interest payments and depreciation.
12  Tax levied directly on income.
13  A good that society thinks everyone ought to have regardless of whether it is wanted by each individual.
14  A measure of the final tax burden on different people once we have allowed for the indirect as well as the direct effects of the tax.

## Exercises

1  (a) Use the data of Table 17-4 of the main text to draw pie-charts showing the shares of the major categories of government expenditure and tax revenue.
   (b) The Conservative administrations of Mrs Thatcher and Mr Major pursued a philosophy based on freedom of individual choice. In part, this meant following policies which allow direct taxes to be reduced. How do you think this will have affected the pattern of revenue shares revealed by your pie-chart?
   (c) How would you expect the pattern of government expenditure to have been affected by the increase in unemployment in the early 1980s?

2  Assume that income tax is levied at a standard rate of 30 per cent on all income over £5000.
   (a) Calculate the marginal and average tax rates at the following income levels:
       (i)  £ 3 000.
       (ii) £ 9 000.
       (iii) £12 000.
       (iv) £20 000.
   (b) Is the tax progressive or regressive?
   Suppose the tax structure is revised so that income over £5000 is taxed at 30 per cent as before, but the rate increases to 50 per cent for income over £10 000.
   (c) Calculate the marginal and average tax rates at the same income levels as in part (a).
   (d) Is the tax more or less progressive than before?

3  This exercise is concerned with the market for a pure public good. In Figure 17-1, D1 and D2 represent the demand curves for the good of two individuals: we assume that for each individual the demand curve shows the marginal private benefit of the last unit of the public good. The line MC shows the private and social marginal cost of producing the public good.
   (a) If DD is to represent the marginal social benefit obtained from the good, what should be the relationship between DD and D1 and D2?
   (b) If the quantity produced is given by OF, what valuation per unit is placed upon the good by individual 1?
   (c) If individual 1 actually pays this amount for the provision of the good, what will individual 2 have to pay?
   (d) What is the marginal social benefit of OF units of this good?
   (e) How does marginal social benefit compare with marginal social cost in this situation?
   (f) What is the socially efficient quantity of this good?

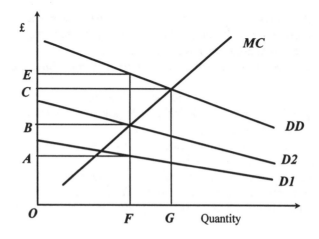

**Figure 17-1    Demand curves for a pure public good**

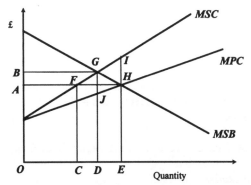

**Figure 17-2    Market for a good in which there is a negative production externality**

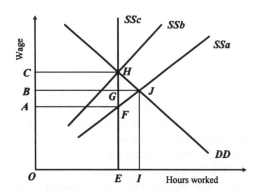

**Figure 17-3    A tax on wages**

4    Figure 17-2 shows the market for a good in which there is a negative production externality such that marginal social cost *(MSC)* is above marginal private cost *(MPC)*. *MSB* represents the marginal social benefit derived from consumption of the good.

*(a)*    If this market is unregulated, what quantity of this good will be produced?

*(b)*    What is the socially efficient quantity?

*(c)*    What is the amount of the deadweight loss to society if the free market quantity is produced?

*(d)*    What level of tax on the good would ensure that the socially efficient quantity is produced?

*(e)*    Suggest an example of a situation in which this analysis might be relevant.

5    A firm engaged in producing a certain good has private costs which are not equal to social costs. Which of the following steps could the government take to increase economic welfare?

*(a)*    Tax the firm if social costs are less than its private costs.

*(b)*    Subsidize the firm if social costs exceed its private costs.

*(c)*    Tax the firm if social costs exceed its private costs.

*(d)*    Subsidize other firms in the same industry if their private costs are less than social costs.

6    Figure 17-3 shows the position in a labour market. *DD* is the demand curve for labour; *SSa*, *SSb* and *SSc* are labour supply curves – but ignore *SSc* for the moment. The 'wage' here is to be regarded as the gross wage. Suppose a tax on wages is imposed.

*(a)*    Of *SSa* and *SSb*, which represents labour supply without the tax, and which shows the post-tax situation?

*(b)*    What is the labour market equilibrium without the tax?

*(c)*    What effect does the tax have on hours worked?

*(d)*    In this situation, what is the wage paid by firms?

*(e)*    What is the wage received by workers?

*(f)*    What area represents tax revenue?

*(g)*    What area represents the deadweight loss?

*(h)*    Identify the areas which represent the incidence of the tax on workers and employers.

Suppose now that the supply of labour is perfectly inelastic at *SSc*, and a tax of AC is levied:

*(i)*    What is the wage paid by firms?

*(j)*    What is the wage received by workers?

*(k)* What area represents tax revenue?

*(l)* What area represents the deadweight loss?

*(m)* Identify the areas which represent the incidence of the tax on workers and employers.

7 The provision of some public services is delegated by central government to local authorities, together with some responsibility for raising finance to fund those activities. The Tiebout model recommends local government jurisdiction areas, but the externalities argument suggests that the geographical jurisdiction areas should be relatively large. Which of the following arguments favour the Tiebout model?

*(a)* People are different and do not want to be treated the same.

*(b)* Public goods are non-exclusive.

*(c)* Differential pricing for residents and non-residents for facilities such as art galleries is difficult to implement.

*(d)* People feel that central government is remote from their needs.

*(e)* Residents mainly consume the public services provided by their own local authorities.

*(f)* Larger jurisdictions enable externalities to be internalized.

*(g)* Smaller jurisdictions maximize people's choices.

8 Table 17-1 shows the sources of tax revenues in a range of countries around the world. Examine these data. What do they reveal about the way that governments in different parts of the world seek to raise revenue?

**Table 17-1   Sources of tax revenue 1995 (% of total)**

|  | UK | Bolivia | Cameroon | India | Malaysia | S Korea | Zambia |
|---|---|---|---|---|---|---|---|
| Income, profits, capital gains | 38.9 | 3.8 | 23.5 | 29.2 | 45.6 | 35.9 | 35.4 |
| Social security contributions | 18.6 | 9.9 | 0.0 | 0.0 | 1.5 | 8.7 | 0.0 |
| Property | 7.0 | 15.4 | 1.6 | 0.1 | 0.6 | 2.6 | 0.2 |
| Domestic goods and services | 35.3 | 59.7 | 34.8 | 38.5 | 31.8 | 37.0 | 51.6 |
| International trade | 0.1 | 10.1 | 38.1 | 32.0 | 15.1 | 7.4 | 12.8 |
| Other | 0.1 | 1.1 | 2.0 | 0.2 | 5.4 | 8.4 | 0.0 |

Source: *Government Financial Statistics Yearbook 1997.*

## True/False

1 Government spending on transfer payments has risen faster than national income since 1956, and continues to do so.

2 Income tax is progressive because the marginal tax rate is greater than the average tax rate.

3 The largest government revenue raiser in the UK in 1991 was taxes on goods.

4 A football match is a public good.

5 Social security payments damage social efficiency by pre-empting resources that would be more productively used in the private sector.

6 Income tax was not introduced in peacetime in the UK until the 1840s.

7 Public goods must be produced by the government.

8 The underlying principle of income tax is the 'benefits principle'.

9 The tax on tobacco tends to be regressive in its effect.

10 The Laffer curve demonstrates that, for many 'big government–big tax' countries, a cut in tax rates would increase tax revenues.

11 Cigarettes are a merit bad.

12 Closer economic integration with other countries undermines the sovereignty of nation-states.

# ECONOMICS IN THE NEWS

## Admit it, Mr Brown: higher taxes are a necessary evil
*(Adapted from The Independent 28 December 1999)*

Try to imagine this exchange when the House of Commons returns next month. Francis Maude: 'Will the Chancellor of the Exchequer please admit what he has so far failed to admit, namely, that the tax burden has risen since Labour came to office in May 1997?'

The Chancellor of the Exchequer: 'I am glad to do so. The tax burden has indeed risen modestly in that period. I have placed a detailed analysis of that increase and subsequent projected increases in the House of Commons library. Let me tell the honourable member that I am proud to belong to a government that has not been frightened of raising taxes in order to procure a juster society. Unlike the honourable gentleman who has revelled in a rash and irresponsible promise to reduce public spending year by year as a proportion of gross national product, whatever the economic circumstances, I have no hesitation in reasserting that taxation is an essential precondition of a safer, healthier and economically successful society.

'First, all of us, including the better off, benefit from the redistribution that I have skilfully begun to carry out in successive budgets (and which is also desirable in itself). After all, the rich benefit as well as the poor from the reduction in crime that should follow lower unemployment and a reduction of inequality, from an increase in the skills and adaptability of our workforce, which will lead to greater national productivity, and from the reduction of congestion that will result from a fast and efficient public transport network. The idea that these highly desirable goals can be achieved while inexorably cutting taxation, as the honourable member's party proposes, will never be believed by the British people. But even if it was, it would still be wrong in principle.'

Such a parliamentary answer from the Chancellor of the Exchequer – let alone the Prime Minister – is highly improbable, of course. It breaks a taboo that, while recent in origin, at least in the Labour Party, has nevertheless put down deep roots. To speak approvingly of taxation, especially of taxation for the purposes of redistribution, remains difficult to the point of impossibility for most New Labour politicians. The 1992 election defeat and the widespread view, promoted most actively after it by Gordon Brown and Tony Blair, that the assumption embedded in Labour's programme – that taxes would have to be raised in order to pay for that programme – was to blame is now too much part of New Labour folklore to allow such statements to be made in public.

But can that taboo ever be lifted? More important, should it be? A provocative pamphlet to be published tomorrow answers 'yes' to both questions. Selina Chen, research fellow at the commission on taxation and citizenship set up by the Fabian Society under the chairmanship of Professor Raymond Plant, attempts to rehabilitate stable tax levels as an essential component of a modern social democracy. Ms Chen is sceptical of the increasingly fashionable view that the global economy and the growth of e-commerce will make it more and more difficult for member states to levy taxes at all. She points to research done for the Plant commission, which casts doubt on the idea that the countries with the lowest taxes will always attract the greatest inward investment and that physical goods are no less taxable because they are ordered by Internet. Second, she points out that modern governments, including the UK's, are – rightly – increasingly taxing 'bads' such as pollution and waste.

More important, however, is her optimism that a social democratic case for taxation can be made more boldly than it is at present and that such a case will need to be made if centre-left governments are to sustain and improve public services such as health, education and transport.

1   Do you agree with the statement in the passage that '…taxation is an essential precondition of a safer, healthier and economically successful society'? What are the economic arguments underlying this point of view?

2   Do you regard the present balance between government intervention and free market forces to be appropriate?

## Questions for Thought

1  How would you expect a switch in policy from direct to indirect taxation to affect income distribution?
2  In looking for a policy to correct for an externality, the authorities have a choice of policies. One possibility is to take action on the quantity side of the market, perhaps by direct regulation, or by selling licences. As an alternative, they may choose to influence market price, either by taxation or by direct price-setting. This exercise explores the circumstances under which this choice is significant, when the authorities have imperfect knowledge of market conditions. First consider Figure 17-4.

Here, $D$ represents the market demand curve, and $MPC$ is marginal private cost. Suppose the authorities know the location of $D$, and that marginal social costs $(MSC)$ are higher than $MPC$, but are uncertain about the position of $MSC$. Specifically, suppose that they perceive $MSC$ to be at $MSCg$, although in fact $MSCa$ represents the actual level.

(a)  Which combination of price and quantity is socially desirable?
(b)  At which combination will the government aim?
(c)  What would be the deadweight loss if the policy adopted is to set price?
(d)  What would be the deadweight loss if the policy adopted is to set quantity?
(e)  Does it matter which policy is adopted?

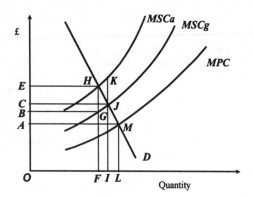

**Figure 17-4    Price or quantity control?**    **Figure 17-5    Price or quantity control?**

Suppose now that the government knows the 'true' level of marginal social cost ($MSC$ in Figure 17-5), but is uncertain about market demand. $Da$ in Figure 17-5 is the actual market demand, but the government perceives it to be at $Dg$.

(f)  Which combination of price and quantity is socially desirable?
(g)  At which combination will the government aim?
(h)  What would be the deadweight loss if the policy adopted is to set price?
(i)  What would be the deadweight loss if the policy adopted is to set quantity?
(j)  Does it matter which policy is adopted?

# 18 Industrial Policy and Competition Policy

## Learning Outcomes

- To explain and contrast the ways in which competition policy and industrial policy seek to offset market failures and improve efficiency
- To discuss the role of patents in stimulating investment in R&D
- To examine why sunrise and sunset industries are vulnerable to market failures
- To consider why a firm's costs might depend on its location and identify reasons for locational externalities
- To define consumer surplus and producer surplus, and use them to analyse the social cost of monopoly power
- To examine the principles behind UK competition policy and evaluate its success in practice
- To distinguish different types of merger and explain why merger booms have occurred.
- To examine the regulation of potential mergers, both in theory and in practice

**IN THIS CHAPTER ...** you will begin to explore the ways in which government intervention attempts to enhance market efficiency. *Industrial policy* is intended to affect market efficiency where there are externalities that affect production decisions of firms. *Competition policy* aims to promote competition amongst firms, to prevent firms from abusing monopoly power. The *Competition Commission* (formerly the Monopolies and Mergers Commission) exists to monitor the behaviour of large firms, and may recommend the breaking-up of existing monopolies, or prevent mergers that would create new monopoly firms.

## Important Concepts and Technical Terms
Match each lettered concept with the appropriate numbered phrase:

| | | |
|---|---|---|
| (a) Competition Commission | (f) Locational externality | (k) Cream-skimming |
| (b) Horizontal merger | (g) Takeover bid | (l) Patent system |
| (c) Industrial concentration | (h) R&D | (m) Industrial policy |
| (d) Deadweight burden | (i) Conglomerate merger | (n) Consumer surplus |
| (e) Vertical merger | (j) Competition policy | (o) Producer surplus |

1   A governmental body set up to investigate whether or not a monopoly acts against the public interest.
2   A voluntary union of two firms whose production activities are essentially unrelated.
3   A situation in which one firm offers to buy out the shareholders of the second firm.
4   A part of government economic policy which aims to enhance economic efficiency by promoting or safeguarding competition between firms..
5   A situation in which a new entrant into a former monopoly market takes over only the profitable parts of the business, thereby undermining scale economies elsewhere.
6   A union of two firms at different production stages in the same industry.
7   The loss to society resulting from the allocative inefficiency of imperfect competition.
8   Government economic policy aiming to offset externalities that affect production decisions by firms.
9   A situation in which activity in an industry becomes focused in a few firms.
10   The excess of consumer benefits over spending.
11   Activity undertaken by private and public sector organizations to discover and develop new products, processes, and technologies.
12   A union of two firms at the same production stage in the same industry.
13   A situation in which one firm's cost curve depends upon the proximity of other similar firms.
14   The excess of revenue over total costs.
15   A temporary legal monopoly awarded to an inventor who registers the invention.

## Exercises

1  Identify each of the following as vertical, horizontal, or conglomerate mergers:
   (a) The union of a motor vehicle manufacturer with a tyre producer.
   (b) The union of a motor vehicle manufacturer with a retail car distributor.
   (c) The union of a tobacco company with a cosmetic firm.
   (d) The union of two firms producing man-made fibres.

2  In Figure 18-1, DD represents the market demand curve for a commodity. If organized as a competitive market, BY would represent the long-run marginal cost curve. However, a monopolist would face the long-run marginal (and average) cost curve AX.
   (a) What would be the price and output of the competitive industry?
   (b) What would be the price and output under monopoly?
   (c) What is the deadweight loss to consumers from the monopoly as compared with the competitive industry?
   (d) What area represents the cost savings of monopoly?
   (e) What area represents monopoly profits?
   (f) Explain why the monopolist and competitive industry might face different cost conditions.

3  Figure 18-2 shows an industry operated as a monopoly, with long-run marginal cost given by LMC.
   (a) Identify the profit-maximizing price and output.
   (b) What is the area representing consumer surplus in this position?
   (c) What is the area representing producer surplus?
   (d) What is the social surplus?
   (e) What would the price-output combination have been in a fully competitive market (assuming that the industry would still face the same cost conditions)?
   (f) What would the consumer surplus be in this situation?
   (g) What would producer surplus be?
   (h) What is the social surplus?
   (i) What position would maximize total social surplus?

4  Which is the 'odd one out' of the following proposed mergers?
   (a) Air France/Sabena.
   (b) Alcatel/Telettra.
   (c) Aerospatiale/Alenia/De Havilland.
   (d) Renault/Volvo.
   (e) Courtaulds/SHIA.

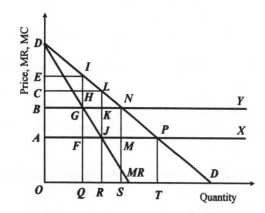

**Figure 18-1  Monopoly and competition**

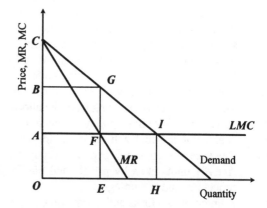

**Figure 18-2  Monopoly and consumer surplus**

5   Which of the following might explain why a firm wished to embark on a conglomerate merger?
    (a)  A wish to retain its share of the market for its main product.
    (b)  A wish to gain control of its supplies of raw materials.
    (c)  The desire to eliminate competition from foreign firms.
    (d)  The desire to diversify and extend its product range.
    (e)  A wish to reduce its dependence on supplies of skilled labour.
    Why was there an increase in the number of conglomerate mergers relative to other forms in the late 1980s?
6   Which of the following might explain why a firm wished to embark on a horizontal merger?
    (a)  The wish to acquire or extend monopoly power.
    (b)  The desire to exploit external economies of scale.
    (c)  The desire to diversity and extend its product range.
    (d)  A wish to gain control of its supplies of raw materials.
7   Which of the following would tend to increase the degree of monopoly power of a firm?
    (a)  The concentration of production into a smaller number of industrial plants.
    (b)  The expiry of a patent.
    (c)  Diversification into a broader range of product lines.
    (d)  An increase in monopoly profits.
    (e)  A reduction in advertising expenditure.
    (f)  A fall in the cross-price elasticity of demand for the firm's product.
8   A market has been operating as a monopoly for many years, with the protection of a barrier to entry. The
    market situation is shown in Figure 18-3.
    (a)  Which if the LMC curves is most likely to be effective?
    (b)  What is the profit-maximizing price-output combination?
    (c)  Identify the consumer surplus in this situation.
    Suppose the market is now opened up to competition:
    (d)  How might this affect costs?
    (e)  What price-output combination might then result under competition?
    (f)  What is consumer surplus in this new situation?
    (g)  In what ways is society better off?

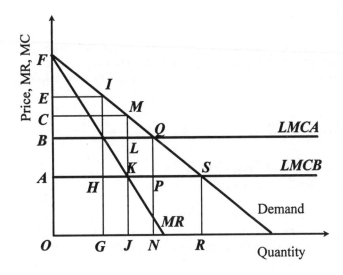

**Figure 18-3   A monopoly and X-inefficiency**

9    Which of the following factors might be seen to affect the social cost of monopoly?
   *(a)* The elasticity of demand for the good.
   *(b)* The steepness of marginal cost.
   *(c)* The resources used in erecting and maintaining barriers to entry, by advertising, holding excess capacity, and so on.
   *(d)* The political influence that accrues to a large company with monopoly power.
   *(e)* The effect of monopoly profits on the distribution of resources.

10   Below are listed a number of policy actions. Identify each as belonging either to competition policy or to industrial policy:
   *(a)* Referral to the Competition Commission of a firm supplying more than 25 per cent of the total market for a particular commodity.
   *(b)* The promotion of R&D.
   *(c)* Assistance for a national firm involved in strategic international competition.
   *(d)* Subsidization of an emerging hi-tech industry.
   *(e)* A patent system.
   *(f)* The restriction of excessive non-price competition (e.g. advertising).
   *(g)* The subsidization of 'lame duck' industries in areas of high unemployment.
   *(h)* The outlawing of explicit price-fixing agreements between firms in an industry.
   *(i)* Nationalization.

## True/False

1    Each firm in an imperfectly competitive market enjoys a degree of monopoly power.
2    The social cost of monopoly in the UK is probably equivalent to more than one-tenth of national income.
3    Competition policy in the UK is more pragmatic than that in the USA.
4    Monopoly may allow social gain through the exploitation of economies of scale.
5    One of the potential benefits of merger activity is that it allows an inspired management to show its worth.
6    We would expect that the law allowing mergers to be referred to the Competition (Monopolies and Mergers) Commission would discourage mergers from taking place.
7    The cost conditions of a firm are always independent of location and the presence of other firms.
8    Consumer surplus is what you have left over at the end of the month.
9    Pre-emptive patenting can be used as an effective strategic barrier to entry.
10   Government expenditure on R&D in the UK is aimed mainly at the advancement of knowledge (via the universities) and at developing new products and processes in the industrial sector.
11   An important part of industrial policy is to subsidize sunrise industries.
12   It is silly to spend money on dole payments; a much better policy is to subsidize declining industries to protect employment.

## ECONOMICS IN THE NEWS

### 1 PepsiCo loses its taste for fast food chains
*(Adapted from the Financial Times, 27 January 1997)*

It seemed a good idea at the time. In the mid 1970s, PepsiCo saw less than stellar prospects for its soft drinks and salty snack operations, and started buying fast food chains to speed up earnings growth. Twenty years later, the strategy is being turned on its head. PepsiCo has announced its decision to get out of the fast foods business by spinning off its restaurant division. From now on, it will be down to soft drinks and salty snacks to put the fizz back into the company's profits.

   In the mid-1970s, the growth potential of the PepsiCo soft drinks business was seen as constrained by its already high penetration of the US market. Overseas, Pepsi-Cola's opportunities were thought to be limited by

Coca-Cola's size, by closed economies and by low income in developing countries. The salty snacks business, meanwhile, was essentially a US affair.

PepsiCo entered the restaurant business with the acquisition of Pizza Hut in 1977, Taco Bell was added the following year and Kentucky Fried Chicken – now KFC – was bought in 1986. The acquisitions were hardly a flop: for a time, amid a big expansion programme, they delivered good profit growth.

Meanwhile, the soft drink and snack businesses did better than expected, helped by strong performances in the US and an unexpectedly rapid opening of world markets.

More recently, however, the group as a whole has run into a series of difficulties. Some have been on the restaurant side, where intense competition in the US fast food market has hurt profits. Others have been on the restaurant side, where Pepsi-Cola burned up money in a quixotic attempt to defeat the mighty Coke in some of its strongest territories. One benefit of the spin-off will be Pepsi-Co's ability to pass on some of its £4.7bn in debt to the restaurant company, giving PepsiCo greater resources for an acquisition, although a spokesperson said that no significant acquisitions were in its business plans.

1    What appeared to be the motivation behind Pepsi-Co's diversification into fast food?
2    What went wrong?
3    To what extent does this reflect the general cycle of conglomerate mergers and demergers during this period?

## 2 Worrying picture of British investment
*(Adapted from the Financial Times, 26 June 1997)*

Most British companies continue to lag well behind their international competitors in their investment in research and development, according to the seventh annual R&D scoreboard published today by the Department of Trade and Industry. UK companies spent a total of £9.6bn on R&D last year, 6 per cent more than in 1995. That represents a small fall in 'R&D intensity', since their total sales rose by 8 per cent.

The UK has the lowest ratio of R&D to sales of any large industrialised country. In 1996, the world's 300 largest spenders devoted 4.4 per cent of sales to R&D – the same intensity as in 1995 – while the 18 British companies in this group saw their R&D fall from 2.5 per cent in 1995 to 2.3 per cent in 1996.

The DTI started the scoreboard in 1991 because industrial analysts believed that a higher investment in manufacturing R&D tended to produce faster growth and greater prosperity in the longer term.

A few British companies stand out as exceptions to the poor general performance. Mr Battle, the science and industry minister, singles out two: Reuters, the financial information company whose R&D expenditure has risen from £110m to £202m since 1993, and Siebe, the fast-growing engineering group whose R&D spending has doubled to £145m over the past three years, Mr Yurko, Siebe's chief executive, makes clear his commitment to use R&D to outperform the competition. 'We have found that, with few exceptions, there is a direct correlation between the amount invested in R&D and the long-term growth rate and prosperity of the competitors in our industry. Simply stated, more R&D means better growth and better profit.'

1    Why does it matter if British firms lag behind in their R&D investment?
2    What is the economic justification for the government to intervene to encourage R&D?
3    What sorts of policies could be adopted?

## 3    Tying the web
*(Adapted from The Guardian, 12 January 2000)*

AOL's $350bn merger with Time Warner (TW) should be scrutinized carefully by the anti-trust authorities to see whether it is good for the consumer. This is vital not just because the merger itself needs to be looked at but because success will trigger a surge of copy-cat mergers across the globe as media companies pay ever higher prices for remaining companies fearing they may be left behind in the race of the Titans. At issue is whether the world wide web – whose founding philosophy is free access and empowerment of the individual – should be dominated by huge media conglomerates or whether plurality is to be the ethos.

AOL's merger was greeted on the markets as a marriage made in heaven to exploit the convergence of computers, telephones and cable. This is because it merges AOL's subscription-driven gateway to the web (with 20m subscribers) with TW's entertainment archive and cable network – a vital asset when the web faces a 'broadband' revolution offering high-capacity links to the home. AOL, which has had many ups and downs in its 15-year life, will be vulnerable without broadband during a period when its subscription-based web model could be challenged by free access.

This merger raises three big issues. First, whether size itself is good if there are no benefits to the consumer. Second, whether AOL will guarantee open access to competitors to its new cable assets. Third, whether there should be guidelines over what happens when media giants own both the conduit and the content sent down them. The problem is this: if there is to be open access to conduit and content then why is there such a pressing need for AOL and TW to merge. If there isn't, and the real motive is to restrict access in order to keep prices higher, then it is a serious matter. The markets are so smitten by an 'internet company' (though actually AOL is a pre-web dial-up service) marrying old technology thereby justifying the inflated prices of web stocks that they haven't had time to consider the real world. Unless this is sorted out now the next giant merger and the one after will point to AOL/TW as a precedent to allow them through the regulatory hoops. It is difficult for net companies, let alone the regulators, to keep up with the dizzy pace of activity. Which is why we must pause in order to decide what sort of future we want and whether it should be moulded by consumers or big corporations.

1    Is big always better from the point of view of firms and consumers?
2    Why should the anti-trust (competition) authorities be especially concerned about market failure in this particular case of a merger?

## Questions for Thought

1    Which do you think is more serious for society – concentration, or collusion?
2    In July 1997, *The Guardian* reported that the director-general of the Office of Fair Trading was accusing the Football Premier league of acting as a cartel, charging artificially high prices for television matches. If the Restrictive Practices Court decided against the League, it would '...be catastrophic for Sky but a huge bonus for the larger Premiership clubs, who would earn far more from TV rights if they were allowed to negotiate their own deals with broadcasters.' Do you think that consumers would benefit from a free market in this instance?
3    Think about the town where you live. If you wanted to buy a house, where in town would you go? If you wanted a newspaper, where would you go? Comment on the difference.

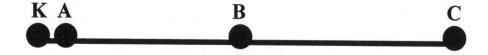

**Figure 18-4    Imagine a beach on a hot and sunny day...**

4    Imagine it is a hot and sunny day in mid-summer. Figure 18-4 represents a beach, on which there are sunbathers, evenly distributed along the beach. At the point *K*, there is a kiosk selling ice cream. Just arriving on the beach is an ice-cream seller with a mobile stall, who aims to maximize profits by selling as many ice creams as possible. Her ice creams are the same brand and quality as those on sale in the kiosk, and she is selling at the same price. Where will she choose to locate her mobile stall on the beach? How would your answer differ if instead of a fixed kiosk, there were two sellers with mobile stalls – where would they choose to be?

# 19 Privatization and Regulation

## Learning Outcomes

- To study the problem of natural monopoly and interpret nationalization, regulation, and market enlargement as possible solutions
- To discuss the ideal of social marginal cost pricing, combined with social cost-benefit analysis of investment decisions
- To examine how two-part tariffs and peak load pricing add to social efficiency (and to private profits if the company remains in the private sector)
- To explore how problems of nationalized industry performance gave rise to pressures for the alternative strategy of privatization and regulation
- To consider arguments for and against privatization, and relate these to the Private Finance Initiative
- To study issues arising in regulation of privatized natural monopolies
- To discuss whether globalization or European integration can solve the problem of natural monopoly by enlarging the market adequately

**IN THIS CHAPTER ...** you will investigate the economics of the choice between public and private ownership of certain industries. An industry may be *nationalized* because it is a *natural monopoly*, because of externalities, or because of distributional or equity considerations. However, are the managers of nationalized industries faced with appropriate incentives? It may be important to monitor *production efficiency*. Do private firms tend to achieve higher productive efficiency than firms in the public sector? The recent wave of *privatization* has provided some interesting empirical observations and insights. In many cases, it has been observed that the performance of nationalized industries *prior* to privatization improved, which may suggest that some inefficiency may indeed have been present, but also suggests that there is nothing intrinsic in public ownership that renders efficiency impossible. Perhaps it is a case of providing managers with appropriate targets and incentives. Government responsibility for these large, previously nationalized activities does not end with privatization: the question of regulation and monitoring remains.

## Important Concepts and Technical Terms

Match each lettered concept with the appropriate numbered phrase:

| | | |
|---|---|---|
| *(a)* Regulation | *(e)* Private Finance Initiative | *(i)* Discount rate |
| *(b)* Privatization | *(f)* Production efficiency | *(j)* Offer price |
| *(c)* Employee buyout | *(g)* Marginal cost pricing | *(k)* Regulatory capture |
| *(d)* Allocative efficiency | *(h)* Nationalization | *(l)* Natural monopoly |

1  The acquisition of private companies by the public sector.
2  The sale of public sector companies to the private sector.
3  An industry having enormous economies of scale such that only one firm can survive.
4  The price at which shares in an enterprise to be privatized are initially sold to investors: this often turned out to be below the free market price established on the first day of trading on the stock market.
5  Measures adopted to ensure that privatized companies do not misuse their market situation.
6  The interest rate used in calculating present values of future streams of benefits or costs.
7  A state in which firms are on the lowest possible cost curve so there is no slack or waste.
8  A state in which the balance of activities in the economy is Pareto-efficient such that no reallocation of resources could increase social welfare.
9  A way of drawing on private sector expertise to finance and manage public projects.
10 A situation in which a regulator gradually comes to identify with the interests of the firm it regulates, eventually becoming its champion, rather than its watchdog.
11 A price system where users pay a price equal to marginal production costs: a system that is not viable for a private natural monopoly as the firm would incur losses.
12 A privatization with all shares being sold to employees of the enterprise; e.g. National Freight Corporation.

## Exercises

1   Which of the following have been advanced as reasons for the nationalization of an industry?
    (a) A natural monopoly situation exists, with large economies of scale meaning that average cost lies above marginal cost.
    (b) Externalities exist, such that the social gains from the provision of a commodity exceed the private benefits for which direct users are prepared to pay.
    (c) There is a need to protect the interests of some members of society who might lose out if profit maximization were the sole criterion for the provision of a service.
    (d) Certain basic industries should be under state control.
    Which of these reasons do you consider to be valid?

2   Which of the following effects is/are not claimed as being associated with privatization?
    (a) An increase in competition – and hence a lowering of costs and prices.
    (b) A reduction in political interference.
    (c) An increase in the efficiency of management.
    (d) A reduction in the money that the government needs to borrow to finance its expenditure programme.
    (e) A reduction of deadweight burden.
    (f) A widening of consumer choice, as private firms must be more sensitive to market demand.

3   Figure 19-1 illustrates an industry which is a natural monopoly, with long-run average costs falling continuously over the relevant range of output.
    (a) If the industry is operated by an unregulated profit-maximizing monopolist, what price and output would be chosen?
    (b) What would be the deadweight loss to society of this decision?
    (c) What would be the level of monopoly profits?
    (d) What would be the socially efficient levels of price and output?
    (e) How would the monopolist act if allowed to produce only at the socially efficient point?

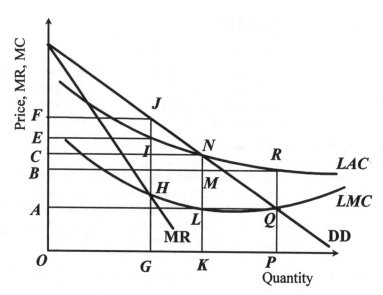

**Figure 19-1    A natural monopoly**

4    Suppose that you are in authority, and are contemplating the privatization of an industry currently within your responsibility. The following thoughts run through your mind. Identify each as being in favour of or against privatization, and assess their validity.

(a) The industry has consistently incurred losses over a period of many years and thus is a drain on the government's coffers.

(b) The industry enjoys substantial economies of scale and is a natural monopoly, so losses are to be expected. Society as a whole benefits from the scale economies, which would be sacrificed if the industry were to be broken up into a number of smaller firms.

(c) In the absence of competition, the industry has been operating less efficiently than it could have done.

(d) If the industry were to be privatized, the shareholders would be such a diverse group of people that they would be no spur to efficiency.

(e) Privatization would enable the industry to be freed from interference by the government in their pursuit of various political objectives.

(f) Keeping the industry under public control would be a safeguard, ensuring that needy groups in society are protected from a withdrawal of service.

(g) The proceeds from the sale of the industry can be used to finance necessary capital investment in other parts of the public sector.

What other arguments might influence your thinking on this matter? On balance, would you decide to privatize or to maintain the status quo?

5    In 1985, factor incomes in public corporations totalled £23.5 billion compared with a figure of £305.7 billion for the UK economy as a whole. Employment in these industries amounted to 1.3 million of a total employed labour force of 24.4 million. Net capital stock (at current replacement cost) was estimated to be £138.0 billion of a total of £649.9 billion (this excludes dwellings). (These figures all come from CSO, *United Kingdom National Accounts*, 1986 edn., HMSO.)

Calculate the percentage share of the nationalized industries (public corporations) in income, employment, and capital. Comment upon the relative labour or capital intensity of this sector and explain why this pattern should have occurred.

6    Suppose that you are the manager of a firm in the private sector considering a capital investment project. Three plans have been submitted for your consideration (all figures are in £ million).

| | | | Externalities | |
|---|---|---|---|---|
| Project | Private benefits | Private costs | Favourable | Unfavourable |
| A | 400 | 380 | 20 | 80 |
| B | 320 | 350 | 120 | 20 |
| C | 350 | 300 | 70 | 80 |

(a) If your aim is to maximize financial profits for your firm, which project do you choose?

(b) Suppose you know that your shareholders are keen to see successful sales figures rather than large profits (so long as there is no financial loss). Which project do you now choose?

(c) Suppose now that the same projects are submitted to the manager of a nationalized industry. Which project would maximize economic welfare for society as a whole?

7    Exercise 3 explored the situation facing a private natural monopoly if forced to produce at the socially efficient point. Let us now extend the analysis to see how the industry might operate if nationalized.

(a) If the nationalized industry produces at the socially efficient point (*OP* in Figure 19-1), what subsidy is necessary?

(b) Under a two-part tariff pricing scheme, what fixed charge would be needed if the subsidy is to be replaced by user charges?

(c) What variable charge would be needed?

(d) At what price and output would the industry just break even?

(e) What would be the deadweight loss to society in this break-even position?

(f) Would the managers of this industry face appropriate incentives to maintain efficiency in production? If not, how is this likely to affect the situation shown in Figure 19-1?

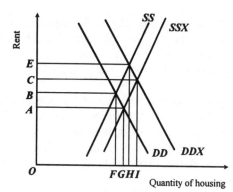

**Figure 19-2    Council housing or rent vouchers?**

8    This exercise considers the relative merits of two alternative schemes for public housing policy: the provision of council housing, and rent vouchers. Figure 19-2 summarizes demand and supply conditions for the schemes. Initial equilibrium in the housing market is shown by demand curve *DD* and supply curve SS.
   *(a)* In this 'without-policy' state, identify equilibrium rent and quantity of housing.
   *(b)* Suppose that the local authority now issues rent vouchers to needy families. Using the figure, describe the response in the housing market, and identify the new equilibrium rent and quantity of housing.
   *(c)* Suppose that, instead of issuing rent vouchers, the local authority provides council housing. How will the market now respond, and what are the new equilibrium levels of rent and quantity of housing?
   *(d)* Which of the two schemes has the greatest effect on the quantity of housing? Why should this be?
   *(e)* Assess the relative merits of the two schemes.
9    Comment on the economic arguments relevant to these characteristics of the Private Finance Initiative (PFI).
   *(a)* The PFI is a natural extension to the transfer of opportunities and assets from the public to the private sector that has been taking place since 1979.
   *(b)* The PFI attempts to introduce competition into the provision of social infrastructure previously seen as the sole responsibility of the public sector.
   *(c)* An intention is to reduce the amount of X-inefficiency entailed in the provision of public goods.
   *(d)* The PFI alters the government's role in the provision of public goods from owner of assets and direct provider of services, to that of purchaser of services from the private sector.
   *(e)* The PFI enables more rapid completion of infrastructure projects.
   *(f)* The private sector tends to view risk differently from their counterparts in Whitehall.

## True/False

1    The deadweight burden of a natural monopoly can be eliminated by forcing the firm to set price equal to long-run average cost.
2    Experience with deregulation of airlines in the USA shows that the removal of legal barriers to entry encourages competition and leads to lower prices and higher usage.
3    To ensure efficiency, investment decisions made by nationalized industries should be made with reference to market rates of interest.
4    Peak load pricing is a system of price discrimination.
5    Privatized industries subject to regulation spend considerable resources in trying to influence the regulator.
6    Incentives for private managers to be efficient are strong because actual and potential shareholders monitor their performance carefully.
7    Private industries are immune from government interference in the pursuit of political aims.
8    Selling off state assets mortgages the country's future.
9    In the period up to 1986, all privatization share offers were under-priced.
10    The most successful of the early privatizations were those involving companies which faced significant competition after privatization.

# ECONOMICS IN THE NEWS

## 1  Russia moves to overhaul monopolies
*(Adapted from the Financial Times, 29 April 1997)*

President Boris Yeltsin yesterday signed a sheaf of sweeping decrees to restructure Russia's natural monopolies and overhaul its inefficient municipal services. This new burst of economic reform, the most radical since 1992–93, aims to inject greater competition in important industries, strengthen public finances and spark growth in an economy which has been dogged by recession since the beginning of the 1990s.

Mr Boris Nemtsov, first deputy prime minister, is spearheading the reform drive. Outlining plans to reform the natural monopolies, he vowed to create a competitive wholesale market for electricity leading to reduced tariffs by the year-end. The government would keep control of a 51 per cent share of UES, the big electricity grid, and retain an integrated power grid, he said. But it would seek an additional £5bn from outside investors to build new power transmission lines. Mr Nemtsov said the government would also exercise stronger control over the railway network and Gazprom, the giant gas monopoly in which the state retains a 40 per cent stake.

In an apparent departure from its monopolies policy, the government announced plans yesterday to turn the Svyazimnvest telecommunications holding company into the dominant carrier of international and long-distance telephone traffic. 'On the one hand, the government is trying to beat up the gas, electricity and railway industries but on the other, is trying to create a new telecoms monopoly', said one western banker in Moscow, speculating the government was not strong enough to tackle every entrenched interest simultaneously.

## 2  Bezeq prepares for hard choices
*(Adapted from the Financial Times, 27 May 1997)*

Bezeq, Israel's state-owned telecommunications company, faces its biggest challenge this week as international telephone lines are opened up to competition under the government's deregulation programmes. Consumers will cash in on what is expected to be a 70 per cent fall in the cost of overseas calls, but the move is set to put enormous pressure on Bezeq's profits as two international consortia plunder what has been a rich monopoly.

There is also more at stake for Bezeq than the dismantling of its exclusive right to handle international calls. Further deregulation is expected when the domestic market is opened up in 1999, and the ability of Bezeq and the two consortia to win over customers to their international telephone networks will be a crucial test of their readiness for this next stage.

'Bezeq is faced with hard choices', says analyst Mr Glora Zarechansky. 'To obtain a sizeable market share, it will have to drop its prices, but its profitability will fall, probably by as much as 20 to 25 per cent. Bezeq believes it should be able to secure a 50 per cent market share in international calls, with the other two consortia each taking about 25 per cent. Initially, Bezeq will have considerable advantages, since it will be able to exploit the infrastructure it has built up. However, where Bezeq will lose out is in revenues from incoming overseas calls. Israel has always been a net receiver of calls, by a ratio of two to one. The revenues received from abroad will be distributed pro-rate to the number of out-going calls handled by each player. It will mean that the three participants will be keen to gain market share. The competition will be very aggressive.

1    How is it possible to foster competition in a natural monopoly without damaging the consumer interest?
2    In the first of the two pieces above, there is a reference to the problems of 'entrenched interest'. Why would you expect this to be a problem?
3    Both passages refer to changes occurring in the telecommunications sector. Why should this be subject to so much change in the late 1990s? If competition is expected to be 'very aggressive', why did it not emerge earlier?

## Questions for Thought

1    Discuss the incentives facing managers in public and private sector enterprises. Think about their relative effectiveness and the potential for improvement.
2    It has been argued that privatization not only raises revenue in the short run, but may also lead to social benefits if improved incentives lead to greater efficiency. Evaluate these arguments, and discuss whether these and other benefits will be maintained in the long run.

# 20 Introduction to Macroeconomics and National Income Accounting

## Learning Outcomes

- To recall that macroeconomics simplifies the components of the economy to study interaction and feedback within the whole system
- To construct an internally consistent set of national accounts
- To explain how the circular flow between households and firms keeps track of real resource flows and the corresponding financial payments
- To bring in the government and the foreign sector, and show the equality of leakages from, and injections to, the circular flow
- To consider that national income and output are poorly measured, and discuss what more comprehensive measures we might wish to include

**IN THIS CHAPTER ...** you will be introduced to macroeconomics, and learn about some key macroeconomic concepts and measurements. You will find that many of the ways of thinking about issues are common to macro and micro: it is mainly the *focus* that is different.

## Important Concepts and Technical Terms

Match each lettered concept with the appropriate numbered phrase:

| | | |
|---|---|---|
| (a) Inventories | (g) Open economy | (m) Investment |
| (b) Exports | (h) Closed economy | (n) Imports |
| (c) Saving | (i) Gross national product | (o) Gross domestic product |
| (d) Depreciation | (j) Personal disposable income | (p) Net income from abroad |
| (e) Current prices | (k) Value added | |
| (f) Constant prices | (l) GNP deflator | |

1  Goods that are produced abroad but purchased for use in the domestic economy.
2  The total income earned by domestic citizens regardless of the country where their factor services were supplied.
3  The output produced by factors of production located in the domestic economy, regardless of who owns those factors.
4  The excess of inflows of income from factor services supplied abroad over the outflows of income arising from the supply of factor services by foreigners in the domestic economy.
5  The purchase of new capital goods by firms.
6  A valuation of expenditures or output using the prices prevailing at some base year.
7  A valuation of expenditures or output using the prices prevailing at the time of measurement.
8  Goods that are domestically produced but sold abroad.
9  That part of income which is not spent buying goods and services.
10  The increase in the value of goods as a result of the production process.
11  A measurement of the rate at which the value of the existing capital stock declines per period as a result of wear and tear or of obsolescence.
12  Household income after direct taxes and transfer payments: the amount that households have available for spending and saving.
13  An economy which does not transact with the rest of the world.
14  Goods currently held by a firm for future production or sale.
15  An economy which has transactions with other countries.
16  The ratio of nominal GNP to real GNP expressed as an index.

# Exercises

Some of the relevant techniques and issues which you will need in the exercises in this chapter were first introduced in Chapter 2.

1    Table 20-1 presents consumer price indices (CPIs) for the UK, USA and Spain.

**Table 20-1    Consumer prices**

| | United Kingdom | | USA | | Spain | |
|---|---|---|---|---|---|---|
| | Consumer price index | Inflation rate (%) | Consumer price index | Inflation rate (%) | Consumer price index | Inflation rate (%) |
| 1988 | 71.7 | | 77.6 | | 68.2 | |
| 1989 | 77.3 | | 81.4 | | 72.9 | |
| 1990 | 84.6 | | 85.7 | | 77.7 | |
| 1991 | 89.6 | | 89.4 | | 82.4 | |
| 1992 | 92.9 | | 92.1 | | 87.2 | |
| 1993 | 94.4 | | 94.8 | | 91.2 | |
| 1994 | 96.7 | | 97.3 | | 95.5 | |
| 1995 | 100.0 | | 100.0 | | 100.0 | |
| 1996 | 102.4 | | 102.9 | | 103.6 | |
| 1997 | 105.7 | | 105.3 | | 105.6 | |
| 1998 | 109.3 | | 107.0 | | 107.5 | |

Source: *International Financial Statistics.*

(a)  Calculate the annual inflation rate for each of the countries.
(b)  Plot your three inflation series on a diagram against time.
(c)  By what percentage did prices increase in each country over the whole period – i.e. between 1988 and 1998?
(d)  Which economy has experienced most stability of the inflation rate?
(e)  Which economy saw the greatest deceleration in the rate of inflation between 1990 and 1993?

Table 20-2 presents some data relating to national output (real GDP) of the same three economies over a similar period, expressed as index numbers.

**Table 20-2    National production**

| | United Kingdom | | USA | | Spain | |
|---|---|---|---|---|---|---|
| | GDP index | Growth rate (%) | GDP index | Growth rate (%) | GDP index | Growth rate (%) |
| 1988 | 91.4 | | 86.7 | | 86.0 | |
| 1989 | 93.4 | | 89.7 | | 90.2 | |
| 1990 | 93.7 | | 90.8 | | 93.6 | |
| 1991 | 91.9 | | 89.9 | | 95.7 | |
| 1992 | 91.4 | | 92.3 | | 96.3 | |
| 1993 | 93.3 | | 94.5 | | 95.2 | |
| 1994 | 97.3 | | 97.8 | | 97.4 | |
| 1995 | 100.0 | | 100.0 | | 100.0 | |
| 1996 | 102.6 | | 103.4 | | 102.4 | |
| 1997 | 106.2 | | 107.5 | | 106.0 | |
| 1998 | 108.5 | | 111.7 | | 110.1 | |

Source: *International Financial Statistics.*

(f)  Calculate the annual growth rate for each of the countries.
(g)  Plot your three growth series on a diagram against time.
(h)  By what percentage did output increase in each country over the whole period?
(i)  To what extent did growth follow a similar pattern over time in these three countries?

2   In a hypothetical closed economy with no government, planned consumption is 150, planned investment is 50, total production is 210.
    (a) How much is total planned expenditure?
    (b) Calculate unplanned stock changes.
    (c) How much is savings in this situation?
    (d) What is actual investment?
    (e) How would you expect producers to react to this situation in the next period?

3   Table 20-3 lists a number of components of UK gross national product from both income and expenditure sides of the account for 1998. All quantities are measured in £ million at current prices and are taken from ONS, *United Kingdom National Accounts*, 1999 edition.

    **Table 20-3   Components of GNP in the UK**

| | | | |
|---|---|---|---|
| Final consumption expenditure* | 545 124 | Capital consumption | 88 771 |
| Subsidies | 7 453 | Stock changes | 3 621 |
| Other indirect taxes** | 17 619 | Fixed investment | 148 202 |
| Net income from abroad | 11 737 | Exports | 224 202 |
| Government final consumption | 153 564 | Employment income | 463 398 |
| Taxes on products*** | 103 634 | Mixed income | 43 379 |
| Profits and rent | 223 212 | Imports | 232 714 |

    Notes:   *   by households and non-profit institutions serving households
             **  Taxes on production, which register on the income side of the accounts only
             *** Taxes on products, which register on both expenditure and income sides of the accounts

    Using the expenditure side of the accounts, calculate the following:
    (a) Gross domestic product at market prices.
    (b) Gross national product at market prices.
    (c) Gross domestic product at basic prices.
    (d) Net national product at market prices.
    (e) Net national income at basic prices.
    (f) Calculate gross domestic product at market prices from the income side of the accounts.
    (g) Can you explain why your answers to (a) and (f) are not identical?

4   Consider five firms in a closed economy: a steel producer, rubber producer, machine tool maker, tyre producer, and bicycle manufacturer. The bicycle manufacturer sells the bicycles produced to final customers for £8000. In producing the bicycles, the firm buys tyres (£1000), steel (£2500), and machine tools (£1800). The tyre manufacturer buys rubber (£600) from the rubber producer, and the machine tool maker buys steel (£1000) from the steel producer.
    (a) What is the contribution of the bicycle industry to GDP?
    (b) Calculate total final expenditure.

5   Table 20-4 (opposite) lists a number of components of UK income accruing to households (and non-profit institutions serving households) in 1998. Also listed are items that affect the resources at the disposal of households, such as taxation etc. The quantities are measured in £ million at current prices and are taken from ONS, *United Kingdom National Accounts*, 1999 edition.
    (a) Calculate the total resources accruing to households – that is, sum the 'incoming' items in the table.
    (b) Disposable income is calculated by deducting the outward payments (such as taxes) from the total resources. This represents the amount that households have in the circular flow to allocate to spending and saving. Calculate disposable income.
    (c) Calculate the savings ratio – i.e. savings as a percentage of disposable income.

**Table 20-4    The household sector**

|  | £ million |  | £ million |
|---|---|---|---|
| Wages and salaries, etc. | 434 474 | Other transfers (in) | 32 215 |
| Social benefits | 170 191 | Other transfers (out) | 20 597 |
| Taxes on income | 88 551 | Other current taxes | 14 892 |
| Gross mixed income | 43 379 | Saving | 37 378 |
| Net property income | 69 794 | Other household income | 45 602 |
| Social contributions | 134 680 |  |  |

6   According to the ONS *United Kingdom National Accounts* (1999 edition), GDP at 1995 market prices was £756 430m in 1997 and £773 380m in the following year. GDP at current market prices was £712 548m in 1995, £754 601m in 1996, and £843 725m in 1998. The implicit GDP deflator was 103.3 in 1996 and 106.3 in 1997.
For the period 1996–98, calculate the annual growth rates of real GDP, nominal GDP, and the price index.

7   The following table illustrates the domestic expenditure and national income of an economy during three consecutive years.

|  | Year 1 (£ bn) | Year 2 (£ bn) | Year 3 (£ bn) |
|---|---|---|---|
| National income | 500 | 600 | 700 |
| Government expenditure | 200 | 250 | 200 |
| Private expenditure | 250 | 300 | 250 |
| Investment | 50 | 200 | 200 |

For each of the three years, evaluate the balance of trade situation facing the economy.

8   The following table refers to one country in two consecutive years:

|  | Index of GNP | Retail price index | Index of population | Average working week (hours) |
|---|---|---|---|---|
| Year 1 | 105 | 102 | 102 | 44 |
| Year 2 | 110 | 106 | 103 | 44 |

On the basis of these figures, evaluate each of the following statements as a description of the changes that took place between year 1 and year 2.
*(a)*  Real GNP increased.
*(b)*  Real GNP per capita increased.
*(c)*  The standard of living of all people within the country fell.
*(d)*  The working population increased in size.

9   Which of the following items are included in the calculation of GNP in the UK and which are excluded?
*(a)*  Salaries paid to schoolteachers.
*(b)*  Tips given to taxi drivers.
*(c)*  Expenditure on social security benefits.
*(d)*  The income of a second-hand car salesman.
*(e)*  Work carried out in the home by a housewife.
*(f)*  Work carried out in the home by a paid domestic.
*(g)*  The value of pleasure from leisure.
*(h)*  Free-range eggs sold in the market.
*(i)*  Blackberries picked in the hedgerows.

## True/False

1   The increase in the quantity of goods and services which the economy as a whole can afford to purchase is known as economic growth.

2   In the period 1980-97, Korea, and Japan grew significantly faster than European countries such as the UK, Switzerland, or France.

3   During the 1980s and 1990s, the UK suffered the highest price inflation in the world.

4   Unemployment in the UK increased tenfold between 1975 and 1985.

5   Given full and accurate measurement, we should get the same estimate of total economic activity whether we measure the value of production output, the level of factor incomes, or spending on goods and services.

6   A closed economy is one with excessive levels of unemployment.

7   The calculation of value added is a way of measuring output without double-counting.

8   In a closed economy with no government, savings are always equal to investment.

9   Gross domestic product at basic prices is equal to gross domestic product at market prices plus net indirect taxes.

10   Depreciation is an economic cost because it measures resources being used up in the production process.

11   Gross national product at current prices is a measure of real economic activity.

12   Gross national product at constant prices is a useless measure of economic welfare because it fails to measure so many important ingredients of welfare.

## ECONOMICS IN THE NEWS

### Black economy 'costs Treasury £20 billion'
*(Adapted from the Financial Times, 26 May 1997)*

Britain's black economy has grown rapidly since the mid-1980s and now costs the Treasury £20 billion a year, an unpublished report for the European Commission has found. The study, by Deloitte & Touche, the accountants, calculates that the black economy last year was worth about £80 billion, the equivalent of 12 per cent of gross domestic product. It estimates that the cost to the exchequer, in lost value added receipts and other taxes, could be the equivalent of nearly one third of last year's income tax revenues. The report is part of a five-country study into the size and budgetary costs of the European shadow economy launched last November by the European Commission. A concerted attack on VAT avoidance announced in the 1996 Budget aimed to raise £700m in its first year. Over the last few years VAT receipts have fallen significantly short of the Treasury's target, but this shortfall has recently been declining as a result of faster economic growth. Previous studies have put the size of the cash economy at about 6-8 per cent of GDP. But Mr Dilip Bhattacharya, and economist at Leicester University who co-authored the report, believes that unmeasured economic activity has risen sharply in recent years. 'In 1984 the shadow economy was running at about 8 per cent of GDP,' he says in the report. 'But there seems to have been a sharp change in behaviour around the time of the 1987 stock market crash.'

1   What factors might have caused the expansion of the 'shadow' economy?
2   Why might we worry about the size of this sector?

## Questions for Thought

1   Reconsider the items listed in exercise 9 of this chapter. Which of these *should* be included in a measure of national economic welfare? What additional items (positive or negative) should be incorporated if the measure is to reflect the quality of life?

2   In many less developed countries, much of economic activity is concentrated in small-scale subsistence agriculture. How would you expect this to affect comparisons of living standards based on GNP measurements? What other difficulties would you expect to encounter in making international comparisons of living standards?

3   Why is it so important to distinguish between real and nominal national income measures?

# 21 The Determination of National Income

## Learning Outcomes

- **To distinguish actual output and potential output**
- **To develop the concept that output is demand determined in the short run, and define short-run equilibrium output**
- **To explain the determinants of desired consumption and desired investment**
- **To derive the level of short-run equilibrium output and show how it changes when there is a shift in aggregate demand**
- **To define the multiplier, and relate its size to the slope of the consumption function**
- **To discuss the paradox of thrift**

**IN THIS CHAPTER ...** you will begin to explain why an economy may settle at a particular level of income at a particular time. The initial simple model assumes that prices and wages are fixed and that there are spare resources. This enables us to neglect the supply side of the economy for the time being and to focus on a *short-run demand-determined Keynesian model*. We also assume no government and no international trade. In aggregate, we may think of consumption being determined mainly by national income, together with an autonomous component. The other component of aggregate demand is investment, which for now we assume to be autonomous. The *aggregate demand schedule* is formed by combining our consumption function with autonomous investment demand. A change in autonomous spending which shifts the aggregate demand schedule moves the economy to a new equilibrium position. But: be warned! No economic model is better than the assumptions on which it is based. So far, our model is very simple indeed, resting heavily on the short-run analysis of a closed economy without government, with wages and prices fixed, and with spare resources.

## Important Concepts and Technical Terms

Match each lettered concept with the appropriate numbered phrase:

| | | |
|---|---|---|
| *(a)* Investment demand | *(f)* Consumption function | *(k)* Unplanned inventory change |
| *(b)* Autonomous consumption | *(g)* Savings function | *(l)* Multiplier |
| *(c)* Potential output | *(h)* Aggregate demand schedule | |
| *(d)* Short-run equilibrium output | *(i)* Marginal propensity to consume | |
| *(e)* Marginal propensity to save | *(j)* Paradox of thrift | |

1 The part of consumption expenditure which is unrelated to the level of income.
2 Firms' desired or planned additions to their physical capital (factories and machines) and to inventories.
3 An unanticipated increase or decrease in the level of stocks held by firms.
4 A relationship showing the level of planned savings at each level of personal disposable income.
5 A curve which shows the amount that firms and households plan to spend on goods and services at each level of income.
6 The level of output the economy would produce if all factors of production were fully employed.
7 The ratio of the change in equilibrium output to the change in autonomous spending that causes the change in output.
8 The situation whereby a change in the amount households wish to save at each income level leads to a change in the equilibrium level of income but no change in the equilibrium level of savings, which must still equal planned investment.
9 The fraction of each extra pound of disposable income that households wish to use for saving.
10 The fraction of each extra pound of disposable income that households wish to use to increase consumption.
11 The level of output in an economy when aggregate demand or planned aggregate spending just equals the output that is actually produced.
12 A relationship showing the level of aggregate consumption desired at each level of personal disposable income.

## Exercises

1  Table 21-1 presents data on real consumers' expenditure and personal disposable income for the UK.

**Table 21-1 Consumption and income, £ billion at constant 1995 prices**

| Year | Households' final consumption expenditure | Real households' disposable income |
|---|---|---|
| 1987 | 372.601 | 385.240 |
| 1988 | 400.427 | 405.462 |
| 1989 | 413.498 | 423.145 |
| 1990 | 415.788 | 438.935 |
| 1991 | 408.309 | 445.552 |
| 1992 | 410.026 | 461.964 |
| 1993 | 420.081 | 475.850 |
| 1994 | 431.462 | 481.924 |
| 1995 | 438.453 | 494.574 |
| 1996 | 454.986 | 505.392 |
| 1997 | 472.701 | 524.501 |
| 1998 | 488.505 | 524.660 |

Source: *Economic Trends Annual Supplement, UK National Accounts.*

(a) Calculate real savings in each year during the period and the percentage of income saved.
(b) Plot a scatter diagram with real consumption on the vertical axis and real personal disposable income on the horizontal axis.
(c) Draw a straight line passing as close as possible to these points on the diagram, and measure the approximate slope of the line.
(d) Under what conditions would you regard this slope as a reasonable estimate of the marginal propensity to consume?
(e) Plot a scatter diagram of real savings against income.
(f) If you were to draw a straight line through these points, how would you expect it to relate to the one you drew in part (c)? Do it, and measure its approximate slope.
(g) Assuming this to be a sensible estimate of the marginal propensity to save, what is implied for the value of the multiplier?

2  Table 21-2 shows some data on consumption and income (output) for the economy of Hypothetica. Planned investment is autonomous, and occurs at the rate of $60 billion per period.

**Table 21-2   Income and consumption in Hypothetica (all in Hypothetical $ billion)**

| Income (output) | Planned consumption | Planned investment | Savings | Aggregate demand | Unplanned inventory change | Actual investment |
|---|---|---|---|---|---|---|
| 50 | 35 | | | | | |
| 100 | 70 | | | | | |
| 150 | 105 | | | | | |
| 200 | 140 | | | | | |
| 250 | 175 | | | | | |
| 300 | 210 | | | | | |
| 350 | 245 | | | | | |
| 400 | 280 | | | | | |

*(a)* Calculate savings and aggregate demand at each level of income.

*(b)* For each level of output, work out the unplanned change in inventory holdings and the rate of actual investment.

*(c)* If, in a particular period, income turned out to be $100 billion, how would you expect producers to react?

*(d)* If, in a particular period, income turned out to be $350 billion, how would you expect producers to react?

*(e)* What is the equilibrium level of income?

*(f)* What is the marginal propensity to consume?

*(g)* If investment increased by $15 billion, what would be the change in equilibrium income?

**3** *(a)* Using the data of exercise 2, use graph paper to plot the consumption function and aggregate demand schedule.

*(b)* Add on the 45° line and confirm that equilibrium occurs at the same point suggested by your answer to 2*(e)* above.

*(c)* Show the effect on equilibrium of an increase in investment of $15 billion.

**4** *(a)* Again using the data on Hypothetica from exercise 2, use graph paper to plot how savings vary with income.

*(b)* Add on the investment line and confirm that equilibrium again occurs at the same income level.

*(c)* Show that an increase in investment of $15 billion leads to a new level of equilibrium income.

*(d)* Explain the process by which this new equilibrium is attained.

**5** Figure 21-1 shows the aggregate demand schedule for an economy, together with the 45° line.

*(a)* Suppose output is *OG*: identify the level of aggregate demand and specify whether there is excess demand or excess supply.

*(b)* What is the size of the unplanned inventory change with output *OG*?

*(c)* How will firms respond to this situation?

*(d)* Identify equilibrium income and expenditure.

*(e)* Suppose output is *OJ*; identify the level of aggregate planned expenditure and specify whether there is excess demand or excess supply.

*(f)* What is the size of the unplanned inventory change with output *OJ* – and how will firms react to it?

**6** Figure 21-2 shows autonomous investment for an economy, together with the savings function showing how savings vary with income. *IB* is the initial level of investment.

*(a)* Identify the initial equilibrium levels of income and savings.

*(b)* Which level of investment represents the effect of an increase in business confidence – a surge in optimistic animal spirits?

*(c)* What is the new equilibrium level of income?

*(d)* What is the multiplier?

*(e)* Which level of investment shows an increase in pessimism on the part of firms?

*(f)* What would be the new equilibrium level of income?

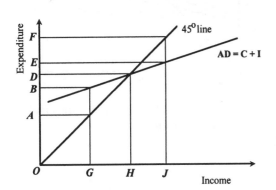

**Figure 21-1    The income-expenditure diagram**

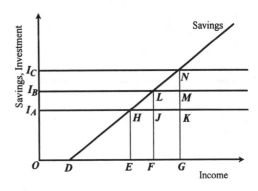

**Figure 21-2    Savings and investment**

**7** Consider a closed economy with no government sector in which consumption *(C)* is related to income *(Y)* by the equation:

$C = A + cY$

*(a)* What is the marginal propensity to consume?

*(b)* How is the level of savings related to income in this economy?

Suppose that $A = 400$, $c = 0.75$ and the level of investment is 500:

*(c)* At what level of national income would savings be zero?

*(d)* What would be the equilibrium level of income?

**8** Figure 21-3 represents a closed economy with no government sector. At the equilibrium level of income, how would you interpret

*(a)* *XY/UX*

and

*(b)* *WY/OW?*

**9** Figure 21-4 shows an economy which initially has an aggregate demand schedule given by AK.

*(a)* What is the initial equilibrium level of income?

*(b)* Suppose there is an increase in the marginal propensity to save: which is the new aggregate demand schedule?

*(c)* What is the new equilibrium level of income?

*(d)* Suppose that, instead, the marginal propensity to consume had increased: which would be the new aggregate demand schedule?

*(e)* What is the new equilibrium level of income?

**10** For the last exercise of this chapter we return to the economy of Hypothetica. Initially, consumption is determined (as before) as 70 per cent of income. Investment is again autonomous and occurs at the rate of $90 billion per period.

*(a)* What is the equilibrium level of income? (If it helps, you might create a table similar to that in exercise 2, for values of output between, say, 250 and 600.)

*(b)* What would be the equilibrium level of income if investment increased by $15 billion?

*(c)* Calculate the value of the multiplier.

Suppose that our Hypothetical consumers become more spendthrift, spending 80 cents in the dollar rather than 70. With investment again at $90 billion per period,

*(d)* Calculate the equilibrium level of income.

*(e)* Calculate the equilibrium level of income if investment increased by $10 billion.

*(f)* Calculate the value of the multiplier.

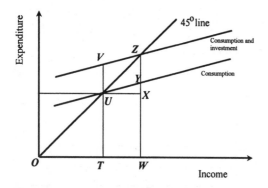

**Figure 21-3   A closed economy with no government**

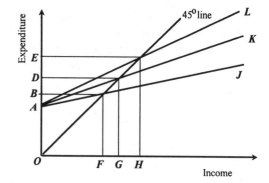

**Figure 21-4   Equilibrium and the marginal propensity to consume**

## True/False

1  Potential output includes an allowance for 'normal unemployment'.
2  The Keynesian model suggests that output is mainly demand-determined.
3  Consumption is linearly related to income.
4  The marginal propensities to consume and save sum to unity.
5  Investment is autonomous.
6  The purpose of the aggregate demand schedule is to separate out the change in demand directly induced by changes in income.
7  Short-run equilibrium occurs when spending plans are not frustrated by a shortage of goods and when firms do not produce more output than they can sell.
8  Unplanned inventory changes are the signal to firms that there is disequilibrium.
9  Planned savings always equals planned investment.
10  The slope of the aggregate demand schedule depends only on the level of autonomous consumption.
11  The multiplier in our simple model tells us how much output changes when aggregate demand shifts.
12  If only people saved more, investment would increase and we could get the economy moving again.

## ECONOMICS IN THE NEWS

### Chancellor urged to halt savings ratio slide
*(Adapted from The Sunday Telegraph, 26 December 1999)*

Chancellor Gordon Brown will be urged this week to take Budget action to halt the plunge in Britain's savings ratio – now at its lowest level since the late 1980s. With retailers enjoying a better-than-expected Christmas and a spending spree expected this week, a report from the Centre for Economics and Business Research, headed by Douglas Williams, former top CBI economist, calls for more generous tax relief in ISAs, special measures to mop up £10bn of demutualization windfalls expected in the next 15 months, and the abolition of stamp duty on share purchases. It also urges more attractive National Savings products and privatization of the marketing of Premium Bonds.

Latest figures show Britain's savings ratio – the amount households put aside as a percentage of disposable income – has tumbled from 7% to 4.3% in the third quarter. The ratio normally falls during upswings as people become more confident about employment and their financial prospects. The surge in household assets – house prices and the value of stocks and shares – has also meant that people rely more on capital gains as a proxy for additional savings. Higher taxes are also discouraging savings. Since 'Prudence' Brown came to office in 1997, the ratio has more than halved, from 9.3%, while the government's finances have improved sharply.

Gavin McCrone of the CEBR, said: 'The replacement of PEPs and TESSAs with ISAs has confused investors, the abolition of the dividend tax credit has made pension funds worse off, while National Savings, which in 1996–97 raised £4.8bn, are now forecast to pay back £900m this year.'

In cash terms, gross savings in the UK peaked at £53.3bn in 1997 but tumbled to £37.4bn last year. The figure is thought to have fallen further this year to £35bn. The latest collapse in the savings ratio will add to concern over a runaway spending boom and fuel pressure for a Budget aimed at encouraging savings. This would also take pressure off interest rates (already set to rise) and the exchange rate.

1  What factors are likely to influence household savings?
2  What is meant by the statement that 'people rely more on capital gains as a proxy for additional savings'?
3  Why should the government be concerned about the savings ratio?

## Questions for Thought

1   In a closed economy with no governmental economic activity, savings and investment are always equal. How, then, does it make sense for economists to talk about situations in which they take different values?

2   Think about the consumption expenditures undertaken by your household. Is income the only factor influencing the aggregate amount? What other factors may help to determine aggregate consumption?

3   Suppose that equilibrium output for an economy entails high levels of unemployment. Does the analysis of this chapter suggest any action which the authorities might take to mitigate the effects of unemployment?

# 22   Aggregate Demand, Fiscal Policy, and Foreign Trade

## Learning Outcomes

- To examine how government spending and taxes affect aggregate demand
- To derive short-run equilibrium output when the model is extended to include the government
- To explain the balanced budget multiplier
- To discuss automatic stabilizers and how the government budget is affected by output fluctuations
- To construct the structural budget and the inflation-adjusted budget
- To consider the link between budget deficits and the build up of the national debt
- To explain the limits to active fiscal policy
- To extend the model of output determination to include the foreign sector

**IN THIS CHAPTER ...** you will see how to extend the model developed in Chapter 21 to incorporate *government* and *foreign trade*. The government spends money on goods and services, and the amount of spending power available to households is affected by taxes and payment of benefits. Decisions about the overall levels of government spending and taxes are *fiscal policy*. Attempts to keep output close to the full-employment level are known as *stabilization policy*. The *balanced budget multiplier* reveals that an increase in government expenditure financed entirely and exactly by net taxation increases equilibrium income. The effect of *taxation* is to reduce the multiplier. However, we cannot judge the fiscal stance of the government merely from the size of the budget deficit, as this may be influenced by whether the economy is in recession. The budget deficit responds to the overall level of activity through *automatic stabilizers* – by which the deficit tends to grow during a recession and diminish in a boom. If the government runs a budget deficit, it needs to borrow from the public to finance it. The size of the accumulated stock of outstanding government debt is known as the *national debt*. An effect of introducing net exports into the model is to reduce the size of the multiplier. As income rises, both households and firms will demand more imported goods and services. With autonomous exports, this implies that the trade deficit tends to be larger at high income levels and may act as a constraint on economic growth.

## Important Concepts and Technical Terms

Match each lettered concept with the appropriate numbered phrase:

| | | |
|---|---|---|
| *(a)* Automatic stabilizers | *(f)* Code for Fiscal Stability | *(k)* Fiscal policy |
| *(b)* National debt | *(g)* Balanced budget multiplier | *(l)* Inflation-adjusted government |
| *(c)* Marginal propensity to import | *(h)* Budget deficit |     deficit |
| *(d)* Stabilization policy | *(i)* Fine-tuning | |
| *(e)* Discretionary fiscal policy | *(j)* The structural budget | |

1   The government's decisions about spending and taxes.
2   Mechanisms in the economy that reduce the response of GNP to shocks.
3   Government actions to control the level of output in order to keep GNP close to its full-employment level.
4   The government deficit adjusted for the difference between real and nominal interest rates.
5   The excess of government outlays over government receipts.
6   The process by which an increase in government spending, accompanied by an equal increase in taxes, results in an increase in output.
7   A commitment by the government to a medium-run objective of financing current government spending out of current revenues.
8   The fraction of each additional pound of national income that domestic residents wish to spend on imports.
9   The government's total stock of outstanding debts.
10   Frequent discretionary adjustments to policy instruments.
11   A calculation of the government budget deficit under the assumption of full employment: a cyclically adjusted indicator of fiscal stance.
12   The use of active fiscal policy in response to economic conditions.

## Exercises

1   Table 22-1 carries us back to the kingdom of Hypothetica, which we visited in Chapter 21. As then, planned consumption is 70 per cent of disposable income, but now the government imposes net taxes amounting to 20 per cent of gross income. Planned investment is still $60 billion and the government plans to spend $50 billion.

**Table 22-1   Government comes to Hypothetica (All values in Hypothetical $ billion)**

| Income/ output | Disposable income | Planned consumption | Planned investment | Government spending | Savings | Net taxes | Aggregate demand |
|---|---|---|---|---|---|---|---|
| 50 | | | | | | | |
| 100 | | | | | | | |
| 150 | | | | | | | |
| 200 | | | | | | | |
| 250 | | | | | | | |
| 300 | | | | | | | |
| 350 | | | | | | | |
| 400 | | | | | | | |

(a)  For each level of income in Table 22-1, calculate disposable income, planned consumption, savings, and net taxes.

(b)  Calculate aggregate demand, showing it at each level of aggregate supply.

(c)  If, in a particular period, income turned out to be $350 billion, how would you expect producers to react?

(d)  What is the equilibrium level of income?

(e)  Calculate the government budget deficit at equilibrium income.

Suppose government expenditure is increased by $22 billion:

(f)   What is the new equilibrium income?

(g)  Calculate the government budget deficit at this new equilibrium position.

(h)  What is the value of the multiplier?

2   (a)  Using the data of exercise 1, plot the consumption function and aggregate demand schedule.

(b)  Add on the 45° line and confirm that equilibrium occurs at the same point suggested by your answers to 1(d) above.

(c)  Show the effect on equilibrium income of an increase in government spending of $22 billion.

3   This exercise concerns the multiplier under different circumstances in a closed economy with and without government. Consumption is determined as 80 per cent of the income available to households. Investment is autonomous at a level of 450, as shown in Table 22-2.

**Table 22-2   The multiplier with and without government**

| Income/ output | Consumption 1 | Investment | Aggregate demand 1 | Disposable income | Consumption 2 | Government spending | Aggregate demand 2 |
|---|---|---|---|---|---|---|---|
| 2000 | | 450 | | | | | |
| 2250 | | 450 | | | | | |
| 2500 | | 450 | | | | | |
| 2750 | | 450 | | | | | |
| 3000 | | 450 | | | | | |

*(a)* Calculate consumption 1 and aggregate demand 1, assuming there is no government.

*(b)* What is the equilibrium level of income?

*(c)* What would be equilibrium income if investment increased by 50?

*(d)* Calculate the value of the multiplier.

Suppose now that the government levies direct taxes of 10 per cent of income and undertakes expenditure of 250, with investment back at 450:

*(e)* Calculate disposable income, consumption 2, and aggregate demand 2.

*(f)* What is the equilibrium level of income?

*(g)* What is the size of the government budget deficit?

*(h)* Use your answers to parts *(b)*, *(e)*, and *(f)* to explain the balanced budget multiplier.

*(i)* What would equilibrium income be if investment increased by 70?

*(j)* Calculate the value of the multiplier.

4   The government in an economy undertakes expenditure on goods and services of £100 million and makes transfer payments amounting to 10 per cent of national income. The rate of direct taxation is 30 per cent.

*(a)* Draw a diagram showing autonomous government expenditure and the way in which net taxes vary with national income.

*(b)* At what level of income does the government have a balanced budget?

*(c)* Within what range of income does the government run a budget deficit?

*(d)* Within what range of income does the government run a budget surplus?

*(e)* What would be the government deficit/surplus if equilibrium income were £400 million?

*(f)* If full-employment income is £750 million, what is the full-employment budget?

5   A government has £100 billion of outstanding debt, on which it must make interest payments at the current nominal rate of 8 per cent. Inflation is running at 6 per cent per annum.

*(a)* Nominal interest payments are included in government expenditure and thus contribute to the government deficit. What is the nominal interest burden?

*(b)* What is the real interest rate? (*Note*: this was discussed in Chapter 14.)

*(c)* What is the real interest burden?

*(d)* If you have followed this line of reasoning through, you may feel suspicious that we have just been manipulating the figures. After all, holders of government bonds must be paid their (nominal) 8 per cent return. How in practice will the government be able to meet the payments?

6   An economy exports £150 million worth of goods each period, this quantity being autonomous. Imports, however, vary with national income such that imports always comprise 20 per cent of income.

*(a)* Draw a diagram which shows imports and exports against national income.

*(b)* What is the trade balance when income is £1000 million?

*(c)* What is the trade balance when income is £500 million?

*(d)* At what level of income are imports equal to exports?

*(e)* If full-employment income is £1000 million, explain how the balance of trade may act as a constant on government policy.

7   This exercise explores the balanced budget multiplier in a closed economy. Investment expenditure is fixed at 450, consumption is 80 per cent of disposable income. Initially, government expenditure is 250 and direct taxes are 10 per cent of income.

*(a)* Identify the initial equilibrium income for the economy.

*(b)* Calculate the amount of consumption expenditure, tax revenue, and the government budget deficit/surplus.

Suppose now that government expenditure is increased by 500 and the tax rate raised from 10 to 25 per cent.

*(c)* Before output has had time to adjust, by how much is disposable income reduced?

*(d)* Calculate the resulting change in consumption expenditure and the net effect on aggregate demand, remembering the increase in government expenditure.

*(e)* What is the new equilibrium income level for the economy?

*(f)* What is the government budget deficit/ surplus?

*(g)* Calculate the balanced budget multiplier.

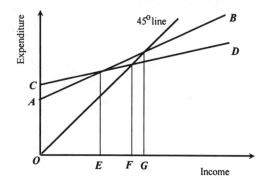

Figure 22-1    Equilibrium in an open economy

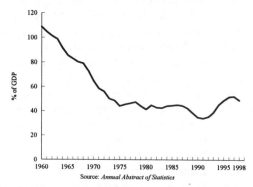

Figure 22-2    UK national debt as a percentage of GDP

8    Figure 22-1 shows aggregate demand schedules with and without foreign trade, together with the 45° line.
   (a) *AB* and *CD* represent aggregate demand schedules with and without foreign trade. (Assume that imports are proportional to income, but exports are autonomous.) Which is which?
   (b) Identify equilibrium income in the absence of foreign trade.
   (c) Identify equilibrium income when there is foreign trade.
   (d) At what level of income is there a zero trade balance?
   (e) Explain whether the presence of foreign trade increases or reduces the size of the multiplier.
9    Figure 22-2 shows the ratio of national debt to GDP in the UK for each year since 1960.
   (a) What is meant by the 'national debt'?
   (b) Discuss the time-path followed by the national debt in this period, paying especial attention to the changes in the 1980s.
   (c) Should the government be concerned at the size of the national debt in the 1990s?
10   Explain why each of the following items may constitute an obstacle to the use of active fiscal policy.
   (a) Monitoring the economy's performance.
   (b) Implementing changes in the spending programme.
   (c) Timing the multiplier process.
   (d) Uncertainty concerning the operation of the multiplier.
   (e) Uncertainty concerning future aggregate demand.
   (f) The possibility of indirect policy effects.
   (g) Endangerment of other policy objectives.
   (h) Uncertainty concerning the level of full employment.

## True/False

1    In the 1990s, direct purchases by government comprised about one-half of national output in most European countries.
2    The effect of net taxes is to steepen the relationship between consumption and national income.
3    An increase in government spending accompanied by an equal increase in taxes results in an increase in output.
4    The effect of net taxes is to reduce the multiplier.
5    For a given level of government spending, an increase in the tax rate reduces both the equilibrium level of national income and the size of the budget deficit.
6    The size of the budget deficit is a good measure of the government's fiscal stance.
7    The structural budget shows the state of the government deficit/surplus if the other components of aggregate demand were such as to ensure the economy was at full-employment output.
8    In a world with significant inflation, it is sensible to count only the real interest rate times the outstanding government debt as an item of expenditure contributing to the overall government deficit.

**9** Income tax, VAT, and unemployment benefit are important automatic stabilizers.

**10** The debt:GDP ratio fell in the UK in the 1980s – as it did in most industrial countries.

**11** Net exports in the UK amount to nearly 30 per cent of GDP.

**12** Direct import restrictions are always good for domestic output and employment as they allow the economy to reach full employment without hitting the constraint of the trade balance.

## ECONOMICS IN THE NEWS

### Pre-Budget statement: surplus to total £46bn over next four years
*(Adapted from The Independent, 10 November 1999)*

Even Gordon Brown admitted there would be a little extra in the kitty during the next few years, revising his estimates of likely government revenues compared with March's Budget. But the Chancellor was less optimistic than many outside forecasters, basing his predictions of future tax revenues on cautious assumptions.

There is no single bottom line in the public finances, but the closest thing to it is the figure for public sector net borrowing (PSNB). Thanks to the economy's better than expected performance, Mr Brown was able to revise down his estimates of how much the government will need to borrow. In fact, he is predicting a surplus of revenues over spending this year and for the next two before returning to a small deficit in 2002–03 and 2003–04. There will be a debt repayment of £3.5bn this year and £3bn in the two following years, and small borrowing requirements of £1bn in 2002–03 and £4bn in 2003–04. This represents an improvement of £6.5bn in net borrowing this year, compared with the forecasts he made in March, tapering off to an unchanged forecast for 2003–04.

Confusion abounds partly because there are so many summary figures. The borrowing total can include or exclude the windfall tax revenues. The government also presents the sums that will be spent on the working families tax credit as negative revenue rather than positive spending – just as the Conservatives presented privatization revenues as negative spending rather than positive taxes. Certainly, the new presentation of the figures can make readers feel there is such a thing as too much transparency. A Treasury guide to analysing the public finances, published alongside yesterday's pre-Budget report, contained a six-page glossary of terms.

However, the basic, prudent principles of tax and spending policies are unchanged. The Code for Fiscal Stability passed a year ago requires the Chancellor to satisfy two rules. The 'golden rule' says the government can only borrow to invest; in other words current, day-to-day spending must balance revenues over the course of the business cycle. Surpluses in good times are therefore needed to offset deficits in bad times, and Mr Brown has pencilled in a comfortable surplus for the next five years. The 'sustainable investment rule' caps borrowing overall by saying net public sector debt must be stable over the cycle at a level preferably below 40 per cent of GDP.

The separate paper published yesterday emphasises that the fiscal projections in the pre-Budget report have a completely different status from those in the Budget. Yesterday's new forecasts are updates that take account of changes in the economy rather than a new statement of policy. The paper also spells out the Treasury's assessment of the impact of fiscal policy. The overall impact is captured in the change from year to year in the PSNB. If it falls, policy is getting tighter. Adjusting this measure to remove the impact of 'automatic stabilizers' such as the fact that tax revenues rise and benefits fall as the economy expands gives the cyclically adjusted PSNB. This measures what the Treasury calls the change in the fiscal stance, the result of policy measures. It is the best measure of the real economic impact of the government's decisions.

The new figures show very little change in the cyclically adjusted PSNB, indicating that the higher actual debt repayments mainly reflect the better performance of the economy. The golden rule means that surpluses in good times have to be banked to cover deficits in bad times. However, even here the Treasury projections build in some caution. They assume the economy can grow at just 2.25 per cent a year on average, requiring a bigger cushion of surpluses when the economy grows at a pace faster than that.

Yesterday's report played down the public sector net cash requirement, which used to be known as the public sector borrowing requirement. Its importance as an economic indicator dates from the days of monetary targeting, but the City still uses the figure to estimate how much gilt-edged stock the government will need to sell. The result of Mr Brown's passion for prudence is that gilts will continue to be in short supply, especially long-term stocks, which pension funds need to meet their minimum funding requirements.

1   What implications are there for the national debt if the government runs a budget surplus, as the passage predicts?
2   The passage suggests that the Chancellor is more cautious in predicting the course of the economy than many other commentators. What is implied for the stance of macroeconomic policy if the government adopts an excessively pessimistic view of the performance of the economy?

## Questions for Thought

1   Examine the effect on the multiplier of the existence of government activity and international trade. Discuss the problem of timing the multiplier process and explore reasons why this model may not provide an adequate explanation of how an economy 'really' works.
2   Discuss the importance of automatic stabilizers. To what extent may imports be regarded as one such automatic stabilizer?
3   What do you regard as the principal shortcomings of the model as developed so far?

# 23  Money and Modern Banking

## Learning Outcomes

- To define the medium of exchange, the key attribute of money
- To consider other functions of money
- To analyse how banks create money by holding fewer reserves than they create deposits
- To relate the monetary base to the money supply via the money multiplier
- To explain different measures of money in the UK and discuss why different measures have been emphasized as the financial sector has changed
- To analyse how modern banks compete for deposits and loans by choosing the interest rates they pay depositors and charge lenders

**IN THIS CHAPTER ...** you will turn your attention to the financial markets by examining the importance of money and banking in a modern economy. In this chapter and the next, you will explore the uses of money and the means which the authorities may adopt in order to control its quantity. In this exploration, you will need to look at the roles of money in a modern economy: as a *medium of exchange, unit of account, a store of value,* and as a *standard of deferred payment.* In defining money, notes and coins (legal tender) are supplemented by customary or IOU money, such as bank deposits. The Bank of England acts as a banker for the commercial banks, who hold a proportion of their reserves as idle cash balances to enable this activity. Like any other private firm, the commercial banks act as profit-maximizers. By granting loans and overdraft facilities, the commercial banks effectively add to the amount of customary money in the economy and can thus affect the size of the existing money stock. The money supply is equal to the monetary base times the money multiplier, reflecting the ability of the banks to create credit.

## Important Concepts and Technical Terms

Match each lettered concept with the appropriate numbered phrase:

| | | | | | |
|---|---|---|---|---|---|
| (a) | Medium of exchange | (f) | M0 | (k) | Money multiplier |
| (b) | Financial intermediary | (g) | Money supply | (l) | Unit of account |
| (c) | Money | (h) | Store of value | (m) | Monetary base |
| (d) | Near money | (i) | Liquidity | (n) | Barter economy |
| (e) | Financial panic | (j) | Reserve ratio | | |

1  Any generally accepted means of payment for the delivery of goods or the settlement of debt.
2  The function of money whereby it enables the exchange of goods and services.
3  The function of money by which it provides a unit in which prices are quoted and accounts are kept.
4  The function of money by which it can be used to make purchases in the future.
5  The quantity of notes and coin in private circulation plus the quantity held by the banking system, sometimes known as the stock of high-powered money.
6  An economy with no medium of exchange, in which goods are traded directly or swapped for other goods.
7  The change in the money stock for a £1 change in the quantity of the monetary base.
8  An institution that specializes in bringing lenders and borrowers together.
9  Assets that are 'almost' as good as money: stores of value that can readily be converted into money but are not themselves a means of payment.
10 A self-fulfilling prophecy whereby people believe that a bank will be unable to pay and, in the stampede to get their money, thereby ensure that the bank cannot pay.
11 Notes and coin in circulation plus bankers' operational deposits with the Bank of England.
12 The value of the total stock of money, the medium of exchange, in circulation.
13 The speed and certainty with which an asset can be converted into money.
14 The ratio of reserves to deposits.

## Exercises

1   Eight individuals in a barter economy have and want the following goods:
   Alice has some haddock but would like some apples;
   Barry has some gin but fancies blackcurrant jam;
   Carol is in possession of doughnuts but wants coconuts;
   Daniel has obtained some jellied eels but really wants doughnuts;
   Eleanor has some figs but would prefer jellied eels;
   Felix fancies figs but has only blackcurrant jam;
   Gloria has coconuts but yearns for gin;
   Henry has apples but would like haddock.
   (a)  Can you work out a series of transactions which would satisfy all concerned?
   (b)  Can you now understand how money is so helpful in making the world go round?

2   Identify each of the following items as legal, token, commodity, or IOU money – or, indeed, as not-money:
   (a)  Gold.
   (b)  £1 coin.
   (c)  Cigarettes.
   (d)  Cheque for £100.
   (e)  Petrol.
   (f)  Camera accepted in part-exchange.
   (g)  A building society deposit.
   (h)  Pigs, turkeys, and cocoa nuts.

3   This exercise shows how the banks can create money through their loan policy. For simplicity, assume that there is a single commercial bank, which aims to hold 10 per cent of its deposits as cash. The public is assumed to have a fixed demand for cash of £10 million. We begin in equilibrium with the following situation:

| Commercial bank balance sheet (£m) | | | | | | |
|---|---|---|---|---|---|---|
| Liabilities | | Assets | | Cash ratio | Public cash holdings | Money stock |
| Deposits | 100 | Cash<br>loans | 10<br>90 | | | |
| | 100 | | 100 | 10% | 10 | 110 |

   Consider the sequence of events that follows if the central bank autonomously supplies an extra £10 million cash which finds its way into the pockets of Joe Public:
   (a)  How will Joe Public react? (Remember the fixed demand for cash.)
   (b)  How does this affect the cash ratio of the commercial bank?
   (c)  How will the commercial bank react to this 'disequilibrium'?
   (d)  How much cash does Joe Public now hold?
   (e)  What will Joe Public do with the excess cash?
   (f)  How does this affect the commercial bank's behaviour?
   (g)  At what point will the system settle down again, with both bank and public back in equilibrium?
   (h)  How does money stock alter as this process unfolds?
   Note: if this sequence of questions does not make any sense to you, you are recommended to tackle them again in conjunction with the commentary provided in the 'Answers and Comments' section.

4   Which of the following characteristics are necessary for an asset to function as money?
   (a)  Backed by a precious metal.
   (b)  Authorized as legal tender by the monetary authorities.
   (c)  Generally acceptable as a medium of exchange.
   (d)  Having value in future transactions.

5    The commercial banks in an economy choose to hold 5 per cent of deposits in the form of cash reserves. The general public chooses to hold an amount of notes and coin in circulation equal to one-quarter of its bank deposits. The stock of high-powered money in the economy is £12 million.
   (a)  Calculate the value of the money multiplier.
   (b)  What is the size of the money stock if both public and banks are holding their desired amounts of cash?
   (c)  Suppose the banks now decide that they need to hold only 4 per cent of deposits as cash. Calculate the value of the money multiplier.
   (d)  What is now the size of 'equilibrium' money stock?
   (e)  Suppose that the banks again choose to hold 5 per cent of deposits as cash, but the public increases its cash holdings to 30 per cent of its bank deposits. Now what is the value of the money multiplier?
   (f)  What is now the size of 'equilibrium' money stock?
   (g)  Does this analysis provide any clues to how the monetary authorities might try to influence the size of the money stock?

6    Suppose that the clearing banks maintain a minimum cash ratio of 12½ per cent.
   (a)  If an individual bank receives a cash deposit of £1000, what additional deposits would the bank feel able to create?
   (b)  What difference would it have made if the cash ratio had been only 10 per cent?
   (c)  Under what circumstances might a bank choose to hold a higher cash ratio than is required by government regulations?

7    Which of the following would be regarded as an asset to a customer of a commercial bank?
   (a)  A current account bank deposit.
   (b)  A special deposit.
   (c)  Trade bills held by the bank as reserve assets.
   (d)  The bank's deposits at the Bank of England.
   (e)  An overdraft.
   (f)  Loans advanced by the commercial bank in US$.

8    In Table 23-1 are listed a number of components of the monetary aggregates in the UK, as at October 1999. These data were taken from the Bank of England's web site at
   http://www.bankofengland.co.uk/mfsd/
   Calculate M0, M2, and M4.

9    Assess the liquidity and likely return of each of the following financial assets:
   (a)  Cash.
   (b)  Equities.
   (c)  Bonds.
   (d)  Bills.
   (e)  Industrial shares.
   (f)  Perpetuities.

**Table 23-1    Some components of UK monetary aggregates**

|  | £ million |
|---|---|
| Wholesale deposits | 252 189 |
| Notes and coin in circulation outside the Bank of England | 29 192 |
| Cash in circulation | 23 521 |
| Banks' retail deposits | 409 345 |
| Building society retail shares and deposits | 109 052 |
| Bankers' operational deposits with the banking department | 186 |

## True/False

1  Dogs' teeth have been used as money.
2  Trading is expensive in a barter economy.
3  Money in current accounts in banks is legal tender.
4  Financial panics are rare in present-day Britain because of the actions of the Bank of England.
5  If the goldsmiths insisted that all transactions were backed by equal amounts of gold in the vaults, then their actions could not cause growth in the money supply.
6  Banks are the only financial intermediaries.
7  The clearing system represents one way in which society reduces the costs of making transactions.
8  The more liquid an asset, the higher the return received.
9  The modern fractional reserve banking system is an intrinsic part of the process of money creation.
10  The monetary base is the quantity of notes and coin in circulation with the non-bank private sector.
11  The more cash that the public wishes to hold, the higher is money supply.
12  Building society deposits are so liquid that they ought to be included in the definition of money.

## ECONOMICS IN THE NEWS

### Smile. Now beenz means more than just virtual cash
*(Adapted from The Scotsman, 10 January 2000)*

From the perspective of driving its mantra into the hearts and wallets of the mainstream, the problem with electronic commerce is that it is so gosh-darned esoteric. Credit cards may work well enough, but they have also generated enough security myths, blunders and genuine fears to render their use downright scary. Likewise, the various forms of e-cash might be particularly safe for small online transactions, but as long as you can't spend it at the shops down the road, it is never going to feel like currency of real value.

Following a joint announcement from web currency creator beenz.com and electronic transaction specialist Mondex International, however, this problem may have been solved. The companies are developing a smartcard capable of carrying beenz, a suite of complementary e-commerce services and good old-fashioned cash that promises to embrace the home PC, mobile phone, digital television and shopping mall with ease. 'At some point, people are finally going to realize there are no such things as online commerce or offline commerce – there is only commerce,' says Charles Cohen, founder and chief technology officer of beenz.com. 'Any distinction that has been made between the two is manifestly false; it's just that, until now, there has been no clear bridge between website and high street.' The products to be included on the card are complementary but distinct. Mondex, functioning in Scotland by means of a pilot scheme involving Edinburgh University, the Bank of Scotland and local retailers, is essentially cash stored in electronic form on cards that can be credited at a variety of outlets. Beenz is a universal web currency launched last year that cannot be bought directly by consumers, but is earned online by visiting, interacting with or shopping at websites – rather like a supermarket loyalty scheme – and can in turn be spent on products offered by participating merchants.

In theory, a consumer with one of the cards could earn beenz in return for purchasing goods using Mondex cash and then spend them at a high street shop. Mondex cardholders would likewise be able to earn beenz at retail outlets by uploading them on to their cards and then spending them online, offering a flexible one-stop payment solution that the brokers believe is the answer to the 21st-century consumer's problems. The benefits to the consumer of such a system are relatively clear. Apart from the convenience of having one card to handle all transactions, as cash is credited to the Mondex function in limited amounts determined by the user, a stolen card would give felons access only to that cash limit and not, as may be the case with a credit card, your entire bank balance.

Of particular relevance when it comes to shopping online with foreign vendors is the fact that problems over economic borders are not, apparently, a problem for Mondex, with each card built with the capacity to recognize up to 15 currencies.

'Liquidity is the key here. Apart from their houses and cars, people want to hold assets that they can spend,' says Cohen. 'In terms of day-to-day living, loyalty points are essentially useless because you can't spend them anywhere; we want to offer them a currency that is useable everywhere, from home to abroad, from online e-tailers to the local pub.' The attraction of the scheme for business is equally plain, largely because Mondex cash transactions are instantaneous and the charges low, with even those directed through a third-party broker costing a few pence in the pound, considerably less than the 15 to 18 per cent frequently levied by credit card companies. A somewhat better rate of return for lower priced items is also offered.

1   To what extent do beenz fulfil the characteristics of money?
2   If beenz were to take off, what would be the effect on money supply?
3   Might network externalities be important in determining the success of beenz? (See the discussion in Chapter 11 if you cannot remember about network externalities.)

## Questions for Thought

1   Discuss why you think that people want to hold money rather than using the funds to earn a return.
2   How do you expect the increased use of credit cards to affect the money supply?

# 24 Central Banking and the Monetary System

## Learning Outcomes

- To explain the key roles of the central bank as banker to the commercial banks and setter of monetary policy
- To examine the channels through which the central bank can affect the money supply
- To explore the role of the central bank as lender of last resort
- To discuss motives for holding money and their relation to the determinants of money demand
- To note that people care about the size of real money balances not nominal balances
- To analyse how money market equilibrium is achieved and recognize that this implies equilibrium in other financial markets as well
- To analyse comparative static experiments that alter money market equilibrium
- To consider why a nominal anchor is needed to tie down the price level, and examine how the central bank uses the interest rate instrument to pursue intermediate targets

**IN THIS CHAPTER ...** you will examine the role of the *central bank* (in the UK this is the *Bank of England*), the demand for money, and the way in which money market equilibrium is reached. This is crucial for understanding the conduct of macroeconomic policy, which in recent years has focused on monetary policy. The Bank of England also acts to ensure that the government can meet its payments when running a budget deficit. The late 1980s saw major changes in financial markets throughout the world, enabled by advances in technology, bringing both deregulation and new forms of regulation. In the face of such developments and moves towards European integration, the role and conduct of central banks are changing.

## Important Concepts and Technical Terms

Match each lettered concept with the appropriate numbered phrase:

| | | |
|---|---|---|
| (a) Monetary instruments | (f) Open market operations | (k) Required reserve ratio |
| (b) Central bank | (g) Interest rate spread | (l) Transaction motive |
| (c) Intermediate target | (h) Lender of last resort | (m) Opportunity cost of holding money |
| (d) Discount rate | (i) Precautionary motive | |
| (e) Asset motive | (j) Gilt repo | (n) Financial Services Agency |

1  The most important bank in a country, usually having official standing in the government, having responsibility for issuing banknotes, and acting as banker to the banking system and to the government.
2  The difference between the deposit rate and the interest rate available on treasury bills.
3  A sale and repurchase agreement: a bank sells a gilt with a simultaneous agreement to buy it back at a specified price on a particular future date.
4  A motive for holding money arising from uncertainty by which people hold money to meet contingencies the exact nature of which cannot be foreseen.
5  Action by the central bank to alter the monetary base by buying or selling financial securities in the open market.
6  The role of the central bank whereby it stands ready to lend to banks and other financial institutions when financial panic threatens the financial system.
7  The interest rate that the central bank charges when the commercial banks want to borrow money.
8  A minimum ratio of cash reserves to deposits which the central bank requires commercial banks to hold.
9  A motive for holding money arising because people dislike risk and are prepared to sacrifice a high average rate of return to obtain a portfolio with a lower but more predictable rate of return.
10  A motive for holding money reflecting the fact that payments and receipts are not perfectly synchronized.
11  A key indicator used as an input to frequent decisions about where to set interest rates.
12  The variables over which the central bank exercises day to day control.
13  The body responsible for the regulation of UK banks.
14  The interest given up by holding money rather than bonds.

## Exercises

1   The following items comprise the assets and liabilities of the Bank of England in October 1999:

|                                              | £ billion |
| -------------------------------------------- | --------- |
| Government securities (Issue Department)      | 13.4      |
| Public deposits                              | 0.2       |
| Advances                                     | 26.1      |
| Government securities (Banking Department)    | 1.3       |
| Notes in circulation                         | 24.8      |
| Bankers' deposits                            | 1.3       |
| Reserves and other accounts                  | 28.6      |
| Other securities (Issue Department)          | 11.4      |
| Other assets (Banking Department)            | 2.7       |

Source: http://www.bankofengland.co.uk/mfsd/.

Identify each item as an asset or a liability and complete the balance sheets for the two departments of the Bank.

2   In a given economy, the public chooses to hold an amount of cash equal to 40 per cent of its bank deposits. The commercial banks choose to hold 5 per cent of deposits in the form of cash in order to service their customers. The stock of high-powered money is £12 million.

*(a)* What is the size of the money supply?

Each of the following four situations represents an attempt by the monetary authorities to reduce the size of money supply. In each case, assume that the banking system is initially as described above.

*(b)* What would be the size of money supply if the central bank imposed a 10 per cent cash ratio on the commercial banks?

*(c)* What would be the size of money supply if the central bank raised its discount rate to such a penalty rate that the banks choose to hold an extra 5 per cent of deposits as cash?

*(d)* What would be the size of money supply if the central bank called for Special Deposits of an amount corresponding to 5 per cent of bank deposits?

*(e)* What would be the reduction in money supply if the central bank undertook open market operations to reduce the stock of high-powered money by £1 million?

3   In what way would you expect each of the following items to affect the demand for real money balances?

*(a)* An increase in real income.

*(b)* An increase in confidence about the future.

*(c)* An increase in the opportunity cost of holding money.

*(d)* A fall in nominal interest rates.

*(e)* An increase in the price level.

*(f)* An increase in the interest differential between risky assets and time deposits.

*(g)* An increase in uncertainty concerning future transactions.

*(h)* A fall in the frequency of income payments – for example, a switch from weekly to monthly payment.

*(i)* An increase in the stock of high-powered money brought about by open market operations by the Bank of England.

4   Table 24-1 overleaf provides information concerning nominal national output, M1, £M3, and interest rates, comparing the years 1979 and 1983 in the UK, a period in which money supply was a well publicized policy target.

*(a)* Calculate an index of real GDP for 1983 based on 1979=100.

*(b)* Explain how you would expect real money holdings to have changed between 1979 and 1983 on the basis of the evidence on GDP, prices, and the interest rate.

*(c)* Calculate an index of real M1 and real £M3 for 1983 based on 1979=100 and discuss whether your answer is consistent with your reasoning in part *(b)* of the exercise.

*(d)* Why is it more difficult for the Bank to control real money stock than it is to control nominal money stock – and why does it matter?

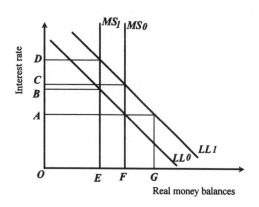

**Figure 24-1    Money market equilibrium**

**Table 24-1    Analysing money holdings 1979–83**

|  | 1979 | 1983 |
|---|---|---|
| Nominal money holdings M1 (end 1979 = 100) | 100 | 151.5 |
| Nominal money holdings £M3 (end 1979 = 100) | 100 | 178.0 |
| Nominal GDP (1979 = 100) | 100 | 137.5 |
| GDP deflator (1979 = 100) | 100 | 139.7 |
| Nominal interest rate on 3-month Treasury bills (%) | 16.65 | 9.28 |

Source: ONS, *Economic Trends Annual Supplement 1986* , HMSO, and *Bank of England Quarterly Bulletin June 1984*.

5    Figure 24-1 shows conditions in the money market. *LL0* and *LL1* are money demand schedules; *MS0* and *MS1* represent alternative real money supply schedules. In the initial state, the money market is in equilibrium with the demand for money *LL0* and money supply *MS0*.

*(a)* Identify equilibrium money balances and rate of interest.

*(b)* Suggest why it might be that the money demand schedule shifted from *LL0* to *LL1*.

*(c)* Given the move from *LL0* to *LL1*, suppose that no adjustment has yet taken place: what is the state of excess demand/supply in the bond market?

*(d)* How does this disequilibrium in the bond market bring about adjustments in the money market?

*(e)* Identify the new market equilibrium.

*(f)* Suppose that money demand remains at *LL1*: what measures could the authorities adopt to move money supply from *MS0* to *MS1*?

*(g)* Identify the new market equilibrium.

6    Which of the following situations would entail an increase in the transactions demand for money?

*(a)* A general rise in consumer prices.

*(b)* An expected general rise in consumer prices.

*(c)* The extension of value-added tax to goods which were previously zero-rated.

*(d)* An increase in the level of real income.

*(e)* An increase in the standard rate of income tax.

*(f)* A fall in interest rates.

7    In which of the following circumstances would a rise in interest rates be expected?

*(a)* A fall in money supply.

*(b)* An increase in money demand.

*(c)* A rise in liquidity preference.

*(d)* A fall in the price of bonds.

*(e)* An increase in consumer prices.

8    Use a diagram to explain how the authorities may attempt to control money stock through interest rates. Comment on the problems of this procedure.

9    Explain how the authorities may attempt to influence interest rates by controlling money stock. Comment on the problems of this procedure.

## True/False

1  There is no possibility that the Bank of England can go bankrupt because it can always meet withdrawals by its depositors by printing new banknotes a little more quickly.

2  The central bank can reduce the money supply by reducing the amount of cash that the commercial banks must hold as reserves.

3  Open market operations are a means by which the Bank alters the monetary base, banks' cash reserves, deposit lending, and the money supply.

4  A reverse repo is where you repossess your car from the loan shark.

5  The initiation of the London repo market increased M4 by about £6 billion in early 1996.

6  When you've tried everywhere else to get money for your holidays, you go to the lender of last resort.

7  Money is a nominal variable, not a real variable.

8  The existence of uncertainty increases the demand for bonds.

9  The best measure of the opportunity cost of holding money is the real interest rate.

10  The central bank can control the real money supply with precision more easily than the nominal money supply.

11  An excess demand for money must be exactly matched by an excess supply of bonds: otherwise people would be planning to hold more wealth than they actually possess.

12  The central bank can fix the money supply and accept the equilibrium interest rate implied by the money demand equation, or it can fix the interest rate and accept the equilibrium money supply implied by the money demand equation; but it cannot choose both money supply and interest rate independently.

## ECONOMICS IN THE NEWS

### £50bn readied for millennium weekend
*(adapted from The Financial Times, 19 October 1999)*

The Bank of England has made available more than £50bn of banknotes – twice the amount currently in circulation – to meet any surge in demand for cash over the millennium weekend. Consumers usually withdraw more money than usual at the end of the year and the peak may be higher this New Year's Eve as revellers order their last round of drinks before the end of the century.

But the Bank is determined to avoid panic over the effects on the financial system of the millennium bug, which could create problems if computers record dates as two digits and so choke on the change from 99 to 00. The Bank expects demand to peak at £30bn, but is pumping another £8bn into the system. On top of that, £12bn is available from commercial banks' stocks and its own reserves. The total of £50bn allows £850 for every man, woman and child. Some extra notes have already been shipped to bank vaults and cash centres. Distributing that bulk of money to regional cash centres involves huge preparations, but bankers are coy about the details for security reasons. 'It's Wembley football pitch 16ft deep in notes. We need from August to Christmas just to deliver them,' said one commercial banker.

To make sure it had enough cash, the Bank stopped destroying old £20 notes at the start of the year and has concentrated its printing on the £10 and £20 notes most in demand for automatic teller machines. Consumer panic over the millennium bug appears to have subsided. Surveys conducted by the banking industry earlier this year showed consumers expected to take out an extra £3bn of cash at the year end. The figure has now fallen to about £1bn.

### Banks mop up surplus millennium liquidity
*(adapted from The Financial Times, 5 January 2000)*

With the turn of the year safely negotiated, central banks yesterday began mopping up the extra cash they made available at the end of 1999 to avert any problems the millennium bug might have caused. Central banks around the world had made additional liquidity available to the money markets in case fears about the millennium bug made it difficult for some banks to fund themselves over the year-end. At the same time, truckloads of new banknotes had been shipped out in case consumers started to make panic cash machine withdrawals. But the millennium weekend passed smoothly for the financial system, and consumers seem to have decided to use their plastic payment cards instead of withdrawing more cash. Visa International, the payment card grouping, reported that it had handled 48m Year 2000 transactions from the south Pacific onwards, even before managers at its Y2K management centre in Foster City, California had rung in the new year. That was 35 per cent more than in the same period of last year.

The European Central Bank said there was surplus liquidity in the euro market as a result of its efforts to prevent any squeezes occurring at the end of the year – a time when some central bankers worried that millennium bug fears might prompt a flight to quality, leaving second tier banks short of cash. 'As the transition to the year 2000 went smoothly, the ECB now considers it appropriate to adjust the liquidity situation accordingly,' it said. Bankers said the end of the millennium had produced some money market effects, but fewer than might have been anticipated.

Absorbing surplus banknotes may take longer. In the UK, for example, the Bank of England had made £50bn of banknotes available to meet demand that was forecast at around £30bn, and which is now thought to have been, in fact, much lower. But Bank officials were at pains to deny that convoys of armoured cars would now have to transport these unneeded notes, neatly packaged in £25,000 bundles, back to its vaults. Instead they will be gradually absorbed into the system.

1    The first passage describes the preparations made by the Bank of England in preparation for the millennium weekend. Under what conditions would they have been necessary? What effect would these measures have had on the UK money supply?
2    The second passage describes the way that central banks went about coping with the aftermath of the millennium non-crisis. What effect would these measures have had on the UK money supply?

## Questions for Thought

1    Imagine that you have a stock of wealth to be allocated between money and bonds, your main concern being to avoid the capital losses which might ensue if the price of bonds falls when you are holding bonds. Suppose that you expect the rate of interest to be at a particular level $Rc$.
    (a) How would you allocate your wealth between money and bonds if the current rate of interest were below $Rc$?
    (b) How would you allocate your wealth between money and bonds if the current rate of interest were higher than $Rc$?
    (c) What would be implied for the aggregate relationship between money holdings and the rate of interest if different individuals have different expectations about future interest rates?
2    Discuss whether monetary policy has any meaning in an economy where we cannot clearly define money supply, and could not control it even if we could.

# 25 Monetary and Fiscal Policy in a Closed Economy

## Learning Outcomes

- **To develop theories of consumption that allow household borrowing against future incomes, and explore motives to smooth out fluctuations in consumption**
- **To study how interest rates and expected future profits affect investment demand by firms**
- **To analyse simultaneously the markets for output and money, realizing output affects money demand and interest rates affect goods demand**
- **To derive IS and LM curves, combinations of output and interest rates that lead to goods market and money market equilibrium**
- **To manipulate the IS-LM model to show how output and interest rates react to shocks in either the goods market or the money market**
- **To recognize that different mixes of monetary and fiscal policy can achieve the same output but at different interest rates**

**IN THIS CHAPTER ...** you will begin to draw the macroeconomic model together, combining an extended version of the income-expenditure model of the real sector with the analysis of money market equilibrium. This will allow you to look more closely and carefully at the policy options facing the government. This will still not be a complete model, and we will continue to assume a closed economy, and to hold prices fixed. In building towards this more complete model, you will need to revisit the topics of *consumption* and *investment*, This entails exploring the way in which the rate of interest affects the level of aggregate demand. Given the connection between the rate of interest rate and money stock, you will also explore the way in which financial variables may be seen to affect 'real' economic activity. This is also revealing about the way in which *crowding-out* may dilute the use of fiscal policy. Also in this chapter you will meet the *IS-LM* model, which enables you to see simultaneous equilibrium in both the real and financial sectors. Fiscal and monetary policy can then be examined in this perspective. The model so far has a 'Keynesian' flavour to it, in its emphasis on aggregate demand. When we do allow prices to be flexible, the supply-side will be seen to be important.

## Important Concepts and Technical Terms

Match each lettered concept with the appropriate numbered phrase:

| | | |
|---|---|---|
| *(a)* Wealth effect | *(e)* Transmission mechanism | *(i)* Demand management |
| *(b)* Investment demand schedule | *(f)* Permanent income hypothesis | *(j)* Ricardian equivalence |
| *(c)* IS schedule | *(g)* LM schedule | |
| *(d)* Crowding out | *(h)* Life-cycle hypothesis | |

1  A function showing how much investment firms wish to make at each interest rate.
2  The upward (downward) shift in the consumption function when household wealth increases (decreases) and people spend more (less) at each level of personal disposable income.
3  The route by which a change in money supply affects aggregate demand.
4  A theory about consumption developed by Ando and Modigliani which argues that people form their consumption plans by reference to their expected lifetime income.
5  A theory about consumption developed by Friedman which argues that consumption depends not on current disposable income but on average income in the long run.
6  The use of monetary and fiscal policy to stabilize the level of income around a high average level.
7  A curve which shows the different combinations of interest rates and income compatible with equilibrium in the money market.
8  The reduction in private demand for consumption and investment caused by an increase in government spending, which increases aggregate demand and hence interest rates.
9  A curve which shows the different combinations of income and interest rates at which the goods market is in equilibrium.
10  A situation in which a reduction in direct taxation has no effect on aggregate demand because individuals realize that tax cuts now will be balanced by higher future taxes.

## Exercises

**Table 25-1    Interest rates and the savings ratio**

|      | Treasury bill rate (%) | Savings ratio (%) |
|------|------------------------|-------------------|
| 1987 | 8.38                   | 5.5               |
| 1988 | 12.91                  | 3.9               |
| 1989 | 15.02                  | 5.6               |
| 1990 | 13.50                  | 7.4               |
| 1991 | 10.45                  | 9.4               |
| 1992 | 6.44                   | 11.5              |
| 1993 | 4.95                   | 11.0              |
| 1994 | 6.00                   | 9.4               |
| 1995 | 6.31                   | 10.3              |
| 1996 | 6.26                   | 9.5               |
| 1997 | 7.13                   | 9.3               |
| 1998 | 5.63                   | 6.4               |

Source: *Economic Trends.*

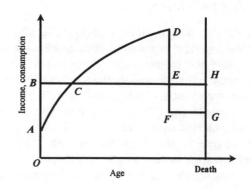

**Figure 25-1    Consumption and the life-cycle**

1   Table 25-1 presents UK data on the savings ratio and interest rates for the period 1987-98.
   (a)  Examine the data and try to detect any trends.
   (b)  Economists often find that visual display of data is more revealing. Draw a graph, plotting the savings ratio and the Treasury bill rate on the same diagram against time.
   (c)  Comment on the apparent relationship between the two series.

2   Figure 25-1 depicts income and consumption during the life-cycle. The path *ACDFG* represents the pattern of disposable income, increasing through the individual's working life and then reducing to pension level on retirement. *OB* represents long-run average, or 'permanent', income. The individual aims at a steady level of consumption through life so as just to exhaust total lifetime income.
   (a)  What level of consumption will be chosen?
   (b)  What does the area *ABC* represent?
   (c)  How is the area *ABC* to be financed?
   (d)  The area *CDE* represents an excess of current income over consumption. Why does the individual 'save' during this period?
   (e)  What does the area *EFGH* (during pension years) represent?
   (f)  How is *EFGH* financed?
   (g)  How would consumption behaviour be affected if the individual begins life with a stock of inherited wealth?
   (h)  Discuss the effect of an increase in interest rates upon the present value of future income and upon consumption.

3   Figure 25-2 opposite presents data for the UK relating to investment according to type of asset since 1965. Comment on the trends revealed by this data – both in terms of the overall trend in the data, and in terms of the pattern as between private and public sector investment.

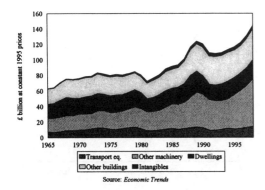

**Figure 25-2    Investment in the UK by sector**

**Table 25-2    Investment opportunities**

| Project | Cost (3) | Expected rate of return (% p.a.) |
|---------|----------|----------------------------------|
| A | 4 000 | 6 |
| B | 6 000 | 12 |
| C | 4 000 | 2 |
| D | 5 000 | 20 |
| E | 3 000 | 10 |
| F | 10 000 | 16 |

4    A firm is appraising its investment opportunities. Table 25-2 shows the projects that are available. Assume that the firm has sufficient internal funds to undertake as many of these projects as it desires without borrowing.

(a)    Which projects will the firm undertake if the market rate of interest is currently 11 per cent per annum?

(b)    Which (if any) projects would be abandoned if the market rate of interest rose from this level by 2 percentage points? Why would this decision be taken?

(c)    Construct a schedule showing how much investment the firm will undertake at different values of the market rate of interest.

(d)    How would you expect this schedule to be affected by an increase in the 'business confidence' of the firm? Relate your answer to Table 25-2.

5    This exercise concerns the transmission mechanism of monetary policy in a closed economy with fixed prices. Suppose that there is a fall in the interest rate.

(a)    What effect does this policy have on the bond market?

(b)    Outline the effect that this will have on consumption and investment.

(c)    What does this imply for aggregate demand?

(d)    How does this change in aggregate demand affect equilibrium output?

(e)    How does this then affect money demand?

(f)    What is implied for the rate of interest, and what further effects may follow?

(g)    What do you expect to be the net effect on equilibrium output?

Please note: if you find that any links in this chain are obscure, you are advised to work through the question in conjunction with the commentary provided in the 'Answers and Comments' section.

6    This exercise concerns the crowding-out effects of fiscal policy in a closed economy with fixed prices. We begin this time with a cut in the rate of direct taxation. As with the previous question, if the chain does not make sense to you, follow the question in conjunction with the commentary.

(a)    How will the policy change initially affect disposable income and aggregate demand?

(b)    What is the subsequent effect on equilibrium output?

(c)    What implications does this have for the demand for real money balances?

(d)    Given fixed money supply, how will this affect bond prices and interest rates?

(e)    How will this feed through to affect aggregate demand?

(f)    What is the effect on equilibrium output?

(g)    Under what circumstances will this crowding-out effect be complete?

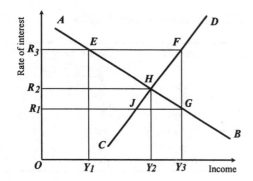

**Figure 25-3   Equilibrium in the goods and money markets**

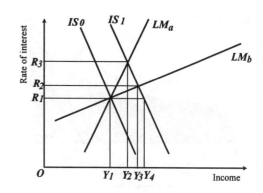

**Figure 25-4   Fiscal policy**

7   Figure 25-3 shows the *IS* and *LM* schedules for a closed economy with fixed prices.
   (a)  *AB* and *CD* are the *IS* and *LM* schedules – but which is which?
   (b)  Comment on the equilibrium/disequilibrium states of the goods and money markets at each of the points *E, F, G, H,* and *J.*
   (c)  How would you expect the economy to react if it is at point *J?*
   (d)  For each of the following items, identify whether the *IS* or *LM* schedule is likely to shift – and in which direction (assume *ceteris paribus* in each case):
     (i)   An increase in business confidence.
     (ii)  An increase in nominal money supply.
     (iii) A reduction in government spending.
     (iv)  A once-for-all increase in the price level.
     (v)   A redistribution of income from rich to poor.
     (vi)  An increase in the wealth holdings of households.

8   Figure 25-4 illustrates the effects of fiscal policy on equilibrium income and interest rate under alternative assumptions about the slope of the *LM* function. In each case, fiscal policy is represented by a movement of the *IS* curve from *IS0* to *IS1*.
   (a)  What is the initial equilibrium income and interest rate?
   (b)  What could have caused the move from *IS0* to *IS1*?
   (c)  What would be the 'full multiplier'.effect of the fiscal policy – that is, if the interest rate remains unchanged?
   (d)  If the fiscal policy is bond-financed and the *LM* schedule is relatively elastic, what is the effect of the fiscal policy on the equilibrium position?
   (e)  If the fiscal policy is bond-financed and the *LM* schedule is relatively inelastic, what is the effect of the fiscal policy on the equilibrium position?
   (f)  Identify the extent of crowding out in each of these situations.
   (g)  What determines the elasticity of the *LM* schedule?
   (h)  How could the authorities arrange policy in order to achieve the 'full multiplier' effect?

9   Figure 25-5 (opposite) illustrates the effects of a restrictive monetary policy on equilibrium income and interest rate under alternative assumptions about the slope of the *IS* schedule. Monetary policy is here represented by a movement of the *LM* schedule from *LM0* to *LM1*.
   (a)  What is the initial equilibrium income and interest rate?
   (b)  What could have caused the move from *LM0* to *LM1*?
   (c)  What is the effect of monetary policy on the equilibrium when the *IS* schedule is relatively steep?
   (d)  What is the effect when *IS* is relatively flat?
   (e)  What factors determine the steepness of the *IS* curve and hence the effectiveness of monetary policy?

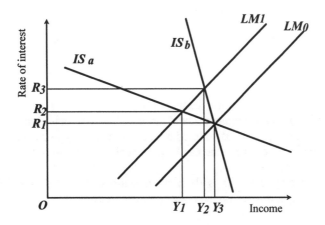

**Figure 25-5    Monetary policy**

**10** It has been argued that individuals realize that reductions in direct taxation in the present will have to be offset by higher taxes in the future, which will have to be paid by them or by their children. This means that tax cuts do not really affect real income in the long run, so consumption plans should not be affected. This argument is known as 'Ricardian equivalence'.

A number of objections have been raised to this line of argument, some of which are listed below.

Which of them may have some validity?

*(a)* Ricardian equivalence implies that government spending on roads has no effect, which is obviously false.

*(b)* Future higher taxes may only be imposed after present taxpayers are dead.

*(c)* There may be breakdowns in intergeneration transfers.

*(d)* Marginal taxes drive distortionary wedges between the price paid and the price received, which may have supply-side effects.

*(e)* There are capital market imperfections which effectively ensure that the government can borrow at a lower interest rate than private citizens.

**11** Suppose you are given the following information:

It is estimated that individuals who receive an increase in disposable income will treat 80 per cent of the increase as being likely to be sustained into the future, and the other 20 per cent as transitory. The marginal propensity to consume out of permanent income is 0.93. Consumption at a zero level of permanent income is estimated to be zero.

*(a)* Give an algebraic expression for consumption.

*(b)* Last year permanent income was £15,000. This year disposable income rose to £25,000. What is this year's estimate of permanent income?

*(c)* What is the marginal propensity to consume out of current income?

*(d)* What do these marginal propensities imply about the Keynesian multiplier for government expenditure and the effectiveness of fiscal policy? (Ignore taxes and the foreign sector.)

## True/False

**1** An increase in transitory income may not have any effect on current consumption.

**2** Tax cuts lead to an increase in current consumption.

**3** The interest rate is the only determinant of investment.

**4** A higher interest rate increases the present value of the expected profit stream from an investment project and hence leads to an increase in investment.

**5** Leasing arrangements and the use of the stock market to finance investment reduce the usefulness of the investment demand schedule in analysing investment decisions.

6    Changes in the rate of interest affect the position of the aggregate demand schedule in the income-expenditure model.

7    When we take into account the money market and interest rate effects, the multiplier on government spending is enhanced.

8    Movements along the *IS* schedule tell us about shifts in equilibrium income caused by shifts in the aggregate demand schedule as a result only of changes in interest rates.

9    The position of the *LM* schedule depends on the price level.

10   Monetary and fiscal policy affect aggregate demand through different routes but have very similar effects.

11   The Heath government in the early 1970s adopted a mix of easy money and easy fiscal policy in an attempt to increase the rate of economic growth, whereas both monetary and fiscal policy were tight during the early years of the first Thatcher administration.

12   The Keynesian model developed so far is deficient because it overemphasizes the demand side of the economy, holds prices fixed, and relies on the existence of spare capacity.

## ECONOMICS IN THE NEWS

### City warns of further interest rate rises
*(Adapted from The Independent, 14 January 2000)*

Interest rates could rise again as early as next month, City experts said after yesterday's widely predicted quarter-point increase. But the cost of borrowing is unlikely to climb much beyond the current 5.75 per cent level. Most analysts believe the highest that rates will climb is around 6.5 per cent.

In its statement, the Bank of England indicated that the pace of growth had triggered the move. It said that, since last month's meeting of the Monetary Policy Committee, the world economy had strengthened, and increases in wealth, income and household borrowing suggested consumer demand at home would remain strong.

The British Chambers of Commerce described the interest rate increase from 5.5 per cent to 5.75 per cent as a 'disappointing blow', while the Engineering Employers' Federation said that interest rate increases were 'hindering essential long-term investment'. Sir Ken Jackson of the AEEU, the largest manufacturing union, said: 'My chief concern is that this rate rise will weaken confidence at a time when manufacturing is starting to recover.'

On the other hand, Digby Jones, the new CBI director-general, said: 'We recognise there is a risk to the inflation target if economic growth is not checked a little. It is better to nudge the tiller now rather than make a major change at a later date.'

None of the main mortgage lenders increased their loan rates immediately but they are expected to do so before long. Michael Saunders, an economist at Salomon Smith Barney, said the housing market meant that UK rates needed to stay relatively high when the economy expanded. If rates were the same as in Germany, he said: 'German households would probably buy bonds, whereas UK households would go to the nearest estate agent, borrow lots of money, buy houses and set a house-price boom in motion.'

1    Explain why high interest rates may be linked to the level of consumer demand.
2    Why might high interest rates hinder long-term investment?
3    The passage argues that there are differences in consumer preferences between German and UK households. Why would this difference be significant?

## Questions for Thought

1    According to the permanent income hypothesis, individuals would not be expected to alter their consumption plans in response to a purely transitory change in income.
    *(a)* How would you expect individuals to react to a temporary reduction in income? Under what circumstances might they be unable to respond in this way?
    *(b)* Suppose the government runs a budget deficit by introducing tax cuts, with the policy being funded by borrowing. How would you expect rational consumers to react?

2  *(a)* How may a firm compare alternative investment projects with different capital costs, different expected income streams, and different expected economic lives?
   *(b)* How would a rise in the rate of interest affect firms' decisions to invest?

3  This exercise requires some facility with simple algebra. Suppose that the following equations represent behaviour in the goods and money markets of a fixed price closed economy:

*Goods market*

Consumption:  $C = A + c(Y - T) - dR$
Investment:   $I = B - iR$
Taxes:        $T = tY$
Equilibrium:  $Y = C + I + G$

*Money market*

Money supply:  $Ms = \bar{M}$
Money demand:  $Md = kPY + N - mR$
Equilibrium:   $Ms = Md$

where $A$ = autonomous consumption, $B$ = autonomous investment, $C$ = consumption, $G$ = government expenditure, $I$ = investment, $M$ = real money, $N$ = autonomous money demand, $P$ = price level, $R$ = rate of interest (%), $T$ = net taxes, $Y$ = income, output. Lower-case letters denote parameters of the model.

(a) Derive an expression for the *IS* curve, i.e. use the equations for the goods market to find a relationship between $Y$ and $R$.

*(b)* Derive an expression for the *LM* curve.

*(c)* Suppose the variables and parameters in the model take the following values:

$A = 700; B = 400; c = 0.8; d = 5; G = 649.6; i = 15; k = 0.25; \bar{M} = 1200; m = 10; N = 200; P = 1; t = 0.2$

Plot *IS* and *LM* curves and read off the approximate equilibrium values of income and the rate of interest.

*(d)* For these equilibrium values, calculate consumption and investment, and confirm that the goods market is in equilibrium.

*(e)* Check that the money market is also in equilibrium.

*(f)* Calculate the government budget deficit or surplus.

# 26 Aggregate Supply, the Price Level, and the Speed of Adjustment

## Learning Outcomes

- To derive the macroeconomic demand schedule, explaining the roles of the real balance effect and the credit channel
- To examine how labour supply and labour demand lead to labour market equilibrium
- To analyse determinants of the equilibrium or natural rate of unemployment
- To show how the equilibrium price level is determined in the classical mode
- To explain why price adjustment, and especially wage adjustment, may be not be rapid
- To use short-run and long-run aggregate supply to trace out the adjustment process
- To explore the effect of a supply shock, both in the short run and the long run

**IN THIS CHAPTER ...** you will see how macroeconomic equilibrium can be attained in a model with flexible prices. The classical model allows both wages and prices to be flexible, so we always end up at full employment. The labour market is added to the model, and *aggregate supply* is seen as the result of interaction between goods and labour markets. We continue to use the *IS-LM* model to ensure goods and money market equilibrium, but recognize that the position of the *LM* curve depends on real money supply, which in turn depends on the price level. This provides a crucial link between price and aggregate demand through the real money supply. As price changes, *LM* moves and hence leads to a new equilibrium level of aggregate demand. The locus of such combinations of price and aggregate demand is known as the macroeconomic demand schedule *(MDS)*, which slopes downwards, reflecting that, as price changes, we slide along the *IS* schedule. This is reinforced by the real balance effect. The intersection of *aggregate supply* and the *MDS* shows the equilibrium price level. Monetary and fiscal policy can now be re-examined.

## Important Concepts and Technical Terms

Match each lettered concept with the appropriate numbered phrase:

| | | |
|---|---|---|
| *(a)* Aggregate supply schedule | *(g)* Involuntary unemployment | *(l)* Lay-off |
| *(b)* Business cycle | *(h)* Real balance effect | *(m)* Price level |
| *(c)* Overtime and short-time | *(i)* Short-run aggregate supply schedule | *(n)* The natural rate of unemployment |
| *(d)* Job acceptance schedule | *(j)* Registered unemployment | |
| *(e)* Voluntary unemployment | *(k)* Labour force schedule | |
| *(f)* Money illusion | | |

1  The average price of all the goods produced in the economy.
2  A schedule showing how many people choose to be in the labour force at each real wage.
3  A temporary separation of workers from a firm.
4  The increase in autonomous consumption demand when the value of consumers' real money balances increases.
5  A schedule which shows the prices charged by firms at each output level, given the wages they have to pay.
6  A schedule which shows the quantity of output that firms wish to supply at each price level.
7  A situation in which people confuse nominal and real variables.
8  The percentage of the labour force that is unemployed when the labour market is in equilibrium.
9  A schedule showing how many workers choose to accept jobs at each real wage.
10  The number of people without jobs who are registered as seeking a job.
11  Devices used by firms to vary labour input without affecting numbers employed.
12  The tendency for output and employment to fluctuate around their long-term trends.
13  A situation in which some people have chosen not to work at the going wage rate.
14  A situation in which some people would like to work at the going real wage but cannot find a job.

# Exercises

1  This exercise explores the relationship between price and aggregate demand. Figure 26-1 shows an economy's *IS* and *LM* schedules. The economy begins in equilibrium with *IS0* and *LM0* being the relevant schedules.

*(a)* Identify equilibrium income, interest rate, and aggregate demand.

Suppose the price level rises to a new level:

*(b)* Which of the *LM* schedules is appropriate?

*(c)* In the absence of the real balance effect, identify the new equilibrium levels of income, interest rate, and aggregate demand.

*(d)* Explain and identify the influence of the real-balance effect.

*(e)* Repeat parts *(b)*, *(c)*, and *(d)* for a fall in price level from its original level.

*(f)* Explain why the price level affects the position of the *LM* curve.

*(g)* Draw a diagram to illustrate the macroeconomic demand schedule with and without the real balance effect.

2  Which of the following characteristics are valid for all points along the macroeconomic demand schedule? Note: more than one response may be valid.

*(a)* Planned spending equals actual output.

*(b)* Planned demand for real money balances is equal to nominal money supply divided by the price level.

*(c)* Demanders of goods receive the quantities they want to buy.

*(d)* The money market is in equilibrium.

*(e)* There is no disequilibrium in the goods market.

3  Figure 26-2 shows the labour market of an economy. *LD* is labour demand, *AJ* is the job acceptances schedule, and *LF* the labour force schedule.

*(a)* What is the equilibrium real wage?

*(b)* Identify the level of employment and registered unemployment.

*(c)* In this situation, what is the natural rate of unemployment, and the quantity of involuntary unemployment?

Suppose the real wage is at *OA:*

*(d)* Identify the level of unemployment, registered unemployment, and quantity of involuntary unemployment.

*(e)* How will the market react?

Suppose now the real wage is at *OC:*

*(f)* Identify the level of employment, registered unemployment, and quantity of involuntary unemployment.

*(g)* How will the market react?

*(h)* Explain why there should be a connection between employment and aggregate supply.

*(i)* What are the implications for aggregate supply if the labour market is always in equilibrium?

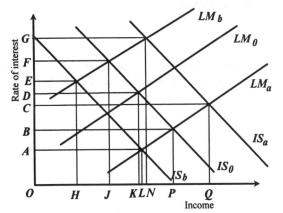

**Figure 26-1    Price and aggregate demand**

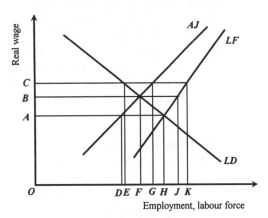

**Figure 26-2    The labour market**

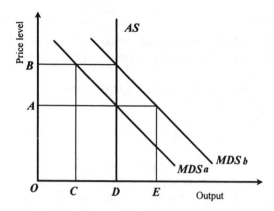

**Figure 26-3   Monetary and fiscal policy**

4   This exercises examines monetary and fiscal policy, using the *MDS* and the aggregate supply schedule. Figure 26-3 shows two macroeconomic demand schedules (*MDSa* and *MDSb*) and the aggregate supply schedule *(AS)*. First, we consider the effects of monetary policy in the classical model – specifically, an increase in nominal money supply.
(a) Identify the 'before' and 'after' *MDS*.
(b) What was the original equilibrium price and output?
(c) What is equilibrium price and output after the policy is implemented?
Next, consider fiscal policy – again in the classical model. Suppose there is a reduction in government expenditure:
(d) Identify the 'before' and 'after' *MDS*.
(e) What was the original equilibrium price and output?
(f) What is the equilibrium price and output after the policy is implemented?
The Keynesian model is characterized by sluggish adjustment. Consider the period *after* the policy but *before* adjustment begins:
(g) Identify price and output.
(h) The *MDS* represents points at which goods and money markets are in equilibrium. In the position you have identified in *(g)*, adjustment has still to take place – so in what sense is the goods market in 'equilibrium'?

5   Consider the following factors. Explore which of them encourage and which discourage rapid adjustment in the labour market. For each of the factors, state whether you expect firms or workers mainly to be affected.
(a) The costs of job search.
(b) Lack of redundancy agreement.
(c) Predominantly unskilled workforce.
(d) Production process well suited to short-time or overtime working.
(e) Concern of firm for its reputation as an employer.
(f) Unemployment at low level.
(g) Acquisition of firm-specific skills.

6   The following symptoms describe the response of an economy to a leftward movement of *either* the demand *or* the supply schedule, in a situation where adjustment is not instantaneous. In each case, deduce whether the shock was to the demand side or the supply side:
(a) A short-run fall in the price level.
(b) Lower long-run output.
(c) No short-run change in price.
(d) Price lower in the long run.
(e) A short-run fall in output.
(f) No long-run change in output.
(g) Price higher in the long run.
(h) Output unchanged in the short run.

7   Which of the following factors would you expect to affect the demand side of the economy and which the supply side? State whether each leads to an increase or a decrease in demand (or supply):
   *(a)* An increase in the number of married women going out to work.
   *(b)* An increase in the price of a vital imported raw material.
   *(c)* An increase in business confidence.
   *(d)* An autonomous increase in money wages.
   *(e)* A fall in nominal money supply.
   *(f)* A shift in the distribution of income from rich to poor.
   *(g)* An increase in the demand for leisure.

8   Consider an economy in which the aggregate supply curve is perfectly inelastic. Which of the following would result from an increase in aggregate demand?
   *(a)* An increase in production.
   *(b)* A decrease in production.
   *(c)* An increase in prices.
   *(d)* An increase in real income.
   *(e)* An increase in money income.

9   Consider an economy in which all resources are fully employed. Which of the following would result in a rise in the general level of prices?
   *(a)* An increase in demand for the country's exports.
   *(b)* An increase in government expenditure.
   *(c)* An increase in personal consumption.
   *(d)* A fall in the productivity of labour.

10  This exercise explores the effects on price and output of a once-for-all increase in nominal money supply in the short, medium, and long runs. These effects are to be examined using Figure 26-4, in which *AS* is aggregate supply, *SASa,b,c* are short-run aggregate supply schedules, and *MDSa,b* are macroeconomic demand schedules.
   *(a)* If Figure 26-4 is to be used to analyse the policy described, and if the economy begins in equilibrium, what are the initial levels of price and output?
   *(b)* How would the economy react to the increase in nominal money supply according to a classical model? Assume that adjustment is sluggish:
   *(c)* Identify the initial reaction of price and output and explain how it comes about.
   *(d)* Using Figure 26-4, describe how adjustment begins and identify the position of the economy in the medium term.
   *(e)* What is the final position of the economy when all adjustment is complete?
   *(f)* Draw a diagram showing how the adjustment process is mirrored in the labour market.
   *(g)* Do you expect adjustment to this change to be slower or more rapid than adjustment to a decrease in nominal money supply?
   *(h)* If the increase in nominal money supply were 10 per cent, what would be the eventual percentage increase in the price level?

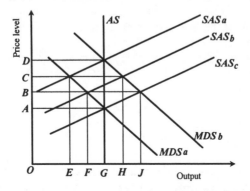

**Figure 26-4    An increase in nominal money supply**

## True/False

1   The position of the *MDS* depends upon the nominal money supply, government spending, and all other variables relevant to the level of aggregate demand.
2   The real balance effect is the decrease in autonomous consumption demand when the value of consumers' real money balances decreases.
3   Full employment is achieved when there is no unemployment.
4   Money illusion is when people are tricked by forged banknotes.
5   The labour market is in equilibrium anywhere on the classical aggregate supply schedule.
6   In the classical model a change in nominal money supply leads to an equivalent percentage change in nominal wages and the price level.
7   Fiscal policy in the classical model leads mainly to an increase in price and only to a modest increase in output.
8   Sluggish wage adjustment is the most likely cause of a slow adjustment of price to changes in aggregate demand.
9   In the short run firms adjust to an increase in labour demand by hiring additional workers.
10  In the model developed in this chapter, the labour market bears the brunt of any short-run disequilibrium.
11  An increase in full-capacity output resulting from a favourable supply shift leads to a higher price and output.
12  In the UK, the supply shocks of 1973 and 1979 were quickly followed by sharp rises in the unemployment rate.

## ECONOMICS IN THE NEWS

### Japan's monetary dilemmas
*(Adapted from The Financial Times, 27 October 1999)*

To print or not to print, that is the question facing Japan's newly independent central bank and its once almighty Ministry of Finance. Japan's monetary dilemmas are as significant as they are fascinating – significant, because this is the world's second-largest economy, and fascinating, because Japan's monetary predicament is unprecedented in the post-war period.

Can the world ask the bank of Japan for still more monetary easing? Yes, like Oliver Twist, it can ask, because it is still hungry. True, nominal interest rates are as low as can be. Yet many indicators suggest monetary conditions have been too tight, rather than too lax. The exchange rate has appreciated by just under 40 per cent since August 1998. Broad money has grown only 3.3 per cent in the year to September. But perhaps the clearest indicator is the persistently sluggish growth of nominal demand. Japan's long-term growth potential is about 2 per cent per year. Even with inflation as low as 1 per cent, nominal demand should be growing at 3 per cent. But it has grown by less than this is every year since 1991, except for 1996.

The Bank's monetary policy board stated this year that its aim was to provide 'the utmost support for economic activity, in order to avoid possible intensification of deflationary pressure and to ensure that the economic downturn will come to a halt'. However, prices have been falling for most of the past 6 years, once allowance is made for the failure of the indices to measure quality improvements. Given this, merely 'to avoid intensification of deflationary pressure' is hardly sufficient.

The Bank argues that deliberate efforts to expand the money supply, beyond that generated beyond its zero-interest rate policies, would be ineffective or dangerous. It would be ineffective because an expansion in bank reserves may not generate any rise in lending.

### Japan tries to jump-start economy
*(Adapted from The Financial Times, 21 December 1999)*

Japan's finance ministry yesterday submitted the country's largest budget, worth Y84,990bn (£512bn) for the next fiscal year. The budget, up 3.8 per cent on this year's, is intended to bolster Japan's stuttering economy, which is in danger of slipping back into a technical recession. Government spending next year will require record issuance of Japanese government debt, and confirm the country as having the worst gross debt as a proportion of gross domestic product among members of the OECD.

'We are crafting a budget to jump-start a full economic recovery,' said Kiichi Miyazawa, finance minister. 'The economic upturn is not yet self-sustaining.' He warned that this would be the last expansionary budget, as Japan could not continue to spend.

The need for government spending was underlined by economic data yesterday. New machine tool orders fell 10.6 per cent year on year during November, underlining weak domestic capital investment.

1   Explain how the policies described in the two passages hope to tackle the problem of recession, and the problems that might be entailed with each.
2   Which strategy seems likely to have the best chance of success?

## Questions for Thought

1   (a)   Explain how cuts in money wages lead to higher output if real wages are initially set at too high a level. Suppose an economy is in $IS$–$LM$ equilibrium, as shown in Figure 26-5. $LMa$ shows the initial $LM$ schedule, $LMb$ shows how the $LM$ schedule moves when the price level falls. $IS$ is the $IS$ schedule, $Y_0$ is equilibrium income, $R_0$ the equilibrium interest rate, and $Y_{fe}$ represents full employment.
    (b)   Re-examine the story you told in part (a). Why might the cut in money wages fail to restore full employment?
    (c)   How might the story be affected if account is taken of the real balance effect?
    (d)   Wopuld you expect fiscal policy to be more or less effective than monetary policy in this situation?
2   The Keynesian concept of the 'liquidity trap' refers to which of the following?
    (a)   The inability of businesses with poor profit performances to obtain funds on loan for investment.
    (b)   The international problems of insufficient funds to finance any growth in world trade and payments.
    (c)   The downward inflexibility of interest rates as the money supply expands above a certain level.
    (d)   The disincentive of high income tax rates on savers depositing money with commercial banks or building societies.
3   In Chapter 25 we saw that 'both fiscal and monetary policy were tight during the early years of the first Thatcher government' (Section 25-6 of the main text). Using the model developed in this chapter, investigate why this policy stance may impose costs on society in the short run. In what respects is the model still deficient in its application to the real world?

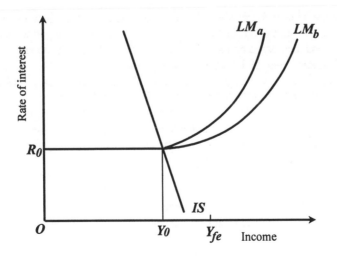

**Figure 26-5   The liquidity trap**

# 27 Unemployment

## Learning Outcomes

- To distinguish classical, frictional, and structural unemployment
- To define voluntary and involuntary unemployment
- To explore determinants of the changing UK unemployment rate
- To assess the success of tax cuts and other supply-side policies in reducing the natural rate of unemployment
- To discuss the private and the social costs of unemployment, and relate them to the source of unemployment
- To discuss the concept of hysteresis and outline channels through which a temporary recession could permanently reduce aggregate supply

**IN THIS CHAPTER ...** you will analyse *unemployment*. The *classical model*, with its emphasis on flexibility, adjustment to full-employment equilibrium, and voluntary unemployment re-emerged at a time when conditions favoured its widespread adoption. The adverse OPEC supply shock of 1979–80 triggered widespread unemployment. In the UK the unemployment rate rose to 1930s levels. Even when unemployment is relatively high, there are typically still substantial flows into and out of unemployment. Various explanations for unemployment will be explored – *frictional, structural, demand-deficient* and *'classical'* unemployment. Also important is the notion of the *natural rate of unemployment* – the rate that occurs when the labour market is in equilibrium. *Supply-side policies* involve the use of microeconomic incentives to affect the level of full employment output.

## Important Concepts and Technical Terms

Match each lettered concept with the appropriate numbered phrase:

*(a)* Replacement ratio
*(b)* Supply-side economics
*(c)* Private cost of unemployment
*(d)* Structural unemployment
*(e)* Discouraged workers
*(f)* Demand-deficient unemployment
*(g)* Hysteresis
*(h)* Social cost of unemployment
*(i)* Frictional unemployment
*(j)* Long-term unemployed
*(k)* Natural rate of unemployment
*(l)* Classical unemployment

1  Those members of the labour force who have remained in unemployment for a time span measured in months rather than weeks – in the UK in 1990, 40 per cent of the unemployed were so classified.
2  People who have become depressed about the prospects of ever finding a job and decide to stop looking.
3  The rate of unemployment when the labour market is in equilibrium.
4  Unemployment which occurs when aggregate demand falls and wages and prices have not yet adjusted to restore full employment – sometimes known as Keynesian unemployment.
5  The ratio of unemployment or supplementary benefit that an unemployed worker gets from the government (transfer payments) relative to the average after-tax earnings of people in work.
6  The unemployment created when the wage is deliberately maintained above the level at which the labour supply and labour demand schedules intersect.
7  The irreducible minimum level of unemployment in a dynamic society: comprising people who are almost unemployable or are spending short spells in unemployment while between jobs.
8  The cost to an worker of being out of work, the largest component being the wage forgone by not working.
9  The use of microeconomic incentives to alter the level of full employment, the level of potential output, and the natural rate of unemployment.
10  A situation experienced by an economy when its long-run equilibrium depends upon the path it has followed in the short run.
11  The cost to society of being below full employment, including lost output and human suffering.
12  Unemployment arising from a mismatch of skills and job opportunities as the pattern of demand and production changes.

## Exercises

1  Remember the economy of Hypothetica? They're now having unemployment problems. Below are presented some data on the flows in the labour market in a particular year. ('Real' data on some of these flows are hard to come by, so any resemblance between these numbers and those for any real economy you know about is purely fortuitous.) Data are in thousands.

At the beginning of the year the labour force is 26 900, of whom 2900 are unemployed. We also have:

| | | |
|---|---|---|
| (i) | Discouraged workers | 600 |
| (ii) | Job-losers/lay-offs | 1500 |
| (iii) | Retiring, temporarily leaving | 100 |
| (iv) | Quits | 700 |
| (v) | New hires, recalls | 2000 |
| (vi) | Re-entrants, new entrants | 500 |
| (vii) | Taking a job (not previously unemployed) | 100 |

(a) How many workers joined and left the unemployed during the year?
(b) How many people joined and left the labour force during the year?
(c) How did the size of the unemployed labour force change during the year?
(d) Calculate the size of total labour force and unemployment at the end of the year.
(e) In the UK in 1998, unemployment began the year at 1.36 million. During the year, 3.16 million joined the register, 3.25 million left it. What would this suggest for the level of unemployment at the end of the year?

2  State whether each of the following reasons for unemployment would be classified as frictional, structural, demand-deficient, or classical, and which represent voluntary or involuntary unemployment:

(a) Unemployment resulting from the decline of the textile industry and expansion of the microcomputer industry.
(b) Individuals between jobs.
(c) People whose physical or mental handicaps render them unemployable.
(d) Unemployment resulting from the real wage being too high for labour market equilibrium.
(e) Unemployment arising from slow adjustment following a reduction in aggregate demand.

3  Table 27-1 presents unemployment rates as a percentage of the national average for the standard regions in Great Britain for 1974, 1989, and 1996. Health warning: this question requires thought!

(a) The figures in the table are ranked in ascending order of unemployment in 1974. Comment on the major differences and similarities revealed in the 1989 and 1996 rankings.
(b) How does the analysis of types of unemployment help you to think about why these regional disparities have arisen and persist through time?

Table 27-1   Regional unemployment rate as a percentage of the national (GB) average

| Region | 1974 (%) | 1989 (%) | 1996 (%) |
|---|---|---|---|
| South East | 60 | 65 | 96 |
| East Anglia | 80 | 60 | 77 |
| West Midlands | 84 | 105 | 101 |
| East Midlands | 88 | 90 | 95 |
| Yorkshire & Humberside | 104 | 123 | 109 |
| South West | 108 | 87 | 85 |
| North West | 136 | 137 | 108 |
| Wales | 148 | 124 | 105 |
| Scotland | 156 | 152 | 103 |
| North | 180 | 160 | 131 |
| Great Britain | 100 | 100 | 100 |

Source: *Economic Trends Annual Supplement.*

4    Table 27-2 shows how labour demand and supply vary with the real wage in a small economy. Suppose the real wage is fixed at $5 per hour:
   *(a)* What is the level of employment?
   *(b)* Calculate the level of unemployment.
   *(c)* How much of the unemployment is involuntary and how much is voluntary?
   Suppose now that workers base their decisions on take-home pay, that the real wage is flexible, and that workers are paying $2 in income tax:
   *(d)* What is the equilibrium wage as paid by firms and the net take-home pay of those employed?
   *(e)* What are the levels of employment and unemployment? Is there excess demand for labour?
   *(f)* How much of the unemployment is involuntary and how much is voluntary?
   Finally, suppose that income tax is removed:
   *(g)* What is the equilibrium real wage?
   *(h)* What are the levels of employment and unemployment? By how much has unemployment changed?
   *(i)* How much of the remaining unemployment is involuntary and how much is voluntary?

5    Suppose that a labour market begins in equilibrium. We are to investigate the effects of a change in real oil prices such as happened in the 1970s, causing many energy-intensive firms to become economically obsolete. The effects of this on the labour market are shown in Figure 27-1.
   *(a)* If Figure 27-1 is to illustrate the situation described, which of the labour demand schedules *LDa* and *LDb* represents the initial position? Explain your answer.
   *(b)* Identify the equilibrium levels of employment and the real wage in this initial position.
   *(c)* What is the natural rate of unemployment?
   Now suppose that the oil price shock occurs.
   *(d)* Assume that the real wage fails to adjust immediately – identify the levels of employment and unemployment.
   *(e)* As real wages adjust, to what equilibrium values of employment and the real wage will the market tend?
   *(f)* What will be the natural rate of unemployment?
   *(g)* Has the natural rate increased, decreased, or stayed the same? Why should that be?

6    Which of the following factors may have contributed to the rise in the natural rate of unemployment in the UK after the 1970s?
   *(a)* An increase in unemployment benefits.
   *(b)* A decline in international competitiveness.
   *(c)* An increase in trade union power.
   *(d)* A decline in world trade.
   *(e)* The recession in British manufacturing industry.
   *(f)* Technical progress.
   *(g)* A decrease in the participation rate of married women.
   *(h)* Changes in employers' labour taxes.

**Table 27-2   Labour demand and supply (in thousands)**

| Real wage ($/hour) | Labour demand | Job acceptances | Labour force |
|---|---|---|---|
| 1 | 130 | 70 | 101 |
| 2 | 120 | 80 | 108 |
| 3 | 110 | 90 | 115 |
| 4 | 100 | 100 | 122 |
| 5 | 90 | 110 | 129 |
| 6 | 80 | 120 | 136 |

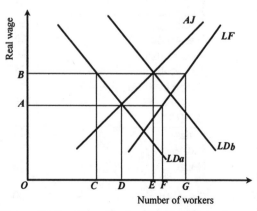

**Figure 27-1   The effects of a supply shock**

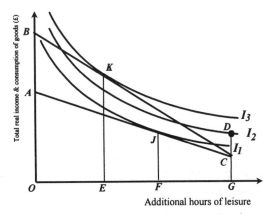

**Figure 27-2    Income tax and the supply of labour**

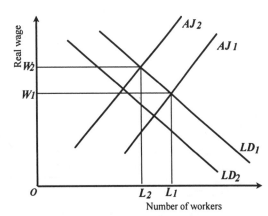

**Figure 27-3    The effects of hysteresis**

7  Below are listed a number of policies which could be used to reduce (or prevent a rise in) the long-run rate of unemployment. In each case, explain the disadvantages of the policy.
   *(a)* Force firms to make high redundancy payments to discourage firms from sacking workers too readily.
   *(b)* The reduction or elimination of unemployment benefit.
   *(c)* Wages cut by an incomes policy.
   *(d)* An expansionary fiscal policy.
   *(e)* Subsidize manufacturing industry.

8  This exercise involves an application of indifference curves, which we first encountered early on in the book. You may wish to remind yourself of their application to labour supply (see Section 12-4 of the main text). Figure 27-2 is to be used to analyse the effects of a cut in the rate of income tax on the supply of labour by an individual (Jayne). $I_1$, $I_2$, and $I_3$ are indifference curves depicting Jayne's preferences for income and leisure. *ACD* and *BCD* are alternative budget lines, which assume that Jayne receives some non-labour income, some of which must be given up if she chooses to work. The horizontal axis is labelled 'additional' hours of leisure as Jayne never chooses to have less than 12 hours of leisure daily.
   *(a)* How would you expect a cut in the income tax rate to affect the budget lines?
   *(b)* This being so, which must be the initial budget line in our story?
   *(c)* Identify Jayne's initial choice point.
   *(d)* At this point, what is Jayne's total income? How many hours does she work?
   *(e)* Identify Jayne's choice point after the income tax cut. How many hours does she now work?

9  Figure 27-3 shows the changing conditions in an economy's labour market. Suppose that this market has moved from an initial equilibrium in which employment was $L_1$ and the real wage was $W_1$, and has now settled at a new long-run equilibrium with employment $L_2$ and real wage $W_2$. *LD* represents labour demand, and *AJ* is the job acceptances schedule. Notice that employment is lower in this final situation. Which of the following arguments could explain the situation?
   *(a)* A temporary recession increases unemployment and discourages potential workers from looking for jobs. This carries over even when the recession is over.
   *(b)* Firms reduce capital stock during a recession, so that labour demand fails to readjust fully when the recession is over.
   *(c)* A recession makes workers less enthusiastic about job search and reduces firms' need to advertise for workers. Previous levels of job search are not recaptured after the recession.
   *(d)* Wage-bargaining is carried out by employed workers (insiders). A recession reduces employment and this situation is exploited by the still-employed workers in negotiating higher real wages for themselves at the recession's end.

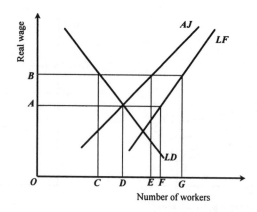

**Figure 27-4    Classical and demand-deficient unemployment**

10  This exercise explores some of the differences between classical and demand-deficient unemployment within our labour market diagram (Figure 27-4).
   *(a)* Identify the equilibrium real wage, employment, and the natural rate of unemployment.
   Now we consider classical unemployment, which is readily shown in Figure 27-4. Suppose that the real wage is stuck at *OB*.
   *(b)* Identify labour demand and the amounts of voluntary and involuntary unemployment.
   This much we have seen already – but how may we show demand-deficient unemployment? We have seen that this unemployment results from sluggish adjustment. Suppose that prices and wages are rigid in the short run, with the price level at too high a level to clear the goods market.
   *(c)* Firms see stocks building up but cannot adjust price immediately – how do they react?
   *(d)* Suppose that the real wage is at *OA*, but firms reduce output to prevent the build-up of stocks, so employ only *OC* workers. Identify the amounts of voluntary and involuntary unemployment.
   *(e)* How does this affect households' incomes?

## True/False

1   The ONS publishes accurate monthly figures of the number of people who are unemployed in the UK.
2   The unemployment rate is lower for women than for men.
3   Minimum wage legislation may result in classical unemployment.
4   The natural rate of unemployment is entirely composed of voluntary unemployment.
5   Shortening the working week and sharing out the work amongst more people is a long-run solution to unemployment.
6   The actual rate of unemployment is always close to the natural rate.
7   A major reason for the increase in unemployment in the UK in recent years has been the changing composition of the labour force, with increasing numbers of young workers and women seeking employment.
8   In the long run the performance of the economy can be changed only by affecting the level of full employment and the corresponding level of potential output.
9   Government expenditure on extra police officers will add less to employment than an equivalent increase in the value of spending on nuclear electricity.
10  When unemployment is involuntary, the case for active policy is stronger, as the private costs are higher.
11  Unemployment is always a bad thing.
12  Freedom of choice is important, so if people choose to be unemployed, society need not be concerned about voluntary unemployment.

# ECONOMICS IN THE NEWS

## 1 Compulsory dress code and tests for job seekers
*(Adapted from The Guardian, 12 January 2000)*

Unemployed people facing job interviews will be forced to take lessons on how to present themselves under an overhaul of the government's flagship New Deal employment programme. A strict dress code will be introduced, with special funds available to help applicants buy suits to impress potential employers. Smart clothing will also be available on loan.

The measures were unveiled yesterday as part of a clampdown on a hard core of the long-term unemployed who refuse work or who lack any of the basic skills that are demanded by companies. Job seekers who decline to take the lessons will have their £40 a week benefit stopped for 14 days, rising to a month if they continue to turn down a place, employment minister Tessa Jowell said. Revealing a 10-point plan, including literacy and numeracy tests, self-presentation lessons, and job coaches, she said a significant number of people were still held back by a poor education.

Appalled by figures which showed that 40% of young people on the ground-breaking programme lacked basic skills, ministers have decided that every person taking part will be screened for learning problems. But they will also be told to dress more snappily. 'First impressions count and the standard dress for interviews is a suit for men and something equally smart for women,' a spokesman at the employment department said. 'We will make funds available for people who have no smart clothes, although it might be possible to get them on loan.' The overhaul, on the second anniversary of the scheme, follows complaints from employers that a lack of basic skills, and a negative attitude in job interviews, are holding job seekers back. Special 'outreach' programmes will also be developed to help people in areas of high unemployment, deprived neighbourhoods and from ethnic minorities. Mrs Jowell said the New Deal had helped almost 170,000 people from long-term unemployment into work. But there were still significant numbers on the programme whose lack of basic skills was preventing them finding a job. The employment department acknowledged it was dealing with people with serious skill shortages, some of whom 'cannot read or write ... they will need a lot of help before they even start applying for jobs.'

One criticism of the programme is that many of those placed in employment would have found jobs anyway. As a result, critics said, the New Deal had failed to help the most disadvantaged. Paul Convery, director of the Independent Unemployment Unit, said that while the programme had been largely successful, it had failed to put 40% of participants into lasting jobs. 'As unemployment is falling, you are ending up not with an easier target but with a tougher challenge: the people now left unemployed are the harder to get into work,' he said.

Mrs Jowell, who presented people from 12 New Deal pilot areas to the prime minister, said some young people had gone from unemployment to management in less than two years and been placed on a 'ladder of opportunity'.

One of those meeting ministers was Daniel Roper, who joined a printing company at Newquay, Cornwall, two years ago, aged 19, after being unemployed for a year. He now manages one of the firm's three shops. John Jay, his employer, immediately bought him smart business clothes. 'Appearances count a lot,' said John's wife, Chrissie, who helps run the business, which has taken on two more New Dealers. 'He's a very dependable lad. We've been very fortunate.'

1    In the passage, what policies are recommended for reducing the level of unemployment?
2    Evaluate the extent to which these policies have a basis in economic reasoning.

## 2 Jobless figures create credibility gap
*(Adapted from the Financial Times, 17 April 1997)*

The measurement of UK unemployment continues to be a source of bitter political controversy as yesterday's row over the latest fall in the registered jobless total indicates. But the credibility of the official figures has been severely undermined. 'Public concern over the validity of unemployment statistics will not go away until the next government takes steps to improve their basis,' Professor Adrian Smith, president of the Royal Statistical

Society, said yesterday. He believes no single figure of unemployment can 'do justice to the complexity of the labour market'.

The difficulty lies in the character of the headline figures that the government uses each month to support its assertion that the labour market is booming. These figures are based on the records of those who claim benefits for being out of work from Employment Service offices. Since May 1979 these statistics have been altered as many as 32 times, most recently in October 1996 as a result of the replacement of unemployment benefit by the more rigorously enforced Job Seekers' Allowance. But the leak yesterday of a government application for European Commission funds to tackle unemployment showed it had acknowledged that the benefit claimant count was 'not fully adequate'. It recognised that a number of groups were excluded from this figure, including

- many young people under the age of 18 who are not normally entitled to claim benefit because a training place is in theory open to them;
- women with a partner who is on means-tested benefit;
- women who have exhausted their insurance benefits and have no call on means-tested benefits because they have a working partner;
- men over 60 who do not have to register as job seekers.

Others excluded are unemployed people disqualified from benefit for misconduct or voluntarily leaving a job, recipients of sickness or invalidity benefit; and those who have exhausted their entitlement to the Job Seekers' Allowance after six months and fail to qualify for income-related allowances. 'The claimant count is of little help if we want to measure the under use of labour in the economy, the unmet demand for work or the social distress caused by unemployment,' said Mr Paul Convery, head of the Independent Unemployment Unit.

A wider indicator of the extent of unemployment comes from the quarterly Labour Force Survey which is based on a sample of 60,000 households. It uses the Geneva-based International Labour Organisation's definition of unemployment which covers those without a job but who have looked for work in the past four weeks and are able to start a job in two weeks. In the UK last winter, that figure was 2.11m, compared with a total of 1.74m in the claimant count.

1   How would an economist want to define unemployment? Why do we wish to do so?
2   Which of the measures discussed in the passage (the claimant count and the ILO measure) correspond most closely to what economic theory would suggests as a definition of unemployment?
3   Which of the categories of people excluded from the count would you *want* to be included?

## Questions for Thought

1   Why was unemployment in the UK higher in the 1980s than in the 1970s?
2   Suppose a society had developed in which there were generally accepted implicit agreements between firms and workers that male workers have lifetime jobs. How would you expect this to affect the nature of unemployment and the efficiency of the labour market?
3   Discuss why it is important that policy to combat unemployment must be tailored to the underlying cause.

# 28 Inflation

## Learning Outcomes

- To analyse the quantity theory of money and discuss when it implies that a higher money supply will simply cause higher prices
- To consider the relation between inflation and nominal interest rates
- To analyse seigniorage, the inflation tax, and why hyperinflations occur
- To examine whether budget deficits lead to increases in the nominal money supply
- To use long-run and short-run Phillips curves to examine the relation between inflation and unemployment
- To explain how the costs of inflation depend on whether or not it was anticipated
- To discuss how central banks independence may remove political temptations to inflate, allowing the private sector to reduce inflation expectations
- To study the Monetary Policy Committee of the Bank of England

**IN THIS CHAPTER ...** you consider *inflation*. We examine the *quantity theory of money*, suggesting a close relationship between money and prices. In this chapter we move from looking at *levels* of economic variables, and instead consider *dynamic* relationships – in particular, the relationship between the *growth* of money stock and *inflation* (the rate of change of prices). Crucial in this is whether inflation has *real* effects. The relationship between inflation and unemployment will be examined, and the importance of expectations about inflation is discussed. You will analyse the *Phillips curve*, the costs of inflation and central bank independence.

## Important Concepts and Technical Terms

Match each lettered concept with the appropriate numbered phrase:

| | | |
|---|---|---|
| *(a)* Fiscal drag | *(f)* Menu costs | *(k)* Stagflation |
| *(b)* Hyperinflation | *(g)* Fisher hypothesis | *(l)* Inflation |
| *(c)* Shoe-leather costs | *(h)* Inflation illusion | *(m)* Inflation accounting |
| *(d)* Inflation tax | *(i)* Quantity theory of money | *(n)* Seignorage |
| *(e)* Phillips curve | *(j)* Indexation | |

1 A rise in the average price of goods over time.
2 The costs imposed by inflation because physical resources are required to reprint price tags, alter slot machines, and so on.
3 A theory which states that changes in the nominal money supply lead to equivalent changes in the price level but do not have effects on output and employment; sometimes summarized in the equation $MV = PY$.
4 The increase in real tax revenue when inflation raises nominal incomes and pushes people into higher tax brackets in a progressive income tax system.
5 A period of both inflation and high unemployment, often caused by an adverse supply shock.
6 The costs imposed by inflation because high nominal interest rates induce people to economize on holding real money balances, so that society must use a greater quantity of resources in undertaking transactions.
7 The adoption of definitions of costs, revenue, profit, and loss that are fully inflation-adjusted.
8 A means of raising finance for government spending *via* the price rises that follow the printing of money.
9 A situation in which people confuse nominal and real changes, although their welfare depends on real variables, not nominal variables.
10 Periods when inflation rates are extremely high.
11 A theory by which a 1 per cent increase in inflation would be accompanied by a 1 per cent increase in nominal interest rates.
12 A process by which nominal contracts are automatically adjusted for the effects of inflation.
13 The value of real resources acquired by the government through its ability to print money.
14 A relationship showing that a higher inflation rate is accompanied by a lower unemployment rate, and vice versa. It suggests we can trade off more inflation for less unemployment, or vice versa.

## Exercises

1  The long-run position of an economy is described by the quantity theory of money

$$MV = PY$$

where $M$ = nominal money stock
$\quad V$ = the velocity of circulation
$\quad P$ = price level
$\quad Y$ = real income.

This economy does not immediately adjust to equilibrium, so we can distinguish both short-run and long-run effects. (Notice, however, that when we observe the economy it is always the case that $MV=PY$, because we define velocity as the ratio of nominal income to nominal money.) The economy begins in equilibrium. Suppose there is a demand shock – namely, a 10 per cent increase in nominal money supply used to finance an increase in government expenditure:

(a)  By what percentage will nominal income change?
(b)  Describe the effects upon real income and the price level in the short run.
(c)  Describe the effects upon real income and the price level in the long run.
Suppose now that the economy, again from equilibrium, experiences a supply shock, say, an increase in the cost of a vital raw material:
(d)  Describe the short-run effect of the supply shock.
(e)  How would the government be likely to act if its primary concern was the level of unemployment?
(f)  What effect would this policy have on the long-run equilibrium position?
(g)  How would the government have been likely to have acted if its primary concern had been the rate of inflation?
(h)  What effect would this policy have had on the long-run equilibrium position?

2  Another 'quantity theory' economy adjusts instantaneously to equilibrium, velocity of circulation being a constant 4. The following observations relate to consecutive years:

|                       | Year 1 | Year 2 |
|-----------------------|--------|--------|
| Nominal interest rate | 9      | 9      |
| Nominal money supply  | 2000   | 2200   |
| Real income           | 4000   | 4065   |

(a)  Calculate the growth rate of nominal money supply.
(b)  What was the rate of inflation between year 1 and year 2?
(c)  Calculate the real interest rate in year 2.
(d)  Calculate real money demand in each of the two years.

3  This exercise shows how taxing capital is complicated by the presence of inflation. Initially, suppose there is no inflation, a nominal interest rate of 3 per cent, and income tax levied at 30 per cent on earnings from interest. Being a money-lender, this fact is of interest to you!
Suppose you lend £5000 to a client for the purchase of a car:
(a)  Calculate your gross earnings from this transaction in the year.
(b)  For how much tax are you liable?
(c)  Calculate net earnings and the after-tax real rate of return on the deal.
Suppose now that the same deal goes through when inflation is 10 per cent per annum, but that institutions have adapted, so the market nominal interest rate is 13 per cent (i.e. the real pre-tax interest rate is still 3 per cent):
(d)  Calculate gross earnings and tax liability.
(e)  Calculate net earnings and the after-tax real rate of interest on the deal.

**Table 28-1    Inflation and unemployment, UK**

| Year | Rate of change of retail price index (% p.a.) | Unemployment rate (%) |
|---|---|---|
| 1972 | 7.3 | 3.1 |
| 1973 | 9.1 | 2.2 |
| 1974 | 16.0 | 2.1 |
| 1975 | 24.2 | 3.2 |
| 1976 | 16.5 | 4.8 |
| 1977 | 15.9 | 5.2 |
| 1978 | 8.3 | 5.1 |
| 1979 | 13.4 | 4.6 |
| 1980 | 18.0 | 5.6 |
| 1981 | 11.9 | 9.0 |
| 1982 | 8.6 | 10.4 |
| 1983 | 4.6 | 11.2 |
| 1984 | 4.9 | 11.2 |
| 1985 | 6.1 | 11.5 |
| 1986 | 3.4 | 11.6 |

Source: Calculated from data in CSO, *Economic Trends Annual Supplement*, HMSO, and Department of Employment, *Employment Gazette*.

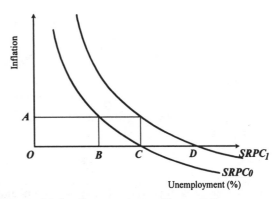

**Figure 28-1    Government policy and the Phillips curve**

4   Table 28-1 presents data on inflation and unemployment in the UK for the period 1972-86.
   *(a)* Plot a scatter diagram with inflation on the vertical axis and unemployment on the horizontal axis. You will find it helpful to mark each point with the year.
   *(b)* To what extent does your diagram support the idea of a trade-off between inflation and unemployment?
   *(c)* In the main text it was pointed out that the government of the day reacted very differently to the oil price shocks of 1973-74 and 1979-80. Use your diagram to compare the differing reactions of the economy following these supply shocks.
5   Figure 28-1 shows two short-run Phillips curves (SRPC0 and SRPC1). SRPC0 corresponds to a situation in which workers expect no inflation.
   *(a)* What is the natural rate of unemployment?
   *(b)* What is the expected rate of inflation if the Phillips curve is SRPC1?
   Suppose that the economy begins in long-run equilibrium with zero inflation and that the authorities adopt a policy of constant monetary growth because they wish to reduce unemployment below its existing level:
   *(c)* Identify the short-run effect on inflation and unemployment.
   *(d)* Explain why this new position for the economy is untenable in the long run.
   *(e)* Towards what long-run equilibrium position will the economy tend?
   Suppose that the government now wishes to return to zero inflation and holds money supply constant:
   *(f)* Identify the short-run impact on inflation and unemployment.
   *(g)* Identify the long-run equilibrium position.
   *(h)* Under what conditions will this long-run equilibrium be attained?
   *(i)* Can you see a role for incomes policy in this process?

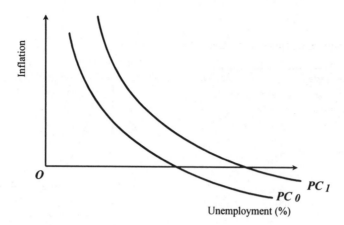

**Figure 28-2   Inflation and unemployment**

6   Which of the following initial causes of inflation stem from the demand side of the economy and which from the supply side?
   *(a)*  An increase in government expenditure on goods and services financed by printing money.
   *(b)*  An increase in the price of oil.
   *(c)*  An increase in value-added tax.
   *(d)*  An increase in income tax allowances for individuals.
   *(e)*  An increase in money wage rates.
   *(f)*  A decrease in the marginal propensity to save of households.

7   Which of the following would result from a rise in the supply of money relative to its demand in an economy operating at full employment under the Quantity theory of money?
   *(a)*  A reduction in the velocity of circulation.
   *(b)*  An increase in the level of real output.
   *(c)*  An increase in the price level.
   *(d)*  An increase in money income.

8   Which of the following items is most likely to have caused the move from $PC_0$ to $PC_1$ in Figure 28-2?
   *(a)*  A decrease in the natural rate of unemployment.
   *(b)*  An increase in wage inflation.
   *(c)*  The expectation of a future increase in the rate of unemployment.
   *(d)*  The expectation of a future increase in the rate of inflation.
   *(e)*  An increase in labour supply.

9   State whether each of the following costs of inflation are real or illusory and whether they apply to anticipated or only to unanticipated inflation:
   *(a)*  Fiscal drag.
   *(b)*  A redistribution of income affecting those on fixed incomes.
   *(c)*  All goods becoming more expensive.
   *(d)*  Shoe-leather and menu costs.
   *(e)*  An increase in uncertainty.
   *(f)*  A fall in the real wage arising from the inflation set off by the monetary expansion following a supply shock.

10   Incomes policy has, and has had, many critics. Explain why each of the following items has been a problem area in the past, and whether it nullifies the potential use of incomes policy in the future:
   *(a)*  The lack of support from other policy instruments.
   *(b)*  Multiplicity of objectives.
   *(c)*  The temporary nature of incomes policy.
   *(d)*  Inflexibility in a changing employment structure.
   *(e)*  Inappropriate incentive structures.

## True/False

1   The UK price level was no higher in 1950 than it was in 1920.
2   Sustained inflation is always and everywhere a monetary phenomenon.
3   The simple quantity theory says that the inflation rate always equals the rate of nominal money growth.
4   According to the Fisher hypothesis, an increase in the rate of money growth will lead to an increase in the inflation rate and to an increase in nominal interest rates.
5   The German hyperinflation of the 1920s was so severe that the government had to buy faster printing presses to print money quickly enough.
6   A large budget deficit necessarily leads to inflation by forcing the government to print money.
7   The velocity of circulation is the speed at which the outstanding stock of money is passed round the economy as people make transactions.
8   The Phillips curve shows that a decrease in unemployment can be achieved at the expense of higher inflation.
9   The menu costs of inflation reflect the fact that the faster the inflation rate, the more frequently menus have to be reprinted if real prices are to remain constant.
10  There are no costs to inflation so long as it can be fully anticipated.
11  In order to incur the permanent benefits of lower inflation, the economy must first undergo a period of low output and employment.
12  Indexation may make inflation tolerable in the long run.

## ECONOMICS IN THE NEWS

### 1   The transmission of monetary policy
*(Quoted from an article by Ben Martin in Economic Review, Volume 17(2), November 1999)*

Monetary policy in the UK involves the setting of an interest rate, the *official rate*, which is used to keep inflation close to a target level. Up to May 1997, the official rate was set by the Chancellor of the Exchequer. Since then the government has delegated the interest rate decision to the Monetary Policy Committee (MPC) of the Bank of England. The MPC has been instructed to set the official interest rate in order to achieve the inflation target of 2.5%.

Changes in the official rate affect the spending decisions of individuals and firms, which, when added up across the whole economy, lead to changes in GDP. When actual GDP is high relative to potential, demand for national output is high relative to supply and this creates inflationary pressure. When actual GDP is low relative to potential, inflationary pressure is low. Exchange rate changes also have short-term implications for inflation: an appreciation of sterling can make prices of imported goods lower and so reduces domestic inflation, and vice versa for a depreciation.

So, if the MPC considers that inflation is expected to be too high compared to the government's target, it may choose to raise interest rates in order to dampen the level of spending being undertaken by households and firms in the economy. It is difficult to say how much a particular increase in the official rate will reduce inflation, but it is generally accepted that increases in the official interest rate eventually reduce inflation, and decreases in the official interest rate eventually result in increases in inflation.

1   Why is it 'difficult to say how much a particular increase in the official rate will reduce inflation'?
2   Why is monetary policy thought to be more effective if entrusted to an independent Bank of England, instead of being run by the Treasury?

## 2   Inflation is lower than figures show – official
*(Adapted from The Observer, 13 July 1997)*

Official statisticians are about to admit that inflation is lower than they had thought, because of flaws in the way the retail prices index is calculated. Any move that significantly cuts the official inflation rate will have an important impact on income taxes – where thresholds normally rise in line with the RPI – and on benefits which are linked to changes in price levels. Since the Bank of England targets inflation when setting interest rates, a lower rate might also lead to cheaper borrowing.

A recent study in the US suggested that the real rate of American inflation is 1.1 per cent lower than officially estimated. But in the UK, the Government's Office for National Statistics (ONS) insists that the biases which distort the RPI are far smaller.

A number of errors in the methods used to calculate the CPI were identified in the US study. They found that:

- The index fails to take account of the extra value for money achieved by better quality goods and services, especially when new products are introduced.
- It misses a lot of substitution by consumers. If the price of apples increases compared with the price of pears, shoppers purchase more pears. However, the CPI does not change quickly enough to reflect this substitution effect.
- It fails to take account of the dramatic price drops that follow the introduction of new goods such as mobile phones.

Unlike the CPI, the RPI is updated annually to minimise the substitution effect. And some of the quality adjustments needed in the CPI are not necessary for the RPI. For example the Boskin Report found that the US index failed to measure improvements in medical treatment. Ten years ago an expensive operation was needed to cure an ulcer; now it can be done with cheap drugs. In America, these advances have a huge impact because of the amount spent on private healthcare. But in the UK most such care is provided by the National Health Service.

However, the ONS, assisted by outside bodies such as the Institute for Fiscal Studies and the Cardiff Business School, is conducting research into several areas where there are concerns that the RPI may not be taking full account of quality improvements in goods including clothing, new cars and computers.

1   Identify the causes of bias in the official figures. Do you find them convincing? (In thinking about the second bullet point, you may wish to recall the analysis of income and substitution effects in Chapter 6.)
2   Appraise the possible consequences of redefining inflation, some of which are set out in the passage. What real effects are likely to follow?

## Questions for Thought

1   Given the relationship between inflation and unemployment outlined in this chapter, which do you think should be the prime target of economic policy?
2   The simple quantity theory assumes that the velocity of circulation is constant. What factors might lead velocity to vary in the short and long runs?
3   Discuss the costs of inflation. Which of these cost items is likely to have encouraged Western governments in their adoption of inflation as public enemy number one?
4   Figure 28-3 opposite shows the way in which the demand for real money balances varies with the rate of interest. Notice that we regard the nominal rate of interest as the opportunity cost of holding money in this context. In Figure 28-3, the real rate of interest is given by *OA*. Remember that the real interest rate is equal to the nominal rate less the inflation rate. Suppose initially that there is zero inflation.
    *(a)*   Identify the level of real money demand.
    Now suppose that the government attempts to finance a deficit by printing money, allowing inflation to rise to *AB*.

*(b)* Identify the nominal rate of interest.
*(c)* What is the demand for real money balances?
*(d)* What area represents the real revenue from the inflation tax?
*(e)* What costs does society bear in this situation?
*(f)* What would you expect to happen to revenue from the inflation tax as the government deficit increases and the economy heads for hyperinflation?

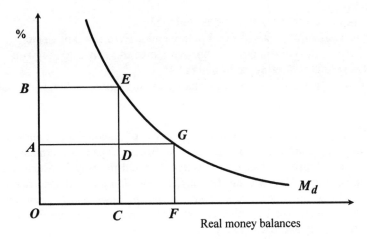

**Figure 28-3    The inflation tax**

# 29 Open Economy Macroeconomics

## Learning Outcomes

- To describe the forex market and discuss how exchange rate regimes differ
- To develop balance of payments accounting, and explain key determinants of current account flows
- To analyse how perfect capital mobility leads speculators to equate expected returns on assets in different currencies
- To define the concepts of internal and external balance
- To analyse the effects of monetary and fiscal policy under fixed exchange rate
- To explore the effects of devaluation in the short run, medium run, and long run
- To analyse what determines floating exchange rates
- To explain how floating rates are affected by changes in monetary policy, fiscal policy, and resource discoveries

**IN THIS CHAPTER** ... you will examine the effects of international transactions on the domestic economy, which are very important for economies such as Britain, Japan or Germany, which rely heavily on exports and imports. You will also see that the *exchange rate* and the way in which it determined has a far-reaching impact on the economy. You will meet both *fixed* and *floating* exchange rate regimes, and find out about the *balance of payments, the real exchange rate, purchasing power parity* – and more! In particular, you will see that there are key connections by which the way that exchange rates are determined can influence the relative effectiveness of monetary and fiscal policy.

## Important Concepts and Technical Terms

Match each lettered concept with the appropriate numbered phrase:

| | | |
|---|---|---|
| (a) Balance of payments | (g) Capital account | (m) Sterilization |
| (b) Purchasing power parity path | (h) Current account | (n) Devaluation |
| (c) Appreciation | (i) Revaluation | (o) Depreciation |
| (d) Real exchange rate | (j) Open economy macroeconomics | (p) Perfect capital mobility |
| (e) Overshooting | (k) Sterling effective exchange rate | |
| (f) Foreign exchange reserves | (l) Exchange rate | |

1  The study of economies in which international transactions play a significant role.
2  The price at which two currencies exchange.
3  A fall in the international value of a currency.
4  A systematic record of all transactions between residents of one country and the rest of the world.
5  A record of international flows of goods and services and other net income from abroad.
6  The stock of foreign currency held by the domestic central bank.
7  A record of international transactions in capital assets.
8  A rise in the international value of a currency.
9  A situation in which speculation causes the nominal exchange rate to move beyond its new equilibrium.
10  A situation in which an enormous quantity of funds will be transferred from one currency to another whenever the rate of return on assets in one country is higher than the rate of return in another.
11  A reduction in the exchange rate which the government commits itself to defend.
12  A measurement of the relative price of goods from different countries when measured in a common currency.
13  An increase in the exchange rate which the government commits itself to defend.
14  The path of the nominal exchange rate that would keep the real exchange rate constant over a given period.
15  An open market operation between domestic money and domestic bonds, the sole purpose of which is to neutralize the tendency of balance of payments surpluses and deficits to change the domestic money supply.

**Table 29-1    The UK balance of payments 1998**

| Item | £m |
|---|---|
| Exports of goods | 164 132 |
| Exports of services | 60 070 |
| Net investment income | 15 174 |
| Net errors and omissions | 8 468 |
| Transfers (net) | –6 526 |
| Imports of goods | 184 897 |
| Imports of services | 47 817 |
| Net transactions in financial assets and liabilities | –9 025 |
| Capital account | 421 |

Source: *Economic Trends Annual Supplement.*

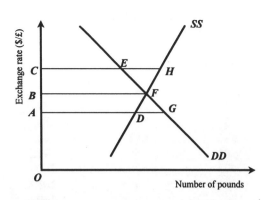

**Figure 29-1    The foreign exchange market**

## Exercises

1  Table 29-1 contains items from the UK balance of payments accounts for 1998, in £ millions. In this version of the accounts, three categories of transactions are distinguished – the current account ( as described in the main text), the capital account (which identifies transactions involving the transfer of fixed assets, mainly by migrants), and the financial account, which covers transactions in financial assets.
   Calculate:
   *(a)* The visible balance.
   *(b)* The invisible balance.
   *(c)* The current account balance.
   *(d)* The overall balance of payments.

2  Figure 29-1 shows the position in the foreign exchange market: *DD* is the demand schedule for sterling and *SS* the supply schedule. Assume a two-country world (UK and USA):
   *(a)* Explain briefly how the two schedules arise.
   *(b)* Identify the exchange rate that would prevail under a clean float. What would be the state of the overall balance of payments at this exchange rate?
   *(c)* Suppose the exchange rate were set at *OA* under a fixed exchange rate regime. What intervention would be required by the central bank? What would be the state of the balance of payments?
   *(d)* Suppose the exchange rate was set at *OC*. Identify the situation of the balance of payments and the necessary central bank intervention.
   *(e)* If the authorities wished to maintain the exchange rate at *OC* in the long run, what sort of measures would be required?

3  This exercise considers the effect of various shocks upon the internal and external balance of an economy. For each shock in Table 29-2, indicate the effects on the assumption that the economy is initially in both internal and external balance.

**Table 29-2    Shocks and balances**

| | Internal: | | External:<br>Current account balance | |
|---|---|---|---|---|
| Nature of shock | Boom | Slump | Deficit | Surplus |
| Reduction in autonomous consumption | | | | |
| Increase in real exchange rate | | | | |
| Tighter monetary and fiscal policy | | | | |
| Increase in world income | | | | |
| Increase in consumption with easier monetary and fiscal policy | | | | |

**Table 29-3    Prices and the exchange rate**

|       | US$/£ exchange rate | UK price index | USA price index | Real exchange rate | 'PPP' exchange rate |
|-------|---------------------|----------------|-----------------|--------------------|---------------------|
| 1985  | 1.30                | 75.0           | 82.4            |                    |                     |
| 1986  | 1.47                | 77.5           | 83.9            |                    |                     |
| 1987  | 1.64                | 80.7           | 87.1            |                    |                     |
| 1988  | 1.78                | 84.7           | 90.5            |                    |                     |
| 1989  | 1.64                | 91.3           | 94.9            |                    |                     |
| 1990  | 1.79                | 100.0          | 100.0           |                    |                     |
| 1991  | 1.77                | 105.9          | 104.2           |                    |                     |
| 1992  | 1.77                | 109.8          | 107.4           |                    |                     |
| 1993  | 1.50                | 111.5          | 110.6           |                    |                     |
| 1994  | 1.53                | 114.3          | 113.4           |                    |                     |
| 1995  | 1.58                | 118.2          | 116.6           |                    |                     |
| 1996  | 1.56                | 121.1          | 120.1           |                    |                     |
| 1997  | 1.64                | 124.9          | 122.9           |                    |                     |
| 1998  | 1.66                | 129.1          | 124.8           |                    |                     |

Source: *Economic Review Data Supplement, September 1999.*

4   Table 29-3 presents data relating to price movements in the UK and the USA and the nominal $/£ exchange rate for the years 1985-98.
   (a)  Using these data, calculate the real exchange rate for the years 1985-98.
   (b)  Plot both real and nominal exchange rates against time.
   (c)  Comment on the path of the real exchange rate during this period.
   (d)  Calculate the purchasing power parity path for the exchange rate relative to 1985.

5   This exercise explores the effects of a devaluation for an economy operating under a fixed exchange rate regime. The economy to be considered adjusts sluggishly to shocks and is initially in a state of both internal and external balance. We consider the effects of devaluation in the short, medium, and long runs.
   *The short run:*
   (a)  What is the immediate effect of the devaluation on international competitiveness?
   (b)  Mention some of the factors that may impede adjustment in the short run.
   (c)  What determines the initial impact on the current account balance?
   *The medium term:*
   (d)  Recall that the economy began at full employment: what does this imply for output and prices in the medium term?
   (e)  Are there any policy measures that could evade this problem?
   *The long run:*
   (f)  Can the lower real exchange rate be sustained in the long run? Explain your answer.
   (g)  Under what circumstances might a devaluation be an appropriate policy reaction?

6   Comment briefly on the short-run effectiveness (or otherwise) of monetary and fiscal policy in each of the following economies:
   (a)  A closed economy.
   (b)  An open economy with fixed exchange rate and perfect capital mobility.
   (c)  An open economy with floating exchange rate and perfect capital mobility.
   (d)  An open economy with floating exchange rate and imperfect capital mobility.

7   Suppose that you have £100 idle which you wish to lend for a year. In Britain the current market rate of interest is 12 per cent, but if you choose you could lend your funds in the USA where the current interest rate is 9 per cent. The present nominal exchange rate is $1.70/£.

(a) What additional piece of information is required to enable you to take a decision on whether to lend in Britain or in the USA?

(b) Suppose that you expect the exchange rate at the end of the year to be $1.50/£: where will you invest?

(c) Where would you invest if you expected the exchange rate to fall only to $1.65/£.

(d) Given that you expect the exchange rate to fall to $1.65/£, where would you invest if the US interest rate were 8 per cent?

(e) Would you suppose expectations about future exchange rates to be stable or volatile? Does it matter?

8   Within a two-country (UK and USA) model, identify the effect on the UK exchange rate of each of the following:

(a) Americans want to buy more British assets.

(b) A fall in the American demand for Scotch whisky.

(c) An increase in the British demand for bourbon.

(d) An increase in the number of US tourists visiting the UK.

(e) A drop in the UK demand for shares in American companies.

(f) An increase in US interest rates.

9   Which of the following (*ceteris paribus*) would move the UK's balance of payments towards a current account surplus?

(a) An increased number of tourists visiting the UK from the USA and Japan.

(b) An increase in dividends from UK investments in the USA.

(c) Increased export earnings from the sale of antique china to Japan.

(d) The hiring of fewer American films for showing in the UK.

(e) The sale of UK investments in American industry.

(f) A fall in the sales of Scotch whisky in the USA.

(g) An increase in official exchange reserves.

10  Consider an open economy which adjusts sluggishly to shocks. A floating exchange rate regime is operating and the economy begins in long-run equilibrium. The authorities initiate a 20 per cent increase in nominal money supply.

(a) What will be the eventual increase in the domestic price level?

(b) What will be the eventual change in the real and nominal exchange rates?

(c) What will be the initial change in domestic interest rates?

(d) Sketch a diagram to show the adjustment path of the nominal exchange rate towards its long-run equilibrium, and comment briefly on the pattern.

## True/False

1   The $/£ exchange rate measures the international value of sterling.

2   Under a fixed exchange rate regime the authorities undertake to maintain the exchange rate at its equilibrium level.

3   Invisible trade is a component of the capital account.

4   In the absence of government intervention in the foreign exchange market, the exchange rate adjusts to equate the supply of and demand for domestic currency.

5   A fall in the international value of sterling makes British goods cheaper in foreign currency and foreign goods more expensive in pounds, and thus increases the quantity of British exports and reduces the quantity of goods imported to Britain.

6   Sterilization of the domestic money supply under fixed exchange rates can be effective only in the short run.

7   Under fixed exchange rates, the ability of an economy to deal automatically with a shock depends on its source.

8   Devaluation need not improve the current account.

9   There is only one real exchange rate compatible with both internal and external balance.

10  The nominal exchange rate always follows the purchasing power parity path.

11  The best policy for the government to adopt is to choose exchange rate and money supply to ensure internal and external balance.

12  The exploitation of North Sea oil led to an increase in the real sterling exchange rate which deepened the recession in the UK in the early 1980s.

## ECONOMICS IN THE NEWS

### The pounding's not over yet
*(Adapted from The Observer, 13 July 1997)*

As you tuck into that lovingly prepared filet mignon in your favourite French bistro this summer, spare a thought for the British manufacturer who probably made the chef's hat. For while the strong pound, which last week brought almost 10 francs, may make the menu seem cheap compared with last year, it's creating havoc for Pal International in Leicester.

The company, which makes hygiene products including chef's hats, exports about 60 per cent of its production, worth £12.5 million a year. 'We are probably the main supplier of chef's hats to the Paris restaurant market,' says chairman Richard Brucciani, who boasts of producing 15 different models. The rapid appreciation of sterling, particularly against European currencies, means that Pal's French sales, which are invoiced in the local currency, are now worth about 30 per cent less than they were this time last year.

This is imposing severe strain on the company. It is being forced to develop business in the Far East to compensate for the shortfall in European markets. Luckily, it already has offices in Singapore.

The financial horror story at Pal is repeated across much of manufacturing industry. Profit margins are being tightly squeezed, and in some cases have turned to losses, as firms battle to remain competitive by holding prices steady in foreign currencies.

The UK's manufacturing base was permanently damaged by a 30 per cent appreciation of sterling's effective exchange rate between 1979, when Margaret Thatcher came to power, and 1981. Bob Anderton, of the National Institute of Economic and Social Research, pointed to a direct link between sterling's appreciation and the downturn in manufacturing. Some commentators have concluded that, in the long run, manufacturing might actually have benefited form the eighties shake-out. Many firms went to the wall, but those that survived were better able to compete. Alan Armitage, head of economics at the EEF, says many firms are trying hard to boost competitiveness by, for example, changing the designs of their products or shopping around for lower prices in bought-in parts.

Currency analysts say sterling is fundamentally overvalued. Its fair value is probably between DM2.50 and DM2.65, says Goldman Sachs. And it will, to the delight of exporters, come crashing down ... but not yet. Eventually, sterling's strength will be sapped by a combination of factors, including a widening trade deficit as imports surge and exports slump, and a narrowing of the short-term interest rate differential between the UK and continental Europe.

The realisation that the UK will join EMU, albeit after the 1999 start date, will also, in the long run, undermine the safe-haven status sterling has acquired, says Avinash Persaud, of JP Morgan. But with EMU still in turmoil, no sign of interest rates going up in Japan or continental Europe, and the current account posting a surplus in the first quarter of the year, it could be a long and painful wait.

1    To what extent is it likely that government policies which lead to higher interest rates will lead to unintended effects on the employment and production structure of an economy?
2    By what mechanism would you expect the exchange rate to reach equilibrium if the analysts are correct in thinking that it is overvalued?
3    What is the current state of sterling as you read this?


## Questions for Thought

1    During the mid-1980s, the government began to pay increasing attention to the exchange rate as a target for economy policy. Why should this be? What implications would it have for the general conduct of policy?

**2**  This exercise offers you a different way of thinking about the balance of payments position for an economy. We argue first that the current account position depends upon income: as domestic income rises, imports also rise and the current account becomes more negative. The capital account depends upon the domestic interest rate relative to the rest of the world. Thus if home interest rates are relatively high, there will tend to be a capital inflow. (We assume that capital is not perfectly mobile; if it were, home interest rates would always be the same as the world level.)

The balance of payments is zero when a current account deficit (surplus) is matched by a capital account surplus (deficit). At a higher level of income, a higher interest rate is required, so that the higher current account deficit can be matched by a larger capital account surplus. This maintains balance of payments 'equilibrium'. We can envisage this as the line $BP$ in Figure 29-2, showing all the combinations of $Y$ and $R$ in which the overall balance of payments is zero. Below the $BP$ line, the balance of payments is in overall deficit, above it there is a surplus. The position of the $BP$ line depends upon international competitiveness and net exports.

We can bring this analysis together with the $IS$-$LM$ curves, as in Figure 29-3. At the intersection of the three lines, we have general equilibrium – zero balance of payments, plus equilibrium in the goods and money markets. We will assume fixed prices for the moment.

*(a)*  Analyse the effects of an increase in money supply in this economy. Assume that the exchange rate is fixed, and that in the short run, goods and money markets remain in equilibrium – but that the balance of payments may be non-zero initially.

*(b)*  Analyse the effects of an increase in government expenditure, again assuming that the authorities are operating under a fixed exchange rate regime.

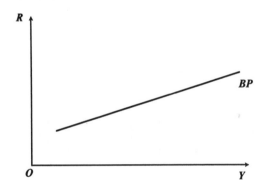

**Figure 29-2   The $BP$ line**

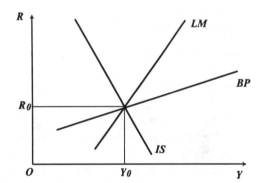

**Figure 29-3   The $BP$ line with $IS$-$LM$**

# 30 Economic Growth

## Learning Outcomes

- To study determinants in the growth of potential output and living standards
- To explain how economics became called the dismal science because Malthus forecast that living standards would fall to starvation levels
- To discuss how, together, technical progress and the accumulation of physical and human capital made Malthus's forecast incorrect
- To study the neoclassical model of economic growth
- To consider how departures from its assumptions can undermine its optimistic conclusion that poor countries enjoy faster growth for a while
- To investigate the growth performance of advanced and less advanced countries
- To analyse whether growth rates could be affected by economic behaviour and economic policy
- To discuss the costs of growth and assess whether growth must be halted in order to preserve the environment

**IN THIS CHAPTER ...** you take a broad view of the macroeconomy. So far, attention has focused on how (and whether) an economy can reach full employment. In the long term, *potential output* may change over time. So, it is time to consider the nature and sources of *economic growth*. You begin with the *production function*, where the level of output depends upon factor inputs and technology. You will see the importance of *capital*, of *renewable* and *depletable* resources, the role of *savings and investment*, and the potential *costs* of economic growth. You will meet some growth theories, including the *convergence hypothesis*, and *endogenous growth*.

## Important Concepts and Technical Terms

Match each lettered concept with the appropriate numbered phrase:

| | | |
|---|---|---|
| (a) Economic growth | (f) Renewable resource | (k) Capital deepening |
| (b) Growth accounting | (g) Depletable resource | (l) Convergence hypothesis |
| (c) Neoclassical growth theory | (h) Capital widening | (m) Endogenous growth |
| (d) Human capital | (i) Steady-state path | (n) Catch-up |
| (e) Embodied technical progress | (j) Solow residual | |

1  The assertion that poor countries grow more quickly than average, but rich countries grow more slowly.
2  The part of output growth not explained by the growth of measured inputs.
3  Capital accumulation which extends the existing capital per worker to new extra workers.
4  In neoclassical growth theory, the trend growth path along which output, capital and labour are all growing at the same rate.
5  The annual percentage increase in the potential real output of an economy.
6  The process by which poor countries may be able to close the gap between them and the rich countries as a result of the convergence hypothesis.
7  A resource which need never be exhausted if harvested with care.
8  Advances in knowledge incorporated in 'new' capital or labour inputs.
9  The stock of expertise accumulated by a worker.
10  The use of growth theory to decompose actual output behaviour into the parts explained by changes in various inputs and the part residually explained by technical progress.
11  Economic growth determined within economic theory, rather than being simply dependent upon external factors such as population growth.
12  A theory of economic growth devised by Bob Solow, which focuses on explaining the long-run growth of potential output, but is not concerned with how the actual rate reaches the potential rate.
13  Capital accumulation which raises capital per worker for all workers.
14  A resource of which only finite stocks are available.

## Exercises

1  Which of the following items reflect genuine economic growth?
   *(a)* A decrease in unemployment.
   *(b)* An increase in the utilization of capital.
   *(c)* An increase in the proportion of the population entering the labour force.
   *(d)* An increase in the rate of change of potential output.
   *(e)* A movement towards the production possibility frontier.
   *(f)* Continuous movement of the production possibility frontier.

2  We have seen that output may be increased either by an increase in inputs or by technical progress. (We neglect economies of scale for the moment.) This exercise explores how this may happen in a practical situation. Below are listed a number of ways by which the output of a word-processor operator might be increased. State whether each involves an increase in input or technical progress.
   *(a)* Modification introduced to improve the quality of the existing computer.
   *(b)* Purchase of a new improved computer.
   *(c)* Making the operator work her or his lunch hour without pay.
   *(d)* Sending the operator to night school to improve her or his technique.
   *(e)* Our word-processor operator gaining experience and producing better quality work.
   *(f)* Introduction of WINDOWS to replace DOS.
   If technical progress is to be measured as a residual, which of the above items will be included?

3  Identify each of the following as a depletable or renewable resource:
   *(a)* Wheat.
   *(b)* Oil.
   *(c)* Whales.
   *(d)* Copper.
   *(e)* Trees.
   *(f)* Rain.

4  This exercise should be approached with a dose of scepticism. Table 30-1 offers some data on output and productivity in three European countries.

**Table 30-1  Output per head and gross product (1980 =100)**

|  | GNP Germany | GDP Italy | GDP UK | Output per person-hour in manufacturing | | |
|---|---|---|---|---|---|---|
|  |  |  |  | Germany | Italy | UK |
| 1974 | 85.4 | 85.9 | 93.2 | 87 | 78 | 95 |
| 1979 | 100.0 | 96.2 | 102.4 | 96 | 96 | 101 |
| 1983 | 99.8 | 98.6 | 104.7 | 110 | 102 | 115 |

Source: *National Institute Economic Review,* August 1984.

   *(a)* Calculate average annual percentage growth rates for gross product and output per person-hour for 1974–79 and 1979–83 for each country.
   *(b)* Explain why these calculations may give a distorted view of the world.

5  Which of the following items might be said to have contributed to the productivity slowdown of the 1970s?
   *(a)* Inflation.
   *(b)* Reductions in company profitability.
   *(c)* The growth of the black economy.
   *(d)* Oil price shock.
   *(e)* The dawning of the post-industrial society.
   *(f)* Completion of recovery from the Second World War.

6   Which of the following policy suggestions are appropriate for improving economic growth in an economy?
    (a) The encouragement of R&D.
    (b) A reduction in marginal tax rates to increase labour supply.
    (c) Investment grants.
    (d) The establishment of training and education schemes to improve human capital.
    (e) An expansion of aggregate demand to increase the level of employment.
    (f) The encouragement of dissemination of new knowledge and techniques.

7   Consider an economy in which there is no technical progress, the labour force grows at a constant rate $n$, and saving is proportional to income. The production function displays diminishing marginal product of capital.
    (a) What is the steady-state rate of economic growth?
    (b) If for some reason the economy is below its long-run growth path, what adjustments take place to enable return to equilibrium?
    (c) What difference does it make to your analysis if labour-augmenting technical progress takes place at a rate $t$?
    (d) What is implied for the long-run relative growth rate of countries if all have access to technical knowledge?
    (e) What factors might impede the process you have described in (d)?
    (f) Explain how externalities in human and physical capital may affect economic growth.
    (g) What role might the government play in the economic growth process?

8   Figure 30-1 illustrates neoclassical growth. The rays $n1k$ and $n2k$ show investment per person needed to maintain capital per person if labour grows at rates $n1$ and $n2$ respectively; $y$ shows how output per person varies with capital per person. Under the assumption that saving is proportional to income, $sy$ shows saving and investment per person.
    (a) Which ray represents the lower rate of growth of the labour force?
    (b) What is the steady-state position for the economy?
    (c) Identify the levels of capital per worker and output per worker in this steady state.
    (d) What is the rate of growth?
    (e) What difference would it make to the steady state if there were a higher rate of growth of labour?
    (f) Would a higher rate of savings mean higher or lower output growth?

9   Figure 30-2 shows the Solow diagram for an economy. When an economy is relatively undeveloped, we might argue that all available resources must be used to try to maintain minimum subsistence survival. In Figure 30-2, $k0$ represents a critical level of capital per person which is just sufficient to generate the critical income level above which people can begin to save. For an economy in each of the positions labelled $A - E$ identify whether capital per person is increasing or decreasing, and the long-run level of $k$ where the economy would settle.

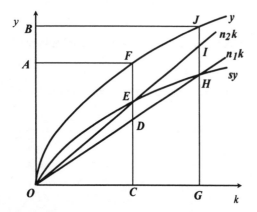

**Figure 30-1   The neoclassical growth model**

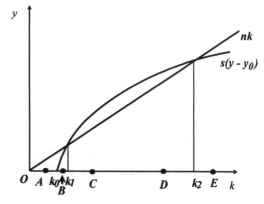

**Figure 30-2   A low-level equilibrium trap**

## True/False

1  Per capita real GDP is a reasonable measure of the living standards of people in a country.
2  An annual growth rate of 2 per cent p.a. leads to a sevenfold increase in real output in less than a century.
3  The purpose of investment is to increase the capital stock.
4  Invention is futile without innovation which in turn requires investment.
5  Sustained growth cannot occur if production relies on a factor whose supply is largely fixed.
6  The potential rate of return on investment in people in the UK is probably quite high.
7  In the neoclassical growth theory, output, capital and labour all grow at the same rate.
8  Capital deepening is needed to extend the existing capital stock to accommodate immigrant workers.
9  Higher savings enables a higher long-run rate of growth.
10 Given the convergence hypothesis, we can expect all poor countries to catch up with the richer countries.
11 Growth may be stimulated by capital externalities: that is, higher capital in one firm increases capital productivity in other firms.
12 A crucial element in the rapid growth of the East Asian Tigers was rapid growth in measured inputs.

## ECONOMICS IN THE NEWS

### Can Asia pull off another miracle in the 21st century?
*(Adapted from Agence France Presse Intl., 26 December 1999)*

'The next century will be the Asian century' – that proud boast by Asian leaders is no longer heard, but analysts say steady reform and restructuring following a financial crisis could well lay the ground for another, more sustainable regional economic miracle. 'The question of an Asian century, to a certain extent, rests on the Asian governments themselves and the key issue is: how far are they willing to go in embracing financial reforms?' said Bill Belchere, head of Asian economics and fixed income research at Merrill Lynch.

The financial crisis which erupted in mid-1997 slammed the brakes on Asia's explosive economic growth and laid bare deficiencies in the region's key financial systems. Belchere said financial reforms were crucial for Asia to ward off increasing competition in the new millennium and, more importantly, to raise rates of return for investors. Citing an example, he said investments by Malaysia, Thailand and South Korea in the last decade made up about 40 percent of their gross domestic products (GDP) but average annual return was only seven to eight percent. Chile and Taiwan however made similar returns by investing only 20 percent of their GDP.

'So it is not difficult to argue that there is a misallocation of resources in much of Asia due largely to a flawed financial sector,' Belchere said. The region should not merely give lip service to reforms in its effort to woo back investors who bailed out of the region following the financial crisis which erupted in mid-1997.

Reputed US professor Paul Krugman, a strong critic of Asia's growth strategy before the financial crisis struck, said the export-driven region could regain its lost lustre in the new millennium. 'It is a story that is starting to look as if it has a happy ending,' he said in a lecture in Bangkok last week, even while noting that much of the region was handicapped by banks burdened with huge bad loans.

Bhanu Baweja, an economist at financial markets research firm IDEAglobal.com, said the financial crisis was a 'short term' problem which could not alter the view on Asian dominance in the 21st century. 'In the big scheme of things, I don't think the Asian crisis – which is going to fade in importance in a few years – is going to alter what Asia is capable of achieving in the next 100 years. 'In terms of return on capital, Asia will be much higher than anywhere else in the world. If I were to buy a stock for the next 100 years, for example, it would be an Asian stock,' he said. Baweja said Asia's growth would be driven by its manpower. 'Already Asia's economies are powering themselves as knowledge societies and in a matter of time the region will be rich in intellectual property,' he said.

1  What is meant by the statement that the Asian region will be 'rich in intellectual property', and why is it important for the prospects for economic growth?
2  Do you think it is coincidence that so many of the successful economies of recent decades have been Asian? What economic arguments are relevant here?
3  What do you think is the significance of the financial reforms discussed in the passage?

## Questions for Thought

1  Explain how the price system helps to deal with the problem of depletion of a scarce resource, but may not always cope with the preservation of a renewable resource.
2  Table 30-2 shows estimates of GNP per capita in 1997 and its average annual real growth rate in the period 1975-97, together with some other information which you may find helpful. To what extent do these data offer support for the convergence hypothesis?
3  What are the major factors affecting the rate of economic growth? Comment on whether the government should introduce a policy to stimulate growth. At which factors should the policy be aimed?

**Table 30-2    GNP *per capita* and other indicators**

| | GNP per capita | | GDP per capita in PPP$ 1997 | Gross domestic investment (% of GDP) 1997 | Adult literacy rate (%) 1997 | Life expectancy at birth (years) 1997 |
|---|---|---|---|---|---|---|
| | US$ 1997 | Average annual % growth rate 1975-97 | | | | |
| Sierra Leone | 160 | −2.2 | 410 | 9 | 33.3 | 37.2 |
| Rwanda | 210 | −0.5 | 660 | 19 | 33.1 | 47.0 |
| Zambia | 370 | −1.7 | 960 | 15 | 75.1 | 40.1 |
| Cameroon | 620 | 0.1 | 1890 | 10 | 71.7 | 54.7 |
| Sri Lanka | 800 | 3.2 | 2490 | 27 | 90.7 | 73.1 |
| China | 860 | 7.8 | 3130 | 35 | 82.9 | 69.8 |
| Peru | 2610 | −0.3 | 4680 | 25 | 88.7 | 68.3 |
| Thailand | 2740 | 5.7 | 6690 | 41 | 94.7 | 68.8 |
| Brazil | 4790 | 1.1 | 6480 | 20 | 84.0 | 66.8 |
| Korea (Rep) | 10550 | 6.8 | 13590 | 35 | 97.2 | 72.4 |
| Italy | 20170 | 2.2 | 20290 | 18 | 98.3 | 78.2 |
| UK | 20870 | 1.9 | 20730 | 16 | 99.0 | 77.2 |
| France | 26300 | 1.7 | 22030 | 18 | 99.0 | 78.1 |
| USA | 29080 | 1.6 | 29010 | 18 | 99.0 | 76.7 |
| Singapore | 32810 | 5.7 | 24070 | 29 | 91.4 | 77.1 |
| Japan | 38160 | 2.8 | 28460 | 37 | 99.0 | 80.0 |

Source: *Human Development Report 1999* and *World Development Report 1998/99*.

# 31 The Business Cycle

## Learning Outcomes

- To distinguish trend growth and economic cycles around this path
- To study theories of why business cycles occur
- To consider whether fluctuations are departures of output from the path of potential output or could also reflect swings in potential output itself
- To investigate whether national business cycles are becoming more correlated as economies become more integrated with each other
- To apply these principles to recent UK business cycles

**IN THIS CHAPTER ...** you will examine the *business cycle*, a term describing the way that an economy passes through phases of slump, recovery, boom, and recession over a four- or five-year period. You will also investigate the suggestion that economies are subject to a political business cycle. Variations in activity during the cycle must be associated with variations in some element of aggregate demand – but which? If we discount the political cycle and regard consumption as relatively rapid in adjustment, we are left with investment as a candidate. We have already argued that investment may be sluggish – and the cycle story is essentially a story about sluggish adjustment. The multiplier-accelerator model offers one explanation. Sluggish adjustment towards equilibrium is one way of explaining business cycles. However, economists of the 'New Classical' school argue that markets clear very rapidly, if not instantaneously. The *real business cycle approach* argues that static analysis such as *IS-LM* cannot capture the dynamic complexity of an economy evolving through time. Households and firms take decisions in the context of the microeconomic theory of intertemporal choice. The way in which they choose to trade off present and future consumption and savings can have important repercussions, and lead to business cycles even when the economy always remains in equilibrium. Common international business cycles may reflect the way that production has become more international, with multinational enterprises planning their operations on a global scale. Financial deregulation that encourages international capital movements provides an additional transmission mechanism.

## Important Concepts and Technical Terms

Match each lettered concept with the appropriate numbered phrase:

| | | |
|---|---|---|
| (a) Slump | (e) Recession | (i) Ceilings and floors |
| (b) Accelerator model | (f) Trend path of output | (j) Real business cycle |
| (c) Recovery | (g) Political business cycle | (k) Real-wage puzzle |
| (d) Boom | (h) Persistence | (l) International business cycle |

1  A period in which the economy is growing less quickly than trend output.
2  The peak of the cycle.
3  A theory that firms guess future output and profits by extrapolating past output growth, so that an increase in the desired level of investment requires an increase in output growth.
4  The smooth path which output follows in the long run once the short-term fluctuations are averaged out.
5  The trough of the cycle.
6  A theory that short-term fluctuations of total output represent fluctuations of potential output.
7  The phase of the cycle following a slump, in which output climbs above its trend path.
8  Constraints which prevent cycles from exploding indefinitely.
9  The idea that national economies follow similar cyclical paths through time.
10  The notion that temporary shocks may have long-term effects, as households and firms take decisions that involve trade-offs between the present and the future.
11  A suggestion that the business cycle is related to the election cycle.
12  The observation that real wages do not follow the expected pattern over the business cycle.

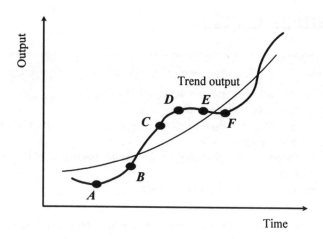

**Figure 31-1   The business cycle**

## Exercises

1   Figure 31-1 shows the path of a hypothetical economy fluctuating around a smooth trend. For each of the labelled points, identify the phase of the cycle.
    How would you interpret the horizontal distance from $A$ to $F$?

2   Which of the following factors might be expected to affect the level of investment?
    *(a)* Past profitability.
    *(b)* The present value of future operating profits.
    *(c)* Real interest rates.
    *(d)* Expectations about future sales.
    *(e)* Past output growth.
    How might a combination of some of these factors give rise to a business cycle?

3   This exercise concerns the multiplier-accelerator model and entails some simple calculations. Suppose we have a fixed-price closed economy with no government, such that
    $Y_t = C_t + I_t$
    where $Y_t$ = national income in time period $t$
    $C_t$ = consumption in period $t$
    $I_t$ = investment in period $t$.
    Further, suppose that consumption in the current period depends upon income in the previous period:
    $C_t = 0.5 Y_{t-1}$
    (0.5 is the marginal propensity to consume).
    Investment comprises two parts, an autonomous element *(A)* and a part which depends upon past changes in output:
    $I_t = A + v (Y_{t-1} - Y_{t-2})$
    where $v$ is the 'acceleration coefficient'.
    Initially, autonomous investment is 30 and the economy is in equilibrium with $Y = 60$, $C = 30$, and $I = 30$.
    We now consider what happens if there is an increase in autonomous investment from 30 to 40. The new equilibrium is $Y = 80$, $C = 40$, $I = 40$, but our model enables us to trace the adjustment path through time. This can be done as in Table 31-1 opposite, under alternative assumptions about $v$, the acceleration coefficient. For $v = 0.2$, we have provided some initial calculations with explanation.

**Table 31-1    A multiplier-accelerator model**

| Time period | v = 0.2 | | | v = 0.8 | | |
| | C | I | Y | C | I | Y |
| --- | --- | --- | --- | --- | --- | --- |
| 0 | 30 | 30 | 60 | 30 | 30 | 60 |
| 1 | 30 | 40 | 70 | 30 | 40 | 70 |
| 2 | 35 | 42 | 77 | | | |
| 3 | | | | | | |
| 4 | | | | | | |
| 5 | | | | | | |
| 6 | | | | | | |

For $v = 0.2$, period 0 shows the original equilibrium. In period 1, investment increases to 40 but consumption has not yet changed. In period 2, consumption is $0.5 \times 70$ and investment is $40 + 0.2 \times (70 - 60) = 42$ and $Y=77$. Complete the remaining entries in Table 31-1, and repeat the exercise for $v = 0.8$: you will find that the adjustment path is very different.

(If you have access to a computer, you may like to set up a spreadsheet to simulate adjustment paths for other values of $c$ and $v$.)

4    Figure 31-2 shows a production possibility frontier *(PPF)* between present and future consumption: this idea first appeared back in Chapter 14, if you want to go back and check it out. $U_0$ and $U_1$ illustrate household preferences between consuming resources now as opposed to in the future.

(a) Mark on your diagram the choice point for society.

Suppose now that there is some temporary technological 'shock' that enables this society to increase its production possibilities.

(b) What effect would this have on Figure 31-2?
(c) What is the effect on present consumption?
(d) What is the effect on future consumption?
(e) What long-run consequences does this have for the society?
(f) Under what conditions would present consumption react differently?
(g) What does all this have to do with business cycles?

5    Which of the following may give rise to persistence, and thus ensure that temporary shocks may have long-run effects?

(a) Diminishing marginal utility of income.
(b) Strong preference for present consumption.
(c) High availability of investment opportunities.
(d) Strong motivation to leave bequests.
(e) Ricardian equivalence.

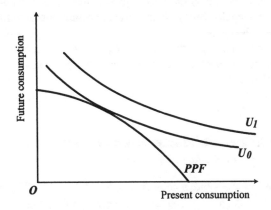

**Figure 31-2    The trade-off between present and future consumption**

6    For this exercise, you need to invoke your imagination a little. Imagine that you are living in a society which has just emerged from a deep recession. Unemployment is falling, real output is rising, prospects are good, you feel confident and ready for anything.

    *(a)*    Your bank writes to you offering to lend you money to spend on consumption at a special rate. Are you more likely to accept the offer than when the economy had been deep in recession, and all was gloom and doom?

    *(b)*    So you borrow. You get yourself a Porsche and an electronic organizer. What has happened to your net indebtedness?

    *(c)*    The clock moves on, the economy does not keep booming for ever. Interest rates begin to rise. Now what has happened to your debt?

    *(d)*    When you had borrowed, you had used your flat in London as collateral. Property prices begin to fall. The shares that you had so eagerly added to your portfolio two years ago are heading for the floor. Do you still feel so confident? What do you do about it?

    *(e)*    What relevance does this have in analysing the events of the 1980s and early 1990s?

7    Which of the following factors may increase the integration of the world economy and thus encourage the international transmission of the business cycle?

    *(a)*    The removal of protectionist policies.

    *(b)*    Improvements in transport and telecommunications.

    *(c)*    The single European market.

    *(d)*    The GATT and the operations of the *WTO*.

    *(e)*    Financial deregulation.

    *(f)*    The integration of the global financial market.

    *(g)*    Policy co-ordination between countries.

8    In exercise 1 of Chapter 20, you calculated growth rates for the UK, USA, and Spain (see 'Answers' Figure A20-2). To what extent do these results support the notion of a common international business cycle?

## True/False

1    In the long run, fluctuations of output around potential output are unimportant.

2    Short-run fluctuations in output can be explained by fluctuations in aggregate demand.

3    Governments cause the business cycle by invoking popular policies in the run-up to elections, and unpopular ones once safely elected.

4    In the multiplier-accelerator model, the less firms' decisions respond to changes in past output, the more pronounced will be the cycle.

5    Changes in stocks help to explain why the economy is likely to spend several years during the phase of recovery or recession.

6    The business cycle cannot exist in theory, because the economy always tends very rapidly to equilibrium.

7    Real wages rise in a slump because cutting back on workers raises the marginal product of labour.

8    Real business cycle theories are usually theories of persistence rather than of cycles.

9    According to real business cycle theory, it is very important for governments to intervene in order to stabilize the economy over the cycle.

10    Increased global integration encourages the international transmission of the business cycle.

11    Recovery from the recession of 1990–91 was slow and weak, because of the huge burden of household debt that had built up during the 1980s.

## ECONOMICS IN THE NEWS

### Tough inflation stance helped build new economic era
*(Adapted from The Financial Post (Canada), 12 January 2000)*

On one of the sports channels last weekend, a commentator declared that 100 years from now, people would still be talking about the Tennessee Titans' trick runback play that gave them a last-second victory over the Buffalo Bills in Saturday's AFC playoff game. I doubt it. Name one thing you talked about recently that happened in 1900 – the last turn of the century excepted.

Something that would be remembered a century from now – if it happened – would be the end of the business cycle: 'Remember those poor devils back in the 19th and 20th centuries, before the invention of Greenspanism, who had to put up with swings in output and employment and actual uncertainty about whether the economy would grow or not? Imagine!'

On this one, colour me sceptical. Still, you do keep reading stories about how the world has changed. Donald S. Allen of the Federal Reserve Bank of St. Louis recently noted that the United States seems to have gone through 'another soft inventory landing.' Since the mid-1980s, inventory growth has seldom exceeded 5% in a quarter, and has gone negative only once or twice. This is in sharp contrast to the mid-1960s and early 1980s, when inventory growth reached or exceeded 10% in several quarters, after which sharply lower growth led to slowdowns in the overall economy.

Inventory cycles have been a classic contributor to the business cycle over the past two centuries. If, as Mr. Allen notes, 'changes in business practices have resulted in improved management of the supply chain,' then that may help dampen fluctuations.

Another change that supposedly is making modern economies less prone to inflation, and therefore less needful of interest-rate purgatives, is globalization. As a result of increasing competition, supply curves are everywhere more 'elastic.' When supply curves are inelastic, even quite sharp increases in prices bring very little increase in output. But if they're elastic, then even quite modest increases in prices bring supply rushing in from all over, thus drastically limiting any price hikes.

If all markets are one, and assuming they aren't all run by AOL, then we have the perfect anti-inflationary environment: Anyone who raises prices – be it a labour union or a corporate board – is punished. And if there is no inflation, there is no need to crash an economy for its own good, the source of many past recessions.

With Asia recovering, with Japan apparently on the mend, with Brazil and Russia no longer imploding, with the American miracle continuing apparently unabated, with more and more countries pushing toward the 3% inflation that marks the upper limit of most people's definition of stable prices, it may be time to start worrying about world over-heating – global economic warming, as it were. At this point, Milton Friedman would interject that 'inflation is everywhere and always a monetary phenomenon.' If governments don't supply money to fuel it, it simply can't take place. If you want to prevent world inflation, tighten world money supply.

Except that there isn't a world money supply. But there are lots of central bankers in the world, and they seem a different breed from their predecessors in the 1960s and 1970s. As far as inflation goes, they're Clint Eastwoods: 'Go ahead. Make my day.' As soon as it shows up, Pow! It will be eliminated.

So long as the markets know this, inflation will stay largely in check. Which means that gentle nudges upward in interest rates will prevent the once-a-decade crunch for which, looking at the calendar, we are just about due.

If everyone understands these new rules, the 1990s may well have been a watershed decade. But it's not computers that will have done it, or globalization, or better management of inventories. It's zero tolerance for inflation.

1    Why should inventory cycles (cycles in stockbuilding activity) be seen as a contributory factor to the business cycle? What is the significance of the supply elasticity in this story?

2    By what route could zero tolerance for inflation influence the business cycle?

## Questions for Thought

1    To what extent can the existence of business cycles be linked with the notion of hysteresis?

2    This exercise considers the political business cycle and uses concepts developed earlier in the book, in particular, notions about indifference curves and short- and long-run Phillips curves.

In Figure 31-3, LRPC is the long-run Phillips curve; SPC0 and SPC1 are short-run Phillips curves reflecting different inflation expectations. The curves I1-I4 are indifference curves which represent how the government perceives the preferences of the electorate for different combinations of inflation and unemployment. The shape of these curves reflects the fact that the two 'goods' are 'bads'! Utility increases from I1 to I2 to I3 to I4. The economy begins in long-run equilibrium with no inflation.

(a) What is the current unemployment level?

(b) What is the perceived utility level of the electorate?

(c) An election approaches; what measures can the government take to make the electorate feel better off? At what point would the economy be in the short run?

(d) What happens as the economy adjusts?

(e) What is the perceived utility level of the electorate?

(f) Supposing that the next election is five years away, where might the economy be taken next, and where might it eventually settle?

(g) Do you think that this model explains the actions of UK governments in recent decades?

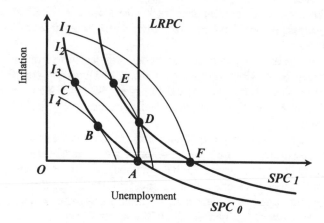

**Figure 31-3   The political business cycle**

# 32 Macroeconomics: Where Do We Stand?

## Learning Outcomes

- To relate different assertions about how the macroeconomy works to differing interpretations of key assumptions behind the analysis
- To discuss the significance of different judgements about how quickly market forces, unassisted by policy, can restore output to full capacity
- To explain how different assumptions about how expectations are formed has an important effect on the speed of adjustment
- To examine the role of the assumption about the speed with which wages adjust to labour market developments
- To consider the potential for hysteresis and more than one long-run equilibrium
- To outline how the major schools of macroeconomic thought differ in their assessments
- To relate these differences to differing recommendations for demand management policy, and for differing judgements about the importance of supply-side policy

**IN THIS CHAPTER ...** you will look back at the material covered during the last 12 chapters, during which we have invoked ever more complicated ways of looking at the macroeconomy. There are many issues on which macroeconomists fail to agree. The purpose of these chapters has not been to convince you of the validity of a particular viewpoint, but to prepare a framework to enable you to make up your own mind. Two economists may agree about the nature of a problem facing an economy, agree about the theoretical analysis of the problem, but yet disagree about the appropriate policy response. This may reflect differing value judgements about the proper objectives of policy. Some disagreements go beyond this. You should be aware of various areas of disagreement, including the formation of expectations, market clearing, the speed of adjustment, and hysteresis. Your position on these issues will form your attitude towards state intervention. You will look at a sequence of snapshots – of New Classical, Gradualist monetarist, Moderate, New and Extreme Keynesians.

## Important Concepts and Technical Terms

Match each lettered concept with the appropriate numbered phrase

| | | |
|---|---|---|
| (a) Exogenous expectations | (e) New Classical macroeconomics | (i) Potential output |
| (b) Moderate Keynesians | (f) Real wage hypothesis | (j) Extreme Keynesians |
| (c) Market clearing | (g) Extrapolative expectations | (k) Hysteresis |
| (d) Rational expectations | (h) Gradualist monetarists | (l) New Keynesians |

1 The level of output that firms wish to supply when there is full employment.
2 A group of economists who insist that markets not only fail to clear in the short run but also may not clear in the long run.
3 The assumption that real wages are rigidly inflexible.
4 A school of economists who believe that the restoration of full employment is not immediate but that adjustment is not too lengthy.
5 A theory of expectations formation which says that people make good use of the information that is available today and do not make forecasts that are already knowably incorrect.
6 A school of economists whose ideas may be summarized as 'short-run Keynesian and long-run monetarist'.
7 Expectations formed on the basis of past experience.
8 Expectations formed independently of the rest of the analysis being undertaken.
9 A situation in which the quantity that sellers wish to supply in a market equals the quantity that purchasers wish to demand.
10 The view that temporary shocks affect the long-run equilibrium.
11 A school of economists whose analysis is based on the twin principles of almost instantaneous market clearing and rational expectations.
12 A school of economists who set out to provide microeconomic foundations for Keynesian macroeconomics.

## Exercises

1   The old joke says that if you were to line up all the economists in the world, they would never reach a conclusion. Which of the following may help to explain why economists sometimes disagree?

   *(a)* Judgements about the relative cost to society of ills like unemployment and inflation involve normative issues on which economists may differ, even if they agree about positive economic theory.

   *(b)* Economists cannot carry out laboratory experiments that enable theories to be proved true or false.

   *(c)* We do not have enough data to allow more than tentative evidence to be presented.

   *(d)* It is not clear whether and how quickly markets clear.

   *(e)* We cannot precisely define the process of expectations formation in the real-world economy.

2   Associate each of the following viewpoints with one of the 'schools' discussed in this chapter.

   *(a)* Full employment will be reached in a reasonable period of time.

   *(b)* Long-run demand-deficient unemployment is feasible.

   *(c)* Short run and long run are indistinguishable because adjustment is rapid.

   *(d)* Short-run stabilization could be important because adjustment may be sluggish.

   *(e)* Policies should be concentrated on the short run.

   *(f)* Expectations are formed rationally.

3   *(a)* What do you expect to be the rate of inflation in the coming year?

   *(b)* What information did you use to form that expectation?

   *(c)* If you had responsibility for setting prices or negotiating wage settlements, would you form your expectations more carefully? What additional information would you seek?

4   Figure 32-1 shows our usual labour market story: *LD0, LD1* represent labour demand curves; *LF* shows the number of people prepared to register in the labour force at each real wage; *AJ* shows those prepared to accept jobs. The economy begins in equilibrium with labour demand *LD0*. An exogenous shock affects labour productivity and reduces labour demand to *LD1*.

   *(a)* Identify the original real wage and unemployment level.

   After the shock:

   *(b)* How would an Extreme Keynesian view the long-run prospects for the labour market?

   *(c)* How would a Gradualist monetarist and a Moderate Keynesian view the labour market in the medium and long terms? How would you distinguish the two?

   *(d)* Identify the new short-run position of the market according to the New Classical school.

   *(e)* How would the groups differ in their approach to policy?

   *(f)* How would the analysis be affected by hysteresis?

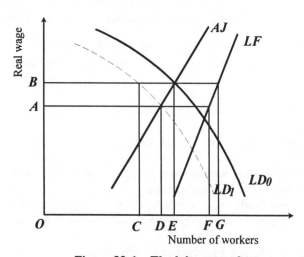

**Figure 32-1   The labour market**

5   Which of the schools are most likely to adopt the following policy measures?
    *(a)* Contractionary monetary policy to combat inflation, as the transitional cost of unemployment will be quite short-lived.
    *(b)* Reduction of money supply to eliminate inflation; output and employment will not be affected.
    *(c)* Import controls to protect domestic employment during an expansion of aggregate demand.
    *(d)* Incomes policy to speed adjustment.
    *(e)* Demand management to stimulate investment and thus raise potential output.
6   Rank the following markets in order of their likely speed of adjustment (most rapid first):
    *(a)* The market for goods.
    *(b)* The money market.
    *(c)* The labour market.
    *(d)* The foreign exchange market.
    Explain your answer.
7   Consider an economy in deep recession which operates under an 'Extreme-Keynesian' perspective.
    *(a)* Draw an *IS-LM* diagram to depict the equilibrium situation for this economy.
    *(b)* On your diagram, show why it is that nominal wage and price adjustments will not be effective in stimulating the level of real output.
    *(c)* Would a monetary expansion be any more effective?
    *(d)* How could such an economy escape from recession?
    *(e)* How would your diagram have differed if you had been considering an economy operating under New Classical or Gradualist monetarist assumptions?
8   Macroeconomics: where do you stand?

## True/False

1   Economists agree about positive issues but disagree on normative matters.
2   A rise in unemployment provides support for Keynesian analysis of the economy in which a deficiency of aggregate demand may move the economy away from full employment.
3   According to the New Classical macroeconomics, government policy can move the economy away from full employment only if agents are surprised by the policy.
4   The New Classicals believe that the dramatic rise in UK unemployment in the early 1980s had almost nothing to do with a fall in aggregate demand.
5   Gradualist monetarists subscribe to the view that an increase in money supply can increase output and employment in the long run, but that the adjustment process is gradual.
6   According to the Gradualist monetarists, the government's chief responsibility is to increase potential output by supply-side policies and by bringing inflation under control.
7   Moderate Keynesians argue that supply-side policies are irrelevant and that attention should be focused on demand management.
8   According to some Moderate Keynesians, demand management may be a significant supply-side policy.
9   Extreme Keynesians argue that supply-side policies are irrelevant and that attention should be focused on demand management.
10  Macroeconomists never consider microeconomic issues.

## ECONOMICS IN THE NEWS

### Brown shows his true colours
*(Adapted from an article by Larry Elliott writing in The Guardian, 25 October 1999)*

Gordon Brown has finally come out. The chancellor has taken a little over two years to define his economic credo and in his Mais lecture last week we found out what it is. Mr Brown is neither a monetarist nor a Keynesian – but something called a post-monetarist. Judging by the contents of the chancellor's lecture, a post-monetarist is someone who has Keynesian objectives – but believes in using monetarist means to achieve them.

The chancellor's argument went like this. Expansionary policies were all very well in the two decades after the Second World War, but this period was a 'special case'. Keynesian demand management failed to tackle the deep structural problems in the economy, and Milton Friedman was right when he said in 1968 that 'the long-term effect of trying to buy less unemployment with more inflation is simply to ratchet up both.' In the 1970s and 1980s, the economy reverted to type, and Friedman's predictions came true in the era of stagflation – unemployment and inflation both rising at the same time. Mr Brown broadly agreed with the analysis of Nigel Lawson in his Mais lecture of 15 years ago that the aim of macroeconomic policy is to keep inflation low and stable, while supply-side reforms should be used to foster higher growth and employment. The chancellor believes his predecessor erred in allowing the economy to get out of control in the 1980s and was mistaken in his belief that deregulation was the answer to higher productivity.

The chancellor has a four-pronged strategy, which is boiled down to four words – stability, employability, productivity and responsibility. That means that keeping inflation at the target of 2.5% provides a base from which welfare-to-work policies and steps to improve the performance of product, labour and capital markets can boost the economy's trend rate of growth. But the fruits of this policy will be frittered away unless wage bargainers avoid short-termism in pay negotiations.

However, a problem with Mr Brown's argument was sketched out by DeAnne Julius, a member of the Monetary Policy Committee, in a lecture the night after Mr Brown's. Ms Julius took a different line: that the 1970s and 1980s have been the 'special case' and the economy is now reverting to a more normal pattern. Before the late 1960s, she said, 'it took world wars or oil price shocks or (working in the opposite direction) the Great Depression to knock inflation off course. Throughout most of the late 19th century, price falls were common.'

All perfectly true. Competition is central to industrial capitalism, and competition tends to hold down prices. What's more, as Ms Julius points out, intensified global competition, the spread of new technologies, and greater price transparency, all mean one thing – the trend in inflation will be downward. In a sentence that might have been aimed at some of her colleagues on the MPC, but could apply equally to the chancellor, Ms Julius said: 'Conventional thinking can be deceptively dangerous when the world is changing. Clinging to old paradigms is at least as risky as embracing new ones before their validity can be fully established. If I am right that the 1970s and the 1980s were the exceptions rather than the norm, we must guard against using paradigms and parameters from those 20 years to shape our views about the present period and projections for the future.'

Milton Friedman's stagflation model suggested that the so-called Phillips curve trade-off between wages (inflation) and unemployment did not work and ultimately any attempts to reduce unemployment by increasing demand would lead to an exponential increase in inflation. That model may have had some brief validity in the 1970s. The staggering increase in unemployment in the 1980s may well have given credence to the idea of a non-accelerating inflation rate of unemployment, a more sophisticated version of Friedman's notion of a 'natural rate' below which the jobless total could not fall without pushing up inflation.

But that isn't what has been happening in the 1990s. Instead, expanding demand in the United States and Britain has led to years of falling unemployment without a sign that inflation is picking up. Moreover, both short-term unemployment and long-term unemployment were falling long before the advent of welfare-to-work policies. The chancellor is to be commended for reaffirming the goal laid out in 1944 of 'high and stable levels of growth and employment'. But there is no real evidence that low inflation coupled with investment incentives will lead to the higher rates of productivity growth that Brown is seeking. Rather periods of high productivity growth have tended to come when periods of technological innovation have been accompanied by strong demand and high employment. As Ms Julius says, perhaps he should get out a bit more.

1   Why should Keynesian demand management policies work in some periods but not in others?
2   If DeAnne Julius is correct in arguing that we cannot use the past to predict the future in a changing world, is there a future for economic analysis?

## Questions for Thought

1   Discuss the proposition that the best stabilization policy is one of non-intervention.
2   Discuss whether government policy should be permitted to react to changing circumstances or whether it should be guided by predetermined rules.
3   Consider the economic policies of the current government and opposition. Can you trace these policies to particular areas of the macroeconomic spectrum?

# 33 International Trade and Commercial Policy

## Learning Outcomes

- To study patterns of international trade
- To explain comparative advantage and the gains from trade
- To analyse how differences in technology or relative factor endowment create comparative advantage
- To examine how scale economies and a demand for diversity lead two-way trade in the same product
- To discuss the welfare economics of levying tariffs, quotas, and export subsidies
- To introduce the principle of targeting and explore first-best and second-best motives for tariffs

**IN THIS CHAPTER ...** you will consider aspects of international trade. Trade has become increasingly important, and here you will see why international trade takes place, discovering that it has its basis in *exchange* and in *specialization*. The gains from international trade are readily demonstrated by the *law of comparative advantage*, formulated by David Ricardo in the early nineteenth century. This rests on international differences in the opportunity cost of goods. The level of the equilibrium exchange rate will reflect the difference in *absolute advantage*. International trade can bring gains in the form of higher output, but the question of distribution remains – the fact that potentially everyone could be made better off does not mean that everyone *will* actually benefit. Measures to influence the pattern of gains are known as commercial policy, and aim to influence trade through taxes (*tariffs*) or subsidies, or through direct restrictions on imports or exports. Many 'justifications' for tariffs have been advanced – most of them invalid. You will also need to examine *non-tariff barriers*. These may take the form of administrative regulations to impede trade. Other policies include export subsidies, which may boost exports, but at the expense of a deadweight loss borne by the domestic consumer. Quotas are quantity restrictions which in practice work in a similar way to tariffs, raising the domestic price of the restricted good, but allowing the foreign supplier to reap extra profits rather than bringing revenue to the home government.

## Important Concepts and Technical Terms

Match each lettered concept with the appropriate numbered phrase:

| | | |
|---|---|---|
| (a) Non-tariff barriers | (e) Export subsidy | (i) Law of comparative advantage |
| (b) Import tariff | (f) Commercial policy | (j) GATT |
| (c) Absolute advantage | (g) Optimal tariff | (k) Factor endowments |
| (d) Import quotas | (h) Infant industry argument | (l) Deadweight loss of a tariff |

1  An import duty requiring the importer of a good to pay a specified fraction of the world price to the government.
2  A commercial policy designed to increase exports by granting producers an additional sum above the domestic price per unit exported.
3  The amounts of capital and labour available in an economy.
4  Government policy that influences international trade through taxes or subsidies or through direct restrictions on imports and exports.
5  Administrative regulations that discriminate against foreign goods and favour home goods.
6  The waste arising from the domestic overproduction and domestic underconsumption of a good where imports are subject to a tariff.
7  A principle which states that countries specialize in producing and exporting goods that they produce at a lower relative cost than other countries.
8  Restrictions imposed on the maximum quantity of imports.
9  The ability to produce goods with lower unit labour requirements than in other countries.
10  Tariffs designed to restrict imports until the benefit of the last import equals its cost to society as a whole.
11  A justification of a tariff on the grounds that a developing industry needs protection until established.
12  A commitment by a large number of countries in the post-war period to reduce tariffs successively and to dismantle trade restrictions, now embodied in the *World Trade Organization* (WTO).

## Exercises

1  Table 33-1 shows how the exports of a number of countries were divided between five commodity groups in 1993.

Table 33-1    Structure of merchandise exports, 1993

| Country | Percentage share of merchandise exports | | | | |
|---|---|---|---|---|---|
| | Fuels, minerals, and metals | Other primary commodities | Textiles and clothing | Machinery and transport equipment | Other manufactures |
| Ethiopia | 1 | 95 | 3 | 0 | 1 |
| Pakistan | 1 | 14 | 78 | 0 | 7 |
| Côte d'Ivoire | 15 | 68 | .. | 2 | 15 |
| Trinidad & Tobago | 58 | 8 | 1 | 3 | 31 |
| Saudi Arabia | 90 | 1 | .. | 2 | 7 |
| Hong Kong | 2 | 5 | .. | 26 | 67 |
| UK | 10 | 9 | 5 | 41 | 35 |
| Singapore | 14 | 6 | 4 | 55 | 21 |
| Germany | 4 | 6 | 5 | 48 | 37 |
| Japan | 2 | 1 | 2 | 68 | 27 |

Source: *World Development Report 1995.*
Note: for Côte d'Ivoire, Saudi Arabia, and Hong Kong, textiles are included in other manufactures.

(a)  What do these figures suggest about the factor and resource endowments in these countries and the pattern of comparative advantage?

(b)  Given recent changes in the composition of world exports (see Section 33-1 of the main text), how would you assess the future prospects for these countries?

(c)  What additional information would you require to feel confident in your answers?

2  This exercise examines the gains from trade in a two-country, two-good model. To simplify matters for the time being, we assume that the two countries share a common currency; this allows us to ignore the exchange rate. The two countries are called Anywaria and Someland; the two goods are bicycles and boots. The unit labour requirements of the two goods in each country are shown in Table 33-2; we assume constant returns to scale.

Table 33-2    Production techniques

| | Unit labour requirements (hours per unit output) | |
|---|---|---|
| | Anywaria | Someland |
| Bicycles | 60 | 120 |
| Boots | 30 | 40 |

(a)  Which of the countries has an absolute advantage in the production of the two commodities?

(b)  Calculate the opportunity cost of bicycles in terms of boots and of boots in terms of bicycles for each of the countries.

(c)  Which country has a comparative advantage in the production of bicycles?

Suppose there is no trade. Each of the two economies has 300 workers who work 40 hours per week. Initially, each country devotes half of its resources to producing each of the two commodities.

**Table 33-3  Production of bicycles and boots, no trade case**

|          | Anywaria | Someland | 'World' output |
|----------|----------|----------|----------------|
| Bicycles |          |          |                |
| Boots    |          |          |                |

**Table 33-4  Production of bicycles and boots**

|          | Anywaria | Someland | 'World' output |
|----------|----------|----------|----------------|
| Bicycles |          |          |                |
| Boots    |          |          |                |

(d)  Complete Table 33-3.

Trade now takes place under the following conditions: the country with a comparative advantage in boot production produces only boots. The other country produces sufficient bicycles to maintain the world 'no-trade' output, devoting the remaining resources to boot production.

(e)  Complete Table 33-4 and comment on the gains from trade.

(f)  On a single diagram, plot the production possibility frontier for each country. What aspect of your diagram is indicative of potential gains from trade?

3  This exercise extends the analysis of the previous one by recognizing that our two economies have different currencies and labour costs. Unit labour requirements are as set out before in Table 33-2. The hourly wage rate in Anywaria is A$5; in Someland it is S$4.50.

(a)  Calculate unit labour costs for the two goods in each country.

(b)  Calculate unit labour costs in terms of Somelandish dollars if the exchange rate is A$1=S$1.8.

(c)  Calculate unit labour costs in terms of Somelandish dollars if the exchange rate is A$1=S$1.2.

(d)  Comment on the range of values for the exchange rate within which trade may take place. Explain your answer.

(e)  Within this simple world, what factors will determine the equilibrium exchange rate?

4  Which of the following factors favour(s) intra-industry trade and which act(s) against it?

(a)  Product differentiation.

(b)  International integration.

(c)  Existence of tariff barriers.

(d)  Availability of economies of scale in the production of individual brands.

(e)  High transport costs.

(f)  Homogeneous commodity.

5  Below are listed a selection of arguments which have been advanced to support the existence of tariffs. Identify each as a 'first-best', 'second-best', or 'non-'argument:

(a)  The need to defend domestic producers against unfair competition based on cheap foreign labour.

(b)  The need to maintain a national defence industry in case of war.

(c)  A desire to restrict imports until the benefits of the last imported unit are equalized with its cost to society as a whole.

(d)  The need to nurture a newly developing domestic industry.

(e)  A wish to prevent dumping by foreign producers.

(f)  The government needs a cheap and easy way of obtaining revenue.

6  Which of the following factors may have adverse effects for a country attempting to protect employment by the imposition of tariffs?

(a)  Retaliation in export markets.

(b)  Loss of consumer surplus.

(c)  Generation of tariff revenue.

(d)  Reduced exploitation of comparative advantage

(e)  Resource cost of production inefficiency.

(f)  Reduced import penetration.

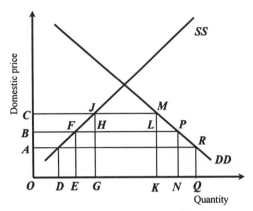

**Figure 33-1    A tariff**

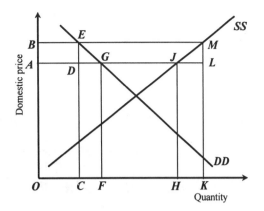

**Figure 33-2    An export subsidy**

7    Figure 33-1 shows the domestic demand (*DD*) and supply (*SS*) of a commodity with and without the imposition of a tariff, the world price being given by *OB*.

(a)  Identify the domestic price and the quantity imported in a situation of free trade.

Suppose now that a tariff is imposed on imports of this commodity.

(b)  Identify the domestic price in the new situation, and the quantity imported.

(c)  By how much does domestic production of this commodity change?

(d)  Identify the area which represents the extra consumer payments for the quantity purchased.

(e)  How much of this accrues to the government as tariff revenue, and how much to domestic producers as additional rents?

(f)  Explain the remaining part of these extra consumer payments.

(g)  Identify the surplus of consumer benefits over social marginal cost which is sacrificed by society in reducing its consumption of this good.

(h)  What is the total welfare cost of this tariff?

8    Figure 33-2 shows the domestic demand (*DD*) and supply (*SS*) of a commodity, the export of which the government wishes to encourage. *OA* represents the world price.

(a)  Identify the domestic price and the quantity exported in a situation of free trade.

The government now imposes an export subsidy.

(b)  Identify the new domestic price and quantity exported.

(c)  By how much does domestic production increase?

(d)  By how much does domestic consumption fall?

(e)  Identify the decrease in consumer surplus.

(f)  What is the social cost of the extra production (i.e. the social cost of producing goods whose marginal cost exceeds the world price)?

(g)  Why would the government wish to introduce this policy?

(h)  How else could the same objective be achieved?

9    Wodgets are available on the world market at a price of £3 each. We consider an economy in which the domestic supply of wodgets is given by:

$Qs = 1000\,p$        (where *p* is the domestic price).

The demand for wodgets is

$Qd = 10\,000 - 1000\,p.$

Assuming there are no tariffs:

(a)  What will be the quantity of wodgets imported?

(b)  What quantity of wodgets will be produced in the domestic market?

If the government places a tariff of £2 on imported wodgets

(c)  Identify the new level of domestic production.

(d)  How much revenue will the government receive from the tariff?

(e)  Calculate the deadweight loss arising from the tariff.

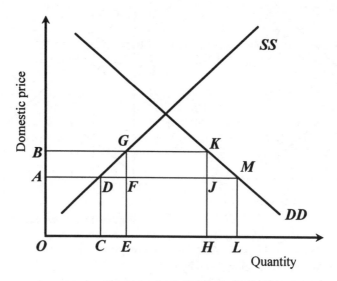

**Figure 33-3    Quota restrictions**

10  The Multi-Fibre Arrangement restricts the increase of imports of many textiles and clothes from the developing into the developed countries including the UK. This exercise explores the effect of such quota agreements on the domestic market using Figure 33-3, which shows the domestic demand curve (*DD*) and supply curves (*SS*) for a commodity. *OA* is the world price.
    (a)  What would be the level of imports in the absence of restriction?
    A quota restriction is now imposed which limits imports to the amount *FJ*.
    (b)  What is the new domestic price?
    (c)  Identify the change in domestic production and consumption.
    (d)  Explain what is represented by the area *FGKJ*.
    (e)  Identify the total welfare cost.
    (f)  Who gains from this, and who loses?

## True/False

1  More than half of world trade is between the industrialized countries.
2  Manufactured goods comprise more than 80 per cent of exports from Asia.
3  International trade is worth while so long as one country has an absolute advantage in production.
4  Comparative advantage reflects international differences in the opportunity costs of producing different goods.
5  If a country has a relatively abundant endowment of a particular factor, it will tend to have a comparative advantage in the production of goods which use that factor intensively.
6  The existence of comparative advantage tends to increase the amount of intra-industry trade.
7  The law of comparative advantage ensures that there are gains from trade which make everyone better off.
8  The imposition of a tariff stimulates domestic consumption.
9  The case for free trade rests partly on the analysis of the deadweight burden arising from the existence of tariff barriers.
10  The need to protect infant industries is a powerful argument in favour of tariff barriers.
11  In the 1990s, tariff levels throughout the world economy were probably as low as they had ever been.
12  Some countries attempt to restrict imports by imposing rigorous or complicated rules concerning the specification of imported goods.

## ECONOMICS IN THE NEWS

### How many Germans does it take to make a light bulb?
*(Adapted from the Financial Times, 21 February 1997)*

The answer to this seemingly light-hearted question is at the core of a ground-breaking deal between one of Germany's biggest unions and the management of Osram, the world's second largest maker of light bulbs. The deal with the IG Metall engineering union, which will safeguard jobs at Osram's plant in Augsburg, southern Germany, is one of the latest examples of how German manufacturers are confronting the future in one of the world's most costly and organized labour markets. In exchange for a commitment on jobs, the union agreed to a more flexible shift system – employees were aware that Osram had been considering transferring plans for a new production line from Augsburg to a plant in Bari, Italy, where labour costs are 40 per cent lower.

The threat was real enough. A big factor behind the recent surge in German unemployment was the shift by many employers to lower-cost production sites, for example in eastern Europe. But as the Osram deal shows, decisions over factory location depend on a variety of factors in addition to labour costs. Productivity, plant flexibility, closeness to customers and the technical content of the work are all included in the equation.

Osram, part of Siemens, Germany's biggest electronics and electrical goods company, says productivity in its German plants is normally higher than elsewhere, reflecting the greater skill of the German workforce. Output per person in its US plants is roughly half that in Germany. Meanwhile it takes 38 times more people to turn out Osram light bulbs in China as in Germany, going a long way to cancel out China's fifty-fold advantage on labour costs.

1   What does this story imply for the German labour market, and future unemployment? Is the answer likely to lie in trying to protect employment in Germany by restricting the level of trade?
2   And how about China? What should the Chinese government do if they wish to remain competitive?

## Questions for Thought

1   The *Financial Times* in April 1997 reported that EU foreign ministers had agreed to take a more flexible approach to import quotas for textiles, despite protests from Portugal that textile jobs would be lost across Europe. Was Portugal right to be concerned?
2   This exercise extends some aspects of the analysis in this chapter of a two-country, two-good world. The two countries are *A* and *B*, the two goods *X* and *Y*. Figure 33-4 focuses on country *A*, illustrating the production possibility frontier (*PPF*) and some indifference curves (*I1*, *I2*) depicting the community's preference for the two goods.

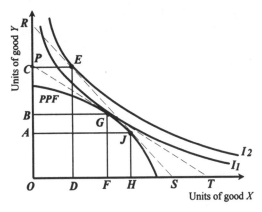

Figure 33-4   Country *A*: production and preferences

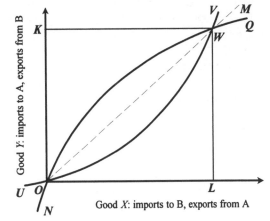

Figure 33-5   Offer curves

Suppose that initially there is no trade, and that the domestic price ratio is given by the line *PT.*

*(a)*   At what point will the economy choose to produce?

*(b)*   If the 'world' price ratio is also given by *PT*, what is implied for comparative advantage and the gains from trade?

Suppose now that the world price ratio is given by *RS*, but the domestic price ratio by *PT*.

*(c)*   What are the implications for the comparative advantage of country *A*?

With international trade in this situation, country *A* can move to any point along *RS* by exporting and importing goods.

*(d)*   At what points will country *A* choose to produce and consume?

*(e)*   Identify exports and imports.

In parts *(d)* and *(e)*, we have seen that the quantities offered for exchange internationally depend upon the terms of trade (the world price ratio) and upon the preferences of people in country *A*. Of course, a similar story could be told for country *B*, showing the offers made for exchange. By examining the offers made by the two countries at different relative world prices, we can gain some insight into the equilibrium terms of trade.

Consider Figure 33-5 on the previous page. The curve *UV* is the 'offer' curve for country *A*: it shows the quantities of good *X* offered in exchange for good *Y* at different terms of trade. The curve *NQ* shows the offer curve for country *B*, constructed in similar fashion.

*(f)*   Interpret the line *OM*, and explain the sense in which the point *W* represents an equilibrium.

# 34   The International Monetary System

## Learning Outcomes

- To consider alternative exchange rate regimes
- To examine the Gold Standard
- To discuss the adjustable peg Bretton Woods system
- To analyse the determination and behaviour of floating exchange rates
- To examine the rise of capital mobility and the reasons for speculative attacks within adjustable peg systems
- To consider ways in which international linkages give rise for motives for co-ordination of national macroeconomic policies
- To study the European Monetary System as an example of monetary policy coordination

**IN THIS CHAPTER ...** you will look at the significance for the world economy of the exchange rate regime adopted by nations. You will investigate whether a fixed or floating exchange rate system is best for the world economy, basing this partly on evidence of the working of various regimes in the past – the 'fixed' systems of the gold standard and the adjustable peg, the more recent experience with a managed float, and the potential for a clean float. There are merits in each of these regimes, but also disadvantages. In this debate, you should be aware that when governments decide on an economic policy, they must remain aware of possible repercussions on other countries. In this sense they operate rather like oligopolists. If a single government allows a rise in the domestic exchange rate in order to combat inflation, an externality is imposed on other countries. *International policy co-ordination* may prevent some of the damage caused by such externalities.

## Important Concepts and Technical Terms

Match each lettered concept with the appropriate numbered phrase:

| | | |
|---|---|---|
| (a) PPP path | (e) Currency board | (i) European Monetary System |
| (b) Adjustable peg regime | (f) Exchange rate speculation | (j) Financial discipline |
| (c) International competitiveness | (g) Gold standard | (k) Speculative attack |
| (d) Capital controls | (h) Managed float | (l) Dollar standard |

1  Measured by comparing the relative prices of the goods from different countries when these are measured in a common currency.
2  The path for the nominal exchange rate that would maintain the level of international competitiveness constant over time.
3  A situation that occurs when a country faces a sharp loss of reserves, a sharp depreciation, or both.
4  An exchange rate system under which the government of each country fixes the price of gold in terms of its home currency, maintains convertibility of the domestic currency into gold, and preserves 100 per cent cover.
5  A regime in which the exchange rate floats but is influenced in the short run by government intervention.
6  An exchange rate system which operated after the Second World War in which countries agreed to fix their exchange rates against the dollar.
7  A feature of fixed exchange rate systems by which governments are forced to pursue policies which keep domestic inflation in line with world rates.
8  The movement of investment funds between currencies in pursuit of the highest return in the light of expected exchange rate changes.
9  Measures introduced by governments to defend pegged exchange rates by prohibiting, restricting or taxing the flow of private capital across countries.
10  A tentative step towards fixed exchange rates involving members of the EU from 1979 onwards.
11  A regime in which exchange rates are normally fixed but countries are occasionally allowed to alter their exchange rate.
12  A constitutional commitment to peg the exchange rate by giving up monetary independence.

## Exercises

1   Below are listed a number of policy actions and situations. In each case, identify the sort of exchange rate regime in operation.

  *(a)* The government carries out open market operations to prevent the exchange rate from falling so rapidly as to endanger the target inflation rate.

  *(b)* The money supply decreases following a balance of payments deficit and a fall in the economy's gold reserves.

  *(c)* A major crisis leads to a devaluation of the domestic currency.

  *(d)* A contractionary fiscal policy is introduced following successive years of balance of payments deficits and falls in the foreign exchange reserves.

  *(e)* The foreign exchange markets are in continuous equilibrium with no government intervention via foreign exchange reserves.

  *(f)* There is a fixed exchange rate regime with automatic government reaction to disequilibrium.

  *(g)* There is a flexible exchange rate system in which the government has some discretion in exchange rate policy.

  *(h)* A country experiencing high rates of inflation relative to other countries also experiences a depreciating nominal exchange rate which in the long run maintains a constant real exchange rate.

2   This exercise and the following one investigate the operation of the gold standard. Suppose the USA has fixed the par value of gold at $20.67 per ounce, and the UK par value is £4.25.

  *(a)* What is the $/£ exchange rate?

  Suppose that you begin with £85 and the exchange rate is $6/£.

  *(b)* How much gold could you buy in the UK?

  *(c)* Suppose instead that you exchange your pounds for dollars: how much gold could you then buy in the USA?

  *(d)* If you then ship the gold back to Britain, what would it be worth in sterling?

  *(e)* For how long would you expect the exchange rate to remain at $6/£?

  *(f)* Describe the likely events should the exchange rate be $3/£.

  Figure 34-1 shows the demand for (*D*) and supply of (*S*) pounds at different exchange rates under the gold standard.

  *(g)* Identify the gold parity exchange rate.

  *(h)* Describe what happens at exchange rate *OC*.

  *(i)* Describe what is happening between exchange rates *OA* and *OC*.

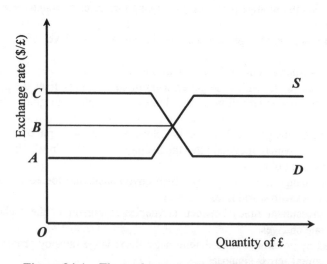

**Figure 34-1   The exchange rate and the gold standard**

3   Two countries, called the UK and the USA, are operating under the gold standard, both countries beginning in both internal and external balance. There is then a fall in the US average propensity to import from the UK at each income level.

  (a)   What is the short-run impact on UK exports and the balance of payments?

  (b)   Describe the effect of this on aggregate demand, output, and employment if UK wages and prices do not immediately respond.

  (c)   How does this affect the exchange rate and UK gold reserves?

  (d)   What does this in turn imply for money supply?

  (e)   Describe how the UK now manages to return to internal and external balance.

  (g)   Briefly outline the effects upon the US economy.

4   Three countries, A, B, and C, are all experiencing relatively high rates of inflation. A floating exchange rate regime is in operation.

  Country A wants to reduce the rate of inflation, so introduces a restrictive monetary policy.

  (a)   What effect does this have on A's exchange rate relative to the other two countries?

  (b)   How does this affect A's competitiveness?

  (c)   Meanwhile, back in B and C, what is happening to the inflation rate?

  Country B now gets worried about inflation and initiates a tight money policy.

  (d)   What effect does this have on 's exchange rate relative to the other two countries?

  (e)   Outline the effects of B's policy on country A.

  We could now, of course, consider what happens when country C decides to have a go at tight money – but instead,

  (f)   comment briefly on the potential advantages of policy harmonization.

5   Which of the following were features of the dollar standard?

  (a)   The provision of an automatic mechanism for resolving imbalances in international payments.

  (b)   The removal of speculation problems, given the fixed nature of the exchange rate.

  (c)   At the fixed exchange rate, central banks were committed to buy or sell dollars from their stock of foreign exchange reserves or dollar holdings.

  (d)   A series of gradual exchange rate adjustments at frequent intervals.

  (e)   100 per cent backing of domestic currencies by dollar reserves.

  (f)   A relatively rapid increase in the world supply of dollars in the late 1960s, partly as a result of the Vietnam war.

6   Which of the following describe the response of an economy to a shock under a system of freely floating exchange rates? (Note: more than one response may be valid.)

  (a)   An autonomous increase in aggregate demand leads to an increase in imports, a balance of payments deficit (in the immediate run), and a depreciation of the domestic currency.

  (b)   A once-for-all reduction in domestic money supply leads to an appreciation of the exchange rate, which may overshoot in the short run.

  (c)   A decrease in aggregate demand leads to a balance of payments surplus and an increase in foreign exchange reserves.

  (d)   Domestic interest rates are increased by government action to slow down a depreciation of the exchange rate.

  (e)   A succession of balance of payments deficits enables the domestic government successfully to request a devaluation of the currency.

7   Which of the following is not a feature of a managed float?

  (a)   In the long run, the nominal exchange rate tends to follow the PPP path.

  (b)   Governments may sometimes intervene to smooth out short-run fluctuations in the exchange rate.

  (c)   The foreign exchange reserves remain constant.

  (d)   The net monetary inflow from abroad need not always be zero.

  (e)   Governments may operate in the foreign exchange market to influence the direction of movement of the exchange rate.

8   In the post-war period, both fixed and floating exchange rate systems have been tried, but there is still no consensus on which is the more effective. Critically evaluate the following statements concerning some of the relevant issues.

*(a)* Flexible exchange rates are better able to cope with major external shocks.

*(b)* Fixed exchange rates offer greater stability of trading conditions.

*(c)* Floating exchange rates enable individual countries to follow independent policies.

*(d)* Fixed exchange rate systems may force governments to adopt other distortionary policy options, such as the imposition of tariffs or import quotas.

## True/False

1   Under the gold standard, 100 per cent backing for the money supply was always strictly adhered to.

2   Victorians were wrong to believe that Britain's trade deficits in the late nineteenth century were the result of laziness or decadence.

3   The crucial difference between the gold standard and the dollar standard was that under the latter there was no longer 100 per cent backing for the domestic currency.

4   The adjustable peg system effectively eliminated speculation by creating a state of certainty regarding future exchange rates.

5   The floating exchange rate regime is flexible but not sufficiently so to cope with substantial differences in inflation rates between countries.

6   In practice, exchange rates have rarely been allowed to float absolutely freely during the period since 1973.

7   The volatility of the exchange rate under a floating system leads to great uncertainty and is likely to reduce the level of international trade and the amount of investment undertaken by firms competing in world markets.

8   Protectionism is more likely to occur under a fixed exchange rate system.

9   Policy harmonization might have allowed the world economy to reduce inflation in the late 1970s/early 1980s at a lower short-run cost in unemployment.

10   The EMS committed the central banks of member countries to intervene in foreign exchange markets whenever any of the currencies threatened to deviate from its par value against other member countries by more than an agreed amount.

11   Countries that have pursued more stringent exchange rate regimes have typically had lower and more stable inflation rates than the rest of the world.

## ECONOMICS IN THE NEWS

### Monetary authority shows it can put its money where its mouth is
*(Adapted from The South China Morning Post, Hong Kong, 17 January 2000)*

The past year will be remembered as the period when Hong Kong, having decisively defeated the speculators against its currency, finally began its long-awaited recovery from the Asian financial crisis. Soon after this crisis erupted in July 1997 and rapidly engulfed most of East Asia, a host of pundits, analysts, and other self-appointed experts opined and declaimed that Hong Kong's linked exchange rate could not stand alone when other regional currencies fell. They felt that the population could not or would not endure the pains of domestic adjustments, that Beijing would not allow Hong Kong to squander its foreign exchange reserves, that depegging or devaluation was a matter of time. Yet 2.5 years later, as the crisis itself was drawing to a close, the Hong Kong dollar's peg to the US dollar remains intact and extraordinarily stable.

How has Hong Kong managed to do this? One obvious but superficial reason is Hong Kong's strong foreign reserves. When the crisis first erupted, Hong Kong had about US$82 billion in reserves, which rose to US$98 billion in January 1998. However, the existence of strong foreign reserves is only a necessary, but not a sufficient condition, for exchange rate stability. For example, both Singapore and Taiwan also had enormous reserves, yet they had chosen 'competitive devaluation' as the soft option.

Hong Kong, however, had both the ability and will to defend its currency against speculators. From January to September 1998, Hong Kong spent about US$10 billion from its reserves to battle speculators, not only in the forex market, but also in the securities markets. On both counts it had won handsomely.

A more fundamental reason for the robustness of the linked exchange rate is that it is a form of currency board arrangement (CBA). Under the currency arrangement, the monetary base must be fully backed by foreign currency assets, and there is consequently an automatic adjustment mechanism, basically similar to that under the classical gold standard. It is true that this gold-standard type of adjustments in interest rates, prices, and wages can be very painful, even brutal. But abandoning the CBA could mean a greater catastrophe, and a replay of the 1982–83 crisis, which nearly brought Hong Kong to its knees. Perhaps mindful of the fact that the linked exchange rate saved Hong Kong from total collapse in 1983, the population has generally supported the present system, despite occasional grumbles.

The robustness of the linked rate must not give rise to any smugness, however, for our currency stability has been achieved at a heavy price in the form of the worst recession in 40 years. Fortunately, the economy has finally turned round after painful adjustments. The growth rate of real GDP has become positive again, rising from 1.1 per cent in the second quarter to 4.5 per cent in the third quarter last year. For 1999 as a whole, the economy should register a growth rate of 1.8 per cent. For 2000, the current prevailing view is that a growth rate of 4 to 5 per cent is achievable, barring unforeseen circumstances.

One final point which is not often appreciated: by refusing to join the game of 'competitive devaluation', China and Hong Kong have played a stabilising role during the financial crisis. Both therefore deserve credit for their responsible behaviour in international financial affairs.

1   Describe how a currency board arrangement operates in practice.
2   Explain why such a linked exchange rate system forces a painful domestic adjustment process on an economy.
3   Discuss whether the benefits of maintaining the linked exchange rate system outweigh the costs of adjustment.

## Questions for Thought

1   Discuss the proposition that governments will not behave responsibly unless forced to.
2   Below are listed four criteria by which an exchange rate regime may be evaluated. Outline the merits and demerits of fixed and floating systems under each criterion:
    (a)  Robustness.
    (b)  Financial discipline.
    (c)  Volatility.
    (d)  Freedom from restrictions on trade and payment.
    To what extent does the UK's post-war experience support the case for fixed or floating exchange rates?

# 35   European Integration

## Learning Outcomes

- To evaluate the success of the programme to create a Single Market in the EU
- To discuss how small integrated European economies, caring about their mutual exchange rates but vulnerable to capital flows, concluded that there was no alternative to monetary union
- To examine the process by which EMU was created and the macroeconomic policies that it will now seek to pursue
- To explore why the UK has traditionally been reluctant to join monetary co-operation in Europe
- To assess progress in Central and Eastern European economies making the transition from central planning to modern market economies

**IN THIS CHAPTER ...** you will investigate some key issues facing Europe. The creation of the European single market began the process of closer integration, and the breaking down of barriers with Eastern Europe offers new challenges. The single market measures involved the abolition of all remaining foreign exchange controls within the EU, together with the removal of *non-tariff barriers,* the elimination of bias in public sector purchasing policies, the virtual removal of frontier controls and progress towards harmonization of tax rates. These measures should have had the effect of stimulating increases in the volume of intra-European trade, and reducing the transactions costs of such trade. This has also enabled the exploitation of more economies of scale, and led to intensified competition. *European monetary union (EMU)* has been seen by some commentators as the logical extension of the *European Monetary System* and the single market measures. The benefits of such a union can only be reached if individual member states are prepared to surrender sovereignty over domestic monetary policy. For EMU to be successful, it was seen to be crucial for member states to have converged in certain key areas of economic policy and performance. The criteria were set down in the *Maastricht Treaty.* In the event, eleven countries established a single currency area in 1999.

## Important Concepts, Technical Terms and Initials

Match each lettered concept with the appropriate numbered phrase:

| | | | | | |
|---|---|---|---|---|---|
| (a) | A monetary union | (e) | CEE | (i) | ERM |
| (b) | EMU | (f) | Optimal currency area | (j) | Federal fiscal system |
| (c) | CAP | (g) | Maastricht Treaty | (k) | ECB |
| (d) | SOE | (h) | Non-tariff barriers | (l) | Cross-border takeovers |

1   Differences in national regulations or practices preventing free movement of goods, services, and factors across countries.
2   The largest programme administered by the EU, involving a system of administered high prices for agricultural commodities.
3   A system by which each member country fixed a nominal exchange rate against each other participant, while jointly floating against the rest of the world.
4   A system in which a group of states agrees to have permanently fixed exchange rates within the union, an integrated financial system and a single monetary authority responsible for setting the union's money supply.
5   Central and Eastern Europe.
6   The joining together of members of the EU in a monetary union.
7   The authority with full responsibility for EU monetary policy.
8   A system under which fiscal transfers between states helps to cushion individual states from the effects of temporary local recession.
9   A group of countries better off with a common currency than keeping separate national currencies.
10   The treaty that set out the agreed route towards monetary union within Europe.
11   A situation in which domestic firms buy into or sell out to firms based in other countries.
12   A common feature of the former centrally planned economies, in which enterprises were owned by the state.

## Exercises

1  The creation of a single European market by 1992 entailed a number of changes for EU members. For each of the following, state whether or not they were part of the 1992 reforms:

(a) The abolition of all remaining foreign exchange controls between EU members.

(b) The removal of frontier controls (delays), subject to retention of necessary safeguards for security, social and health reasons.

(c) The harmonization of all tax rates in EU member countries.

(d) The removal of all non-tariff barriers to trade within the EU.

(e) The creation of an economic area without frontiers in which the free movement of goods, persons, services, and capital is ensured.

(f) Mutual recognition of regulations such that, for instance, a doctor who qualified in England could practice medicine in any other EU country.

(g) The adoption of a common currency within the EU.

2  Which of the following constitute non-tariff barriers to trade?

(a) Differences in patent laws between countries.

(b) Safety standards which act to segment national markets.

(c) Voluntary export restraints – bilateral agreements whereby an exporting country agrees to limit exports to a quota.

(d) Taxes imposed on imported goods.

(e) Sanitary requirements for imported meats and dairy products which are more stringent than for domestic goods.

(f) Quota limits on the import of particular commodities.

(g) Packaging and labelling requirements.

3  The entry of sterling into the Exchange Rate Mechanism of the European Monetary System was delayed until 1990. A number of reasons were put forward for this delay, some of which are listed below. In each case, consider the strength of the case made against entry.

(a) Sterling was a petrocurrency because of North Sea oil, and is thus subject to volatility because of possible fluctuations in the price of oil.

(b) With London and Frankfurt being the only decontrolled financial centres in Europe, it would be inconvenient for the UK to join the ERM, as this would require the co-ordination of monetary policy.

(c) A significant proportion of UK trade is conducted with countries outside the EU.

(d) UK inflation was being controlled independently by the policies of the government in power, so the additional stability of the ERM was unnecessary.

(e) Independence of domestic monetary policy is important for the UK.

(f) The EMS was a result of muddled thinking, so it is better to bide time until things settle down.

You might like to discuss with your fellow students the extent to which these arguments continue to apply in the context of joining the single currency.

4  Which of the following is/are characteristic of a monetary union?

(a) Fixed exchange rates within the union.

(b) A single currency.

(c) Freedom of capital movement.

(d) A single monetary authority for setting the union's money supply.

(e) A common interest rate policy.

(f) A federal government

(g) A federal fiscal system.

5  Consider a country that is part of a monetary union that has no federal system of fiscal transfers. Suppose that for some reason – perhaps trade union pressure – firms in the economy face an increase in costs which is passed on by producers in the form of higher prices. This exercise traces the path taken by the economy as it adjusts towards equilibrium.

(a) If the cost increase is restricted to firms in the domestic economy, what is the effect on competitiveness?

*(b)* Given that the exchange rate cannot adjust because of the rules of the monetary union, what is the effect on exports?

*(c)* What will be the consequences for output and employment?

*(d)* By what process will the economy now return to equilibrium?

*(e)* The Delors Report favoured the placing of ceilings on government budget deficits so that the return to equilibrium could not be encouraged by domestic fiscal policy. Would such expansionary fiscal action be effective, and why should it be outlawed?

*(f)* Explain how a system of federal fiscal transfers would alter the sequence of events.

6   Identify each of the following as a cost or a benefit of 1992 or European Monetary Union:

*(a)* Greater efficiency in resource allocation.

*(b)* The removal of frontier controls.

*(c)* Loss of protection of domestic activity.

*(d)* Loss of sovereignty over interest rates.

*(e)* Intensified competition.

*(f)* Enhancement of labour mobility.

*(g)* Reduction of trade between Britain and the Commonwealth.

*(h)* Exchange rate certainty.

*(i)* Fuller exploitation of economies of scale.

*(j)* Establishment of a credible pre-commitment to controlling inflation.

*(k)* Inflexibility in adjusting to a loss of competitiveness.

*(l)* A reduction in transaction costs.

*(m)* A politically acceptable way for moving towards European integration.

7   Figure 35-1 shows the situation facing a small country in Euroland. With the interest rate being set by the ECB, the country faces a fixed interest rate $r_0$, so the *LM* curve is effectively horizontal. $Y_0$ represents potential output, but the country is in recession with the *IS* curve stuck at $IS_A$.

*(a)* How far would the interest rate need to fall for the economy to reach potential output?

*(b)* Is this a feasible solution?

*(c)* What steps could the government of the country take in order to reach $Y_0$?

*(d)* In the absence of intervention from the domestic government or the ECB, will the economy ever get to $Y_o$? If so, by what mechanism?

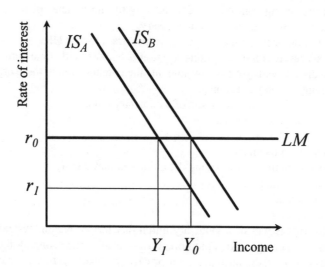

**Figure 35-1   A small country in Euroland**

8   For the UK, 1992 brought problems which had not been wholly anticipated. Instead of the smooth integration into the single market and progress towards even closer integration through monetary union, the UK was forced to suspend its membership of the ERM, bringing the temptation to retreat back to being the solitary island. Which of the following do you see as the best way forward, and why? Which is the most likely course?

*(a)* Give up the whole idea of joining the single currency, and go back to flexible exchange rates, thus retaining national sovereignty.

*(b)* Speed up the process of transition to EMU, and thus minimize vulnerability to speculative pressure.

*(c)* Return to the idea of sedate progression towards EMU, but introduce policies such as the Tobin tax which would reduce the power and influence of the short-term speculators, and thus avoid the problems such as that which led to the UK's exit from the ERM.

9   Imagine that you are a planner working in one of the centrally planned economies of Eastern Europe in the early 1980s. (You may wish to tackle parts of this question in conjunction with the commentary in the 'Answers and Comments' section.)

*(a)* The rules of the economy do not permit the industry for which you are responsible to make profits, so profit maximization cannot be your objective: on what basis do you take decisions about the number of workers to hire and the amount of output to be produced?

*(b)* How do you think prices will come to be fixed?

*(c)* If the output of your industry (e.g. steel) is used for defence goods, industrial goods, and consumer goods, how will priorities be determined?

*(d)* What is likely to be the state of equilibrium or disequilibrium in the market for consumer goods?

*(e)* Discuss the incentives for workers and management.

*(f)* Reforms are introduced to move the economy towards a more market-oriented system. What is the likely effect upon prices, especially in the market for consumer goods?

*(g)* Must inflation occur?

*(h)* Under what conditions will the market reforms be successful?

*(i)* By the time you get to tackle this question, market reforms in Eastern Europe will have progressed even further. Discuss the degree of success that has been achieved.

## True/False

1   The swing in thinking against big government and extensive regulation of the economy accelerated the moves towards European integration.

2   A bank registered in Germany was, after 1992, permitted to operate in France or the UK.

3   The 1992 reforms created a European economic area almost as large as the United States or Japan.

4   1992 outlawed tariffs on trade between EU members.

5   Cross-border takeovers and mergers of European firms will effectively preserve market power and prevent gains from the intensified competition that was intended to follow the 1992 reforms.

6   English and Scottish banknotes both circulate in Scotland, proving that a monetary union need not have a single currency.

7   The Maastricht Treaty was an agreement by all EU member-nations to achieve monetary union by 1997.

8   Countries gain most by keeping their monetary sovereignty when they are not integrated with potential partners, have a different structure and hence are likely to face different shocks, and cannot rely on domestic wage and price flexibility as a substitute for exchange rate controls.

9   The EU Structural Funds provide a system of federal fiscal transfers which can help countries suffering from a temporary loss of competitiveness.

10   The Bank of England's MPC is more transparent in its operations than the ECB.

11   The high standards of education and health provision in the countries of Eastern Europe put them in a better position to be able to attain large productivity gains than many of today's less developed countries.

12   The substantial debts incurred by Eastern European countries to Western creditors are a substantial obstacle to further development.

## ECONOMICS IN THE NEWS

### 1   Toyota threat to quit UK over euro
*(Adapted from The Guardian, 18 January 2000)*

The head of one of the world's biggest car companies reignited the debate over the single currency yesterday with a warning for the government that its £1.5bn investment in the UK would be at risk if Britain stayed out of the euro. Executives of Japan's biggest car manufacturer, Toyota, which employs thousands of workers at plants in Derbyshire and Clwyd, said they could no longer sit on the fence as Britain decides whether or not to enter EMU. 'Waiting for a decision is really hurting us and it is time to state very clearly to the British public that we want Britain to join the single currency,' said Shoichiro Toyoda, honorary chairman and former chief executive officer of Toyota.

The comments are sure to increase the pressure on the government and come days after the trade and industry secretary, Stephen Byers, admitted that big business was telling ministers that they must make a decision on the euro early in the next parliament.

Toyota's broadside echoes earlier calls by senior figures from industry to sign up to the single currency. The chairman of Rover Group, Prof W. Samann, told reporters recently that full membership of the euro would 'consolidate BMW's investment' in Britain. Naoyuki Akikusa, the president of Fujitsu, went further last year. 'If the UK were to join in 2002, that would be OK. But if 2020 – that would pose a big problem.'

Toyota managers said yesterday that its UK operations, including a new £200m plant at Burnaston, Derbyshire, would be at risk if the strong pound continued to push its British operations deep into the red. The company said its British operation had suffered its worst performance ever last year as a result of the sharp strengthening of sterling against the euro. This currency fluctuation hurts the competitiveness of the 200,000 Toyota cars produced each year in the UK, 70% of which are sold elsewhere in Europe.

The comments, which represent the clearest indication yet of Japanese frustration with Britain's prevarication on the euro, will send shudders through manufacturing industry. Trade union figures show that more than 1m jobs could be lost unless the government signs up for the single currency within 30 months.

For inward investors one of the UK's strongest attractions has been the combination of flexible labour markets and strong trading links with Europe – up to 60% of exports – but the strength of the pound vis-à-vis the euro is undermining the competitiveness of British-based manufacturers.

Since its opening in 1992, Toyota's Burnaston factory has expanded rapidly and its output almost doubled last year to 200,000 cars. The Deeside plant in Clwyd is one of the world's largest engine plants. Together, they have created 3,300 jobs directly, as well as four times that amount among suppliers, in two of Britain's employment blackspots.

Even if Toyota decides only to freeze its current scale of operations, it would be a setback for Britain. Any hesitancy it expresses about the UK is bound to trigger doubts among other Japanese investors.

1   What features of the UK economy make it attractive for Japanese firms as a location for manufacturing activity?
2   Why should membership of the single currency area be so important for Japanese car firms?

### 2   One side of the coin
*(Adapted from an article by James Forder in Economic Review, Volume 17(3), February 2000)*

There are really two economic issues that need to be considered in thinking about European integration. One is whether the member states of the European Union are likely to be well served, in principle, by having the same currency. The second is whether the particular arrangements made for managing that currency in the Maastricht Treaty and certain later agreements are desirable. On each issue people are to be found on both sides, and with no particular tendency for those who think a single currency harmful also to think the Maastricht arrangements are undesirable, or vice versa.

The basic point in favour of a single currency is that it reduces transactions costs in trade and travel, and eliminates uncertainty about future exchange rates. These are both supply side benefits. The first releases the factors of production involved in currency transactions for employment in a genuinely productive activity. The second promotes the efficient allocation of international investment.

The basic cost, however, is in the loss of economic policy autonomy. This is something different from the political idea of sovereignty, which is about the *right* to control one's policy. Autonomy is about the *ability* to control it. In a single currency area, there cannot be different interest rates in different places. This is fundamentally because of the opportunity for arbitrage. Hypothetically, if there were different interest rates in France and Germany, borrowers in the high interest country would seek to borrow in the low interest one, whilst lenders were doing the opposite, and the two interest rates would converge.

What we really learn from this of course is not that it is definitely the case that the whole European Union would benefit from a single currency, but rather that there are both costs and benefits when we think about enlarging a currency area. The two extreme cases are where every individual has their own currency and where the whole world shares a single currency. The first case would be hopeless since in effect we would be in a barter economy. The second – a common world currency – might perhaps not be bad, but it is a fair bet that transactions between some areas would be so slight that there would be little benefit in reducing transactions costs between them, and yet perhaps large costs if they are forced to adopt the same interest rate policy. The question is then one of where one draws the line. Do we suppose that the right sort of size for a currency area is as large as the European Union, or more like the size of the United Kingdom?

1   Is the UK economy sufficiently integrated with the rest of Europe to ensure that the savings in transactions costs are substantial?
2   Do you think that the ECB will be rigorous in pursuing price stability than the Bank of England's MPC?
3   To what extent is the UK likely to share common patterns of economic activity across the business cycle with the rest of Europe?
4   If you balance the benefits against the costs of membership of the single currency, do you think that the UK should join?

## Questions for Thought

1   Germany has become a major force within the EU, because of the strength of its economy. Explore the way in which this affects other members of the EU and the build-up towards EMU.
2   Discuss the UK's entry and exit from the ERM. Do you believe that re-entry is in the UK's best interests? Has it yet happened?
3   'The pressure for reform in Eastern Europe came more from discontent with past performance than from belief in the superiority of capitalist economies.' Do you think this overstates the situation?
4   Discuss the extent to which Euroland meets the conditions of an optimal currency area.

# 36  Problems of Developing Countries

## Learning Outcomes

- To analyse why poor countries are poor and explore ways in which they may do better in the future
- To identify the handicaps with which developing countries begin
- To examine whether reliance on comparative advantage, usually the export of primary products, is a secure route to prosperity
- To discuss the role of industrialization and the export of manufactures
- To study the problems that have arisen in seeking development through foreign borrowing
- To explore the role that structural adjustment can now play in future development
- To assess the importance of aid from rich countries

**IN THIS CHAPTER ...** you will examine the global maldistribution of income, by which a vast number of people in *less-developed countries (LDCs)* live in conditions of dire poverty. The LDCs have long felt that they have been exploited by the rich nations, and in 1974 they used the forum of the United Nations to call for a *New International Economic Order (NIEO)*. Progress since then has been at best mixed. Some countries (mainly in South East Asia) have enjoyed remarkable success in economic growth, but the *relative* position of most LDCs has worsened. Here you will investigate reasons for low growth rates in the LDCs, as well as looking at some of the possible routes that could be taken to bring improved success in the future. If a key factor in the failure to develop is the lack of resources, then the question of development resolves into a question of how countries can better mobilise resources, either within the domestic economy, or by drawing in resources from abroad, through trade, aid, borrowing, or direct investment. You will also look at the relationship between the LDCs and the more developed countries, and at the difficulties caused by the high indebtedness of a number of LDCs.

## Important Concepts and Technical Terms

Match each lettered concept with the appropriate numbered phrase:

| | | |
|---|---|---|
| (a) Import substitution | (e) New protectionism | (i) Aid |
| (b) Less developed countries | (f) Export-led growth | (j) Debt rescheduling |
| (c) Primary commodities | (g) Price volatility | (k) International debt crisis |
| (d) Buffer stock | (h) Newly industrialized countries | (l) Structural adjustment |

1  An organization aiming to stabilize a commodity market, buying when the price is low and selling when the price is high.
2  Agricultural commodities, minerals, and fuels: goods that may be inputs into a production process but are not outputs from such a process.
3  Attempts by some industrial countries to protect domestic industries from competition from LDCs.
4  Assistance from the rich North to the poor South in the form of subsidized loans, gifts of food, or machinery or technical help, and the free provision of expert advisers.
5  A situation in which LDCs have difficulty in meeting their debt repayments and interest payments, such that interest rates rise, aggravating the situation still further.
6  The pursuit of supply-side policies aimed at increasing potential output by increasing efficiency.
7  Production and income growth through exports rather than the displacement of imports.
8  A group of countries that have successfully developed local industries and are growing rapidly and exporting manufactures.
9  The low-income nations of the world, ranging from the very poor, such as Ethiopia and India, to the nearly rich, such as Argentina and Mexico.
10  A policy of replacing imports by domestic production under the protection of high tariffs or import quotas.
11  A situation in which prices are subject to extreme movements from year to year.
12  A procedure whereby countries with difficulties in meeting their debts are either lent new money to meet existing loans or allowed to pay back the original loan over a longer time scale than originally negotiated.

# Exercises

1   Table 36-1 lists some data relating to various welfare measures for eight countries throughout the world. (They will be identified in the 'Answers' section.) The list of countries includes low-income, lower middle-income, upper middle-income, and high-income economies. Try to associate each country with the appropriate income category. Which of the countries would you classify as LDCs?

**Table 36-1    Welfare indicators**

| Country | Average annual per cent growth rate of population 1975-97 | Per cent of GDP from agriculture 1998 | Life expectancy at birth (years) 1997 | Infant mortality rate (aged under 1) per 1000 live births 1997 | Population with access to safe water (%) 1995 | Adult literacy rate (%) 1997 |
|---------|-----|-----|------|-----|-----|------|
| A | 1.7 | 11 | 68.8 | 33  | 89  | 94.7 |
| B | 1.4 | 7  | 72.9 | 22  | 65  | 96.5 |
| C | 2.6 | 40 | 57.3 | 83  | 59  | 38.1 |
| D | 1.0 | 2  | 76.7 | 7   | 98  | 99.0 |
| E | 2.3 | 17 | 68.3 | 35  | 83  | 94.6 |
| F | 2.1 | 5  | 72.2 | 31  | 95  | 90.1 |
| G | 2.5 | 49 | 42.4 | 119 | 48  | 44.6 |
| H | 0.2 | 2  | 77.2 | 6   | 100 | 99.0 |

Source: *Human Development Report 1999, World Development Report 1999/2000.*
Note: Figures in italics are for a different year.

2   Demand for a primary product is stable, but the supply is subject to large fluctuations from year to year. The producers of the product decide to operate a buffer stock to stabilize revenue. Table 36-2 shows how demand varies with price.
Suppose the buffer stock is operated in such a way that price is stabilized at $70 per unit.
*(a)* In the first year of the buffer stock, supply turns out to be 450 (thousand) units. What would the equilibrium price have been without the buffer stock? How must the buffer stock act to stabilize price at $70?
*(b)* Supply is 350 in the second year. Identify what equilibrium price would have been, the quantity bought or sold by the buffer stock, and the cumulative quantity of the commodity held by the buffer stock.
*(c)* In the following five years, supply turns out successively to be 375, 425, 400, 325, and 475. Trace the cumulative quantity held by the buffer stock.
*(d)* What price would on average have kept the buffer stock stable?

**Table 36-2    Demand for a primary product**

| Price per unit ($) | Quantity demanded ('000 units) |
|--------------------|-------------------------------|
| 100 | 300 |
| 90  | 325 |
| 80  | 350 |
| 70  | 375 |
| 60  | 400 |
| 50  | 425 |
| 40  | 450 |
| 30  | 475 |
| 20  | 500 |

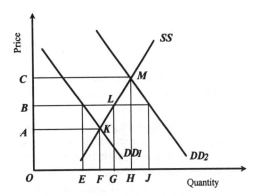

**Figure 36-1    Commodity price stabilization**

3   Consider the market for a primary commodity in which supply is stable, but the position of the demand schedule varies with the business cycle experienced by the industrial nations. The position is illustrated in Figure 36-1 on the previous page.

*SS* represents the supply curve. When the industrial nations are in the trough of the cycle, demand is at *DD1*; at the peak, demand for the commodity is *DD2*.

(a)  Identify equilibrium price and revenue at the trough of the cycle.

(b)  Identify equilibrium price and revenue at the peak of the cycle.

Suppose now that a buffer stock is established with the aim of stabilizing price at *OB*.

(c)  Identify quantity supplied and total revenue if demand were such as to make *OB* the equilibrium price.

(d)  Describe the actions of the buffer stock and revenue accruing to producers in the trough of the cycle.

(e)  Describe the actions of the buffer stock and revenue accruing to producers in the peak of the cycle.

4   Consider two economies, representative of low-income and high-income nations. In the period 1965-85, the low-income country experiences a faster annual growth rate of 2.9 per cent per annum compared with 1.6 per cent per annum for the higher-income economy. Suppose the low-income country begins with GNP per capita of $380, compared with $8460 for the high-income economy. Calculate the absolute difference between GNP per capita in the two countries, and investigate whether the differential widens or narrows over a five-year period given the above growth rates.

5   Table 36-3 presents data on growth rates and the share of manufactures in exports for a selection of countries.

**Table 36-3    Industry, growth and trade**

| Country | Annual real per capita GNP growth 1975–95 (%) | Share of manufactures in exports (%) | |
|---------|---------|---------|---------|
| | | 1960 | 1993 |
| A | 1.5 | 3 | 53 |
| B | –1.8 | 1 | 17 |
| C | 3.2 | 0 | 73 |
| D | 5.8 | 26 | 84 |
| E | 0.7 | 29 | 37 |
| F | 5.7 | 80 | 93 |
| G | 0.3 | 5 | 26 |
| H | 7.0 | 14 | 87 |
| I | 3.8 | 4 | 14 |

Source: *World Development Report, Human Development Report.*

Identify the newly industrialized countries.

6   Which of the following would be regarded as typical features of the LDCs?

(a)  Low productivity in agriculture.

(b)  High dependence on primary commodities.

(c)  Meagre provision of infrastructure.

(d)  Low population growth.

(e)  Low propensity to import.

(f)  Rapidly expanding labour force.

Which of these features might be seen as the most damaging to prospects for economic development?

7   This exercise explores issues of static and dynamic comparative advantage in the context of LDCs.

(a)  Many LDCs have a relative scarcity of physical and human capital, as compared with natural resources or unskilled labour. Where is their comparative advantage likely to rest?

*(b)* Does the historical pattern of primary product prices have implications for the product specialization suggested by your answer to *(a)*?

*(c)* Might an import substitution policy serve to alter a country's comparative advantage? What are the disadvantages of this approach?

*(d)* Discuss whether export promotion is likely to be a superior strategy.

8   The transfer of aid between countries involves both (rich) donors and (poor) recipients. In this exercise, we explore some of the motivations on each side. If you find the questions to be obscure, please tackle them in conjunction with the commentary provided.

*(a)* It might be argued that donors provide aid for humanitarian motives. Does your experience of the governments of industrial nations suggest this to be a sufficient explanation for aid flows?

*(b)* What political motivations might donors have for granting aid?

*(c)* Many aid transactions involve the movement of commodities between countries, either directly or as an indirect result of aid. How might donor countries advance their own economic self-interest through the granting of aid?

*(d)* From the recipients' perspective, why might there be political reasons for accepting aid?

*(e)* The economic motivation for accepting aid seems obvious ... but might there be disadvantages for an independent country?

*(f)* Why should free trade be superior to aid for encouraging development?

9   Consider Table 36-4 and then relate the figures to the statements that follow.

**Table 36-4   Debt indicators for developing countries, 1980–83**

| Indicators | 1980 | 1981 | 1982 | 1983 |
|---|---|---|---|---|
| Ratio of debt to GDP | 19.2 | 21.9 | 24.9 | 26.7 |
| Ratio of debt to exports | 76.1 | 90.8 | 90.8 | 121.4 |
| Debt service ratio | 13.6 | 16.6 | 16.6 | 20.7 |
| Ratio of interest service to GNP | 1.5 | 1.9 | 1.9 | 2.2 |
| Total debt outstanding and disbursed ($ billion) | 424.8 | 482.6 | 538.0 | 595.8 |
| *of which* Official | 157.5 | 172.3 | 190.9 | 208.5 |
| Private | 267.3 | 310.3 | 347.1 | 387.3 |

Note: calculations are based on a sample of 90 developing countries.
Source: *World Development Report 1984.*

Which of the following statements are supported by the figures in Table 36-4?

*(a)* The size of debt relative to GNP was increasing steadily during the period.

*(b)* An increasing share of exports was being taken up by the servicing of existing debt.

*(c)* Borrowing from commercial banks and other private sources grew in importance relative to borrowing from official sources.

*(d)* During the period, the amount of debt grew such that, even if an entire year's exports were devoted to paying off the debt, it would not suffice.

Since the early 1980s, the debt situation does not seem to have improved dramatically. Table 36-5 offers more recent data for a number of countries in Sub-Saharan Africa.

Table 36-5    Debt indicators for some Sub-Saharan African countries

| Country | Debt service ratio (debt service as % of exports of goods and services | | Total external debt | |
|---|---|---|---|---|
| | 1980 | 1997 | As % of GNP 1997 | US$ billions 1997 |
| Ethiopia | 7 | 12 | 159 | 10.1 |
| Mozambique | .. | 19 | 233 | 6.0 |
| Uganda | 17 | 22 | 57 | 3.7 |
| Côte d'Ivoire | 39 | 27 | 165 | 15.6 |
| Tanzania | 26 | 13 | 97 | 7.2 |
| Ghana | 13 | 30 | 89 | 6.0 |
| Kenya | 21 | 22 | 65 | 6.5 |

Source: *Human Development Report 1999.*

10   Table 36-6 shows data for two countries relating to a range of social indicators.

Table 36-6    Social indicators for two countries

| Indicator | Country X | Country Y |
|---|---|---|
| Life expectancy at birth (years) 1993 | 72 | 56.3 |
| Adult literacy (%) 1993 | 89.6 | 60.8 |
| Combined school enrolment ratio (%) 1993 | 66 | 48 |
| Infant mortality per 1000 live births 1993 | 17 | 62 |
| Population per doctor 1988-91 | 7143 | 12500 |
| Daily calorie supply per capita 1992 | 2275 | 1981 |
| Pupil:teacher ratio (primary) 1992 | 29 | 20 |

Source: *Human Development Report 1996.*

Which of these two countries would you expect to have the higher GNP per capita?

## True/False

1   In 1997, 35 per cent of the world's people lived in low-income countries with an average income for the year of about £220 per person.
2   A major problem of the LDCs is the lack of both physical and financial capital.
3   The tribal customs prevalent in some LDCs inhibit the development of enterprise and initiative.
4   The law of comparative advantage proves that the best route to prosperity is for the LDCs to export primary commodities to the rest of the world.
5   The reduction of price volatility by the use of a buffer stock is most necessary and most successful when demand and supply are relatively elastic.
6   Import substitution is doomed to failure because it involves the concentration of resources into industries in which an economy has a comparative disadvantage.
7   On average, the NICs grew twice as rapidly as the rich industrialized nations during the 1970s.
8   Debt rescheduling has avoided default by a number of LDCs on external loan repayments; such defaults would have had major repercussions on financial institutions in the leading countries.
9   Structural adjustment programmes are measures designed by rich countries to keep poor countries in their place.
10   The quickest way to equalize world income distribution would probably be to permit free migration between countries.
11   More aid is what is needed to solve the problems of the LDCs.

## ECONOMICS IN THE NEWS

### UN sets $80 billion as price of ending world poverty
*(Adapted from the Financial Times, 29 May 1997)*

Extreme poverty could be eradicated across the world in the early part of the 21st century, according to the 1997 United Nations Human Development Report. It says the developing world has made progress in the last 30 years that took the industrial world a century to accomplish. More than 75 per cent of the world's population can now expect to live beyond 40. Child mortality rates have halved since 1960, malnutrition has fallen by a third, and adult illiteracy by a third. But, the report warns, there is no room for complacency: 800m people world-wide do not have enough to eat, and 1.3 billion people live on less than 60p per day.

The report introduces the notion of 'human poverty', which focuses on lack of capabilities, rather than low income alone. This is based on measurement of life expectancy, education levels and overall material provision. On this basis, the report estimates that a quarter of the developing world lives in poverty. Sub-Saharan Africa has the highest proportion of people in human poverty, and its fastest rate of growth. Between 1990 and 1994 per capita income in Sub-Saharan Africa fell by 2.4 per cent. Africa has failed to attract foreign investment, and excessive military expenditure and foreign debt repayment have been a drain. The problems are worsened, says the report, by the increasing incidence of Aids, and violent conflict in 30 African countries. In looking to the future, the authors emphasize that developing countries need first to help themselves – to suppress conflict, corruption and organized crime and to invest in human capital. Poor macroeconomic policy, and the failure to uphold the rule of law and to enforce contracts has deterred foreign investment. To break this downward spiral, and to eradicate income poverty, the report proposed a six-point plan:

- Promoting the political rights of poor people, and making clean water, education, health care, and social safety nets available to all.
- Promoting sexual equality to ensure equal rights, equal access to education, equal access to health care, and equal access to land and credit for women.
- Higher levels of growth, and 'pro-poor growth' that reduces inequality and helps the poor, and those in rural areas.
- Managed globalization to help the poorest countries, through fairer world trade, concessional assistance, debt relief, and the promotion of basic education and skills.
- A democratic voice for the poor in developing countries, to allow them to advance their own interests peacefully.
- Special support from the international community in conflict prevention and peacekeeping, debt relief for human development and poverty eradication, and more aid better directed to the poor.

The report says that basic social services could be made available to all people in developing countries at the cost of $40 billion over the next 10 years. A further investment of $40 billion over 20 years could spur pro-poor growth, and eradicate income poverty across the world. With this price tag for eradicating poverty, the report concludes that 'political commitment, not financial resources is the real obstacle to poverty eradication'.

Evaluate this six-point plan in the light of the economic analysis that you have encountered during your study of economics, and evaluate the prospects for future development of poor countries.

## Questions for Thought

1  Is it feasible for LDCs to achieve economic development without external assistance? What implications would arise if some LDCs defaulted on their international debt?

2  In the late 1990s, an initiative was launched by which highly-indebted poor countries (HIPC) could qualify for debt forgiveness is they could demonstrate their commitment to a programme of structural adjustment over a period of years. Discuss the economic reasoning underlying this idea.

3   The performance of many LDCs (especially in Africa) in terms of economic growth has been disappointing in recent decades, with a number of countries having lower real GNP per capita in the 1990s than they did in the mid-1960s. To what extent does this reflect market failure, and to what extent does it result from policies adopted and events occurring in the industrial economies?

4   Suppose that you are asked to make an assessment of the economic performance of a number of countries. Explain why such a task would be an exercise in normative economics.

# ANSWERS

# AND

# COMMENTS

## Chapter 1   Economics and the Economy

### Important Concepts and Technical Terms

| 1 | (f) | 4 | (d) | 7 | (i) | 10 | (b) |
|---|-----|---|-----|---|-----|----|-----|
| 2 | (k) | 5 | (h) | 8 | (c) | 11 | (l) |
| 3 | (j) | 6 | (a) | 9 | (g) | 12 | (e) |

### Exercises

1  (a)  The straight line PPF$_a$ in Figure A1-1 represents the production possibility frontier for this society.

  (b)  *PPF$_b$* is the new production possibility frontier. The change in technology enables more coconuts to be 'produced' than before, without any reduction in output of turtle eggs.

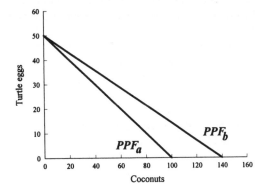

**Figure A1-1     The effect of technical change**

**2** *(a)* Combinations *(i)* and *(iv)* lie on the production possibility frontier and thus represent points of *efficient* production. Combinations *(ii)* and *(v)* lie outside the frontier and are thus *unattainable* with the resources available. Combination *(iii)* lies within the frontier, and is a point of inefficient production. Not all the available resources are being fully or effectively used.

*(b)* 100 watches must be given up for the 20 cameras when the society begins at (300, 40).

*(c)* 200 watches must be given up for the 20 cameras when the society begins at (200, 60).

*(d)* The difference in shape results from the law of diminishing returns. On the tropical island, the amounts produced by a worker did not vary according to whether other workers were engaged in the same activity. In the cameras and watches case, this is not so: as more workers are used to produce cameras, the additional output produced falls. This is explained in Section 1-2 of the main text.

**3** *(a)* C. *(b)* D. *(c)* A. *(d)* B.

**4** *(a)*, *(d)*, *(g)* and *(h)* are positive statements, containing objective descriptions of economies and the way they work. *(b)*, *(e)* and *(i)* are normative statements which rely upon value judgements for their validity. Statement *(c)* contains elements of both: it includes a (positive) statement of fact about the distribution of world population and income but also rests on a (normative) value judgement that this was 'too unjust'.

**5** *(a)*, *(d)*, *(g)* and *(h)* deal with economy-wide issues, and are thus the concern of macroeconomics. *(b)*, *(c)*, *(e)* and *(f)* are devoted to more detailed microeconomic issues.

**6** *(a)* C. *(b)* A. *(c)* B.

**7** *(d)*.

**8** Only *(a)* would be untrue for a economy. Remember though, that no pure command economy actually exists. Countries of the former Soviet bloc began to make the transition to being market economies in 1989–91, but even in their heyday they could not have been described as 'pure' command economies.

## True/False

**1** False: the claim of economics to be a science rests not on its subject matter, but upon its methods of analysis.

**2** False: see Section 1-1 of the main text.

**3** True.

**4** True.

**5** True.

**6** False: while being closer to a command economy than many others. China increasingly tolerates and encourages the existence of some private markets as it moves towards a more market-based system.

**7** Sorry, this was a trick question! This is another example of a normative statement, which rests on a subjective value judgement. As a result it can never be proven to be either true or false.

**8** False: don't forget services! The production of services may be more difficult to measure than that of goods, but is important none the less.

**9** True: many disagreements between economists reflect differences in beliefs and values (normative statements). rather than differences of opinion about objective analysis.

### ECONOMICS IN THE NEWS

**1** The passage mentions a number of potential benefits for traffic using the bridge, especially in terms of shorter journey times, congestion and reliability in bad weather. In the long run, when the cost of construction of the bridge has been recouped, the tolls will be removed, bringing even more benefits. Notice that we are here discussing the benefits to society, or to the users of the bridge, rather than the private company which has been involved in building and running the bridge.

**2** When we come to think about costs, we might initially think in terms of the financial costs involved in building the bridge, and perhaps we would also want to consider any possible damage to the environment that had been caused. Indeed, the passage mentions a specific sum of £39m that the taxpayers and the users of the bridge will have had to fork out.

3   When it comes to balancing the costs and benefits in order to evaluate whether building the bridge was a good decision, the question of costs becomes more complicated. The passage indicates that the main concern in deciding to build the bridge had been to compare the benefits of private and public financing of the project. However, what is also clear is that the NAO's conclusion was that insufficient attention had been paid to opportunity cost. In other words, when considering a project such as this, the concern should be to compare the net benefits of the project with the *next best alternative*. The question should be asked as to how the links with the Isle of Skye could be best provided if the bridge under private finance did not go ahead. If the question had been asked that way, using the simple notion of opportunity cost, then the answer would have been obvious: the next best alternative might be to improve or maintain the existing ferry service. This may indeed be an inferior service, but the question is whether it is £39m+ inferior!

## Questions for Thought

1   *Hint:* It is rare that an economic issue involves only one of the three basic questions.
2   *Hint:* So far, we have only considered an economy in a single time period. Here, the production of one of the goods directly affects what can be produced in the future.
3   Country A (which is Uganda) remains very heavily dependent upon agriculture; the share of industrial activity here rose very little between 1965 and 1997. In contrast, Country B (Indonesia) has seen a marked expansion of industry, but agriculture remains important, with a 16 per cent share in GDP. The trend towards industrialization and away from agriculture has been much more rapid in Country C; this is South Korea, one of the so-called newly industrialized countries (NICs) of East Asia. Country D (Japan) displays the more stable characteristics of an industrial economy, but with an expanding service sector. Box 1-2 in the main text discusses some of these issues. Problems of less-developed countries are discussed again at the end of our tour of economics.

# Chapter 2 The Tools of Economic Analysis

## Important Concepts and Technical Terms

| | | | | | | | |
|---|---|---|---|---|---|---|---|
| 1 | (g) | 5 | (c) | 9 | (k) | 13 | (n) |
| 2 | (m) | 6 | (i) | 10 | (e) | 14 | (l) |
| 3 | (f) | 7 | (d) | 11 | (b) | | |
| 4 | (j) | 8 | (a) | 12 | (h) | | |

## Exercises

1   *(a)*, *(c)* and *(d)* comprise information for the same variables at different points in time: they are thus time series. *(b)* and *(f)* are straightforward *cross-section* data series, observing different individuals or groups of individuals at an instant in time. *(e)* is a different sort of data set: it is a cross-section repeated at different points in time. It thus combines features of both cross-section and time series. Often known as *panel data*, such series are rare because of the expense of collecting the information and the difficulty in recontacting the same individuals in different periods.

2   *(a)* Simple observation of the figures does not take us very far. It is clear that agricultural employment decreased in this 20-year period for all the countries in the table, but the differences in the size of employment in the six countries is substantial. Employment in France fell by a large number, but to assess the proportional change, we need to carry out some calculations.
   *(b)* See Table A2-1, overleaf.
   *(c)* The index numbers enable much more ready comparison of the countries. We can now see clearly that the proportional decrease was at its greatest in France – a fall of 51.8 per cent over the decade. The smallest relative change was in the UK, with only a 27.7 per cent decrease.

3    *(a), (b)*: see Table A2-2.

   *(c)* Inflation for the non-smoking teetotaller is calculated directly from the price index for 'other goods and services'. Our non-smoking teetotaller experiences similar (but slightly lower) inflation rates to the representative person, but the difference is relatively minor. This suggests that the rate of change of prices of alcohol and tobacco did not differ greatly from other prices in this period. This will not always be the case, for example when the government chooses to increase taxes and duties on these goods in excess of the rate of inflation. Prices of alcohol and tobacco had increased by much more relative to the 1987 base year.

   *(d)* The charts, shown in Figures A2-1 and A2-2, reinforce this analysis.

**Table A2-1    Agricultural employment in six European countries (thousands)**

| Country | 1970 | 1990 | Index 1970=100 |
|---------|------|------|-----------------|
| Belgium | 177 | 100 | 56.5 |
| Denmark | 266 | 147 | 55.3 |
| Greece | 1279 | 900 | 70.4 |
| France | 2751 | 1325 | 48.2 |
| Italy | 3878 | 1895 | 48.9 |
| UK | 787 | 569 | 72.3 |

**Table A2-2    Price indices, 1994–98 (1987 = 100)**

|  | 1994 | 1995 | 1996 | 1997 | 1998 |
|--|------|------|------|------|------|
| Price index, alcohol and tobacco | 161.6 | 169.4 | 176.4 | 184.2 | 193.9 |
| Price index, other goods and services | 141.9 | 146.6 | 149.8 | 154.2 | 159.1 |
| Aggregate price index | 144.1 | 149.1 | 152.7 | 157.5 | 162.9 |
| Inflation |  | 3.5 | 2.4 | 3.1 | 3.4 |
| Inflation for non-smoking teetotaller |  | 3.3 | 2.2 | 3.0 | 3.2 |

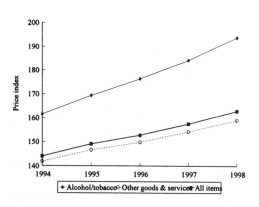

**Figure A2-1    Price indices, 1994–98**

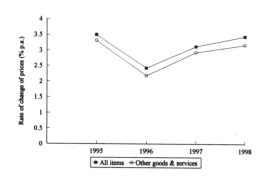

**Figure A2-2    Inflation 1995–98**

4    *(a)* See Figure A2-3 opposite.

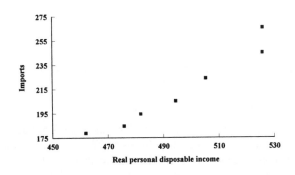

**Figure A2-3    Imports and income at 1995 prices (£ billion)**

*(b)–(d)* There seems to be a positive association between real imports and household income. We might perhaps expect households to buy more imported goods at higher levels of real income, but this is not likely to be the only variable affecting imports. For instance, changes in the relative price of UK and foreign goods or changes in demand by UK firms for imported raw materials also influence the overall level of real imports. Indeed, we would expect that as real incomes increase, firms will need to import increased amounts of materials and machinery. You may have thought of other factors. When we focus upon this simple association, these elements are all covered by our assumption that 'other things are equal' and may explain why the scatter of points in Figure A2-3 does not form a precise relationship.

5   *(a)* ii. *(b)* iii. *(c)* iv. *(d)* i.
    If we are considering just these simple relationships the fitting of a straight line would not be appropriate for *(b)* or *(c)*.
6   *(a)* An aggregate price index is required as a basis for comparison: we need the price of clothing relative to that of other goods.
    *(b)* Real price index for clothing and footwear:

| 1994 | 1995 | 1996 | 1997 | 1998 |
|------|------|------|------|------|
| 83.6 | 80.9 | 78.4 | 76.6 | 73.6 |

    Method:
    The 1994 figure is the price of clothing divided by the aggregate price index, all multiplied by 100.
    *(c)* Prices for clothing have increased much less than other prices, so their real price has fallen since 1987, and continues to do so.
7   *(a)* The model states that the quantity of chocolate bars demanded depends upon their price, and upon the level of consumer incomes. You will find that this question is answered in Chapter 3 of the main text where this example is used as an illustration.
    *(b)* With income held constant, we would expect to see less chocolate bars demanded at a higher price – that is, we expect a *negative* association between these variables.
    *(c)* With the price of chocolate bars held constant, an increase in income would probably lead to an increase in the quantity demanded – that is we expect chocolate bars to be a normal good, and thus we look for a *positive* association.
    *(d)* A complete model would also incorporate the price of other goods, and consumer preferences, as we would expect these to affect the demand for chocolate bars.
8   We calculate $3 \times 170 + 2 \times 186 + 5 \times 173 = 1747$. Then we must divide by the sum of the weights ($2 + 3 + 5 = 10$), giving answer *(c)*.

**9** *(a)*   12 552 + 12 949 + 12 747 + 13 520 = 51 768.

   *(b)*   12 929 + 13 193 + 13 109 + 14 029 = 53 260.

   *(c)*   Quarter 1  Quarter 2  Quarter 3  Quarter 4
         103.0      101.9      102.8      103.8

The results of this calculation look very much like an index of some kind – and that is exactly what they *do* represent. In fact, this calculation provides us with a price index based on 1995 = 100, known as the 'implicit deflator' of consumers' expenditure, or sometimes as the 'consumer price index'. It is always the case that

$$\text{Variable at current prices} = \text{Variable at constant prices} \times \frac{\text{Price index}}{100}$$

**10**   When asked to 'describe a trend', it is always tempting to go into great detail about all the ups and downs of the series. However, as economists it is more important for us to be able to filter the data and identify the salient features. It sometimes helps to lay a pencil on to the diagram so that it follows the overall trend of the line. For this graph, we see that the savings ratio remained relatively stable until the early 1970s, then rose steadily until 1980. The period after 1980 is less clear, with the 1980s showing a marked decline in the savings ratio, only recovering with the dawn of the 1990s, but then falling again towards the end of the period. The behaviour of savings is discussed in Box 21-2 and Section 31-5 of the main text.

## True/False

**1**   False: admittedly economists cannot easily carry out laboratory experiments. This does not prevent us from applying scientific methods to economic problems, and making the best we can of available information. There are other non-experimental sciences – astronomy, parts of biology, etc.

**2**   True: see Section 2-9 in the main text.

**3**   True: but we must be careful not to manipulate our charts to distort the picture so as to prove a point.

**4**   False: the association may be spurious – perhaps both variables depend upon a third one, or both happen to be growing over time.

**5**   True: but not invariably.

**6**   False: 'other things equal' is an assumption enabling us to simplify and to focus upon particular aspects of our model. However, we cannot ignore these other factors which affect the position of our curves and contribute to our explanation.

**7**   False: we may often assume a linear function for simplicity, but there are also many economic relationships that are nonlinear.

**8**   False: facts cannot speak for themselves and can be interpreted only in the light of careful and informed reasoning.

**9**   True: of course they have other uses also.

**10**   False: 'positive' refers to the direction of association between two variables.

**11**   False: inflation measures the *rate of change* of the price level.

**12**   True.

### ECONOMICS IN THE NEWS

**1**   This may seem a strange question to have asked, because the government has long treated low inflation as the prime target of macroeconomic policy. However, the whole wording of the passage seems to indicate a different perspective, with talk of prices on the high street being 'hit hard'. Thus from a retailer's point of view, falling prices may mean bad news. From the perspective of consumers, the story is naturally very different. For the government's target of low inflation to be achieved, it is almost inevitable that some prices will have to fall, so that *on average*, prices rise only slowly. As this book progresses, we will argue that prices have a crucial role to play in guiding the allocation of resources in a society. If this role is to be effectively met, then relative prices must change smoothly in response to changes in the pattern of consumer demand.

2   The simple model outlined in the text argues that the quantity demanded of a good will depend upon a number of factors. In particular, the price of the good (and the prices of other competing goods) will be important, together with consumer incomes and other factors, such as consumer preferences. These factors will be explored more carefully in a later chapter, but the passage helps to point our way forward by raising a number of important questions that we will need to consider. For example, there is the question of why prices of clothing and footwear might be showing a downward trend, as seems to have been happening. The importance of consumers' *expectations* about future price changes is also mentioned as being an important influence of current prices. However, you should also notice that some of the factors mentioned seem to have nothing to do with consumer demand. For example, reference is made to the earthquakes in Korea and Taiwan, which caused disruption to the *supply* of computer chips. In other words, before we can fully understand how markets are operating we will need to think about the supply conditions of commodities, as well as the factors affecting demand. However, all in good time…

## Questions for Thought

1   This question requires careful treatment. The preferred calculation uses the ratio of the weighted sum of the prices in year $Y$ to that in the base year; that is,

$$\frac{(2 \times 12) + (5 \times 80) + (3 \times 70)}{(2 \times 10) + (5 \times 100) + (3 \times 50)} \times 100 = 94.6$$

Notice that if we first calculate the index for each commodity and then take a weighted average – as if calculating a retail price index – we do *not* get the same answer. In this instance, we would get 106. This serves to illustrate that the retail price index calculation is not an exact one.

2   Quantity of school lunches demanded = f{?}.
    What items would you put in brackets? An obvious one is the price of school lunches – but what else would you include? Perhaps the price of competing 'goods', individual preferences, time of year, income, whatever.

3   The 'classic' method of visually depicting relative shares is by means of a pie-chart. For instance, if we want to illustrate the way in which sectoral shares changed in South Korea between 1965 and 1997, we could draw pie-charts as in Figure A2-4, which show very clearly how agriculture declined relative to industry and services.
    However, in practical terms, there are two problems with using pie-charts. First, they are a pain to draw: it is time-consuming to calculate the angles and so on, unless you have a computer to do it for you. I expect you remember this from GCSE days. Second (and more seriously), pie-charts are fine for looking at one or two sets of data, but the eye finds it difficult to assimilate more than a small number of pie-charts together. If we wanted to compare all four countries shown in Table 1-1, a 'stacked bar chart' may be more appropriate. The data for 1997 are shown using this technique in Figure A2-5.

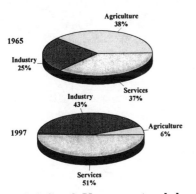

Figure A2-4  South Korea: sectoral shares

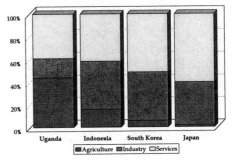

Figure A2-5  Sectoral shares 1997

**4** One way of thinking about this issue is in terms of the demand for additional children. We might argue that a family taking a decision about whether to have another child may balance the marginal benefits they expect against the marginal costs. Remember that 'costs' in this context will include opportunity cost. So, if having an additional child means that one parent has to forego earnings by remaining out of the labour market, then this must be included in the calculation. We might argue on this basis that improved education and job opportunities for women in many less-developed countries may increase the opportunity cost of having children, and thus lead to a slowing of the population growth rate. (See 'Making choices' by Peter Smith, in *Economic Review, September 1997.*)

## Chapter 3   Demand, Supply, and the Market

## Important Concepts and Technical Terms

| | | | | | | | |
|---|---|---|---|---|---|---|---|
| 1 | *(b)* | 4 | *(e)* | 7 | *(c)* | 10 | *(j)* |
| 2 | *(h)* | 5 | *(a)* | 8 | *(d)* | 11 | *(i)* |
| 3 | *(f)* | 6 | *(l)* | 9 | *(k)* | 12 | *(g)* |

## Exercises

**1**  *(a)*  See Figure A3-l.
   *(b)*  Excess demand of 60 million tins/year.
   *(c)*  Excess supply of 30 million tins/year.
   *(d)*  50 million tins/year at a price of 24p.
   *(e)*  60 million tins/year at a price of 28p.

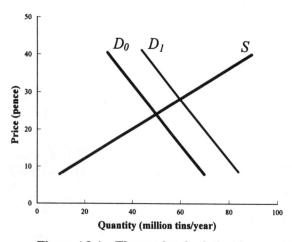

**Figure A3-1   The market for baked beans**

2    See Table A3-1.
3    The movement could have been caused by *(b)*, *(a)* or *(g)*. Factors *(a)* and *(f)* would move the demand curve in the opposite direction; factors *(c)* and *(e)* would move the supply curve.

**Table A3-1    Movements of and along a curve**

| Change in 'other things equal' category | Shift of demand curve | Movement along demand curve | Shift of supply curve | Movement along supply curve |
|---|---|---|---|---|
| Change in price of competing good | ✓ | | | ✓ |
| Introduction of new technique of production | | ✓ | ✓ | |
| A craze for the good | ✓ | | | ✓ |
| A change in incomes | ✓ | | | ✓ |
| A change in the price of a material input | | ✓ | ✓ | |

4    The shift could have been caused by *(b)* or *(c)*. *(a)* may have been a response to a change in demand but will not initiate a shift in the demand curve. If the change in price results from a shift in supply, the result will be a movement *along* the demand curve.
5    The movement could have been caused by *(a)* or *(e)*. Factor *(c)* would move the supply curve in the opposite direction; factors *(b)* and *(d)* would move the demand curve.
6    *(a)* and *(b)* are likely to be normal goods. *(c)* and *(e)* are likely to be inferior goods – as incomes rise, we might expect the demand for these commodities to fall, as consumers find they can afford other alternatives. In the case of *(d)* there may be arguments both ways. As incomes rise, more people may afford televisions, tending to increase demand. However, if more people switch to colour televisions, the demand for old-fashioned monochrome televisions may decline. In the UK now it is likely that monochrome televisions are inferior goods, if indeed they are available at all!
7    The answer here depends very much upon individual preferences! Most would regard strawberries and fresh cream as being complements. Others may like raspberries and/or ice cream with their strawberries. However, in the final analysis, most goods will turn out to be substitutes – if you spend more on strawberries, you must spend less on other goods.
8    *(a)*    $P2, Q3$.
     *(b)*    $P1$.
     *(c)*    $Q1$.
     *(d)*    $(Q4 - Q1)$.
     *(e)*    $P2$. A minimum price will be effective only if set above the equilibrium level.
     *(f)*    $Q3$.
     *(g)*    None.
9    *(a)* or *(b)* could cause a rise in house prices. Factors *(a)* and *(d)* will lead to movements of the supply curve, whereas (b) and (c) affect the demand curve. Try drawing a diagram to see the effects of these movements.
10   *(a)*    See Figure A3-2 overleaf.
     *(b)*    Price 18p, quantity 44 units. So far, so good. It's the next bit that's tricky: the key is to think through the supplier's decision process. Suppose the market price is 20p: 5p of this goes in tax to the government, and the supplier receives 15p – at which price we know he or she is prepared to supply 35 units per year. Using this sort of argument, we can construct a new supply schedule showing how much will be supplied at each (gross of tax) price.
     *(c)*    The new supply curve is given by S*S* in Figure A3-2; the vertical distance between SS and S*S* is 5p.
     *(d)*    Price 21p, quantity 38 units. Notice that price does not rise by the full amount of the tax.

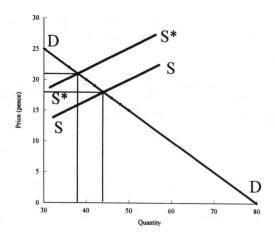

**Figure A3-2    A tax on good $X$**

## True/False

1   False: the demand curve itself shows how buyers respond to price changes.
2   False: some goods may be 'inferior'.
3   True.
4   False: there may be periods when markets adjust sluggishly towards equilibrium. Government intervention may prevent adjustment to equilibrium.
5   False: an inferior good is one for which demand falls as incomes rise.
6   True: see Box 3-1 of the main text.
7   True.
8   False: if effective, such legislation may lead to a fall in employment (see Section 3-9 of the main text).
9   True: but a more precise economist's view of complementarity awaits in Chapter 6.
10  False: see exercise 10.
11  True: see Section 3-8 of the main text.

## ECONOMICS IN THE NEWS

1   A failure in the harvest would be shown in a demand and supply diagram as a leftward shift in the supply curve. Equilibrium price would then rise to reflect the relative shortage of peanuts. This is clearly expressed in the passage, at the end of the second paragraph.
2   Towards the end of the passage, we read that farmers in the US were increasing the land devoted to growing peanuts. This is exactly what we would expect, as we have argued that producers will be prepared to sell more at a higher price. Notice the effects, however. The article suggests that the likely effect of the US farmers' action will be to lead to a fall in price. In other words, in terms of the diagram that you sketched in part 1, the supply curve shifts back towards its original position (or further, of course).
3   However, rather than there being a fall in price, the problems with Chinese peanuts led to further rises in prices – to $1000 per tonne, which was about 15 per cent higher than the norm. The fall in China's output was not solely due to a poor harvests, but also reflected movers by farmers to switch cultivation to other crops.

## Questions for Thought

1   The market in this situation will be displaying a state of excess supply: producers are prepared to supply more of the commodity at the given price than consumers are prepared to demand. From the perspective of the producers, they are likely to find that their stocks of unsold goods begin to build up. In subsequent periods, producers are likely to react to this by reducing the price to induce higher sales, and by reducing the amount of the commodity being produced. As producers do this and the price begins to fall, we would expect some consumers who previously curtailed their consumption because of the high price to increase their demand for the good. If the price is set *below* the equilibrium price, the reverse forces are likely to be seen: producers will find that their stocks of the commodity are run down, and they may find that some consumers are trying to jump the queue by offering a higher price for the good. In other words, there is excess demand and, perhaps, rationing as not all consumers can buy although they would like to. Thus price will tend to be bid up, and producers will tend to increase their supply of the good as the price rises. This is one way in which we can argue that if the market is left to its own devices, price will tend to move towards the equilibrium level: the level at which demand just matches supply. Much economic analysis relies on this sort of adjustment towards equilibrium, as we will see as we delve more deeply into economics. Further discussion in economics centres around why the adjustment may not always happen – but that is a story for later.

2   The result depends crucially on the steepness of the demand curve: the coffee market is discussed in Chapter 5 of the main text.

3   There are many such examples: in particular, we may consider whether a pair of goods are complements or substitutes.

4   Hint: see Box 3-3 in the main text.

# Chapter 4   Government in the Mixed Economy

## Important Concepts and Technical Terms

| | | | | | | | |
|---|---|---|---|---|---|---|---|
| 1 | *(i)* | 4 | *(j)* | 7 | *(l)* | 10 | *(g)* |
| 2 | *(d)* | 5 | *(a)* | 8 | *(f)* | 11 | *(k)* |
| 3 | *(e)* | 6 | *(b)* | 9 | *(c)* | 12 | *(h)* |

## Exercises

1   (a) The only years in which government revenue exceeded expenditure were 1970 and 1988–90. In 1987 the two were almost equal. For the rest of the period there was a budget deficit.

   (b) We do not really have enough information in Figure 4-1 to explain the fall in government debt between 1980 and 1989. It seems unlikely that the budget surpluses of 1988 and 1989 offer sufficient explanation. However, we should be aware that the government's borrowing requirement during the 1980s was tempered by receipts from privatization.

   (c) There are a number of reason why a government might not be able to make rapid adjustments to its involvement in the economy. Many long-term capital projects commit funds for particular uses over a long time horizon (e.g., the Channel Tunnel), so that some expenditure items cannot be rapidly reduced. The recession of the early 1980s aggravated the situation, requiring an increase in the funds devoted to the payment of unemployment and other welfare benefits.

   (d) We cannot comment here, as we do not know when you will be tackling this question. Make sure that you have data on total government expenditure and revenue (including capital transactions). Notice that we used GDP at current market prices to measure 'national income'. One interesting question is whether the New Labour government under Tony Blair will adopt a different attitude towards revenue and expenditure.

2   *(a)* $S_y$.
    *(b)  AEGC.*
    *(c)  (i)   AEFB.*
    *(ii)  BFGC.*
3   *(b)* is a tax contributing to local authority revenues; *(e)* is a payment for nursing services rendered.
4   If you were to re-read Section 4-2 of the main text, you would find each of these items discussed as possible justifications for government intervention. Each may be considered to be an example of a form of market failure. As far as item *(a)* is concerned, some economists argue that government attempts to dampen the business cycle do more harm than good. However, expenditure and revenue-raising decisions should not be taken in isolation from the state of the business cycle. National defence (item *(b)*) is an example of a public good, where the free-rider problem leads to potential market failure. Similarly externalities *(c)*, information problems *(d)* and imperfect competition *(e)* all represent forms of market failure. Modern governments also indulge in income redistribution *(f)*. All these issues will be re-examined in a later section of the book. The extent to which these various interventions may be successfully implemented remains contentious.
5   *(a)* Defence is the closest here to being a 'pure' public good, in the sense that all citizens of a country 'consume' nearly equal amounts of defence: this is not true of any of the other goods mentioned. Of course, different individuals may obtain differing amounts of utility from their consumption of defence.
6   The correct answers here are *(c)* and *(f)*: the key feature of merit goods is that the government wishes to make sure that they are consumed by individuals. The 'merit' lies in the good, not in the consumer; thus response *(b)* is incorrect. Notice that answer *(a)* refers to a public good.
7   Items *(c)*, *(e)* and *(f)* are all part of the explicit costs of constructing the road, and thus are reflected in market prices. However, the other items are all examples of externalities, some positive, some negative. In deciding whether to go ahead with building the motorway, all these factors should be taken into account if the society as a whole is to be best served.
8   *(a)–(e)* 3, i.e. a majority.
    *(f)* This is one illustration of the 'paradox of voting', by which we see that voters' preferences may fail to allow consistent decision making.
    *(g)* Single-peaked (see Section 4-3 of the main text).
9   *(a), (e), (g)* and *(h)*.

## True/False

1   True: but such restrictions have been much relaxed with the break-up of the former Soviet Union and other 'socialist' states (see Section 4-1 of the main text).
2   Not really true: in most capitalist economies the government regulates markets in one way or another (see Section 4-1 of the main text).
3   False: the initial experience of the transition economies was painful, and the data suggest that government plays a key role in supporting successful market economies: see Box 4-1 in the main text.
4   False: UK government spending was lower than France, Germany or Sweden, but higher than other economies such as Japan or the USA (see Table 4-2 of the main text).
5   True: see Table 4-3 of the main text.
6   True: see Box 4-2 of the main text
7   True.
8   True: but in the case of merit goods (bads), the government may intervene because it believes it has a clearer view of what is in society's best interests.
9   False: see Section 4-3 of the main text
10  True.

## ECONOMICS IN THE NEWS

1   Remember the distinction between public and merit goods. The definition of a public good in the main text is a good that, even if it is consumed by one person, is still available for consumption by others. A classic example mentioned in the article is that of street lighting. This clearly meets the definition of a public good. Similarly, street paving and the fixing of potholes come to mind as examples. However, there is a grey area of which we should be aware. In principle, we could exclude people from consumption of good roads, in the sense that we could impose a toll on a particular stretch of street. Similar sorts of arguments could be made about the self-cleaning public toilets.

   Merit goods are goods that society thinks people should consume. Such goods can be controversial. For example, one good mentioned in the passage is neighbourhood art. Could this be a merit good? If the City Council take the view that art is good for you, whether you want it or not, then presumably they would appeal to the merit good argument to justify their spending. Of course, a cynic might argue that neighbourhood art is a way of discouraging informal graffiti that imposes maintenance costs on the Council. Yet another way of looking at this is in terms of externalities. There may be negative externalities attached to graffiti, but positive externalities connected with neighbourhood art. So, perhaps the Council is correcting a rather different form of market failure. We will leave you to discuss with your fellow students the status of the Seattle Chinese Garden, skateboard park, the farmers' markets and the Civic Centre.

   Another interesting point to notice is the fact that the Seattle City Council may spend on all of these goods, but does not provide all of them directly. This issue is raised in the main text, Section 4-2.

2   As explained in the main text, Councils act as the agents of their electorate, and thus need to undertake the sorts of expenditures that the voters desire. However, we cannot predict which of the items would correspond with *your* preferences. This also raises questions of how voters' preferences can be gauged by the Council, and of accountability. See Section 4-3 for a fuller discussion of these matters.

## Questions for Thought

1   See Section 4-1 of the main text.
2   In tackling this question, the first issue to examine is that of interpreting the word 'effectiveness'. In other words, we must consider the objectives of the government in imposing taxes on tobacco. Evidence suggests that the demand for tobacco products is relatively insensitive to price changes, so if a tax raises the price of cigarettes, demand will not alter greatly; people will continue to smoke cigarettes. If the government's aim is to raise revenue, then the tax will be effective. However, if the objective is to discourage smoking (perhaps because tobacco is seen to be a 'demerit' good), then the tax may not be seen as effective. It may then be necessary to find other ways of affecting demand: by health warnings on cigarette packets, banning advertising, etc.
3   An important justification for the government to provide health care is that it is a merit good. In other words, this is a good that society thinks that people should consume. There may also be externalities involved: society may not wish to bear the social cost of knowing that people in the community are suffering. In the case of some types of health care there may be more obvious externalities. Vaccination against some diseases may have benefits that individuals do not perceive clearly, but the prevention of epidemics will benefit society as a whole. In this case, there may be an information problem as well, where people do not think that vaccination against polio or whooping cough is necessary, for example. Section 4-2 of the main text introduces many of the issues, although detailed discussion is reserved for a later chapter.

## Chapter 5   The Effect of Price and Income on Demand Quantities

## Important Concepts and Technical Terms

| | | | | | | | | | |
|---|---|---|---|---|---|---|---|---|---|
| 1 | *(i)* | 4 | *(k)* | 7 | *(n)* | 10 | *(j)* | 13 | *(l)* |
| 2 | *(b)* | 5 | *(a)* | 8 | *(f)* | 11 | *(g)* | 14 | *(h)* |
| 3 | *(d)* | 6 | *(e)* | 9 | *(m)* | 12 | *(c)* | | |

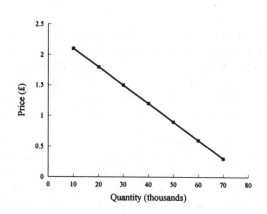

**Figure A5-1  The demand curve for rice popsicles**

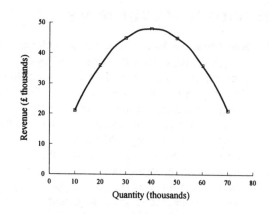

**Figure A5-2  Total spending on (revenue from) rice popsicles**

## Exercises

1  *(a)*  See Figure A5-1.

*(b)*  The demand curve being a straight line, the response to a 30p reduction in price will always be an increase of 10 000 in the quantity demanded – at least within the range of prices shown.

*(c)* and *(d)* See Table A5-1.

**Table A5-1  The demand for rice popsicles**

| Price per packet (£) | Quantity demanded (thousands) | Total spending (revenue) (£ thousands) | Own price elasticity of demand |
|---|---|---|---|
| 2.10 | 10 | 21 | −7 |
| 1.80 | 20 | 36 | −3 |
| 1.50 | 30 | 45 | −1.67 |
| 1.20 | 40 | 48 | −1 |
| 0.90 | 50 | 45 | −0.6 |
| 0.60 | 60 | 36 | −0.3 |
| 0.30 | 70 | 21 | |

Notice that we cannot calculate the elasticity for a reduction in price at a price of 30p, as we are not told what happens to demand if price falls below this level. We could, of course, calculate elasticities for price increases instead.

*(e)*  See Figure A5-2.

*(f)*  At a price of £1.20.

*(g)*  At a price of £1.20. Expenditure is always greatest at the point of unit elasticity.

*(h)*  *(i)*  At prices above £1.20.

  *(ii)*  At prices below £1.20.

Notice in this exercise how the value of the elasticity varies at different points along the demand curve, although its slope does not change. This means that you should remember not to describe a linear demand curve as being either 'elastic' or 'inelastic': it is both, depending on where we measure it.

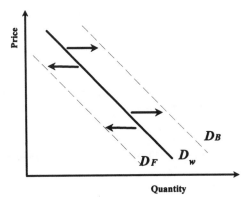

Figure A5-3    The demand for wine in Mythuania

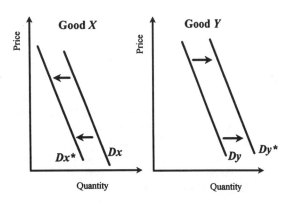

Figure A5-4    The effect of income on demand

2   (a)   For the own-price elasticities we need to use the top left–bottom right diagonal of Table 5-2. For instance, the response of the demand for food to a one per cent change in the price of food is –0.25. The demand for food is thus inelastic, as we might expect. The demand for beer is also inelastic, although the response is stronger than for food. The demand for wine is elastic (– 1.20).

   (b)   Using the cross-price elasticities in the first column of the table, we see that an increase (say) in the price of food will lead to a fall in the quantity of wine demanded but an increase in the quantity of beer demanded. This implies that, in response to the change in the price of food, food and wine may well be complements, but food and beer seem more likely to be substitutes.

   (c)   An increase in the price of food causes a contraction in the demand for wine, shifting the demand curve to $D_F$ in Figure A5-3 (food and wine are complements). The cross-price elasticity of demand for wine with respect to the price of beer is positive, indicating that these goods are substitutes. The demand curve moves to $D_B$.

3   See Table A5-2.

**Table A5-2    Using the income elasticity to categorize goods**

|  | Income Year 1 £100 | Income Year 2 £200 | Budget share (year 1) | Budget share (year 2) | Income elasticity of demand | Normal (No) or inferior (I) good | Luxury (L) or Necessity (Ne) |
|---|---|---|---|---|---|---|---|
| Good A | £30 | £50 | 30% | 25% | 2/3 | No | Ne |
| Good B | £30 | £70 | 30% | 35% | 4/3 | No | L |
| Good C | £25 | £20 | 25% | 10% | –1/5 | I | Ne |
| Good D | £15 | £60 | 15% | 30% | 3 | No | L |

4   If the price of electricity increases, other things being equal, we would expect households to switch to alternative energy sources – perhaps installing gas central heating or using gas for cooking. However, such changes will not take place immediately, so in the short run the demand for electricity will be relatively inelastic *(DD)*. The long-run demand curve is thus represented by *dd*, the more elastic of the two.

5   For goods X and Y see Figure A5-4. The demand curve for good Z would remain static: with an income elasticity of demand of zero, a change in income has no effect upon demand.

6   The terminology 'inferior' and 'normal' goods used by economists habitually creates confusion among students. The terms are used to describe the way in which demand for a good varies with changes in *income*.

Thus in tackling this question, it is the income elasticity that is important. We can see that good *(a)* is an inferior good: demand falls when income rises. Good *(d)* is a normal good, having a positive income elasticity. In the remaining cases *(b)*, *(c)* and *(e)*, we would say that an economist would not describe them either as inferior or as normal goods.

A positive own-price elasticity suggests a very unusual demand curve, with an increase in price leading to an increase in demand. This curiosum will be encountered in Chapter 6.

7    For Flora, tea and coffee are substitutes (cross-price elasticity positive), whereas sugar and coffee are complements (cross-price elasticity negative). Sugar and tea would probably display a cross-elasticity close to zero, or slightly negative.

8    Increased by 25 per cent.

9    Estimates of own-price elasticities for commodities close in definition to those in the table may be found in Section 5-1 of the main text.

10   *(a)*  See Figure A5-5.
     *(b)*  A positive relationship.
     *(c)*  Bacon seems to be a normal good, with consumption increasing with income. However, the rate at which consumption increases slackens off at higher incomes: this is very clear in the diagram.
     *(d)*  See Figure A5-6.
            Such a curve showing the relationship between the consumption (quantity) of a good and income is sometimes known as an *Engel curve*.

11   So, here we have an economy that is prospering; real incomes are expected to increase rapidly. The best prospects are seen for the Bechans (best chance) sector, with a strong positive income elasticity of demand. Demand is likely to grow for the OK-ish sector, but at a slower rate than income itself grows. Zegroes will face zero growth, as the income elasticity is zero, whereas there is no hope for the Nohoes, with a strong negative income elasticity.

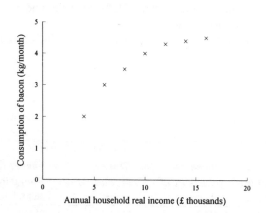

**Figure A5-5    The relationship between consumption of bacon and income**

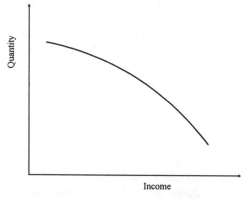

**Figure A5-6    The relationship between consumption and income for an inferior good**

## True/False

1    True: see Section 5-1 of the main text.
2    False: if in doubt, see your answers to exercise 1 of this chapter.
3    False.
4    True: see main text Section 5-2 and also exercise 1 of this chapter.
5    False: the more narrowly defined the commodity, the more likely it is that there are readily available substitutes. Demand will thus tend to be highly sensitive to price.
6    False: only if the income elasticity is greater than 1 – see your answers to exercise 3 of this chapter.
7    False.

8   False: if relative prices are unchanged, and incomes increase at the same rate as prices, the pattern of expenditure will not change.

9   False: see main text Section 5-3.

10  True: again see main text Section 5-3.

11  False: somebody somewhere must be producing 'inferior' goods.

12  True.

## ECONOMICS IN THE NEWS

1   If you read the passage, you will see that the character of football attendance changed substantially during the period. In the early post-war years of discomfort and danger, it seems likely that attendance at football matches was an inferior good. As people's real incomes rose, they were less likely to attend matches, seeking alternative forms of entertainment that may previously have been beyond their means. The advent of widespread access to TV may have contributed to this. However, once the football clubs began to get their act together by improving facilities, and improving the comfort and attractiveness of matches, it seems that attendance became a normal good, increasing with real incomes.

2   The article on which this brief passage was based offers some evidence on this issue, and if you have access to the *Economic Review* in the library, you might wish to consult it. This evidence does seem to suggest that giantkilling is less common than it used to be. So, perhaps the argument has something to commend it. Whether it is a complete explanation is quite another matter.

## Questions for Thought

1   Price volatility will be discussed much later on (Chapter 36).
    *Hint:* Think about the main factors influencing elasticity and sketch some diagrams to assess the effect on price of a supply shift under alternative assumptions about the demand elasticity.

2   Factor *(d)* lies at the heart of this question. Consumers are likely to respond more strongly to a change in the price of a commodity if there are substitutes readily available. The other factors can be interpreted in the light of this. A 'necessity' can be seen as a commodity for which there are no close substitutes: so demand will be relatively inelastic. When a commodity is very narrowly defined (e.g. a particular brand of detergent), then there will tend to be more substitutes (other brands) available, so demand may be relatively elastic. For some commodities, consumers may be unable to adjust demand in the short run, whereas flexibility (elasticity) may be greater in the long run. If you have an oil-fired central heating system, there is no substitute for oil in the short run.

3   Volatility caused by weather conditions is of course an influence on the supply side, and is similar to the discussion of the market for peanuts that we saw in Chapter 3. However, it is also probable that demand-side factors will influence the market. For instance, changes in preferences over time, between coffee and tea, may have a big influence on demand. If demand falls to the extent that coffee producers cannot sell all their output, then they are likely to decrease acreage devoted to coffee, so that in the long run a new equilibrium will be reached. This shows you how prices can act as a signal to guide the allocation of resources so as to match the pattern of demand. In fact, the coffee market is even more complicated, as there is a so-called 'futures' market in coffee, whereby coffee can be bought and sold at an agreed price at some day in the future. Peter Smith discusses some aspects of the coffee market in the 'Data and Response' column of the *Economic Review* in September 1997.

4   There are many ways in which this information might be useful to you. Peter Smith discusses a very similar question in the 'Question and Answer' column of the *Economic Review,* September 1993.

# Chapter 6   The Theory of Consumer Choice

## Important Concepts and Technical Terms

| | | | | | | | |
|---|---|---|---|---|---|---|---|
| 1 | *(b)* | 4 | *(k)* | 7 | *(e)* | 10 | *(c)* |
| 2 | *(j)* | 5 | *(l)* | 8 | *(d)* | 11 | *(a)* |
| 3 | *(g)* | 6 | *(i)* | 9 | *(h)* | 12 | *(f)* |

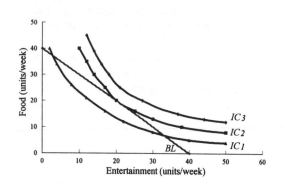

**Figure A6-1   Ashley's indifference curves**

**Figure A6-2   The income expansion path**

## Exercises

1   If you are doubtful about how to draw a budget line, the simplest way to go about it is to calculate how much of each good Ashley could buy if he were to spend his entire allowance on it. Mark these two points on the graph (one on each axis) and join them. This exercise should reveal that a change in one price alters the *slope* of the budget line, leaving the other intercept unchanged. An equal proportional change in both prices, e.g. *(d)* compared with *(a),* has the same effect as a change in income, e.g. *(e)* compared with *(a)* – namely, the budget line changes in position but not in slope.

2   *(a)*  See Figure A6-1.
   *(b)*  *IC3.*
   *(c)*  *IC1.*
   *(d)*  Bundle C confers most utility, being on *IC3.*
       Bundles A and D are both on *IC2* and would be ranked equally.
       Bundle B confers less utility, being on *IC1.*
       Bundle E is below *IC1* and confers least utility.
   *(e)*  No, we need to know Ashley's budget constraint.
   *(f)*  *BL* in Figure A6-1 is the relevant budget line: it just touches indifference curve *IC2* at (2OE, 20F). This point represents the highest level of satisfaction that Ashley can reach given his budget constraint.

3   *(d).*

**4**  (1)  *d*        (4)     *e*
       (2)  *c*        (5)     *b*
       (3)  *a*        (6)     *f*

**5**  *(a)*  See Figure A6-2.

*(b)*  As income expands, consumption of good *X* increases (*X* is a normal good) but consumption of good *Y* decreases (*Y* is an inferior good).

*(c)*  Upward-sloping to the right.

*(d)*  No. In a two-good world, it is not feasible for both goods to be inferior. For instance, suppose income falls with prices constant – clearly, the consumer could not consume more of both goods, as would be the case if both were inferior!

**6** *(a)*  As the price of good *X* varies, the budget line changes its slope, while still cutting the *Y* axis at the same point: we can draw a series of budget lines, each tangent to an indifference curve on the diagram. This is done in Figure A6-3.

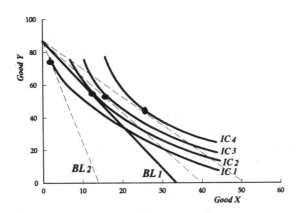

**Figure A6-3   The effect on purchasing pattern of a change in the price of *X***

*(b)*  Yes, if we know Christopher's money income, we can calculate the price of *X* corresponding to each budget line and we can read off the demand for *X* at each price. Indeed, we can get a rough idea of the demand curve by reference to the intercepts of the budget lines on the *x*-axis. If we call the original price '1', then the relative price for budget line *BL2* is approximately 33/14=2.36. (33 is the *BL1* intercept and 14 the *BL2* intercept.) Reading off the *X* quantities, we get the following:

| Price | Quantity |
|-------|----------|
| 2.36  | 2        |
| 1     | 15       |
| 0.75  | 24       |
| 0.59  | 32       |

You might like to plot these on a diagram. This analysis provides the theoretical underpinning of the demand curve. We see that its position and slope will depend upon income and upon preferences.

*(c)*  The demand for good *Y* increases as the price of *X* increases, indicating a strong substitution effect.

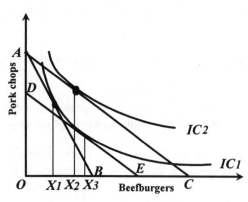

**Figure A6-4   The effect of a price fall**

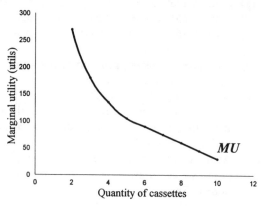

**Figure A6-5   Frank's MU schedule for cassettes**

7   If only tastes change, $Q$ remains unattainable, so the answer cannot be *(a)*. Options *(c)* and *(d)* both move the budget line closer to the origin: *(e)* leaves the budget line unchanged. Hence, the answer is *(b)*. Try sketching in the budget lines.

8   *(a)* See Figure A6-4.
   For a price *fall* we need to discover the resulting increase in real income. We do this by drawing in a new budget line *(DE)* which is parallel to the new budget line *AC* and tangent to the 'old' indifference curve *IC1*. The substitution effect is from *X1* to *X3* and the real income effect from *X3* to *X2*. This way of analysing the real income effect is sometimes known as the 'compensating income variation method'. It entails answering the question, 'What level of money income at the *new* relative prices would just allow Debbie to attain the original utility level?' If you are sure you have understood this, read on – otherwise, be warned that we are about to confuse you! We *could* have asked an alternative question – namely, 'What level of money income at the *old* relative prices would be equivalent to Debbie's *new* utility level?' We would analyse this by drawing another 'ghost' budget line parallel to *AB* at a tangent to *IC2* – try it on your diagram if you like. This is sometimes known as the 'equivalent income variation method'.
   *(b)* As drawn, beefburgers are a normal good, although the income effect is relatively small.
   *(c)* They work.
   *(d)* If beefburgers were an inferior good.

9   *(a)* Yes, it is quite consistent for him to choose to be at point *F*: it merely requires that his indifference curves are sufficiently steep that *F* (previously unattainable) lies on a higher indifference curve than *E*.
   *(b)* If Eliot is consistent in his preferences, there is no way he would choose to be at *G*. Both *E* and *G* were available options in the initial period; indeed, initially Eliot could have chosen a point to the north-east of *G*, with more of both goods – but yet he chose to be at *E*. If he now chooses *G*, it must be because of a change in tastes. You can confirm this by drawing indifference curves tangential to points *E* and *G*: you will find that they *must* intersect, indicating inconsistency.
   *(c)* CE.
   *(d)* They have changed: see comment on 9*(b)*.

10   *(a)* 2 cassettes give Frank 630 utils, and 10 magazines give him 371, a total of 1001 utils.
   *(b)* See columns (2) and (5) of Table A6-1 opposite.
   *(c)* See Figure A6-5.
   *(d)* No, because we have not taken into account the relative prices of the two goods.
   *(e)* He could afford just 4 cassettes, which would give him 945 utils – less than his original choice.
   *(f)* See columns (3) and (6) of Table A6-1 opposite.

(g) Frank maximizes utility by adjusting his expenditure such that $MU_m/P_m$ is equal to $MU_c/P_c$. You will see from Table A6-1 that this occurs when he buys 3 cassettes and 5 magazines. His total expenditure is unchanged, but he now receives 1042 utils.

**Table A6-1    Frank's utility from magazines and cassettes**

| | Magazines | | | Cassettes | | |
|---|---|---|---|---|---|---|
| Number consumed | (1) Utility (utils) | (2) Marginal utility | (3) $\frac{MU_m}{P_m}$ | (4) Utility (utils) | (5) Marginal utility | (6) $\frac{MU_c}{P_c}$ |
| 1 | 60 | | | 360 | | |
| 2 | 111 | 51 | 34 | 630 | 270 | 36 |
| 3 | 156 | 45 | 30 | 810 | 180 | 24 |
| 4 | 196 | 40 | 26.7 | 945 | 135 | 18 |
| 5 | 232 | 36 | 24 | 1050 | 105 | 14 |
| 6 | 265 | 33 | 22 | 1140 | 90 | 12 |
| 7 | 295 | 30 | 20 | 1215 | 75 | 10 |
| 8 | 322 | 27 | 18 | 1275 | 60 | 8 |
| 9 | 347 | 25 | 16.7 | 1320 | 45 | 6 |
| 10 | 371 | 24 | 16 | 1350 | 30 | 4 |

## True/False

1  True: see Section 6-1 of the main text.
2  True.
3  True.
4  True: see Section 6-1 of the main text,
5  False: the individual can always improve on such a point.
6  False: the slope depends only on the prices.
7  True.
8  False: see Section 6-3 of the main text,
9  True.
10  True: see Section 6-3 of the main text.
11  False: if the income effect is working against the substitution effect, then $X$ must be an inferior good.
12  False: in general, consumers potentially gain by freedom to choose (see Section 6-6 of the main text).

## ECONOMICS IN THE NEWS

1  We have argued that the demand for any commodity depends upon three key factors: the relative price of the good, consumer incomes, and preferences. We can see all three factors at work in this passage. It seems that the governments of these countries have been attempting to influence the demand for domestically produced cars by tariffs and taxes which affect the relative price. Foreign car manufacturers see the market in south-east Asia as promising because of the rapid growth of consumer incomes, in conjunction with the large populations. In the case of Malaysia, the income growth seems to be seen as being more important than the population size, given that Malaysia has higher income per head than the other countries mentioned in the article. The question of preferences is less explicitly mentioned in the article, although there is some hint that ambitious road building programmes are likely to boost the demand for car ownership. This might be seen as affecting demand via preferences – if congestion is reduced through an improved road system, then more people want to own cars.

**2** This question goes rather beyond the material we have covered so far. However, the suggestion in the passage is that governments of these countries are racing to industrialize. The car industry offers one activity in which technology transfer from industrial economies has been possible. Malaysia's Proton Saga (now exported to the UK) is one prime example of this. Governments here are seen to be more concerned to increase domestic production of cars than to worry about traffic congestion. Congestion is an example of an *externality*, which we encountered briefly in chapter 4, and will meet again later in the book.

## Questions for Thought

**1** *Hint:* These effects are sometimes referred to as the 'bandwagon' and 'snob' effects. The slope of the market demand curve will be affected. This discussion anticipates chapter 11, in which we meet the notion of network externalities.

**2** Some hints:

  *(a)* What happens as you move along an indifference curve? What happens to utility if the quantity of $Ya$ stays constant but quantity of 'good' $Xa$ increases? (Possible example: medicine and sweets?)

  *(b)* Even if you like cream doughnuts, how would you feel about eating 50 of each – or more?

  *(c)* What would be the substitution effect of a price change? (Possible example: right and left shoes?)

**3** Consider Figure A6-6. The shape of the indifference curves reflects our individual's preferences between income and leisure. At the wage rate represented by $BL1$ the choice is at $A$: 16 hours of leisure are chosen and hence 8 hours of work. The dashed budget line shows a higher wage rate. As we have drawn it, our individual chooses less leisure, more work. This topic will be examined again later on, when we find that the reaction to an increase in the wage rate could be to work more or fewer hours (Section 12-4 of the main text).

**4** The answer is *(d)*; this is explained in the Appendix to Chapter 6 in the main text.

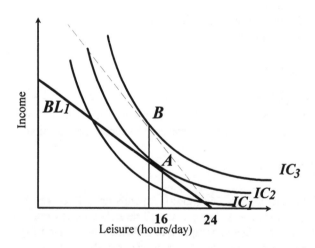

**Figure A6-6   The choice between income and leisure**

## Chapter 7    Business Organization and Behaviour

## Important Concepts and Technical Terms

| | | | | |
|---|---|---|---|---|
| 1  (l) | 4  (n) | 7  (e) | 10  (h) | 13  (g) |
| 2  (m) | 5  (j) | 8  (b) | 11  (a) | 14  (o) |
| 3  (k) | 6  (i) | 9  (d) | 12  (c) | 15  (f) |

## Exercises

1  (a)  Partnership.
   (b)  Partnership.
   (c)  Company.
   (d)  Sole trader.

**2**

**Lex Pretend & Sons Limited**

*Income Statement for the year ending 31 December 1999*

| | | |
|---|---|---|
| Revenue:  5000 units of good $X$ sold at £40 each | £200 000 | |
| 4000 units of good $Y$ sold at £75 each | 300 000 | |
| | | £ 500 000 |
| **Deduct expenditures** | | |
| Wages | 335 000 | |
| Rent | 25 000 | |
| Travel expenses | 19 000 | |
| Advertising | 28 000 | |
| Telephone | 8 000 | |
| Stationery and other office expenses | 15 000 | |
| | | 430 000 |
| Net income (profits) before tax | | 70 000 |
| Corporation tax at 30% | | 21 000 |
| Net income (profits) after tax | | £ 49 000 |

3  (a)  £27 000.        (d)  £2500.
   (b)  £28 000.        (e)  £50 500.
   (c)  £21 000.        (f)  £4500.

**4**

**GSC Limited**

*Balance Sheet 31 March 2000*

| Assets | | Liabilities | |
|---|---|---|---|
| Cash in hand | £ 30 000 | Accounts payable | £  40 000 |
| Accounts receivable | 55 000 | Wages payable | 25 000 |
| Inventories | 80 000 | Salaries payable | 30 000 |
| Buildings | | Mortgage | 180 000 |
| (Original value £300 000) | 240 000 | Bank loan | 50 000 |
| Other equipment | | | |
| (Original value £250 000) | 200 000 | Total | 325 000 |
| | | Net worth | 280 000 |
| Total assets | £605 000 | | £ 605 000 |

**5** See Table A7-1.

**Table A7-1 Profits, MR and MC**

| Total production (units/week) | Price received (£) | Total revenue | Total costs | Profit | Marginal revenue | Marginal cost |
|---|---|---|---|---|---|---|
| 1 | 25 | 25 | 10 | 15 | | |
| | | | | | 21 | 13 |
| 2 | 23 | 46 | 23 | 23 | | |
| | | | | | 14 | 15 |
| 3 | 20 | 60 | 38 | 22 | | |
| | | | | | 12 | 17 |
| 4 | 18 | 72 | 55 | 17 | | |
| | | | | | 3 | 20 |
| 5 | 15 | 75 | 75 | 0 | | |
| | | | | | 0 | 23 |
| 6 | 12½ | 75 | 98 | −23 | | |

Profits are maximized at an output level of 2 units per week.

**6** *(b).*
**7** *(a).*

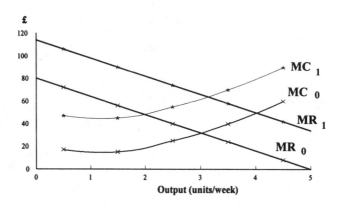

**Figure A7-1  Marginal cost and marginal revenue**

*(b)* Marginal cost *(MC0)* intersects marginal revenue *(MR0)* at an output level of about 3 units per week.

*(c)* Total revenue continues to increase while marginal revenue is positive. After an output level of about 5 units per week marginal revenue would become negative. Total revenue is thus maximized at 5 units per week.

*(d)* *MC1* in Figure A7-1 represents the new marginal cost schedule, $MC1 = MR0$ at an output level of about 2 units per week: a cost increase thus causes output to fall.

*(e)* *MR1* in Figure A7-1 represents the new marginal revenue schedule $MC0 = MR1$ at an output level of about 4 units per week: i.e. output has increased.

**8** All of these could provide motivation for decision-makers in firms, although some may be relevant mainly where there is a separation of ownership and control. In such a situation, there may be a conflict of interest between owners and managers (the principal-agent problem). The shareholders (owners/principals) may prefer the firm to maximize profits, but the managers (agents) may prefer to maximize sales, market share or growth. For more discussion of firms' motivations, see Section 7-3 of the main text. The separation problem is most important where it is difficult for the owners to monitor the actions of managers: for example, where there are many small shareholders.

Economists tend to focus on profit maximization *(a)* as being a reasonable approximation to reality – and convenient for analysis.

## True/False

1   True: see Section 7-1 of the main text.
2   False: the balance sheet sets out assets and liabilities of a firm at a particular date.
3   False: of course, nobody wants to end up with worthless shares, but shareholders are only liable for the amount they put into the firm and no more.
4   False: opportunity cost must also be considered.
5   True.
6   True: see Section 7-2 of the main text.
7   False.
8   True: see Section 7-5 of the main text.
9   False: unless you can convince your bank manager that all will be well, the long term may never come!  Most new businesses (and many old ones) need to borrow to help them through periods of low cash flow.
10  True: see Section 7-4 of the main text.
11  True: remember exercise 7?
12  False!
13  True: see Section 7-5 of the main text.
14  True: see Box 7-2 of the main text.

## ECONOMICS IN THE NEWS

1   The airline business has been highly competitive since deregulation, which has allowed airlines to fix fares and compete freely on routes within the EU. However, the prevalence of these deals and offers does not prove that firms do not maximize profits. Remember that the profit maximizing position for a firm is not a question of charging the highest possible price, but a question of locating the point at which marginal cost equals marginal revenue. For an airline, the marginal cost of taking additional passengers onto a plane that is not full may be very low, so it may pay to sell off marginal seats at a low price. This is the case especially where different passengers may pay different prices for the same journey. This is an issue to which we will return later.
2   The strategic interaction between firms may complicate the story further, making it even more difficult to judge whether firms are seeking to maximize profits. There may be circumstances in which a firm will forego maximum profits in the short run in order to improve the prospects for profit in the long run. However, we need to gain some more understanding of the economic principles of firm behaviour before we pursue this issue in more depth. The airlines may not be unique in experiencing this level of competition, but they are a very visible example, partly because the transition to a deregulated market is still not complete.

## Questions for Thought

1   Some hints may be found in Section 7-5 of the main text: it will also be discussed again in Chapter 8.
2   If you are reading this, you have decided that the opportunity cost is not excessive – or you would have hurried on to the next chapter! Opportunity cost is involved every time we make a choice between alternatives: spending money in one way precludes us from buying other items; taking time to do something prevents us from doing something else.

3    *(a)* One possibility is that the managers' aims will be to ensure job security and to safeguard a good salary. These objectives *may* not coincide with profit maximization, especially if the managers' salaries are seen to be associated with sales or market share.

     *(b)* The problem is that it may not be a straightforward matter for you to monitor the managers, or to assess whether output and price have been set so as to maximize profits.

     *(c)* The managers may be aware that a hostile takeover could well be followed by changes in management. This may provide an incentive for profit maximization, which may reduce the likelihood of a takeover

     *(d)* The threat of a hostile takeover may lead to short-termism. It may be more difficult to undertake long-term investment if the firm becomes vulnerable to takeover in the transition. Box 7-2 in the main text argues that firms in the UK and USA suffer in this way relative to firms in Germany or Japan, where there is a different approach to corporate finance.

     *(e)* You need to find some way of setting appropriate incentives for the managers, perhaps by seeing that they hold some shares in the company. If you are anxious about the long-term position of the company, then you might wish to take measures to reduce the probability of a takeover or to limit its effects on the existing management Box 7-2 in the main text explores these and other issues in more depth.

# Chapter 8    Developing the Theory of Supply: Costs and Production

## Important Concepts and Technical Terms

| | | | | | | | | | |
|---|---|---|---|---|---|---|---|---|---|
| **1** | *(a)* | **4** | *(m)* | **7** | *(d)* | **10** | *(j)* | **13** | *(g)* |
| **2** | *(l)* | **5** | *(n)* | **8** | *(i)* | **11** | *(b)* | **14** | *(k)* |
| **3** | *(h)* | **6** | *(f)* | **9** | *(e)* | **12** | *(c)* | | |

## Exercises

1    *(a)* and *(b)*. The calculations for *(a)* are needed to tackle part *(b)*. Total costs for each technique are set out in Table A8-1; the preferred technique for each output level has been indicated by lines of enclosure. At low levels of output, technique A provides the least-cost method of production – notice that this technique is relatively labour-intensive, using more labour but less capital than the alternatives. However, as output levels increase, technique B becomes more efficient, and then technique C takes over when output reaches 6 units/week – this being the most capital-intensive technique.

     *(c)* If labour becomes more expensive relative to capital, we expect the firm to move towards more capital-intensive techniques. In particular. we expect a move away from technique A in this exercise – and this is what happens, as you can see in Table A8-2.

     *(d)* See Table A8-2.

**Table A8-1    Total cost and the choice of technique**

| Output (units/week) | Total cost technique A | Total cost technique B | Total cost technique C |
|---|---|---|---|
| 1 | 2 600 | 2 800 | 3 200 |
| 2 | 5 000 | 5 200 | 5 600 |
| 3 | 7 400 | 7 600 | 8 000 |
| 4 | 10 200 | 10 000 | 10 800 |
| 5 | 14 200 | 13 600 | 14 000 |
| 6 | 19 800 | 18 200 | 17 600 |
| 7 | 27 200 | 24 200 | 21 800 |

**Table A8-2    Total cost and the choice of technique after the change in labour cost**

| Output (units/week) | Total cost technique A | Total cost technique B | Total cost technique C |
|---|---|---|---|
| 1 | 3 500 | 3 400 | 3 600 |
| 2 | 6 900 | 6 200 | 6 400 |
| 3 | 10 300 | 9 000 | 9 200 |
| 4 | 14 300 | 11 800 | 12 400 |
| 5 | 20 100 | 16 000 | 16 000 |
| 6 | 28 300 | 21 500 | 20 000 |
| 7 | 39 200 | 28 700 | 24 700 |

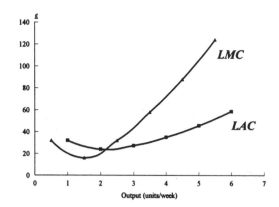

**Figure A8-1    Long-run average cost and long-run marginal cost**

2    (a)  See Table A8-3.

**Table A8-3    Output and long-run total cost**

| Output (units/week) | Total cost (£) | Long-run average cost | Long-run marginal cost |
|---|---|---|---|
| 0 | 0 | | |
| | | | 32 |
| 1 | 32 | 32 | |
| | | | 16 |
| 2 | 48 | 24 | |
| | | | 34 |
| 3 | 82 | 27.3 | |
| | | | 58 |
| 4 | 140 | 35 | |
| | | | 88 |
| 5 | 228 | 45.6 | |
| | | | 124 |
| 6 | 352 | 58.7 | |

(b)  See Figure A8-1.

(c)  At 2 units/week.

(d)  It is always the case that $LMC=LAC$ at the minimum point of $LAC$ – thus the intersection is at 2 units/week of output.

3    (a)  Up to 2 units/week.

(b)  In excess of 2 units/week.

(c)  2 units/week.

(d)  This point represents the switch-over from falling $LAC$ to rising $LAC$ from increasing to decreasing returns to scale.  *At that point*, the firm has constant returns to scale.

4    (a) is a tempting response, but incorrect: diminishing returns to a factor do not require that the extra units used diminish in quality; nor need total product fall: it is marginal product that diminishes.  Response (c) is an interesting observation (in jargon, this describes a 'pecuniary external diseconomy of scale'), but it is not pertinent to diminishing returns.  If you think about it you will realize that (d) described increasing returns to a factor.  (e) is concerned with revenue rather than costs.  This leaves us with (b) as the correct response: diminishing returns are indeed concerned with the returns to the variable factor.

5    All of them.

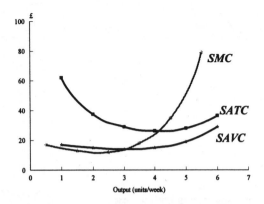

**Figure A8-2   Short-run average total cost, short-run average variable cost, and short-run marginal cost**

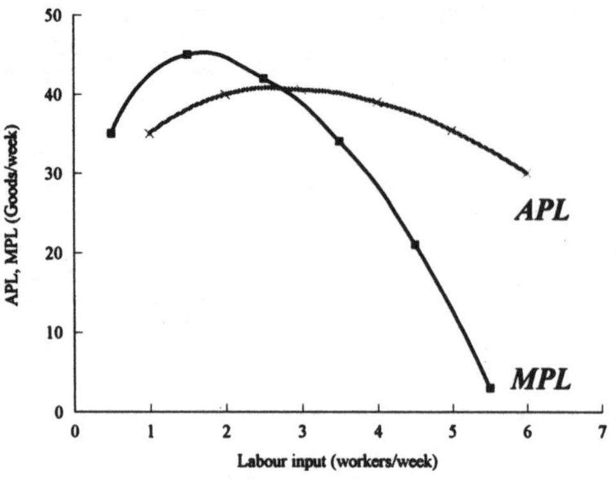

**Figure A8-3   Average and marginal product of labour**

6   *(a)*  See Table A8-4.

**Table A8-4  Short-run costs of production**

| Output (units/week) | SAVC Short-run average variable cost | SAFC Short-run average fixed cost | SATC Short-run average total cost | STC Short-run total cost | SMC Short-run marginal cost |
|---|---|---|---|---|---|
| | | | | | 17 |
| 1 | 17 | 45 | 62 | 62 | |
| | | | | | 13 |
| 2 | 15 | 22.5 | 37.5 | 75 | |
| | | | | | 12 |
| 3 | 14 | 15 | 29 | 87 | |
| | | | | | 18 |
| 4 | 15 | 11.25 | 26.25 | 105 | |
| | | | | | 35 |
| 5 | 19 | 9 | 28 | 140 | |
| | | | | | 79 |
| 6 | 29 | 7.5 | 36.5 | 219 | |

*SAFC* = £45 divided by output;  *SATC* = *SAVC* + *SAFC*;  *STC* = *SATC* multiplied by output.

*(b)*  See Figure A8-2.
*(c)*  In the short run, the firm cannot adjust its capital input. If it wishes to change the level of output, it must do so by altering labour input.  However, with capital input fixed, diminishing returns to labour set in rapidly, such that the marginal product of labour falls. For this reason, the marginal cost of producing more output may be very high in the short run.

7   *(a)*  See Table A8-5 opposite.

**Table A8-5   Output and labour input**

| Labour input (workers/week) | Output (goods/week) | Marginal product of labour | Average product of labour |
|---|---|---|---|
| 0 | 0 | | |
| | | 35 | |
| 1 | 35 | | 35 |
| | | 45 | |
| 2 | 80 | | 40 |
| | | 42 | |
| 3 | 122 | | 40.6 |
| | | 34 | |
| 4 | 156 | | 39 |
| | | 21 | |
| 5 | 177 | | 35.4 |
| | | 3 | |
| 6 | 180 | | 30 |

*(b)* See Figure A8-3.

*(c)* MPL turns down close to 1½ workers/week: this is the point at which diminishing returns set in.

*(d)* MPL must cut APL at its maximum point – i.e. just below 3 workers/week.

*(e)* A change in the level of capital input affects the *position* of MPL and APL. An increase in capital would move these curves upwards.

**8** *(e)*, *(f)*.

**9** *(a)* OC can be produced at minimum average cost.

   *(b)* Decreasing returns to scale.

   *(c)* That corresponding to SATC2.

   *(d)* The firm would have no choice in the short run but to produce using SATC2. In the long run, it would pay to expand to SATC3.

   *(e)* See Figure A8-4.

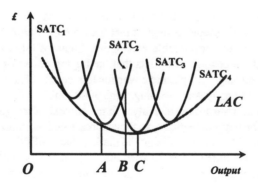

**Figure A8-4   Short-run (and long-run) average cost**

10

| Price (£) | Short-run decision | | | Long-run decision | | |
|---|---|---|---|---|---|---|
| | Produce at a profit | Produce at a loss | Close down | Produce at a profit | Produce at a loss | Close down |
| 18 | ✓ | | | ✓ | | |
| 5 | | | ✓ | | | ✓ |
| 7 | | | ✓ | | | ✓ |
| 13 | | ✓ | | ✓ | | |
| 11.50 | | ✓ | | | | ✓ |

Notice that firms will never choose to produce at a loss in the *long run*.

## True/False

1  False: it may seem like that sometimes, for economists often assume for simplicity that there are only these two factors.  In reality, there may be others: managerial input raw materials, energy – even bandages for the rest room!  (See Section 8-1 of the main text.)

2  True: of course, the economies of scale may persist to quite high output levels (see Section 8-4 of the main text).

3  True: this was discussed in the writings of Adam Smith in the eighteenth century.

4  False: not all industries experience significant economies of scale.

5  False: remember exercise 10?

6  False: price and average revenue are the same if all output is sold at the same price.

7  False: reference must also be made to the average condition, to see whether the firm should close down (see Section 8-6 of the main text).

8  True: see Section 8-7 of the main text.

9  True: see Section 8-5 of the main text.

10  True: see Section 8-4 of the main text.

11  True: sunk costs are sunk: what is important is the level of variable costs (see Box 8-2 in the main text).

12  False: the $LAC$ curve touches each $SATC$ curve but never cuts one.

## ECONOMICS IN THE NEWS

1  We do not always think of service sectors like the insurance market as being able to exploit economies of scale. However, the passage certainly seems to suggest that the Royal & Sun Alliance merger was successful in allowing the new company to tap considerable economies. Some of these may have come through the application of IT advances, but the passage also hints that the buying power of the newly-merged company may have brought benefits in securing '...the same cover for less cost...' The other reflection of economies of scale is the fact that the new company was shedding some 5000 jobs.

2  Competitiveness is not a straightforward issue to analyse in the context of merger activity. there is a tendency to expect mergers to be anti-competitive, as they increase concentration. However, it is possible that merger activity will have the effect of equalizing the market shares of firms in an industry, with the end result of increasing the competitive interactions between the firms. It seems that thus may be the case here, especially within the international insurance market, where the new company may be more able to compete on equal terms with foreign firms.

## Questions for Thought

1  In your discussion of this question, you will have to explore the issue of economies and diseconomies of scale. Average costs decline up to the 'minimum efficient scale' as a result of indivisibilities in the production process, specialization and (in some cases) benefits of large scale (see Section 8-4 of the main text). However, the level of output at which the minimum efficient scale is reached varies from industry to

industry, with the type of activity and technology involved. These are some of the issues that you will need to consider. Do try to think up some examples of industries in which there are likely to be significant economies of scale, and also industries where the minimum efficient scale is likely to be at a relatively low level of output. This process of relating theory to reality is an excellent way of confirming your understanding of the concepts.

2   *Hint:* Remember the long-run/short-run distinction.

3   There was some brief discussion of this at the end of Chapter 7 in the main text.

4   The scope for economies of scale in many industries has been greatly affected by the IT revolution. Box 8-1 in the main text talks about this a bit and we devote the whole of Chapter 11 to the information economy. The changing nature of capital and technology in many industries has affected the extent of economies of scale – not always in the same direction: notice how you can now buy spectacles almost anywhere without having to wait while lenses are ground in some remote central factory.

# Chapter 9   Perfect Competition and Pure Monopoly: The Limiting Cases of Market Structure

## Important Concepts and Technical Terms

| 1 | (a) | 4 | (k) | 7 | (e) | 10 | (h) |
|---|-----|---|-----|---|-----|----|-----|
| 2 | (j) | 5 | (l) | 8 | (c) | 11 | (i) |
| 3 | (g) | 6 | (f) | 9 | (d) | 12 | (b) |

## Exercises

1   (a)   Profits would be maximized at output *OA* in Figure A9-1 (overleaf) where *MC=MR*.

   (b)   Profits would be calculated by the excess of average revenue over average cost, multiplied by output – in Figure A9-1 (overleaf), this is the area *PBCD*.

   (c)   This firm is making profits over and above 'normal profits', which are included in average cost. It is thus probable that Figure A9-1 represents short-run equilibrium, as we would expect other firms to be encouraged to enter the industry by the lure of these supernormal profits. However, it could be a long-run equilibrium if this firm enjoys a cost advantage – perhaps a better geographical location. In this case, further entry would depend upon the marginal firm's performance.

   (d)   A decrease in demand would lead initially to a fall in the price of the good, and firms such as the one represented in Figure A9-1 would experience a reduction in profits. In the long run, firms would be able to adjust their input structures to the new conditions, so that price would drift up again. (See Section 9-4 of the main text for a similar analysis of an increase in demand.)

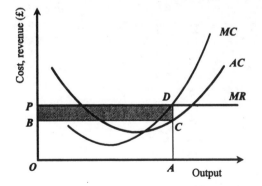

**Figure A9-1 A firm under perfect competition**

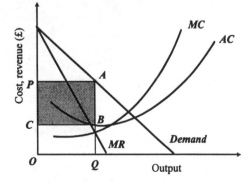

**Figure A9-2 A monopolist**

2   (a)  *OB*: the price at which the firm just covers its variable costs.
    (b)  *CD*.
    (c)  *CDRP*: total cost less variable cost.
    (d)  Between *OB* and *OD*.
    (e)  The supply curve in the short run is the portion of the *SMC* curve above point *K*.
    (f)  Above *OD*.

3   (a)  Profit would be maximized at output *OQ* in Figure A9-2 where *MR* = *MC*.
    (b)  The demand curve shows that the monopolist could sell *OQ* output at a price *OP*.
    (c)  Profits would be calculated. as before, as the excess of average revenue over average cost, multiplied by output – this is the area *PABC*.
    (d)  A decrease in demand would affect both 'Demand' and *MR* curves in Figure A9-2, moving them to the left. *MC* and *MR* will now intersect at a lower level of output, so the monopolist will produce less.

4   (a)  *MR* = *LMC* at the output level *OD*.
    (b)  *OC*.
    (c)  *LAC* is just tangent to the demand curve at this point, so the monopolist makes only normal profits: supernormal profits are zero.
    (d)  If the monopolist were forced to charge a price equal to marginal cost, then an output of *OH* is indicated, with price *OB*. However, notice that in this situation *LAC* exceeds average revenue and the monopolist would close down, unless the authorities were prepared to offer a subsidy.

5   (a)  See Table A9-1.
    (b) and (c)  See Figure A9-3.
    (d)  4.
    (e)  4.
    (f)  4.

6   (a)  *OC*.
    (b)  *OE*.
    (c)  *OB*.
    (d)  *OF*.

7   (d).

### Table A9-1   A monopolist's revenue curves

| Demand ('000s/ week) | Price (£) (average revenue) | Total revenue | Marginal revenue |
|---|---|---|---|
| 0 | 40 | 0 | |
| | | | 35 |
| 1 | 35 | 35 | |
| | | | 25 |
| 2 | 30 | 60 | |
| | | | 15 |
| 3 | 25 | 75 | |
| | | | 5 |
| 4 | 20 | 80 | |
| | | | -5 |
| 5 | 15 | 75 | |
| | | | -15 |
| 6 | 10 | 60 | |
| | | | -25 |
| 7 | 5 | 35 | |

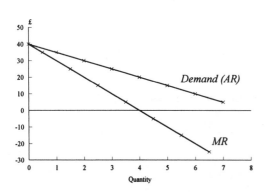
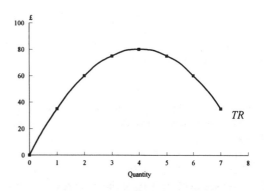

**Figure A9-3   A monopolist's revenue curves**

**8**   Option *(a)* relates only to a monopoly situation: the monopolist chooses output where $MC = MR$. at which point *AR* (hence the chosen price) exceeds *MR*.. Thus *(h)* also applies only to the monopolist. In the case of situation *(b)*, a firm under perfect competition has no influence over price, and thus faces a horizontal demand curve such that $AR = P = MR$. Situation *(c)* expresses the condition for firms to maximize profits, so applies to all market situations in which firms attempt to maximize profits, whether perfect competition, monopoly, or other forms of market structure which we will encounter in the next chapter. Option *(d)* is a feature of the long-run situation under perfect competition if firms are equally efficient, it could also relate to a monopolist, but this depends upon the position of the average cost curve relative to the demand curve. In many cases. we expect the monopolist to be able to make positive profits even in long-run equilibrium, depending on the strength of barriers to entry. Situations *(e)* and *(f)* relate to a monopoly situation. A monopoly will only remain a monopoly if new firms can be excluded from the market by some means. In the case of *(f)*, a firm under perfect competition can only choose output, and must accept the price as given; the monopolist can choose a combination of price and output, but is still subject to the demand curve. Perfect competition assumes that there are no barriers to entry *(g)*; it is this characteristic that leads to the long-run equilibrium position for the industry which we will see later is highly desirable for society as a whole, where price is set equal to marginal cost (situation *(i)*). This is in contrast to monopoly. in which price can be set above marginal cost.

**9**   *(d)*.

**10**  *(a)*  Under perfect competition, industry equilibrium would be where demand (D) equals supply *(LRSS)* – that is, at price *OA* and output *OG*.

   *(b)*  In the short run the monopolist will set marginal revenue *(MRm)* equal to short-run marginal cost *(SMCm)*. Output is reduced to *OF* and price increased to *OB*.

   *(c)*  In the long run, the monopolist will close down some plants and equate *MRm* with long-run marginal cost *(LMCm)*. Output is reduced further to *OE* and price raised to *OC*.

   *(d)*  The monopolist will still operate each individual plant at its minimum *LAC*. *LAC* is thus given by *OA* – and profits by the area *ACHK*.

## True/False

**1**   True.

**2**   False: the increased flexibility in the long run makes the long-run supply curve flatter than in the short run.

**3**   False: the firm is said to be making just normal profits when economic profits are zero (see Section 9-2 of the main text).

4  False: such an industry is a natural monopoly (see Section 9-8 of the main text).

5  False: we must also consider the quantity that would be supplied by firms who are not currently operating in the market, but who would enter if market price were at a higher level.

6  False: a monopolist will never produce on the inelastic part of the demand curve (see Section 9-7 of the main text).

7  False: draw the diagram to check.

8  False: even where efficiency is the same. the monopolist has influence on price and can use this market power to make supernormal profits.

9  False.

10  True.

11  True.

12  True: see Section 9-10 of the main text.

## ECONOMICS IN THE NEWS

1   As the passage makes clear, Eurostar faces competition from other transport providers between London and Paris and Brussels. In particular, the rise of the low-price airlines has made inroads onto Eurostar's expected market, in addition to the expected competition from the ferry companies. Eurostar would still maximize profits at the MC=MR position, but the presence of competition affects the shape and position of the demand curve, which in turn affects marginal revenue.

2   The passage highlights a number of ways in which Eurostar is trying to improve its profitability. When there is excess capacity on the train, the marginal cost of enticing an additional customer is low. It thus pays Eurostar to encourage demand from additional passengers at off-peak times. This will tend to appeal more to some groups of passengers than others, given differing elasticities of demand. A business traveller heading for a meeting will have inelastic demand for travel at a convenient time, so will be prepared to pay a higher price than a casual traveller who may be prepared to travel at a relatively unpopular time in order to take advantage of lower prices. So, the key characteristic of the consumers that enables the firm to charge different prices is their elasticity of demand. Question 3 in 'Questions for Thought' of this chapter explores the theory behind this. We will return to the question of price discrimination in Chapter 11 (The Information Economy).

## Questions for Thought

1   *Hint:* What could threaten the monopolist's long-term position? A crucial factor determining whether a monopolist will decide to take full advantage of its market position is the strength of the barriers to entry. If the monopolist thinks there is a possibility that other firms may be able to enter the industry, then there may be a reluctance to make large profits, for fear of attracting attention. It is also possible that the monopolist may not want to attract the attention. It is also true that the monopolist may not want to attract the attention of the government: this will be discussed further in Chapter 18.

2   In approaching this question, think in particular about the situation for the firm when the industry is in long-run equilibrium. This may be contrasted with the monopoly position, where the firm always produces below minimum efficient scale.

3   (a)  *OcM:* the output at which *LMC=MR* in the combined market.

    (b)  *OcN* (=*O1E*), this being the price to clear the combined market.

    (c)  At the price of *O1E* demand in market 1 would be *O1H,* and demand in market 2 would be *O2K.* Notice, of course, that the scales of the three diagrams are common, and that *O1H+02K=OcM.*

    (d)  Marginal revenue is *O1B* in market 1 and *O2I* in market 2. This large difference has important implications for profits.

*(e)* In part *(d)*, it was clear that marginal revenue in market 2 was much higher than in market 1. If the monopolist can increase sales in market 2 and reduce sales in market 1, the additional revenue from the former will more than offset the lost revenue of the latter, and profits will increase. It will pay to continue this switching until marginal revenue is equal in the two markets.

*(f)* To equalize marginal revenue in the two submarkets, the monopolist would sell in market 1 at a price of $O_1F$ and in market 2 at a price of $O_2J$; sales would be $O_1G$ and $O_2L$, respectively. Again, $O_1G + O_2L = OcM$.

Notice that this analysis depends upon the nature of the commodity (cannot be resold), the separation of the market, and the differing elasticities of demand in the two markets.

It is also worth noticing that if *LMC* cut *MR* much further to the left in Figure 9-7(c), it could be that without discrimination no sales at all are made in market 2.

4 *(a)* *AML.*

   *(b)* *CMH.*

   *(c)* Part has gone to the monopolist as profits *(ACHK)*; the remainder (triangle *KHL*) is a 'deadweight loss' to society. We may argue that this is the irrecoverable loss to society that results from the presence of monopoly in this market.

# Chapter 10   Market Structure and Imperfect Competition

## Important Concepts and Technical Terms

| 1 | *(b)* | 4 | *(j)* | 7 | *(f)* | 10 | *(l)* | 13 | *(n)* |
|---|-------|---|-------|---|-------|----|-------|----|-------|
| 2 | *(a)* | 5 | *(k)* | 8 | *(e)* | 11 | *(m)* | 14 | *(c)* |
| 3 | *(i)* | 6 | *(h)* | 9 | *(g)* | 12 | *(d)* |    |       |

## Exercises

1 *(a)* D.

   *(b)* B.

   *(c)* A.

   *(d)* C.

   *(e)* E: we haven't talked about monopsony yet, but it was defined in Chapter 9.

   *(f)* B/C: although a monopolist in the supply of rail transport, the supplier would doubtless be aware of potential competition from other forms of transport, and would thus perhaps behave more like an oligopolist than a monopolist. We discussed the example of Eurostar in 'Economics in the News' in Chapter 9, p. 45.

2 *(a)* A, because of the existence of substantial economies of scale relative to market size.

   *(b)* B, E: in both industries, the biggest three firms supply a small proportion of the market. In addition, it is clear that no great scale economies exist, in that the minimum efficient size is very small relative to market size.

   *(c)* C, D seem capable of supporting just a handful of firms.

   *(d)* Oligopoly is unlikely to arise in either B or E, with the large number of firms likely to be present in these industries. Could A be an oligopoly? It is perhaps not impossible: we cannot know for sure, as we only have the three-firm concentration ratio; nor do we know whether the firm(s) is (are) actually operating at minimum efficient scale. The monopolist may be prevented by law from exploiting his position – or may have other 'industries' with which to compete (see example *(f)* in exercise 1). The steepness of the average cost curve below minimum efficient scale is also important. For more details, see Section 10-1 in the main text.

3 *(b)*, *(c)*, *(d)*, *(e)*, *(f)* and *(h)* are all typical characteristics of such an industry – see Section 10-2 of the main text. As for the other factors:

*(a)* In long-run equilibrium, firms find themselves in tangency equilibrium with average revenue just covering average costs – so no monopoly profits are to be reaped in the long run. If this were not so, then there would be an incentive for more firms to enter the market.

*(g)* Monopolistic competition is typified by a large number of firms, so the opportunities for collusion are limited.

4  *(a)* *MR=MC* at output *OG*.

   *(b)* *OF*

   *(c)* Yes: the area *EFLK*.

   *(d)* This must be a short-run equilibrium. The presence of supernormal profits will attract new entrants into the industry, causing our firm's demand curve to become more elastic at any price and to shift to the left. This is because of the increased availability of substitutes and because the firm loses some customers to the new entrants. The process continues until the typical firm is in tangency equilibrium, with its demand curve just touching the long-run average cost curve, making only normal profits.

5

| Influence | Encourages collusion | Favours non-co-operation |
|---|:---:|:---:|
| | (Tick one column) | |
| Barriers to entry | ✓ | |
| Product is non-standard | | ✓ |
| Demand and costs are stable | ✓ | |
| Collusion is legal | ✓ | |
| Secrecy about price and output | | ✓ |
| Collusion is illegal | | ✓ |
| Easy communication of price and output | ✓ | |
| Standard product | ✓ | |

6  The figure shows the typical shape of the famous 'kinked demand curve'. A feature of this model is the stability of prices, so we can accept statement *(a)*. The price discrimination model can also produce a demand curve with a kink in it – but in that case, the kink faces the other way (see Figure 9-7). We thus reject *(b)*. As this is an oligopoly model, and the 'kink' occurs because the firm is aware of its rivals' actions, statement *(c)* is likely to be acceptable. Statement *(d)* has no foundation.

7  *(a)* Given that Y produces 'low', you (X) can make profits of 15 by also producing 'low' or 20 by producing 'high'. For this period, you maximize profits by producing 'high' – but notice that, in so doing, you reduce the profit made by Y.

   *(b)* With you producing 'high', firm Y must also produce 'high' to maximize profits.

   *(c)* Given the answer to *(b)*, it seems probable that Y will indeed produce 'high', in which case your only option is also to produce 'high'. In actual fact, your dominant strategy is to produce 'high' – it pays you to do this whatever Y does if we are concerned only with the single time period.

   *(d)* If we start thinking in terms of a sequence of time periods, it should be clear that both firms could be better off if both agree to produce 'low'. If you can be sure that firm Y will produce 'low' and will continue to do so, then it will pay you to decide to produce 'low' also.

   *(e)* One possibility is to announce a punishment strategy. You threaten to produce 'high' in all future periods if Y cheats on the agreement. The threat is credible only if Y believes that you would actually find it in your best interests to carry it out.

   *(f)* One possibility is to enter into a pre-commitment to produce 'low', restricting your own future options.

   *(g)* The arguments here are similar, but the penalties if both firms produce high are much more severe. If firm X announces its intention of producing 'high', firm Y knows that it can only survive by producing 'low'. However, X would also go under if Y produces high, so Y could also announce its intention of producing high, and the question then is whether one firm (or both) will give way. This is sometimes known as the 'chicken' game, because of its similarity to the game of chicken in which two cars rush headlong towards each other, testing each other's nerves. We could still end up with the firms destroying each other if neither gives way.

8   *(a)* is an innocent barrier: if the minimum efficient scale is high relative to market demand, then we are heading towards a natural monopoly situation. *(b)* may well be strategic: potential entrants will perceive that staying in this market will require R&D expenditure and may thus be deterred. Also, R&D expenditure may lead to the generating of patents *(c)* for the future, further preventing entry. Firms have been known to take out a whole range of patents on items that may or may not prove profitable, thus being ready to exploit any ideas that turn out well. Having said that, it may be in society's best interests for firms to undertake R&D expenditure, and the patent system is in place to ensure that there is some incentive for innovation and invention. Items *(d), (e),* and *(f)* are other ways in which the incumbent firm(s), may deter potential entrants; you will find more detailed discussion in Section 10-6 of the main text. The final item *(g)* could be either innocent or strategic. Existing firms may have 'innocent' advantages in locations or experience which make it difficult for new entrants to compete. On the other hand, the advantage may be another offspring of past R&D effort, and thus partly strategic. Indeed, the closer we look at these barriers, the more difficult it becomes to distinguish between the innocent and the strategic. Take barrier *(f)*, for example. A firm may hold excess capacity in order to add credibility to an announced threat of predatory pricing. This is a strategic move. However, a firm may install additional capacity in the expectation of a future increase in demand for its product. This is simply good business practice.

9   With the protection of the patent, the monopolist may have enjoyed a period making profits above the opportunity cost of capital, as we examined in Chapter 9. The patent barrier will have prevented entry of other firms who might have been attracted by the lure of profits. When the patent expires, the market becomes contestable, and these other potential competitors are likely to attempt entry. As entry takes place, the former monopolist's demand curve is likely to shift to the left and to become more elastic, as some customers switch to the new firms. Do you recognize this story? We are back in the world of monopolistic competition, and heading for long-run tangency equilibrium.

10   We cannot offer comments on this, as we do not know what firms operate in your neighbourhood.

## True/False

1   True.
2   True.
3   False: in these conditions a monopoly would be unlikely (see Section 10-1 of the main text).
4   True: see Section 10-2 of the main text.
5   True: a firm's behaviour is determined by its perceptions about the actions of other firms. Thus, firms will be prepared to raise price if it is known that all firms face an increase in costs.
6   False: the kinked demand curve may be the most famous of oligopoly models, but, as this chapter has shown, it is by no means the only way in which economists have tried to analyse such markets.
7   False: 'dominant' has nothing to do with winning; the question is whether the strategy dominates other possible strategies the firm can adopt, given what other firms may do. See Section 10-4 of the main text.
8   True: this is also discussed in Section 10-4 of the main text.
9   Not necessarily true: for this tactic to be successful, it must be apparent that the threat of a punishment strategy is a credible one.
10   This may be 'true' in the short run, but it could be 'false' in the long run: if there is a threat of new entry into the industry, it may pay to use limit pricing to deter potential entrants.
11   True: see Section 10-5 of the main text.
12   True: see Section 10-6 of the main text.

## ECONOMICS IN THE NEWS

1   The passage refers to a number of possible barriers to entry. In particular, branding and advertising, which can raise the fixed costs associated with entry into a market. Branding can be seen as a way in which a firm tries to affect the elasticity of demand of its customers. If consumers have loyalty to a brand, their demand will tend to be less elastic, as they do not perceive other brands as being close substitutes. This means that reputation counts for a lot, and new firms find it more difficult to gain entry to a market. It also refers to the way that bricks-and-mortar companies are making more and better use of the internet to promote their products.

2   Competition seems fierce, but although the passage refers to the way that 'the market is flooded', it does not sound very much like perfect competition. The references to branding and niche markets are more suggestive of monopolistic competition. We will return to discuss market structures within the information economy in the next chapter.

## Questions for Thought

1   No hints are offered for this question: think about it!

2   *(a)* In the market as a whole (panel *(c)*), profits are maximized where $MCc=MRc$ at output $Oce$.

    *(b)* Price will be set at $OcW$ (= $OaE$ = $ObL$).

    *(c)* Accepting the cartel level of marginal revenue (at $OcX$ = $OaF$ = $ObN$), firm A produces $OaK$ and firm B, $ObS$. Notice that $OaK + ObS = Oce$ (although it may not look like that in Figure 10-4, where the horizontal scale of panel *(c)* has been compressed to squeeze it on to the page).

    *(d)* Firm A makes profits of $EFGJ$ and firm B makes $LMQP$. Firm A's cost advantage is reflected in a much higher level of profit, and a higher market share.

    *(e)* If firm B were to act as if it were a price-taker at $ObL$, it would attempt to maximize profits by increasing output to $ObV$, where $MCb$ = perceived $MR$. This again illustrates the tension inherent in a cartel situation.

    *(f)* Of course, firm B is not really a price-taker in this market, and if firm B increases output from $ObS$ to $ObV$, market price will fall (in panel *(c)*), and overall cartel profits will fall. Indeed, price could fall to such an extent that firm B (with its high average cost) makes losses. This is especially likely if firm A also begins to increase output.

3   Perhaps the key question to ask in this context is what information the tobacco manufacturers are really conveying by advertising. It cannot be that they want to tell us that their products will kill us, so what else could it be? Psychologically, perhaps they are merely looking to transmit a subliminal message to existing consumers to encourage them to continue smoking their particular brand. Another way of thinking about this is that one piece of information that we do learn from tobacco advertising is simply that the tobacco firms are prepared to spend lots of money on advertising ... i.e. we might interpret this as a sign of commitment to the market, and to maintaining the quality of the product.

4   From the economist's point of view, there is no doubting the value of the model of perfect competition. It provides a key benchmark against which we can compare the resource implications of alternative market structures. By seeing how real-life markets diverge from the perfectly competitive ideal, we may be able to analyse whether society is suffering a loss of overall welfare. We may even be able to do something about it by framing an appropriate policy to encourage competition and improved resource allocation.

# Chapter 11   The Information Economy

## Important Concepts and Technical Terms

| | | | |
|---|---|---|---|
| 1  *(b)* | 4  *(e)* | 7  *(d)* | 10  *(k)* |
| 2  *(f)* | 5  *(a)* | 8  *(c)* | 11  *(i)* |
| 3  *(h)* | 6  *(l)* | 9  *(j)* | 12  *(g)* |

## Exercises

1   Section 11-1 of the main text discusses the characteristics of information, or e-products. The key feature is that they can be digitally encoded, which means that they can be transmitted rapidly, accurately and cheaply. This clearly excludes tangible goods such as the pencil, refrigerator and computer. Of course, in their own way, each is critical to the transmission of information. Indeed, the computer is a key part of the infrastructure that has enabled the information economy to take off as it has. Why did we include the

refrigerator in this list, when it seems such an odd one out? As this book is being prepared, the TV programme *Tomorrow's World* has recently highlighted a refrigerator connected to the internet which enables the consumer to keep a shopping list up to date by monitoring what is removed from storage. The other items on the list may be information products, although attendance at live music concerts and football matches is not yet a thing of the past.

**2**   *(a)*   We doubt that you would subscribe sight unseen, as this is an example of an experience product – one that you need to sample in order to evaluate its worth.

    *(b)*   All these things may be an inducement. Reputation of the provider *(i)* may reassure you as to the quality of the product, especially if you have personal experience on which to draw *(iii)*, or if you can sample the product in person in order to evaluate it *(ii, iv)*. Firms providing services over the internet often use such offers to try to attract customers. As for *(v)*, we all do strange things at times of panic!

**3**   *(a)*   Production costs (A) in this context are the fixed costs of producing an information product, whereas reproduction and distribution are variable costs.

    *(b)*   The fixed costs entailed in producing an information product are often substantial. The compilation of an electronic dictionary, or the recording of a soundtrack may be large. However, it is a characteristic of information products that the variable costs, of reproduction and distribution (for example, via the internet) may be negligible.

    *(c)*   With large fixed costs and negligible marginal costs, there are likely to be large economies of scale in the production of these goods and services.

**4**   *(a)*   C.

    *(b)*   D.

    *(c)*   The more people that use the network, the more attractive it becomes to others. For example, the more people with email accounts, the more useful does email become. So, the demand curve shifts to the right – to:

    *(d)*   $D_B$ would be the demand curve, and F the equilibrium quantity demanded.

    *(e)*   See the demand curve $D_L$ in Figure A11-1.

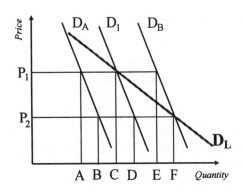

**Figure A11-1   Demand with a network externality**

**5**   There is a sense in which each of these goods is subject to some versioning. Books are discussed in Section 11-3 of the main text. Price discrimination is achieved by issuing a book first in hardback only, then subsequently in paperback – and in some cases at remaindered prices at an even later date. This picks up different groups of buyers. Railways and air travel are 'versioned' through the provision of First Class or Business Class travel arrangements. Computer software also comes in different versions – sometimes a basic version is issued free, with consumers having the option to purchase a 'professional' edition once they become tied in to the product. As for sausages, look in your local Tesco or other supermarket. You will find basic sausages on sale, but also 'finest' designer sausages in a variety of flavours.

6   *(a)* This describes the attribute of an experience product – until you have tried it you cannot judge it.

   *(b)* However, once you have bought a piece of information, you don't need to buy it again. This complicates things for the producer, who cannot give you the product to sample without destroying its value to you. However, a number of ways of getting around this have been devised.

   *(c)* One of the big problems with information is that there is so much of it about! It is easy to get into a situation of information overload, where there is so much information that it is useless to you because you cannot find your way around it. this is where search engines become invaluable.

   *(d)* This relates to the issue of switching costs. Once you become committed to a product, you may find that the costs of switching become substantial. The cost of reformatting all your files so that you can use a new word processor or graphics package may be more hassle than you are prepared to face.

   *(e)* Finally, this relates to the existence of network externalities. Fax machines only caught on when lots of people had them, more than a century after the technology was invented.

7   *(a)* £95: Your costs of £30, and the client's hassle costs of £65.

   *(b)* It does not seem likely to be worth while, as the switching costs exceed the expected profit stream.

   *(c)* Now perhaps it is viable.

   *(d)* You could afford to offer the client a couple of months' free access that would compensate her for the hassle of switching, or you could devote some funds to advertising the product to convince her that there were benefits in switching.

   *(e)* It would make sense for Comp.or to find a way of exaggerating the switching costs to make it more difficult for her to change to your product.

8   *(a)* At these prices, Anna would buy pizza, and Bob would buy treacle tart, so revenue would be £6.

   *(b)* Now, Anna would still buy pizza, Bob would still buy treacle tart, and Caroline would buy both. Revenue would be £8.

   *(c)* Now the supermarket gets the best possible deal. By bundling the goods in this way, Anna buys pizza (at £3), Bob buys treacle tart (also at £3), and Caroline buys both (for £4). Revenue is £10.

   *(d)* The Reward Card schemes run by supermarkets enable them to keep a close watch on who buys what, and at what prices. They can use this information to devise tailored deals for individual customers.

   This exercise is based on an example used by Robin Mason in 'Reward cards: who profits?' in *Economic Review*, Volume 17(1), September 1999.

9   Given that most information products display substantial economies of scale, it is virtually impossible for perfectly competitive markets to develop, as the largest firm is always in a position of cost leadership relative to smaller firms. The market is thus likely to develop into a monopoly (Windows runs on an estimated 90 per cent of PCs around the world), or possibly a sequence of monopolistically competitive markets, in which there is much product differentiation serving niche consumer groups.

## True/False

1   False: the expected increase is much larger. In early 2000, it was predicted that e-commerce would rise from £13bn to £150bn in Western Europe between 1999 and 2002.

2   False: it took even less time than this – see Figure 11-1 in the main text.

3   True, at least to some extent. Suppliers of information products need to adopt a strategy that allows you to sample the product without giving you all of it – see Section 11-2 of the main text.

4   True: see Section 11-2 of the main text.

5   True: see the discussion of switching costs in Section 11-2 of the main text. Of course, there may be a price at which a user may be prepared to switch, if the benefits of the new package are sufficiently attractive.

6   True: see the discussion of network externalities in Section 11-2 of the main text.

7   False: the existence of strong economies of scale makes perfect competition an extremely unlikely result – see Section 11-3 of the main text.

8   True: see Section 11-3 of the main text.

9   True: bundling is discussed in Section 11-3 of the main text.

10  It depends ... strategic alliances may enable cost reductions, and enable firms to deliver an improved product to consumers. However, we also know that collusion between firms in an oligopoly market may lead to a deadweight loss for society by impairing resource allocation.

11  False: the Europeans resolved this issue in the early 1990s, enabling rapid expansion and access to economies of scale that were denied to US firms. See Section 11-4 of the main text.

12  False: this chapter has shown how economics provides insights into the effects of the information revolution – see Section 11-5 of the main text.

## ECONOMICS IN THE NEWS 1

1  Web-selling has developed quite rapidly, and it is no surprise that relatively early websites were designed to be functional rather than user-friendly. So, part of the criticism may simply reflect the prototype nature of some of the sites. However, notice that the passage also refers to the way that the easyJet site may have hit problems *because* it has been around for a longer period. There is a temptation to build in extra knobs and whistles on to a site, rather than focusing on the key elements that need to be present. It must also be remembered that some sites sell advertising to related firms. When you are registered with a site so that it knows some of your personal details, the advertising can be tailored to your own interests, as expressed in the sort of pages that you visit. This illustrates another feature of the information economy that may be of benefit to advertising firms – and to consumers.

2  The last paragraph highlights the key attribute of network externalities, if the ploy is successful. The more people join the network from a particular locality, the better the discounts that could be negotiated, and the more value there is to be gained form joining the network.

3  We cannot comment on this question, for obvious reasons.

## ECONOMICS IN THE NEWS 2

1  In principle, books could be digitized and sold directly in electronic form. Indeed, this *Economics Workbook* is being sent to the publishers in electronic camera-ready format. However, there is a limit to the amount of text that people are prepared to read on screen, and in the case of this book, it would be much less useful to you if it were only provided on screen. However, the sale of books via the internet seems to work quite well. You may wish to read the latest Terry Pratchett, and are prepared to buy it without browsing through it first. Or you may know that a particular book is required for your course. Buying through the internet makes sense. They are non-perishable and easily handled by the postal service. However, the article also highlights one of the problems of internet selling. Namely, that it relies on the physical infrastructure of the postal service. When this slows down, as it does every Christmas-time, then internet buying becomes less attractive.

2  At the time this article came out, buying through the internet was still in its infancy. It seems likely that the pattern of book sales reflects the tastes and preferences of the early internet users. Medics, aspiring managers, computer buffs, economists and students seem to be the groups at the forefront. This is perhaps not surprising. On the other hand, if you are buying a cookery book or a book for children, it may be more important for you to see the book before buying it. You want to see the quality of the pictures, and so on. This is less easy (although not impossible) via the internet. As more people gain access to the web, and as firms become more accustomed to advertising on the web, this pattern is likely to change.

## Questions for Thought

1  Economics has a simple story to tell about internet pricing – if you price a good at zero, too much of the good will be demanded, and there is likely to be a congestion problem. Even if marginal costs of providing the service are zero, some fixed charge needs to be levied to cover the fixed costs. This issue is discussed more fully by Martin Chalkley in 'Internet Economics' in *Economic Review*, Volume 16(4), April 1999.

2   Firms are often reluctant to lose their individual identities by merging into a single firm, and sometimes the management culture of different companies makes a merger difficult to manage. Strategic alliances offer much more flexibility. If market conditions change, then it is not too difficult to disentangle the two partners, whereas the demerging of companies is far more costly. At the end of the day, it comes down to transactions costs. There are costs involved with both mergers and alliances. Mergers impose inflexibility costs, and others. In an alliance, each firm must monitor how the other partner is working. The question is which set of costs is the greater. Presumably Microsoft and Intel decided that the costs of a merger were excessive as compared to the potential benefits.

3   We are not going to pronounce on this topic one way or the other. The discussion in the main text of the economic principles surrounding this case should give you plenty of material to enable discussion of the topic with your fellow students. Indeed, by the time you read this, the matter may have progressed further than the interim judgement of the US Justice Department against Microsoft.

# Chapter 12   The Analysis of Factor Markets: Labour

## Important Concepts and Technical Terms

| | | | | | | | |
|---|---|---|---|---|---|---|---|
| 1 | (d) | 5 | (f) | 9 | (c) | | |
| 2 | (a) | 6 | (j) | 10 | (g) | | |
| 3 | (i) | 7 | (l) | 11 | (b) | | |
| 4 | (k) | 8 | (h) | 12 | (e) | | |

## Exercises

1   (a), (b)  See Table A12-1.
   (c)  See Figure A12-1 (overleaf).
   (d)  Adding the wage cost line to Figure A12-1 shows that profit will be maximized at 2 units of labour input – the firm will continue to hire labour as long as the MRPL exceeds the wage.
   (e)  With 2 units of labour input, total revenue is 80 × 10 = 800.
        Capital cost is 200; wage cost is 280 × 2 = 560.  Profits are 800 − 200 − 560 = £40.

### Table 12-1   Output and labour input, etc.

| Labour input (workers/ week) | Output (goods/ week) | Marginal physical product of labour (MPL) | Price (£) | Total revenue | Marginal revenue per unit output | Marginal value product of labour | Marginal revenue product of labour |
|---|---|---|---|---|---|---|---|
| 0 | 0 | | | 0 | | | |
| | | 35 | | | 12 | 420 | 420 |
| 1 | 35 | | 12 | 420 | | | |
| | | 45 | | | 8.44 | 450 | 378 |
| 2 | 80 | | 10 | 800 | | | |
| | | 42 | | | 4.19 | 336 | 176 |
| 3 | 122 | | 8 | 976 | | | |
| | | 34 | | | −1.18 | 204 | −40.12 |
| 4 | 156 | | 6 | 936 | | | |
| | | 21 | | | −10.86 | 84 | −228 |
| 5 | 177 | | 4 | 708 | | | |
| | | 3 | | | −116 | 6 | −348 |
| 6 | 180 | | 2 | 360 | | | |

**2**   *(a)*   *OD.*
      *(b)*   *OC.*
      *(c)*   *OA.*
      *(d)*   *OB.*
      *(e)*   Both tend to reduce labour demand.

**3**   See Figure A12-2.
      *(a)*   With the wage rate at £2.50, and with £20 unearned income, the maximum earnings for 24 hours would be 20 + 24 × 2.5 = £80 (but wouldn't George be tired!) The budget line is thus *BL1*.
      *(b)*   *BL1* is at a tangent to *IC1* at about 15 hours' leisure – so George works 9 hours.
      *(c)*   The budget line moves to *BL2*.
      *(d)*   George now chooses to work more hours and take only about 13 hours leisure.
      *(e)*   The 'income' effect can be seen by adding a new budget line parallel to *BL2*, tangent to *IC1*. This is *BLx* in the diagram. This shows leisure to be a normal good for George.

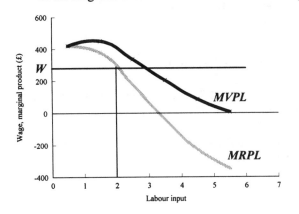

**Figure A12-1   MVPL, MRPL**

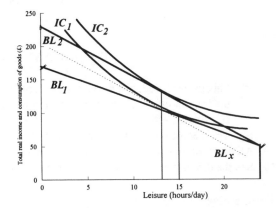

**Figure A12-2   An individual's supply of labour**

**4**   *(a)*   Wage would be *OB* and employment *OJ*.
      *(b)*   As demand for its product declines, the industry must reduce prices: this will affect the marginal revenue product of labour and reduce labour demand. In the diagram, this could be represented by a move to *D'L* with a new equilibrium at wage *OA* and employment *OI*. The supply curve is not affected.
      *(c)*   As wages increase elsewhere, clerical workers will prefer to leave in quest of better pay, so the supply of labour to our industry falls to S'L. In the new equilibrium, wage is *OE* and employment *OH*. The demand curve is not affected.
      *(d)*   With demand *D'L*, supply *SL* and wage *OB* there is excess supply of labour – i.e. unemployment. There are *GJ* workers who would like to obtain work in the industry, but cannot at that wage rate.

**5**   *(a)*   *OP.*
      *(b)*   *OPYZ.*
      *(c)*   *PRWY.*
      *(d)*   *OQ.*

**6**   *(a)*   *OAED.*
      *(b)*   *ABE.*
      *(c)*   Economic rent would be higher, transfer earnings correspondingly lower.

**7**   *(b).*

**8**   See Figure A12-3 (opposite).
      *(a)*   The isoquants are labelled *I10, I20,* and *I30* on the diagram (see Appendix to Chapter 12, main text.)
      *(b)*   The isocost line is given by the line *L1 K1*.
      *(c)*   The isocost line is tangent to the *I30* isoquant, so the maximum possible output is 30 units, for which the firm uses 290 units of labour and 21 units of capital.
      *(d)*   The new isocost is *L2 K1*.
      *(e)*   20 units of output, using 200 units of labour and 20 units of capital.

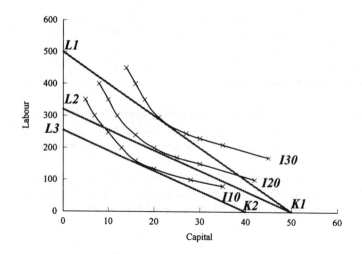

**Figure A12-3   Cost minimization for a firm**

*(f)* Labour use is reduced by 31 per cent and capital use by only 4.8 per cent. This is as we would expect – the 'output effect' leads to a reduction in both inputs, but the change in relative factor prices leads to a substitution effect towards capital.

*(g)* The isocost line *L3 K2* shows that the firm produces 10 units of output, with 160 labour and 16 capital.

9   All of them: these are discussed in Section 12-7 of the main text.
10   See the discussion in Section 12-7 of the main text.

## True/False

1   False: non-monetary differences in working conditions will give rise to an equalizing wage differential (see the introduction to Chapter 12 in the main text).
2   False: the firm will tend to employ relatively more capital, but will probably employ less of both (see exercise 8 of this chapter).
3   True.
4   True: statements 3 and 4 are equivalent (see Section 12-2 of the main text).
5   True.
6   False: $MRPL < MVPL$.
7   False: this ignores the effect of changing industry supply upon output price (see Section 12-3 of the main text).
8   False: an individual may choose to enjoy more leisure and work fewer hours (see Section 12-4 of the main text).
9   True.
10   True: see Section 12-5 of the main text.
11   True: see Section 12-6 of the main text.
11   True: see Section 12-7 of the main text.

## ECONOMICS IN THE NEWS

1   This is one of those questions where the answer begins with the words 'It depends...' In a perfectly competitive labour market, we would expect that the imposition of a minimum wage above the equilibrium wage would inevitably mean a reduction in employment as firms slide along their demand for labour curve. The market is held out of equilibrium, the short side dominates, and there is unemployment. However, if the labour market is not competitive, a different result may occur. In particular, if there is a sole employer in a

market, acting as a monopsonist, then employment could actually *increase* as a result of the introduction of a minimum wage. This is explained in Box 12-3 in the main text. The passage refers to a rather different argument – namely that there cold be knock-on effects, with other workers negotiating wage increases to maintain their differentials. However, there does not seem to be any evidence that this has been happening.

2   Many of the arguments for a minimum wage are couched in terms of protecting the low-paid, which is an argument about equity rather than efficiency. Many of the arguments against the minimum wage are efficiency arguments, in the sense that the imposition of a minimum wage introduces an inflexibility into the labour market that prevents free-market equilibrium from being reached.

3   We cannot answer this question, of course, as we do not know when you are reading the passage – and we leave you to make up your own mind about the desirability of the policy. However, we hope that you will base your view on sound economic reasoning.

Notice that some aspects of the minimum wage issue are discussed by Patricia Rice in the *Economic Review,* November 1997.

## Questions for Thought

1   The methods are equivalent: think about the nature of short-run marginal cost.
2   (a)  Point *A*.
    (b)  The budget line is given by the line *BC* in Figure A12-4.
    (c)  If Helen were to work, then she would choose to be at point *X*, where the budget line is at a tangent to *IC1*. Here she would be working 6 hours per day. However, she will not in fact do this, as she obtains more utility by not working and being at point *A* on indifference curve *IC2*.
    (d)  The effect of overtime, paid at a premium rate, is to kink the budget line after 8 hours' work, shown by the line *CDE* in Figure A12-4.
    (e)  Helen can now reach a tangency point with *IC3* and will work $(12 - L0)$ hours.
3   (a)  The isocost which has a tangency point with the *3X* isoquant is *C2* (tangency at point *C* in Figure 12-8).
    (b)  The distance from *G* to *C* is much smaller than from *C* to *F*: more labour is needed to increase output from *3X* to *4X* than from *2X* to *3X*. We are observing diminishing returns to a variable factor, in this case, labour.
    (c)  Notice the relative distances between these points *ABCDE*. At first the isoquants move closer together, but then they get further apart as output increases. At first, there are economies of scale, but then diseconomies set in: the long-run average cost curve is U-shaped.

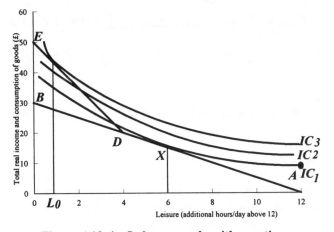

**Figure A12-4   Labour supply with overtime**

# Chapter 13    Human Capital, Discrimination, and Trade Unions

## Important Concepts and Technical Terms

| 1 | (b) | 4 | (f) | 7 | (e) | 10 | (c) |
|---|-----|---|-----|---|-----|----|-----|
| 2 | (a) | 5 | (j) | 8 | (d) | | |
| 3 | (i) | 6 | (h) | 9 | (g) | | |

## Exercises

1  (a)  Total benefits amount to 2500 + 9000 = 11500.  Total costs amount to 3000 + 7000 = 10000 (both in 'present value' terms).  Ian would thus choose further education, as the benefits outweigh the costs.

   (b)  If Ian were to fail to obtain the qualification, then the additional future income would not be forthcoming. In the calculations, Ian would reduce his valuation of this item.

   (c)  Joanne would place a lower valuation on the non-monetary benefits of student life. Whether or not she decides to continue in education depends upon how little she expects to enjoy herself.

   (d)  Keith is likely to use a different discount rate when assessing the present value of future costs and benefits. On the other hand, he could place a high valuation on 'student life', so again his decision could go either way.

2  (a)  See Figure A13-1.

   (b) (i) Group C.        (ii) Group B.        (iii)        Group A.

   Profiles based upon authentic UK information may be seen in Section 13-1 of the main text.

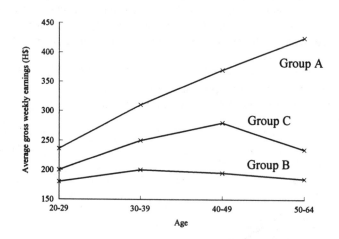

**Figure A13-1  Age-earnings profiles for three groups of workers**

3    (a) and (c) could be explained in terms of differences in occupational structure, and of themselves do not provide evidence of discrimination. It is possible that differences in occupational choice may reflect earlier discrimination in educational opportunities, but that is a separate issue. Observation (b) avoids the occupational explanation, but differences in pay here may reflect employers' different evaluation of the future productivity of men and women rather than overt discrimination. Observation (d) offers the strongest evidence of discrimination, as here we have a closely defined skill level and presumably similar marginal products of black and white workers, and yet we observe differences in earnings. For more discussion see Section 13-2 of the main text.

4    *(a)*  Wage *OA*, employment *OH*.

     *(b)*  *OC*.

     *(c)*  *DBDB*: the demand curve becomes more elastic.

     *(d)*  Wage *OC*, employment *OD*.

     *(e)*  *OB*.

5    These are all arguments that have been advanced to explain the differential in pay between men and women. Factor *(a)* is true, but we can adjust for it by considering pay of full-time workers only – and we find that the differential is still substantial. Men do tend to work in different occupations and industries *(b)*, partly because of biological differences *(f)*, which make men more suited for heavy physical labour. In the past, there has also been a tendency for manufacturing activity to be male-dominated, and for services to be more female-based. As the structure of the economy has changed, this has been one factor which has led to an ever-increasing proportion of females in total employment. Firms may often perceive that women are more likely to have their working-life interrupted by the demands of child-bearing and rearing. This may lead them to offer less training to women *(c)*, and perhaps to promote them less rapidly, as they see that the returns on their training expenditure may be lessened by these career interruptions. Educational choices made by females tend to be different from those of males *(d)* and *(e)*: there is still a tendency for fewer females to take mathematical or scientific subjects, and for fewer women to proceed to higher education. This may mean that they end up in lower-paid occupations. Some of these factors can be taken into account in calculations of the wage differential between the genders, but it seems that some differential remains, so that there is still some discrimination *(g)* in levels of pay offered by employers to males and females, but it is probably less widespread than in earlier years.

6    *(a)*  The earnings forgone by not accepting employment in another occupation, perhaps in manufacturing industry.

     *(b)*  The high future expected returns will attract some people into the profession; others may prefer to earn now; others may not feel themselves well-suited to life in a white-collar or professional occupation.

     *(c)*  The manufacturing sector in the UK has been in decline for a number of years now, and unemployment is especially high among young people. This may lower the opportunity cost of undertaking professional training, as alternative earnings opportunities may be limited. This is thus likely to lead to an increase in the demand for training, and ultimately entry to the profession. Of course, there will still be some individuals who realize that their talents and abilities are not likely to lead them to receive high returns in the professions.

     *(d)*  In the long run, the results are unclear. The changing structure of the economy may continue to move against manufacturing activity, such that the demand for members of the professions continues to expand. On the other hand, the increased numbers of qualified entrants to the profession will have an effect on the supply curve. If you sketch a demand and supply diagram, you will be able to check out the possible effects of these movements for yourself.

7    Trade unions will be in a relatively strong situation when *(a)* there is excess demand for labour, or when *(b)* there is a closed shop. However, if *(c)* the *MRPL* is below the wage rate, then their position in arguing for even higher wages is considerably weakened. Similarly, when *(d)* unemployment is at a relatively high level, employers will have less need to bid for labour by offering higher wages. If *(e)* the demand for labour is highly inelastic, the trade union's position is relatively strong, for it may be able to negotiate higher wages with very little fall in employment levels. However, if the union *(f)* faces a monopsony buyer of labour, it will find that its own market power is partly matched by that of the employer.

8    *(a)*  These rates of return compare very favourably with the rates of return typically expected on investment projects involving physical assets, especially in Africa and Latin America. This emphasizes the importance of human capital, especially in less developed countries.

     *(b)*  Education levels in many less developed countries are much lower than in the industrial countries, whether we measure in terms of literacy rates or mean years of schooling received. Thus, the returns to investing in education are high, because there is so much potential. None the less in many cases investment in human capital remains low, either because physical capital is more tangible and therefore seems more important, or simply because of lack of resources.

(c) Private returns are maximized at 'higher' levels in Africa and Asia, and are equal in Latin America and the industrial countries.

(d) Social returns, however, are higher at secondary level in all the country groups.

(e) Unfortunately, in many less developed countries the political influence of those who are likely to benefit from higher education has distorted resource allocation away from the secondary (and primary) sector in favour of higher education. Higher education tends to be heavily subsidized, but open only to a minority, in spite of the fact that higher social returns are available in the secondary stage.

(f) A further problem is that different groups in society will perceive the returns from education in different ways. A poor rural family may expect to gain much less from education, and to face higher costs than a rich urban family. This may be especially the case in terms of the opportunity cost of education; for example, it may be that a poor family sees a child in school as a child not working in the fields. This may be especially significant at secondary school level. This may help explain the political pressures mentioned in (e).

## True/False

1    True.

2    False: workers with general training are highly mobile between firms, so it pays the firm to offer low pay during training but relatively high pay to the qualified worker (see Section 13-1 of the main text).

3    False: degree training may act as a signalling device.

4    False: this statement ignores the opportunity cost of further schooling and the different marginal utilities of income of rich and poor families.

5    True: and notice it is the perception that is important, not the actuality (see Section 13-2 of the main text).

6    False: the difference in pay may reflect other factors, such as occupational choice, educational training, and so on. This is not to say that there may not be discrimination in some covert or overt form in some parts of the economy.

7    True: see discussion in Section 13-2 of the main text.

8    False: the true figure is just over one-half (see Section 13-3 of the main text).

9    False: we should not compare these low-paid workers with other groups of workers, but rather should ask what rates of pay they would have received in the absence of the union.

10    True.

11    False: see the evidence presented in Section 13-3 of the main text.

## ECONOMICS IN THE NEWS 1

1    Remember that the estimates here are averages across individuals – there is no guarantee that you will reap these returns … but keep hoping.

2    There is some evidence here, in that the relative earnings of men and women are closer for graduates than for non-graduates.

3    Again, remember that the study (as reported here) does not distinguish between subject of study. A key issue for this question is the extent to which university education acts as a signal about innate talent and ability, and the extent to which employers are looking for specific training.

## ECONOMICS IN THE NEWS 2

1    Clearly there are many factors that can influence an individual's earnings which would need to be taken into account, such as occupation, industry, gender, race, and so on.

2    *Hint:* A key question is whether we expect trade unions to have more or less power and influence at different stages of the business cycle.

3    We leave you to think about this one.

## Questions for Thought

1   This issue is tackled towards the end of Section 13-1 of the main text. It is one example where there may be a divergence between the interests of the individual and those of society at large. This sort of situation is reconsidered in Chapters 16 and 17.
2   This issue is discussed towards the end of Section 13-3 of the main text.
3   We would normally expect that a trade union will bargain for higher wages, and that this would be at the cost of accepting a lower employment level. There is one exception to this, however. Consider Figure A13-2.

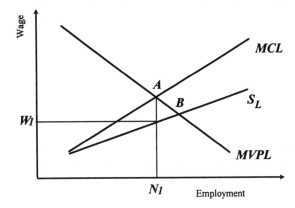

**Figure A13-2   Do trade unions always reduce employment?**

Suppose a firm operating with perfect competition in the product market is a monopsonist in the labour market. $S_L$ represents the supply curve of labour and $MCL$ the marginal cost of labour as faced by the firm: $MVPL$ constitutes the demand curve for labour. Before the trade union appears on the scene, the firm employs $N_1$ at a wage of $W_1$. When the firm is unionized, it is possible to negotiate with the firm to be at any position along the $MVPL$. At any point along the section $AB$ it is possible for the union to negotiate both an increase in wages and an increase in employment. This is a very special case, which is why this question appears in the 'Questions for Thought' section of the chapter.

4   If we regard the trade union as a monopoly seller of labour, then we can think of $DL$ as being the equivalent of the '$AR$' curve faced by the monopolist. Associated with this $AR$ curve there is of course also an '$MR$' curve, which we can think of as the 'marginal returns' from selling labour. This will have the form as shown in Figure A13-3, with a slope twice as steep as $DL$. If we then think of $SL$ as being the equivalent of the marginal cost curve of the monopolist, then the returns to selling labour ('profits') are maximized where $MR=SL$, at employment level $N_T$ and wage $W_T$.

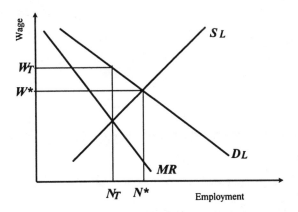

**Figure A13-3   A trade union in a labour market**

## Chapter 14   Capital and Land: Completing the Analysis of Factor Markets

### Important Concepts and Technical Terms

| 1 | (c) | 4 | (i) | 7 | (k) | 10 | (d) | 13 | (j) |
|---|-----|---|-----|---|-----|----|-----|----|-----|
| 2 | (a) | 5 | (m) | 8 | (f) | 11 | (e) | 14 | (g) |
| 3 | (l) | 6 | (n) | 9 | (b) | 12 | (h) | | |

### Exercises

1  *(a)*  Stock.
   *(b)*  Stock.
   *(c)*  Flow.
   *(d)*  Stock.
   *(e)*  Flow.
   *(f)*  Flow.

2  *(a)*  The rate of interest may be calculated as the constant annual coupon payment (£10) divided by the bond price (£62.50), i.e. 10/62.5 = 0.16, or 16 per cent.
   *(b)*  13 1/3 per cent.
   *(c)*  Price of bond = present value = coupon value/interest rate; i.e. price = 10/0.08 = £125.

3  *(a)*  12 per cent.
   *(b)*  12 − 14 = −2 per cent (approximately).
   *(c)*  With a negative real rate of interest, Lucy would do better to spend the money now, as the return on money saved is not sufficient to compensate for changing goods prices.
   *(d)*  The real rate of interest would then be +2 per cent, and Lucy might be encouraged to save the money and spend later – unless she is impatient for the goods!

4  To calculate the break-even price for the machine, we simply sum the present value rows of Table A14-1, with the following results:
   *(a)*  £1851.85 + £1714.68 + £6350.66 = £9917.19.
   *(b)*  £9841.59.
   *(c)*  £11705.51.

### Table A14-1   Present value calculations

| | Year 1 | Year 2 | Year 3 |
|---|--------|--------|--------|
| Stream of earnings | 2000 | 2000 | 2000 |
| Scrap value | | | 6000 |
| Present value | | | |
| *(a)* r = 8% | 1851.85* | 1714.68* | 6350.66 |
| Present value | | | |
| *(b)* r = 10% | 1818.18 | 1652.89 | 6010.52 |
| Present value | | | |
| *(c)* r = 8%; inflation = 7% | 19820.20 | 1960.59 | 7764.72 |

* The present value of £2000 in one year when the rate of interest is 8 per cent is calculated as:
  2000 / (1.08) = 1851.85
  After two year, the calculation is $2000 / (1.08)^2$.

The present value calculations for *(c)* are based on a real interest rate of 1 per cent – i.e. after 1 year:
  2000 / 1.01 = 1980.20
(See the Appendix to Chapter 14 of the main text for details.)

**5**   *(a)* Equilibrium will occur when the rental rate is the same as the two sectors, and when their joint demand exhausts the supply of land. This happens when the rental is *OA*, at which level, *OD* land is used for agriculture and *OH* for industry. (Note that *OD=HJ*.)

   *(b)*  In the short run, land use cannot change, so *OD* is used for agriculture and *OH* for industry.

   *(c)*  The rental rate in agriculture increases to *OC*, but the rental in industry remains at *OA*.

   *(d)*  In the long run, the high rental rate in agriculture relative to that on industrial land encourages the transfer of land from industry to agriculture. This continues until the rental is the same for both sectors. This occurs at rental *OB*, with *OE* land in agricultural use and OG in industry. *OE + OG = OJ.*

**6**  *(a)*   Annual cost of the machine is calculated as the real interest cost plus the cost of maintenance and depreciation; i.e. $25000 \times (0.10 - 0.08 + 0.12) = £3500$. This is the required rental – the proceeds necessary for the firm to cover the opportunity cost of buying the equipment.

   *(b)*  An increase in the inflation rate reduces the real interest cost of the loan, so the required rental falls to £3000.

**7**  *(a)*   In order to identify the initial position, we need first to understand what change is to take place. A reduction in the wage, which makes capital relatively more expensive, will shift the demand curve for capital to the right. Thus, *DB* in Figure 14-2 must be the initial position: quantity is *OD*, and the rental on capital is *OB*.

   *(b)*  The rental rate on capital when the market is in long-run equilibrium represents the opportunity cost of capital.

   *(c)*  After the wage cut, we find that capital is fixed in the short run at *SSC*, and the rental rate will thus increase to *OC*, with quantity remaining at *OD*.

   *(d)*  This position cannot be sustained: the rental *OC* is now above the opportunity cost of capital, *OB*, so capital will be attracted into this industry.

   *(e)*  The industry will settle in the long run when the rental on capital has returned to the original (long-run equilibrium) rate of *OB*; the quantity of capital is now *OH*.

   *(f)*   We normally think of these additions to capital in an industry as being investment.

**8**   All statements are valid: see Section 14-11 of the main text.

**9**   The straight line *OA* in Figure A14-1 would represent a perfectly equal distribution of income. *LC1* represents the distribution of original income in the UK and *LC2* the distribution of post-tax income – noticeably nearer to the straight line. *LC3* shows that the distribution of after-tax income in Brazil in 1995 was very skewed. For further discussion, see Bhanoji Rao and Peter Smith in *Economic Review*, February 1994.

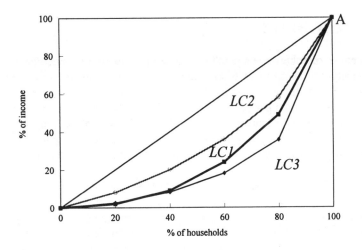

**Figure A14-1   Lorenz curves**

10 *(a)* *D* is the equilibrium, where the price line, *PPF*, and indifference curve all touch.

  *(b)* *OE* represents maximum current consumption, *OC* is actual consumption, so the difference *CE* is savings.

  *(c)* *OA*: but starvation may set in before the 'future' is reached if no resources are currently consumed.

  *(d)* By the slope of the *PPF*.

  *(e)* The rate of interest.

11 Suppose the interest rate increases. The consumer's trade-off between current and future consumption changes, as more future consumption can be obtained for a given sacrifice in the present. Thus, the substitution effect suggests that savings will increase with the interest rate. The real income effect is likely to operate in the reverse direction: at higher interest rates less saving is required to generate a given future income level. We cannot be certain of the net effect, but it is probable that the substitution effect will win – that is, higher interest rates will tend to encourage savings.

12 *(b)* and *(f)* would cause the *PPF* to steepen.

  *(a)* affects the shape of the society's indifference curves.

  *(c)* and *(d)* affect the slope of the price line.

  *(e)* refers to a movement along the *PPF*.

## True/False

1 False: not government bonds: see the introduction to Chapter 14 in the main text.

2 True.

3 False: the rental payments must be discounted to give the present value.

4 False: it is the real interest rate that matters.

5 True.

6 False: even in the short run, capital services can be varied to some extent by overtime working, shift adjustment, etc. (see Section 14-5 of the main text).

7 True.

8 True to an extent: but, as with labour, all land is not the same and some land may in practice command relatively high rentals because of its characteristics.

9 True.

10 True: see Section 14-10 of the main text.

11 False: declined from 64.3 to 63.4 per cent (see Section 14-11 of the main text).

12 True: see Section 14-11 of the main text.

## ECONOMICS IN THE NEWS

1 The personal income distribution may tell us something about how income is distributed among the members of a society, but is only part of the picture. To get a complete view, we might need to look at a range of indicators. Common ways of doing this are to look at the ratio of average income of the richest 20 per cent to that of the poorest 20 per cent, or to count the number of people below some 'poverty line'. This in itself creates new problems, because we need to find some way of defining such a poverty line, and we may wish to recognize that poverty may be a *relative* concept as well as an absolute one. Some writers have argued that a key part of poverty is when an individual is excluded from activities considered normal within a society.

2 Notice that this is a rather value-laden question. For starters, it presumes that you regard it as being desirable to narrow the gap between rich and poor. Decisions on the key policies then also bring further value judgements into play. Taxation is one obvious way of tackling the gap. The use of direct taxes on income that impinge more heavily on the rich, coupled with transfer payments to the poor is one possibility. However, in framing such policies, it is important to be careful about the incentives being provided. It is desirable neither to tax the rich so heavily that they have no incentive to work, nor to provide benefits to the poor at such a level that they do not wish to work either. The question is one of balance, and we shall return to this in Chapter 17. Notice that the minimum wage has also been highlighted as an anti-poverty policy. We discussed this in Chapter 12.

## Questions for Thought

1   The distinction between economic rent and transfer earnings was discussed in Section 12-6 of the main text.

2   Clearly, energy is a crucial input to almost every production process, and there is an extent to which we can think of energy as being a potential substitute for other factors. For instance, we may think of choices of technology which allow alternative combinations of labour, capital, and energy. This became important especially after the oil price shocks, where the sudden change in the real price of energy caused a search for more energy-efficient techniques of production.

# Chapter 15   Coping with Risk in Economic Life

## Important Concepts and Technical Terms

| 1 | (c) | 4 | (m) | 7 | (f) | 10 | (d) | 13 | (i) |
|---|-----|---|-----|---|-----|----|-----|----|-----|
| 2 | (a) | 5 | (n) | 8 | (j) | 11 | (e) | 14 | (h) |
| 3 | (l) | 6 | (k) | 9 | (b) | 12 | (g) |    |     |

## Exercises

1   (a)  Maureen is risk-averse.
       Nora is a risk-lover.
       Olga is risk-neutral.
     (d)  You may well have been risk-averse like Maureen in choosing not to buy in (b). However, Maureen tells us that if she had lots of money, she might accept the deal. This, of course, reflects the diminishing marginal utility of wealth (see Section 15-1 of the main text).

2   Risk-pooling occurs in situations (b), (c) and (e), where relatively large numbers of people face the risk, each with a relatively small likelihood of needing to claim.

3   Moral hazard is present in cases (a), (b) and (d). In case (d), the probability of rain is unaffected by the insurance, but the size of the bills is not. (c) and (e) are concerned with adverse selection.

4   (a)  £24.
     (b)  £12.
     (c)  £18.
     (d)  50 per cent.
     (e)  Still £18.
     (f)  The chance that both industries hit bad times together is now only 25 per cent, so you have reduced the risk by diversifying.

5   (a)  3.
     (b)  4.
     (c)  5. See Box 15-3 of the main text.
     (d)  2.
     (e)  1.

6   If the efficient markets theory of the stock market is correct, then any method relying on past information is doomed to failure, as current share prices already incorporate the effects of past information. The best hope is to be the first trader to respond to new relevant information – i.e. option (e). If the market were a casino, then option (b) might be as effective as anything else (see Section 15-5 of the main text).

7   (c) and (e) are correct: a share with negative beta tends to move against the market, and thus reduces the risk of a portfolio. Most shares move with the market, and thus have a beta close to 1.

8   (a).

## True/False

1 False: on the contrary, the risk-lover gains utility from risk (see Section 15-1 of the main text).
2 True.
3 True: see Section 15-2 of the main text.
4 True.
5 False: see Section 15-3 of the main text.
6 True: see Section 15-4 of the main text.
7 True: this was James Tobin's characterization.
8 False: it is precisely when share returns are negatively correlated that diversification is most successful.
9 False: low-beta shares will be highly valued (see Section 15-4 of the main text).
10 True: see Section 15-5 of the main text.
11 False: whether or not prices would be stabilized is irrelevant: the point is that a forward market in cars is not a viable proposition (see Section 15-6 of the main text).
12 False: he or she would be speculating.

## ECONOMICS IN THE NEWS

1 The investor's attitude towards risk.
2 We cannot comment on your answer to this, as we don't know you well enough!
3 If you are a risk-averse sort of investor, you will probably have chosen a balanced portfolio, as a diversified mix of investments offers safety – so long as the chosen nations and sectors do not all dip at the same time. A risk-lover will go for the excitement, perhaps choosing a narrower range of high-risk but high-return assets.

### Questions for Thought

1 See Section 15-3 of the main text.
2 and 3 See Section 15-5 of the main text.
4 Moral hazard may be thought to be a potential problem in the case of unemployment insurance. In the case of health insurance, adverse selection is a possibility.

## Chapter 16   Introduction to Welfare Economics

## Important Concepts and Technical Terms

| | | | | | | | |
|---|---|---|---|---|---|---|---|
| 1 | *(d)* | 4 | *(g)* | 7 | *(f)* | 10 | *(i)* |
| 2 | *(a)* | 5 | *(k)* | 8 | *(e)* | 11 | *(j)* |
| 3 | *(b)* | 6 | *(l)* | 9 | *(h)* | 12 | *(c)* |

## Exercises

1 *(a)* D, F, and H each make at least one of our two subjects better off without making the other worse off. For instance, at D Ursula is better off, and Vince no worse off. Both are better off at F.
   *(b)* C and E.
   *(c)* B and G cannot be judged either superior or inferior to A: in each case one individual is better off, but at the expense of the other. This does not mean that 'society' is indifferent between A, B, and G. The three points represent distributions of goods between which the Pareto criterion cannot judge.

*(d)* *C, E.*

*(e)* *A, B, G.*

*(f)* *D, F, H.*

2 *(a)* £10, this being the purchase price of books.

  *(b)* 2, reflecting the ratio of prices (marginal utility) of the two goods.

  *(c)* Marginal cost of the last book was £10, last unit of food, £20. Under perfect competition, equilibrium price = marginal cost (this was discussed in Chapter 9).

  *(d)* As 'job satisfaction' is equal in the two sectors, so also will be the wage rate in equilibrium – otherwise there would be movement of labour.

  *(e)* 2:1.

  *(f)* 2, reflecting the difference in the marginal physical product of labour.

  *(g)* The allocation is Pareto-efficient – there is no feasible reallocation of resources which will make society better off. If you have had difficulty following the chain of arguments in this exercise, you should re-read Section 16-2 in the main text, where a similar exercise is discussed in more detail.

3 *(a)* Price *OC*, quantity *OG*.

  *(b)* The new supply curve is *SA*. Equilibrium price would be *OD*, quantity *OF*. Tax is *AD*.

  *(c)* Marginal social cost is *OA*. Marginal consumer benefit is *OD*. This allocation is socially inefficient, as too few books are being produced.

  *(d)* Price *OK*, quantity *OP*.

  *(e)* It is not a satisfactory allocation because marginal social cost *(OM)* is greater than marginal private benefit *(OK)* at this price: 'too much' food is being produced.

  *(f)* The books tax causes a distortion, such that *MSC* represents the true marginal social cost in terms of the utility forgone by using resources in food rather than books.

  *(g)* The preferred output would be *ON* at price *OL*, where the marginal social cost equals the marginal social benefit of food production. This could be achieved by a tax of size *JL*. This topic is discussed in Section 16-3 of the main text.

4 *(b)*, *(c)*, and *(e)* all indicate that distortions exist which lead to market failure. *(a)* – traffic congestion – is not evidence of market failure. Just as the optimal level of pollution may not be zero, so there may be some 'optimal' level of congestion. As far as *(d)* is concerned, it is not the divergence of marginal social and private benefit which matters: the issue is whether marginal social cost is equated to marginal benefit.

5 Pavement-fouling imposes a cost on society in that it reduces the utility of other people or forces someone to bear the cost of clearing it. The absence of a charge for dog ownership would tend to lead to there being more dogs than is socially efficient. Many economists would argue that a price control (increasing the fee) is preferable to a quantity control.

6 *(a)* E.

  *(b)* *MSCY*: the marginal social cost lies below the marginal private cost to the individual firm when production externalities are beneficial (see Section 16-5 of the main text).

  *(c)* *J*: this is the point where the marginal social cost equals the marginal social benefit.

  *(d)* The area *EHJ*.

7 *(a)*: firm initially produces 7 units of output, where *MPC* = *MR*, and then restricts output to 3 units where (*MPC* + *MSC* of pollution) = *MR*.

8 *(b)* and *(e)*: these options relate directly to the Pareto criterion.

9 Here, all the options are correct. If the local authority wants to increase revenue, it is vital that demand be inelastic (as we saw way back in Chapter 5). If the authority wishes to relieve congestion, as the wording implies, then this is tantamount to saying that option *(b)* holds. Option *(c)* is closely allied to *(a)*, in that demand would not be likely to be inelastic if there were alternative car parking facilities in the town centre.

10 In approaching any issue involving externalities, the aim for society is to reach a position in which marginal social cost is equal to marginal social benefit. As far as pollution is concerned, we must balance the benefits of pollution reduction against the costs entailed in achieving it. This analysis suggests that the total elimination of pollution would not necessarily take society to its most preferred position. This is explained more fully in Section 16-5 of the main text.

Figure A16-1 (opposite) may help to explain what is going on here. Suppose we have an industry in which private firms face costs given by *MPC*, but in which production causes pollution, such that society faces higher marginal costs given by *MSC*. If firms are free to produce as much as they like, equilibrium is attained at *Q*, although you can see in the figure that Q* would be preferred. The shaded area represents the deadweight loss imposed on society by being at *Q* instead of at *Q\**. This is the excess of *MSC* over *MSB* between *Q\** and *Q*. However, the question was about the optimal level of pollution, and whether this would be zero. Clearly in Figure A16-1 it is not zero – *MSC* > *MPC* even at *Q\**.

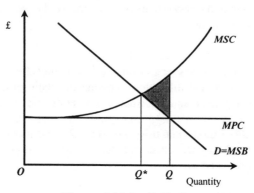

**Figure A16-1    Pollution**

## True/False

1   True.
2   True: see Section 16-1 of the main text.
3   False: one non-competitive market is sufficient distortion to prevent Pareto efficiency.
4   False: the second-best theory says it is better to spread the distortion across all sectors (see Section 16-3 of the main text).
5   True; given our definition of market failure (see Section 16-4 of the main text).
6   True.
7   False: the reverse is so (see Section 16-6 of the main text).
8   False.
9   False: the optimal level of pollution need not be zero.
10   True: see Section 16-7 of the main text.
11   False: no economy could afford such priority. (See an article by Anil Markandya and Pamela Mason on 'Air pollution and health', in *Economic Review* 17(2), November 1999.)
12   True.

## ECONOMICS IN THE NEWS

1   The fundamental idea here is that congestion is a source of market failure. The marginal motorist on the road not only incurs congestion, but also imposes congestion on others, so that marginal private costs are below marginal social costs. Figure A16-1 was used to discuss pollution, but could equally be used to analyse congestion. Electronic road pricing is one way of trying to deal with this problem. By imposing a congestion charge, that marginal motorist can be forced to face up to the full marginal social cost of his or her journey. This will then encourage appropriate decisions by road users. You will see from the passage that technology has advanced to the point where the charges can be calculated quite precisely to match the particular time of day.
2   If the aim is to control congestion on the roads, then it is car usage that is more important than car ownership. Singapore has attempted to control car ownership for many years, as is mentioned in the passage. This is done through various taxes, licences and permits. In 1989 an econometric study indicated to the Singaporean government that the demand for cars was more income elastic than price elastic, suggesting that

higher taxes or registration fees would not stem the growing demand for cars – given that real incomes were growing very rapidly. Hence the introduction of a quantity control system in 1990, limiting the number of new cars allowed onto the roads. It has also been argued that once having incurred the very high cost of car purchase in Singapore, car owners are likely to be highly insensitive to road charges.

3   Working in Singapore's favour is that it does not have to be concerned about inter-city roads, as there are none. For an economy like the UK the road system is much more complex and there is much greater variance in the road capacity in different regions and towns. It is thus more difficult to devise an appropriate road-pricing scheme. Having said that, such schemes have been tried in some cities.

## Questions for Thought

1   The topic of nuclear energy remains a contentious one: there are many private and social costs and benefits which need to be considered before an objective evaluation can be reached. One aim of this chapter has been to offer you a framework for thinking about issues such as this.

2   The granting of property rights would entitle these suffering people to compensation – perhaps from the football club for damage and disruption, or from noisy neighbours (re-read Section 16-5 of the main text).

# Chapter 17   Taxes and Government Spending

## Important Concepts and Technical Terms

| | | | | | | | |
|---|---|---|---|---|---|---|---|
| 1 | *(b)* | 5 | *(n)* | 9 | *(j)* | 13 | *(f)* |
| 2 | *(l)* | 6 | *(k)* | 10 | *(a)* | 14 | *(e)* |
| 3 | *(g)* | 7 | *(i)* | 11 | *(c)* | | |
| 4 | *(m)* | 8 | *(d)* | 12 | *(h)* | | |

## Exercises

1   *(a)*   See Figure A17-1.

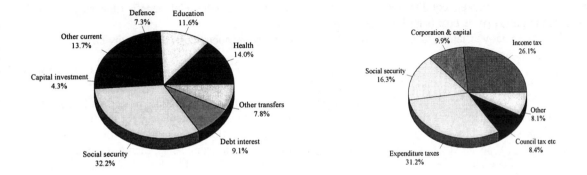

**Figure A17-1   Patterns of government expenditure and revenue, 1998**

*(b)* We would expect to find an increase in the share of expenditure taxes, and a fall in the share of direct taxes – especially income tax. For instance, in the very first Budget of the first Thatcher government in 1979, the Chancellor reduced the rate of income tax, but introduced increases in VAT. If we were to see a pie-chart for 1978, we would expect to observe 'Income tax' with a larger slice, and 'Taxes on expenditure' with a smaller one.

*(c)* The increase in unemployment will have had a number of effects. On the expenditure side, we would expect in particular to see an increase in payments of social security benefits. On the revenue side, we would expect there to have been some fall in receipts from income tax.

2   See Table A17-1.

**Table A17-1   Marginal and average tax rates (All figures expressed in percentage terms)**

| Income level (£) | Scheme A (30% tax on income over £ 5 000 | | Scheme B (30% tax on income over £ 5 000) (50% tax on income over £ 10 000) | |
|---|---|---|---|---|
| | Marginal rate (%) | Average rate (%) | Marginal rate (%) | Average rate (%) |
| 3 000 | 0 | 0 | 0 | 0 |
| 9 000 | 30 | 13.3 | 30 | 13.3 |
| 12 000 | 30 | 17.5 | 50 | 20.8 |
| 20 000 | 30 | 22.5 | 50 | 32.5 |

Both schemes are progressive, with average tax rates rising with income: Scheme B is more progressive, as intuition suggests, with average rates rising more rapidly.

3   *(a)* As this good is a pure public good, one individual's consumption of the good does not prevent others from also consuming it; thus the marginal social benefit *DD* should be the vertical summation of *D1* and *D2* – and we have of course drawn it that way.

*(b)* *OA*.

*(c)* If individual 1 actually pays *OA* for this good, then individual 2 need not pay at all in order to consume it. One of the characteristics of a public good is that individuals cannot be excluded from consuming it. This is at the heart of the 'free-rider' problem entailed with public goods.

*(d)* The marginal social benefit is given by the *DD* schedule – i.e. the amount *OE*.

*(e)* At this point marginal cost is at *OB*, which is well below marginal social benefit, suggesting that too little of the good is being produced.

*(f)* At *OG*, where marginal social benefit is equal to marginal cost. For further discussion of public and merit goods, see Peter Smith in the 'Question and Answer' column of the Economic Review, April 1994.

4   *(a)* In a free market, equilibrium in the market is where marginal social benefit (demand) is equal to marginal private cost (supply) at *OE* quantity (and price *OA*).

*(b)* The socially efficient quantity is where *MSB* equals marginal social cost: the quantity *OD*.

*(c)* The triangle *GHI*.

*(d)* The tax required is that which would induce producers to take decisions on the basis of *MSC* rather than *MPC*. A tax of the amount *GJ* would accomplish this.

*(e)* There are a number of possible examples. An obvious one might be pollution, or traffic congestion.

5   In a situation where social costs are less than private costs, there will be a tendency for too little of the good to be produced, so a subsidy to firms might be appropriate. Option *(a)* would have the opposite effect. Conversely, if social costs are above private costs (as they were in exercise 4), then too much of the good will be produced in a free market, and a tax is the appropriate response. This eliminates option *(b)* and leads us to option *(c)* as being the correct answer.

6   *(a)* *SSa* is labour supply without the tax; *SSb* is the post-tax supply curve.

*(b)* Wage *OB*; hours *OI*.

*(c)* Reduced from *OI* to *OE*.

(d)  *OC*.

(e)  *OA: AC* is the amount of the tax.

(f)  Tax revenue is *ACHF*.

(g)  *FHJ*.

(h)  Workers *ABGF*; firms *BCHG*. (Compare this with exercise 2 in Chapter 4.)

(i)  *OC*.

(j)  *OA*.

(k)  *ACHF*.

(l)  There is no distortion.

(m)  The tax falls entirely on the workers.

7  To an extent, statements *(f)* and *(g)* encapsulate the central arguments. The Tiebout model emphasizes the importance of choice to individuals, which may be more readily facilitated by having small jurisdictions *(g)*. We may see statements *(a)*, *(d)*, and *(e)* as being in support of this view. However, public goods by their very nature are non-exclusive *(b)*, so when jurisdiction areas are relatively small, non-residents are able to avail themselves of the facilities provided: a beneficial externality, which may be difficult to accommodate within the market price system. Statement *(e)* ceases to be valid. Expanding the area of jurisdiction reduces this effect *(f)*.

8  The diversity in pattern of tax revenues is substantial. Some of these differences may be easier to explain than others. For example, social security systems are still largely absent in many developing countries, so it may not be a great surprise to see the zero entries for Cameroon, India and Zambia. In some societies, governments do not find it politically easy to levy direct taxes on income. From the data, it seems that Bolivia is a prime example of such a society. Countries that are open to international trade, and that rely heavily on exports, tend to avoid taxes on international trade. With the successive tariff reduction rounds of the post-war period, such taxes are little used by the industrial countries anyway, as you can see in the case of the UK. Countries like Cameroon and India continue to remain heavily dependent on taxes on international trade and transactions. We will discuss this issue more carefully later in the book. UK's VAT forms part of the taxes on domestic goods and services. For some countries, such as Bolivia and Zambia in the table, indirect taxes on goods offer a relatively straightforward method of raising revenue.

## True/False

1  False: the decline in unemployment in the late 1980s brought with it a fall in the ratio of transfer payments to national income.

2  True.

3  True: see Section 17-1 of the main text.

4  False: in the case of a football match, there is the possibility of exclusion (see Section 17-2 of the main text).

5  False: this is an example of a transfer payment, which serves to redistribute income between groups in society (see Section 17-2 of the main text).

6  True: see Section 17-3 of the main text.

7  False: this is not necessarily so. The key feature of public goods is that the government should determine how much is produced, but this need not entail direct production.

8  False: see Section 17-3 of the main text.

9  True: this results from the typical consumption patterns of 'rich' and 'poor'.

10  False: the statement is too strong. It may be that this effect would be evident in some countries, but it has by no means been proved and many economists remain sceptical (see Section 17-4 of the main text).

11  True: see Section 17-2 of the main text.

12  True: see Section 17-6 of the main text. Whether we mind this happening may be a different matter.

## ECONOMICS IN THE NEWS

1  We do not know whether or not you agree with the statement, but we hope that the discussion in this chapter and elsewhere in the book so far will have given you a good view of the economic arguments to be brought

to bear on this question. The question is not clear-cut, as we need to look for balance. If there is market failure, then the government may be justified in intervening. We have referred to a number of areas in which such market failure may be present, and some of these are mentioned in the passage – for example, the provision of public services such as health, education and transport, or the need to tax 'bads' in society, like pollution and waste. On the other hand, there is the danger that if the government intervenes with too much enthusiasm, then distortions will be introduced, which may mean that resources are not allocated as efficiently as they might be.

2   Again, judgement has to come in for you to evaluate the present balance according to your own beliefs, but (we hope) backed up with sound economic reasoning.

## Questions for Thought

1   *Hint:* Is income tax a progressive or a regressive tax? How about expenditure taxes?
2   *(a)* Where $D$ (marginal social benefit) = $MSCa$; price $OE$, quantity $OF$.
   *(b)* Where $D$ *(MSB)* = $MSCg$; price $OC$, quantity $OI$.
   *(c)* Setting price at $OC$, quantity will be $OI$. At this point, marginal social cost exceeds marginal social benefit, and the deadweight loss is given by the area $HJK$.
   *(d)* Setting quantity at $OI$, price will be $OC$; the deadweight loss is again $HJK$.
   *(e)* No: the loss is the same in both cases.
   *(f)* Where $Da$ = $MSC$; price $OP$, quantity $OU$.
   *(g)* Where $Dg$ = $MSC$; price $ON$, quantity $OR$.
   *(h)* Setting price at $ON$, quantity will be at $OW$, at which point $MSC$ exceeds $MSB$ *(Da)*. The deadweight loss is area $VXY$.
   *(i)* Setting quantity at $OR$, price will be $OQ$. Now marginal social benefit exceeds $MSC$: too little of this commodity is being produced. The deadweight loss is now $TSV$.
   *(j)* The price- and quantity-setting policies no longer produce the same outcome. In Figure 17-5, the deadweight loss is smaller under a price-setting regime than a quantity-based policy. Notice that this may not always be the case; the outcome will depend upon the steepness of both the demand curve and the $MSC$ curve. You could see this by sketching a version of Figure 17-5 in which $MSC$ was steeper, and $D$ was flatter.

# Chapter 18   Industrial Policy and Competition Policy

## Important Concepts and Technical Terms

| 1 | (a) | 4 | (j) | 7 | (d) | 10 | (n) | 13 | (f) |
|---|-----|---|-----|---|-----|----|-----|----|-----|
| 2 | (i) | 5 | (k) | 8 | (m) | 11 | (h) | 14 | (o) |
| 3 | (g) | 6 | (e) | 9 | (c) | 12 | (b) | 15 | (l) |

## Exercises

1   *(a)* and *(b)* are examples of vertical mergers. If in *(a)* the vehicle manufacturer took over the tyre producer, this could be described as 'backward vertical integration' – the vehicle firm is expanding activity back down the production process. A vehicle firm expanding by buying car distributors would be indulging in 'forward vertical integration'.
   *(c)* represents a conglomerate merger – there is no direct production link between tobacco and cosmetics.
   *(d)* is an example of a horizontal merger where the firms presumably hope to benefit from economies of scale.

2   (a)   Price *OB*, output *OS*.
    (b)   Price *OC*, output *OR*.
    (c)   The area *KLN*.
    (d)   *ABKJ*.
    (e)   *ACLJ*.
    (f)   The most likely explanation is that the monopolist is able to exploit economies of scale.
3   (a)   Output *OC*, price *OE*.
    (b)   *BCG*.
    (c)   *AGBF* . Notice that this area also represents monopoly profits.
    (d)   This is the sum of consumer and producer surpluses – that is, the area *ACGF*.
    (e)   Output *OH*, price *OA*.
    (f)   *ACI*.
    (g)   There is no producer surplus in this position: firms are only making normal profits.
    (h)   *ACI*. Notice that this is appreciably larger than *ACGF*, which was the social surplus under monopoly. Another way of looking at this is that the difference between the surplus in the two situations (i.e. *FGI*) represents the social cost of monopoly.
    (i)   The same as *(e)*.
4   (c): this was the only merger blocked by the EC Commission (see Box 18-5 in the main text).
5   (d). As to why conglomerate mergers became important in the late 1980s, this may partly have been a result of the opportunities offered by financial deregulation, partly the idea that diversification offered security, and partly other factors. Notice that the trend towards conglomerate mergers was to some extent reversed in the early 1990s. See Section 18-5 of the main text.
6   (a) and (b).
7   (f): this is the only factor mentioned which leads to a reduction in competition. If you sketch a diagram, you will see that, if cross elasticity falls and thus the demand curve becomes steeper, the deadweight loss to society increases.
8   (a)   *LMCA*.
    (b)   Output *OG*, price *OE*.
    (c)   The triangle *EFI*.
    (d)   As the market opens up, it is possible that there will be a reduction in X-inefficiency, causing costs to fall to *LMCB*.
    (e)   Output *OR*, price *OA*.
    (f)   *AFS*.
    (g)   Most obviously, consumer surplus has increased greatly, although the monopolist (who is also a member of society!) is no longer making large profits. The other gain is in productive efficiency, in the sense that resources are being more effectively used in the production of this good.
9   All of them.
10  Policies *(a)*, *(f)*, and *(h)* are elements of competition policy. Item *(i)* can also be viewed in this way, being one way of tackling the 'natural monopoly' problem. The other policies would be regarded as belonging to industrial policy.

## True/False

1   True: see Section 18-3 of the main text.
2   False: few estimates have been set so high, although Cowling and Mueller set it as high as 7 per cent.
3   True: see Section 18-4 of the main text.
4   True – but society may wish to take steps to ensure a just distribution of the monopoly profits.
5   This could be regarded as true or false – it depends upon your point of view. Most economists would tend to be sceptical.
6   True enough, but the extent to which this directly affects merger activity is not clear. A study by Pickering in the *Journal of Industrial Economics*, March 1993, suggests that 'about one-third of all merger proposals referred to the MMC have been abandoned on reference'. There may be several reasons for such abandonments.

7   False: this ignores locational externalities, which may be significant (see Section 18-2 of the main text).
8   False: see Section 18-3 of the main text for a discussion of this important concept.
9   True.
10  False: more than one-half of such expenditure in the UK is related to military defence.
11  Not necessarily true: it is important to approach this question carefully – see Section 18-1 of the main text again.
12  Often false: if structural change must take place, then it may be unwise to try to resist it; better to manage the adjustment. However, unless new industries can be developed to replace old ones, it may sometimes be desirable to ease the transition by temporarily subsidizing lame ducks.

## ECONOMICS IN THE NEWS 1

1   The suggestion in the passage is that PepsiCo perceived that it had reached saturation point in its prime market (soft drinks). So, if it wanted to be able to expand sales revenues, it needed to diversify into new products. Hence the interest in fast foods. We might think that this was a logical move, as there might be expected to be potential links between the two businesses.
2   The passage is brief, but contains a few hints of what might have happened. On the one hand, it seems that PepsiCo found itself facing intense competition in the fast food sector (although it should be noticed that they did enjoy some success here). On the other hand, it seems that PepsiCo also persisted in trying to compete with Coke, which in retrospect may not have been an ideal move. One of the dangers of diversification may be that the management team of a company may become over-stretched. Indeed, Edith Penrose pointed out that the size and ability of the management team may be a vital constraint on the growth of firms, and the diseconomies of scale that may arise form this management constraint is sometimes referred to as the *Penrose effect*. We do not have enough information to say whether this was a factor in this particular case.
3   The PepsiCo experience was echoed in a number of other mergers and demergers that took place. It seems that merger activity (especially conglomerate mergers) happens in waves. There are periods when diversification is all the rage, but then there seem to be periods in which firms break up again.

## ECONOMICS IN THE NEWS 2

1   The final paragraph suggests that 'more R&D means better growth and better profit', which seem to be two good reasons for wanting high R&D. It may be regarded as especially important in the context of increasing international competitiveness.
2   We have argued that government intervention may be justified in the presence of market failure. In the case of R&D, this may take the form of externalities. Firms may not fully perceive (or stand to gain from) the benefits from R&D.
3   There are various policy measures that could be adopted to encourage more expenditure by firms on R&D – tax relief or patent protection, for instance.  These are discussed in the main text in Section 18-1.

## ECONOMICS IN THE NEWS 3

1   The argument expressed at the beginning of the passage is that the AOL–TW merger is likely to lead to increasing concentration in this rapidly-growing sector. Back in Chapter 11, we suggested that the production of information products would be likely to be characterized by substantial economies of scale, and that this was likely to lead to the development of monopoly firms, as the largest firms would always be in a position of cost leadership relative to competitors.  Whether this is good or bad for the consumers will depend upon how the firms operate in practice.  If the market remains contestable, then they may not be able to exploit their monopoly power by restricting output and raising price.  In this case, consumers may benefit from 'bigger'.

2    Some people might have concerns about firms having a monopoly on the provision of some information. The use of the media as a propaganda device, angling news in a particular way was famously and graphically described in George Orwell's novel *1984*. However, this is rather different from the normal concerns about imperfect competition and the abuse of monopoly power.

## Questions for Thought

1    Concentration is not bad for society of itself. A market may be dominated by very few firms, but if those firms are competing vigorously with each other, there is no reason to suppose that society will suffer. However, where firms collude to avoid competition, then society may incur the deadweight loss from the abuse of market power. None the less, legislation in the US has been more preoccupied with the evils of concentration than with collusion. In the UK, a more pragmatic attitude has seen individual cases judged on their own merits.

2    This section of the chapter is headed 'Questions for Thought', so you cannot expect answers too easily. This is not a straightforward example of a cartel. Ask yourself who suffers from the alleged collusion, and who gains.

3    In many towns around in the world, you will find that real estate agents are concentrated in one particular part of town, but you can buy a newspaper almost anywhere.

4    You might at first think that the best location for our mobile ice-cream seller would be at $C$, as far away from the competition as possible. But if you think more carefully about it, you will realize that the best she could do then is to sell to half of the sunbathers – the half who will be nearer to her than to the kiosk. However, if she located at $B$, then she would sell to all the sunbathers between $B$ and $C$, and to half of the rest. However, even better is to locate at $A$, close to the kiosk, and then sweep up the whole market. Similar arguments apply if there are two mobile sellers, although they are not both operating strategically, anticipating each other's actions. They will end up next to each other in the middle of the beach. This result was noted many years ago by an economist called Hotelling.

# Chapter 19    Privatization and Regulation

## Important Concepts and Technical Terms

| | | | | | | | |
|---|---|---|---|---|---|---|---|
| 1 | *(h)* | 4 | *(j)* | 7 | *(f)* | 10 | *(k)* |
| 2 | *(b* | 5 | *(a)* | 8 | *(d)* | 11 | *(g)* |
| 3 | *(l)* | 6 | *(i)* | 9 | *(e)* | 12 | *(c)* |

## Exercises

1    All have been advanced at one time or another: see Section 19-1 of the main text. The validity of these arguments has been questioned, partly because managers of nationalized industries have been seen to face poor incentives for efficiency – hence the great privatization debate.

2    In recent privatization debates, many claims have been made, covering most of those mentioned, with the probable exception of *(e)*. Some of the effects may be of limited significance in practice or of only short-run relevance. For instance, effect *(d)* is important only in the short run, when the proceeds from the sale of an industry can be used to help fund expenditure. Time alone will reveal the importance of these effects. Discussion of rail privatization may be found in an article by Antony Dnes in the *Economic Review,* September 1997.

3   (a)  *LMC = MR* at output *OG*, price *OF*.
    (b)  The area *HJQ*.
    (c)  *EFJI*.
    (d)  *P = LMC* at output *OP*, price *OA*.
    (e)  At this point, long-run average costs *(OB)* exceed average revenue *(OA)*, and a private monopolist would be forced out of business.

4   Thoughts *(a), (c), (e),* and *(g)* might incline you towards privatization, but the remainder represent the opposite point of view. Unless you have strong prior views taking you in one direction or the other, I expect you found it quite difficult to weigh up the arguments and come to a firm decision. As you learn more about economics, you will find that there are many areas like this where there are no clear-cut or definitive answers.

5   From the figures given, public corporations in 1985 accounted for 7.7 per cent of national income, 5.3 per cent of employment, and 21 per cent of net capital stock (excluding dwellings). The clear implication is that these industries are relatively capital-intensive. This should be no great surprise, as it is in such capital-intensive industries that we would expect fixed costs to be important, creating the conditions for a potential natural monopoly. With the privatization programme of the 1980s, these proportions have decreased: the corresponding figures for 1988 were respectively 5.4, 3.5 and 16.5 per cent.

6   Tabulating the net private and social gains from each of the projects, we find the following

| Project | Financial profit (loss) | Net overall gain (loss) |
|---------|------------------------|-------------------------|
| A       | 20                     | (40)                    |
| B       | (30)                   | 70                      |
| C       | 50                     | 40                      |

The net overall gain (loss) column takes account of both private and social costs and benefits.
    (a)  Profits are maximized by choosing project C – but notice that the net overall gain, while positive, is smaller than the private gain accruing to the firm.
    (b)  Revenue is maximized by project A, but this is clearly bad news for the community at large, as this project shows a net overall loss.
    (c)  The project that maximizes economic welfare generally is project B, although this entails a financial loss for the enterprise.

7   (a)  The necessary subsidy would be represented by the area *ABRQ*.
    (b)  The fixed charge is needed to cover the withdrawn subsidy *(ABRQ)*; the per unit charge would be *AB*.
    (c)  The variable charge would need to cover marginal cost: *OA*.
    (d)  Where *AC = AR*, at output *OK*, price *OC*.
    (e)  The area *NLQ*.

8   (a)  Rent will be *OB* and the quantity of housing *OF*.
    (b)  By offering rent vouchers to the needy, the demand for housing will be increased, from *DD* to *DDX*; rents will rise to *OE*, and the quantity to *OG*.
    (c)  In this situation, the supply of housing will increase from SS to *SSX*; in equilibrium, rents fall to *OA* (demand is still at *DD*, of course), and the quantity of housing rises to *OH*.
    (d)  As the figure was drawn, there is little difference in the effect of the quantity of housing, although there is a dramatic difference in rent levels. In practice, the result will depend upon the elasticities of demand and supply in the market.
    (e)  Clearly the major difference between the two schemes is the effect upon rent. This in turn will have an effect on income distribution, with landlords gaining perhaps substantially from the voucher scheme.

9   (a)  A belief in the efficacy of free market forces had been growing for some time when Mrs Thatcher became Prime Minister in 1979. During the period of her administrations, great efforts were made to disengage the government – to withdraw from sectors of the economy where it was believed that market forces could be effective. The PFI was one such initiative, launched in November 1992 after the main wave of privatization was seen to be complete.

*(b)* It had long been argued that the public sector needed to take a lead in the provision of social infrastructure such as roads or hospitals, where it is not obvious as to how it is possible for there to be competition in provision. The PFI handles this by putting such projects out to competitive tendering, undertaking to buy back the services to flow from the projects after completion.

*(c)* A key reason for doing this is to provide improved incentives for efficiency. When the public sector is solely responsible for social infrastructure, it is argued that there is little true accountability. As a result, a certain amount of X-inefficiency creeps in. It was hoped that this would be squeezed out through the operations of the PFI.

*(d)* This is indeed how the scheme is intended to work. Instead of owning a hospital or a road, the public sector purchases the flow of services provided by these assets from the private sector.

*(e)* Early indications are that this may be happening. For example, one of the earliest projects launched under the PFI was The Princess Margaret's Hospital in Swindon. The outline business plan for the project was approved in December 1993, and the planned opening ceremony is due to take place in September 2002. This contrasts with the original hospital built in the area, which took 24 years from conception in 1950 to completion in 1974. Of course, whether it will open to schedule remains to be seen at the time of writing…

*(f)* This is certainly an issue to be taken into account, as we expect the private sector to be concerned with a rather shorter time horizon than the government. We would also expect a private firm to use a very different discount rate, partly reflecting risk-averseness but also acknowledging that the government may take social returns as well as private returns into account.

Further discussion of the PFI may be found in an article by Danny Myers ('The private finance initiative: a progress report') in *Economic Review*, 15(4), April 1998. A glimpse of a PFI was seen in 'Economics in the News' in Chapter 1 of this Workbook.

## True/False

1  False: the deadweight burden would be reduced but not eliminated.
2  False: the initial effects were encouraging to those who believe in free markets, but subsequently the establishment of strategic barriers to entry eroded these benefits (see Box 19-1 in the main text).
3  False: nationalized industries should use a lower discount rate, and undertake some projects that the private sector would consider unprofitable.
4  True: peak-time users pay higher prices to reflect the higher marginal cost of supplying them.
5  True: see Section 19-1 of the main text.
6  False: in practice, individual shareholders have little influence and face a free-rider problem (see Section 19-3 of the main text).
7  Not always true: for instance, private oil companies operating in the North Sea have been faced with petroleum revenue tax, often at very high rates.
8  There is no simple true/false response to this one: in part, it depends upon how the proceeds are disposed.
9  False: most were under-priced, in the sense that the opening free market price was higher than the offer price. However, Enterprise Oil opened at the offer price and Britoil opened below it. (Section 19-4 of the main text.)
10  True.

## ECONOMICS IN THE NEWS 1 and 2

1  The danger is in forcing firms to duplicate expenditure on fixed costs, causing a fundamental misallocation of resources. After all, the reason that many natural monopolies were nationalized in the first place was to enable the exploitation of economies of scale without running the risk of a firm abusing monopoly power in the market. There may be some parts of some natural monopoly where there could be effective competition, but the authorities need to be careful. We might argue that the incentives for managers may not improve greatly if they become accountable to a dispersed and uncoordinated group of shareholders who may not choose to exercise their powers.

2   If the people running state enterprises have political power, they may be able to protect themselves against major changes.
3   Partly this may reflect international agreements being orchestrated by the WTO. There have also been major technological changes in telecommunications which have affected the extent of scale economies in the industry. Competition from the mobile phone companies has revolutionized the telecommunications market in many parts of the world.

## Questions for Thought

1   This issue is discussed at some length in Section 19-3 of the main text.
2   We know this is a big question, covering much of the material of this chapter. However, it will do you no harm to try to marshal your thoughts and to focus on the salient points. This is part of the economist's skill.

## Chapter 20    Introduction to Macroeconomics and National Income Accounting

## Important Concepts and Technical Terms

| | | | |
|---|---|---|---|
| 1  *(n)* | 5  *(m)* | 9  *(c)* | 13  *(h)* |
| 2  *(i)* | 6  *(f)* | 10  *(k)* | 14  *(a)* |
| 3  *(o)* | 7  *(e)* | 11  *(d)* | 15  *(g)* |
| 4  *(p)* | 8  *(b)* | 12  *(j)* | 16  *(l)* |

## Exercises

1   See Table A20-1.

Table A20-1    Inflation

| | United Kingdom | | USA | | Spain | |
|---|---|---|---|---|---|---|
| | *Consumer price index* | *Inflation rate (%)* | *Consumer price index* | *Inflation rate (%)* | *Consumer price index* | *Inflation rate (%)* |
| 1988 | 71.7 | | 77.6 | | 68.2 | |
| 1989 | 77.3 | 7.8 | 81.4 | 4.9 | 72.9 | 6.9 |
| 1990 | 84.6 | 9.4 | 85.7 | 5.3 | 77.7 | 6.6 |
| 1991 | 89.6 | 5.9 | 89.4 | 4.3 | 82.4 | 6.0 |
| 1992 | 92.9 | 3.7 | 92.1 | 3.0 | 87.2 | 5.8 |
| 1993 | 94.4 | 1.6 | 94.8 | 2.9 | 91.2 | 4.6 |
| 1994 | 96.7 | 2.4 | 97.3 | 2.6 | 95.5 | 4.7 |
| 1995 | 100.0 | 3.4 | 100.0 | 2.8 | 100.0 | 4.7 |
| 1996 | 102.4 | 2.4 | 102.9 | 2.9 | 103.6 | 3.6 |
| 1997 | 105.7 | 3.2 | 105.3 | 2.3 | 105.6 | 1.9 |
| 1998 | 109.3 | 3.4 | 107.0 | 1.6 | 107.5 | 1.8 |

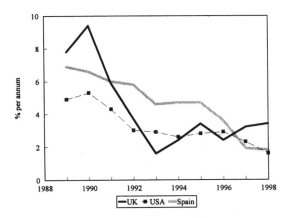

**Figure A20-1**
**Inflation in the UK, USA and Spain**

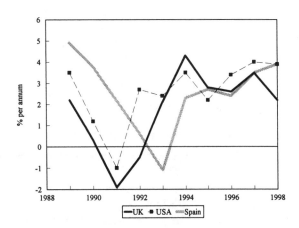

**Figure A20-2**
**Economic growth in the UK, USA and Spain**

*(a)* The annual inflation rate is calculated from the consumer price index using the method described in Section 2-4 of the main text. Thus for the UK, the inflation rate for 1988–89 is calculated as:
$100 \times (77.3 - 71.7) / 71.7 = 7.8\%$.

*(b)* See Figure A20-1.

*(c)* UK 52.4 per cent. USA 37.9 per cent. Spain 57.6 per cent.

*(d)* USA.

*(e)* Inflation fell substantially in all three countries, but the UK had experienced greater acceleration and much higher inflation in 1989 and 1990, so thus started at a higher level in 1990.

*(f)* The growth rates are calculated in the same way as the inflation rates: see Table A20-2.

**Table A20-2   National production and economic growth**

|      | United Kingdom | | USA | | Spain | |
|------|:--------------:|:-----------------:|:---------:|:-----------------:|:---------:|:-----------------:|
|      | GDP index | Growth rate (%) | GDP index | Growth rate (%) | GDP index | Growth rate (%) |
| 1988 | 91.4  |      | 86.7  |      | 86.0  |      |
| 1989 | 93.4  | 2.2  | 89.7  | 3.5  | 90.2  | 4.9  |
| 1990 | 93.7  | 0.3  | 90.8  | 1.2  | 93.6  | 3.8  |
| 1991 | 91.9  | −1.9 | 89.9  | −1.0 | 95.7  | 2.2  |
| 1992 | 91.4  | −0.5 | 92.3  | 2.7  | 96.3  | 0.6  |
| 1993 | 93.3  | 2.1  | 94.5  | 2.4  | 95.2  | −1.1 |
| 1994 | 97.3  | 4.3  | 97.8  | 3.5  | 97.4  | 2.3  |
| 1995 | 100.0 | 2.8  | 100.0 | 2.2  | 100.0 | 2.7  |
| 1996 | 102.6 | 2.6  | 103.4 | 3.4  | 102.4 | 2.4  |
| 1997 | 106.2 | 3.5  | 107.5 | 4.0  | 106.0 | 3.5  |
| 1998 | 108.5 | 2.2  | 111.7 | 3.9  | 110.1 | 3.9  |

*(g)* See Figure A20-2.

*(h)* UK 18.7 per cent; USA 28.8 per cent; Spain 28.0 per cent.

**2** *(a)* Planned consumption plus planned investment is $150 + 50 = 200$.

*(b)* Production less expenditure is $210 - 200 = 10$. This quantity represents an unplanned addition to inventories.

*(c)* Income less consumption is $210 - 150 = 60$.

*(d)* Planned investment plus stock changes is $50 + 10 = 60$.
Thus actual investment = actual savings.

*(e)* Producers have not sold as much output as they expected and witness an increase in stock levels. Two responses are possible: to reduce output or reduce price. As we begin to build our model of an economy in the next chapter, we will initially assume that prices are fixed – so the response to an unplanned increase in stocks will be to reduce output.

**3** It may be helpful to begin by translating these terms into the notation of the main text:

| Item | Notation in main text |
|---|---|
| Final consumption expenditure | C |
| Fixed investment *plus* stock changes | I |
| Government final consumption | G |
| Exports | X |
| Imports | Z |
| Taxes on products *less* subsidies | Te |

The remaining terms should be familiar, although you may not have encountered the item "other indirect taxes". These taxes are on expenditure by firms, and do not register in the expenditure-side calculation.

*(a)* GDP at market prices is $C + I + G + X - Z = 842\ 162$.

*(b)* GNP at market prices is GDPmp + net income from abroad = $853\ 736$.

*(c)* GDP at basic prices is GDPmp $- Te = 745\ 818$.

*(d)* NNP at market prices is GNPmp – capital consumption = $764\ 965$.

*(e)* Net national income at basic prices is NNPmp $- T_e = 668\ 784$.

*(f)* From the income side, GDPbp = profits/rent + employment income + mixed income + $T_e$ + other indirect taxes = $843\ 789$.

*(g)* In an ideal world, the two methods should give the same results. However, in practice the problems of accurate measurement are too great. If you look in the ONS Blue Book you will see that there is a 'statistical discrepancy' item, which is used in the accounts to create consistency between the estimates.

**4** The simplest way to clarify this question is to tabulate the transactions as in Table A20-3, and then calculate the value added entailed in each transaction. This was done in Section 20-4 of the main text.

| (1) Good | (2) Seller | (3) Buyer | (4) Transaction value (£) | (5) Value added(£) |
|---|---|---|---|---|
| Steel | Steel producer | Machine tool maker | 1000 | 1000 |
| Steel | Steel producer | Bicycle manufacturer | 2500 | 2500 |
| Rubber | Rubber producer | Tyre producer | 600 | 600 |
| Machine | Machine tool maker | Bicycle manufacturer | 1800 | 800 |
| Tyres | Tyre producer | Bicycle manufacturer | 1000 | 400 |
| Bicycles | Bicycle manufacturer | Final consumers | 8000 | 4500 |

Check that you understand how column (5) is obtained.   For instance, value added by the bicycle manufacturer is the transaction value (£8000) less the value of goods used up in the production process – namely, tyres (£1000) and steel (£2500) – but not the machine, which is not 'used up' but kept for future use also.

*(a)* The contribution is the sum of the value added in column (5) = £9800.

*(b)* Total final expenditure is composed of two elements – consumers' expenditure on bicycles (£8000) and the bicycle manufacturer's purchase of machine tools (£1800), totalling £9800.

5  *(a)*

| | |
|---|---:|
| Gross mixed income | 43 379 |
| Wages and salaries etc | 463 474 |
| Other households income | 45 602 |
| Net property income | 69 794 |
| Social benefits | 170 191 |
| Other transfers (in) | 32 215 |
| Total resources | 824655 |

*(b)*

| | |
|---|---:|
| Taxes on income | 88 551 |
| Other current income | 14 892 |
| Social contributions | 134 680 |
| Other transfers (out) | 20 597 |
| Total outgoings | 258 720 |
| Disposable income | 565 935 |

*(c)* Savings ratio = 100 x 37378 / 565935 = 6.6%.

6  The key relationship to remember is that the GDP deflator is the ratio of nominal GDP to real GDP expressed as an index; i.e. price index = nominal GDP divided by real GDP ($\times$ 100).

For any year, if we have two of these pieces of information, we can calculate the third. For instance, for 1998 the question furnishes the two GDP measures and we calculate the price index. Once we have our complete series, we can calculate the growth rates. Notice that 1995 is the base year, so nominal GDP equals real GDP, and the price index is 100. Results are summarized in Table A20-4. The information that was provided in the question is emboldened.

**Table A20-4   Real and nominal GDP**

| | (1) GDP at 1995 market prices (£m) | (2) Rate of growth of (1) (% p.a.) | (3) GDP at current market prices (£m) | (4) Rate of growth of (3) (% p.a.) | (5) Implicit GDP deflator | (6) Rate of change of (5) (% p.a.) |
|---|---|---|---|---|---|---|
| 1995 | 712 548 | | 712 548 | | 100.0 | |
| 1996 | 730 767 | 2.6 | 754 601 | 5.9 | 103.3 | 3.3 |
| 1997 | 756 430 | 3.5 | 803 889 | 6.5 | 106.3 | 2.9 |
| 1998 | 773 380 | 2.2 | 843 725 | 5.0 | 109.1 | 2.7 |

7  The key to tackling this question is in the expenditure-side national income accounting identify, which states that:

$Y = C + I + G + NX$

The question provides information about national income (Y), private expenditure (C), investment (I) and government expenditure (G), so we can calculate net exports (NX) as:

$NX = Y - (C + I + G)$.

For year 1,

$NX = 500 - (200 + 250 + 50) = 0$.

Thus in year 1, we infer that exports and imports exactly balanced each other. The balance of trade was thus zero – neither in surplus nor in deficit.

In year 2, the expenditure items (especially investment) rose by more than national income, so the net exports were –150, a balance of trade deficit.

In year 3, government and private expenditures fell while national income continued to rise. The balance of trade moved into surplus (+50).

8  (a)  In order to calculate real GNP, we need to deflate the GNP index by the price index. This process reveals an increase in the real GNP index from 102.9 to 103.8, an increase of 0.8 per cent.

(b)  We can see that the population of the country increased by about 1 per cent from year 1 to year 2: a slightly more rapid rise than in real GNP. Statement (b) is thus false: real GNP per capita fell.

(c)  The fact that real GNP per capita fell does not imply that all people were worse off in year 2. We do not know about the distribution of income in the country.

(d)  The total population increased between year 1 and year 2, but without knowing about the age distribution and about people's decisions about labour force participation, we can say nothing about changes in the working population.

9  The general rule to adopt is that, if an item can be valued and is reported, then, so long as it is notionally part of GNP, it will be included. This includes (a), (b), (d), (f), and (h), although we cannot always guarantee the full reporting of all these items. Item (c) relates to a transfer payment and is not notionally part of GNP. (e) is immeasurable. (g) cannot easily be valued, although GNP will include wages paid to those responsible for providing leisure services. Hedgefruit are neither valued nor reported, unless you choose to visit a pick-your-own fruit farm!

## True/False

1  True: see Section 20-1 of the main text.

2  True: see Section 20-2 of the main text.

3  False: many other countries, especially in Latin America, have experienced much more rapid inflation than the UK – for instance, the average annual rate of inflation in Brazil between 1990 and 1997 was 475.2 per cent! (See *World Development Report* 1998/99.)

4  False: although unemployment did increase substantially at this time, it was by no means as high as tenfold – it just felt that way!

5  True: see Section 20-3 of the main text.

6  False, and silly: whether an economy is 'closed' or 'open' depends upon whether it is open to international trade – not upon the rate of closure of firms (see Section 20-4 of the main text).

7  True.

8  It is true that actual savings will always equal actual investment in such an economy: this results from the way we choose to define these variables. There is no necessity, however, for planned savings and investment to be always equal.

9  False: indirect taxes must be *deducted* from GDPmp to give GDPbp.

10  True.

11  False: if measured at current prices, GNP incorporates price changes – this is nominal GNP, not real GNP.

12  False: real GNP may not be an ideal measure of welfare, but it is the best measure we have which is available on a regular basis.

## ECONOMICS IN THE NEWS

1  The passage provides few clues as to the reasons for the increase in the size of the so-called 'black economy'. There is some reference to VAT avoidance, as the 1996 Budget had included measures to combat this. But this does not necessarily help in this context, as the issue is about why the shadow economy may have become more important. An increase in VAT rates might be expected to lead to greater avoidance, but this cannot be a full explanation here. The other hint in the passage is the reference towards the end to the 1987 stock market crash. This seems to hint that the crash may have induced an increase in the shadow economy.

2 Whether we worry about this may partly depend upon who we are! If we are the government or the Treasury, concerned about raising tax revenues, then of course we might be concerned if more people are avoiding paying tax. As economists, the concern may be different. If we are trying to monitor the growth rate of an economy, or perhaps to compare living standards across countries, then changes in the size of the shadow economy are likely to distort our measurements. An increase in the shadow economy at the expense of formal economic activity will cause economic growth to be understated by the official figures.

## Questions for Thought

1 Some discussion of more comprehensive measures is included in Section 20-5 of the main text. In particular, notice the multidimensional approach introduced by Tony Blair in 1999. This is discussed in *Economic Review Data Supplement*, September 1999.
2 The existence of unrecorded economic activity will bias downwards the measurements of GNP in whatever country. In making international comparisons, we may also have to face problems with income distribution and currency conversions.
3 You might like to illustrate your discussion by using your answers to exercise 6.

## Chapter 21    The Determination of National Income

## Important Concepts and Technical Terms

| 1 | (b) | 4 | (g) | 7 | (l) | 10 | (i) |
|---|-----|---|-----|---|-----|----|-----|
| 2 | (a) | 5 | (h) | 8 | (j) | 11 | (d) |
| 3 | (k) | 6 | (c) | 9 | (e) | 12 | (f) |

## Exercises

1 *(a)* See Table A21-1.

**Table A21-1    Consumption, income, and saving**

| Year | Real consumers' expenditure (£ bn) | Real personal disposable income (£ bn) | Real savings (£ bn) | Savings ratio (%) |
|------|-----|-----|-----|-----|
| 1987 | 372.601 | 385.240 | 12.639 | 3.3 |
| 1988 | 400.427 | 405.462 | 5.035 | 1.2 |
| 1989 | 413.498 | 423.145 | 9.647 | 2.3 |
| 1990 | 415.788 | 438.935 | 23.147 | 5.3 |
| 1991 | 408.309 | 445.552 | 37.243 | 8.4 |
| 1992 | 410.026 | 461.964 | 51.938 | 11.2 |
| 1993 | 420.081 | 475.850 | 55.769 | 11.7 |
| 1994 | 431.462 | 481.924 | 50.462 | 10.5 |
| 1995 | 438.453 | 494.574 | 56.121 | 11.3 |
| 1996 | 454.986 | 505.392 | 50.706 | 10.0 |
| 1997 | 472.701 | 524.501 | 51.800 | 9.9 |
| 1998 | 488.505 | 524.660 | 36.155 | 6.9 |

*(b)* See Figure A21-1.

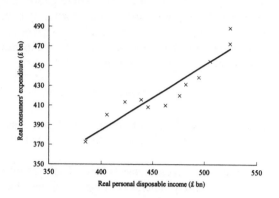

**Figure A21-1  Consumption and income**

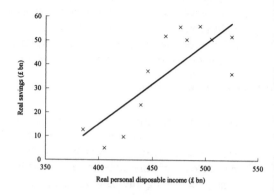

**Figure A21-2  Savings and income**

*(c)* We drew our line using a statistical procedure called 'regression': its slope is 0.662.

*(d)* In focusing upon this simple relationship between consumption and income, we have made a number of assumptions, especially concerning autonomous consumption. We have also assumed that the relationship can be viewed as a straight line. Only if all these assumptions are valid can we regard our estimate of the marginal propensity as 'reasonable'. This must be interpreted in the light of economics (what we are trying to measure) as well as of statistics (how we try to measure it).

*(e)* See Figure A21-2.

*(f)* Given $Y = C + S$, there must be a close correspondence between the two lines. If we write $C = a + bY$, then it is easily seen that $S = -a + (1 - b) Y$. It should thus be no surprise that the slope of the savings line is $1 - 0.662 = 0.338$.

*(g)* $1/0.338 = 2.959$.

Again, we should interpret this figure with caution.

2  *(a)* and *(b)*: answers are contained in Table A21-2.

**Table A21-2  Income and consumption in Hypothetica (all in Hypothetical $ billion)**

| Income (output) | Planned consumption | Planned investment | Savings | Aggregate demand | Unplanned inventory change | Actual investment |
|---|---|---|---|---|---|---|
| 50 | 35 | 60 | 15 | 95 | −45 | 15 |
| 100 | 70 | 60 | 30 | 130 | −30 | 30 |
| 150 | 105 | 60 | 45 | 165 | −15 | 45 |
| 200 | 140 | 60 | 60 | 200 | 0 | 60 |
| 250 | 175 | 60 | 75 | 235 | 15 | 75 |
| 300 | 210 | 60 | 90 | 270 | 30 | 90 |
| 350 | 245 | 60 | 105 | 305 | 45 | 105 |
| 400 | 280 | 60 | 120 | 340 | 60 | 120 |

*(c)* With income at 100, aggregate demand is 130, so that stocks will be rapidly run down. Producers are likely to react by producing more output in the next period.

*(d)* With income at 350, aggregate demand is only 305 and producers will find that they cannot sell their output, so stocks begin to build up. They are thus likely to reduce the output in the next period.

*(e)* Only at income of 200 do we find that aggregate demand equals aggregate supply – or, equivalently, that planned investment equals planned savings. This then is the equilibrium level of income.

(f) As income increases by 50, consumption increases by 35, so the marginal propensity to consume is 35/50 = 0.7.

(g) An increase of investment of $15 billion to $75 billion would carry equilibrium income to 250 – an increase of 15/0.3 = 50.

3 (a) See Figure A21-3.

(b) Figure A21-3 confirms that equilibrium occurs at income of 200 – where the aggregate demand schedule meets the 45° line.

(c) The increase in investment shifts the aggregate demand schedule, giving a new equilibrium at income of 250.

4 (a) See Figure A21-4.

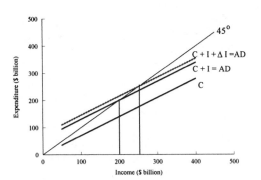

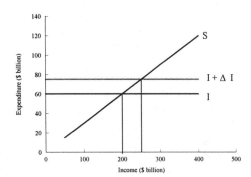

**Figure A21-3 The income-expenditure diagram**   **Figure A21-4   Savings and investment**

(b) Equilibrium is again seen to be at income of 200.

(c) Equilibrium at the new level of investment is at income of 250.

(d) The increase in investment initially affects income, inducing higher savings; the process continues until planned savings equal planned investment.

5 (a) Aggregate demand is *OB*: there is excess demand at this point.

(b) Inventories will be run down to the extent of the excess demand, measured by *AB*.

(c) We expect firms to increase output in the next period.

(d) Income *OH* = planned expenditure *OD*.

(e) Aggregate planned expenditure is *OE*: there is excess supply at this point.

(f) Inventories will increase to the extent of the excess supply – namely, *EF*. Firms are likely to respond by reducing output.

6 (a) Income *OF*, savings *OIB*.

(b) *OIC*.

(c) *OG*.

(d) *LM/NM*.

(e) *OIA*.

(f) *OE*.

7 (a) *c*.

(b) Given $S = Y - C$
$S = Y - A - cY$,
or $S = -A + (1 - c) Y$

(c) With $S = -400 + 0.25\ Y$
if $S = 0$, $Y = 1600$.

(d) We now have $C = 400 + 0.75\ Y$, and equilibrium occurs when aggregate supply equals aggregate demand: i.e. when $Y = C + I$
that is, when $Y = 400 + 0.25\ Y + 500$.

Solving for $Y$, we find that equilibrium is at $Y = 3600$.

**8** (a) *XY/UX* is the slope of the consumption schedule: the marginal propensity to consume.

   (b) At equilibrium *W*, *WY/OW* represents the ratio of consumption to income: the average propensity to consume.

**9** (a) *OG*.

   (b) *AJ*.

   (c) *OF*.

   (d) *AL*.

   (e) *OH*.

**Table A21-3   Hypothetica revisited**

| Income (output) | Planned consumption (MPC = 0.7) | Aggregate demand 1 | Aggregate demand 2 | Planned consumption (MPC = 0.8) | Aggregate demand 3 | Aggregate demand 4 |
|---|---|---|---|---|---|---|
| 250 | 175 | 265 | 280 | 200 | 290 | 300 |
| 300 | 210 | 300 | 315 | 240 | 330 | 340 |
| 350 | 245 | 335 | 350 | 280 | 370 | 380 |
| 400 | 280 | 370 | 385 | 320 | 410 | 420 |
| 450 | 315 | 405 | 420 | 360 | 450 | 460 |
| 500 | 350 | 440 | 455 | 400 | 490 | 500 |
| 550 | 385 | 475 | 490 | 440 | 530 | 540 |
| 600 | 420 | 510 | 525 | 480 | 570 | 580 |

**10** (a) The column in Table A21-3 headed 'Aggregate demand 1' shows that equilibrium income is = 300 (because consumption is then 0.7 × 300 = 210. So C + I is 210 + 90 = 300). Given the multiplier relationship, we could also calculate equilibrium as $Y = 1 / (1 - MPC) = 90 / 0.3 = 300$.

   (b) Using 'Aggregate demand 2' or $Y = 105 / 0.3$, we see that equilibrium output is now 350.

   (c) The multiplier can be calculated as the ratio of the change in equilibrium income to the initiating change in investment (i.e. 50 / 15 = 3.33', or we simply calculate $1 / (1 - MPC) = 1 / 0.3 = 3.33'$.

   (d) With the higher propensity to consume, we get column 'Aggregate demand 3' and an equilibrium of 450: 1 / (1-MPC) = 90 / 0.2} = 450.

   (e) Using 'Aggregate demand 4', equilibrium income is now 500.

   (f) 50 / 10 = 5.

## True/False

**1** True: see introduction to Chapter 21 in the main text.

**2** True.

**3** False: we make this simplifying assumption very often – but it is no more than assumption and may not always be accurate (see Section 21-2 of the main text).

**4** True: we have set up the model such that income is either spent or saved.

**5** False: we have assumed investment to be autonomous to keep the model simple for the time being; later we will treat it more realistically and consider its determinants.

**6** True: see Box 21-1 of the main text.

**7** True: see Section 21-4 of the main text.

**8** True again.

**9** False: this statement is true only in equilibrium. We note that savings and investment plans are formulated independently by different agents and need not always be equal (see Section 21-5 of the main text).

**10** False: the slope depends upon the marginal propensity to consume; the position depends partly on the level of autonomous consumption (see Section 21-6 of the main text).

**11**  True: see Section 21-7 of the main text.
**12**  False: this is an expression of the paradox of thrift (see Section 21-8 of the main text).

## ECONOMICS IN THE NEWS

**1**  In this chapter, we have tended to treat savings rather passively, as 'not-consumption'. In other words, households take decisions about how much of their disposable income to devote to consumption – and the rest is savings. Clearly this is a simplification of reality. The passage hints that the expectations of households about the future are likely to be important, for example. We also saw back in Chapter 14 that decisions between current and future consumption are likely to depend upon the rate of interest. So, we will need to come back to this issue a bit later on.

**2**  The idea here is that if a prime reason for savings is to accumulate assets, perhaps with retirement in mind, then capital gains increase the value of assets held by households, and may then reduce the need for present savings.

**3**  The link between savings and investment may be crucial here. If saving provides funds for investment, then savings will have an influence on the long-run capacity of the economy to produce. However, as usual the story is not so simple, and we need to take other factors into account before we can be confident about this explanation.

### Questions for Thought

**1**  Remember the distinction between planned and actual (see Section 21-5 of the main text).
**2**  We will reconsider consumption theory in Chapter 25.
**3**  This question looks ahead to Chapter 22.

# Chapter 22   Aggregate Demand, Fiscal Policy, and Foreign Trade

## Important Concepts and Technical Terms

| | | | | | | | |
|---|---|---|---|---|---|---|---|
| **1** | *(k)* | **4** | *(l)* | **7** | *(f)* | **10** | *(i)* |
| **2** | *(a)* | **5** | *(h)* | **8** | *(c)* | **11** | *(j)* |
| **3** | *(d)* | **6** | *(g)* | **9** | *(b)* | **12** | *(e)* |

## Exercises

**1**  *(a), (b).* See Table A22-1.

**Table A22-1   Government comes to Hypothetica**

| Income/ output | Disposable income | Planned consumption | Planned investment | Government spending | Savings | Net taxes | Aggregate demand |
|---|---|---|---|---|---|---|---|
| 50 | 40 | 28 | 60 | 50 | 12 | 10 | 138 |
| 100 | 80 | 56 | 60 | 50 | 24 | 20 | 166 |
| 150 | 120 | 84 | 60 | 50 | 36 | 30 | 194 |
| 200 | 160 | 112 | 60 | 50 | 48 | 40 | 222 |
| 250 | 200 | 140 | 60 | 50 | 60 | 50 | 250 |
| 300 | 240 | 168 | 60 | 50 | 72 | 60 | 278 |
| 350 | 280 | 196 | 60 | 50 | 84 | 70 | 306 |
| 400 | 320 | 224 | 60 | 50 | 96 | 80 | 334 |

*(c)* At income $350bn, aggregate demand amounts only to $306bn; producers will see stocks building up and reduce output in the next period.

*(d)* Equilibrium is where aggregate demand equals aggregate supply, at income $250bn. Equivalently, equilibrium occurs where I + G = S + NT – again, of course, at income $250bn.

*(e)* Government spending is $50bn; net taxes are 0.2 × $250bn = $50bn. The budget is in balance.

*(f)* With government spending at $72bn, equilibrium income increases to $300bn.

*(g)* Government spending is now $72bn and net taxes are 0.2 × $300bn = $60bn: the government is running a deficit of $12bn.

*(h)* The multiplier is 50 / 22 = 2.27. Equivalently, it is 1 / {1 – c (1 – t) } = 1 / (1 – 0.56) = 2.27.

2 *(a)* Notice in Figure A22-1 that the aggregate demand schedule is now less steep than previously (namely, Figure A21-3) – this is the result of the taxation.

*(b)* The diagram confirms that equilibrium occurs at income $250bn – where the aggregate demand schedule cuts the 45° line.

*(c)* The increase in government spending moves the aggregate demand schedule to *AD'*, giving a new equilibrium income of $300bn.

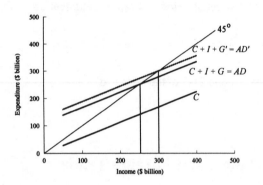

**Figure A22-1  The income-expenditure diagram with government**

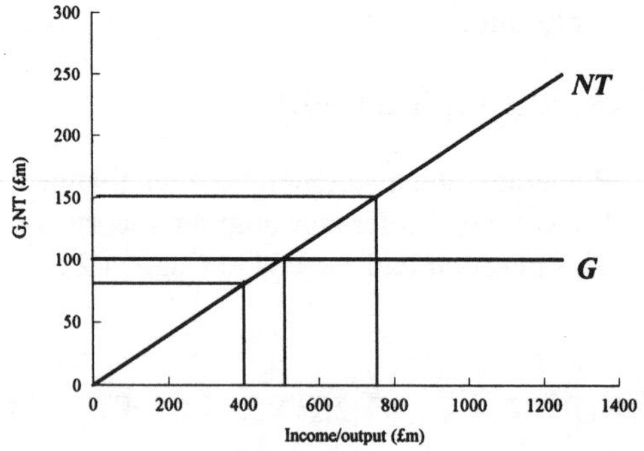

**Figure A22-2  The government budget**

3 *(a)* See Table A22-2.

**Table A22-2  The multiplier with and without government**

| Income/ output | Consumption 1 | Investment | Aggregate demand 1 | Disposable income | Consumption 2 | Government spending | Aggregate demand 2 |
|---|---|---|---|---|---|---|---|
| 2000 | 1600 | 450 | 2050 | 1800 | 1440 | 250 | 2140 |
| 2250 | 1800 | 450 | 2250 | 2025 | 1620 | 250 | 2320 |
| 2500 | 2000 | 450 | 2450 | 2250 | 1800 | 250 | 2500 |
| 2750 | 2200 | 450 | 2650 | 2475 | 1980 | 250 | 2680 |
| 3000 | 2400 | 450 | 2850 | 2700 | 2160 | 250 | 2860 |

*(b)* 2250.

*(c)* 2500.

*(d)* 250 / 50 = 5.

*(e)* See Table A22-2.

*(f)* 2500.

*(g)* Zero.

*(h)* With the introduction of government, equilibrium income has increased from 2250 to 2500, even though the government is spending no more than is collected through taxation (see Section 22-2 of the main text).

*(i)* 2750.

*(j)* 250 / 70=3.57.

**4** *(a)* See Figure A22-2 (opposite).

*(b)* £500m.

*(c)* Up to £500m.

*(d)* At income above £500m.

*(e)* Net taxes at this point would be £80m, so with government expenditure at £100m, the government budget deficit is £20m.

*(f)* A surplus of £50m.

**5** *(a)* £100bn × 0.08 = £8bn.

*(b)* We can approximate the real interest rate as the difference between the nominal rate and the rate of inflation (see Section 14-2 of the main text). In this context, the real interest rate is 8 − 6 = 2 per cent.

*(c)* £100bn × 0.02 = £2bn.

*(d)* It's not really cheating: although the government must pay out the £8bn in nominal interest payments, tax revenues will increase with inflation, clawing back part of this amount. If national income is also increasing in real terms, this will add further to tax revenues. It is valid to take these effects into account.

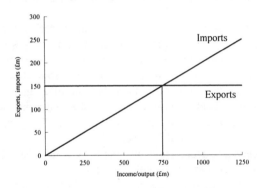

**Figure A22-3   Imports and exports**

**6** *(a)* See Figure A22-3.

*(b)* At this income level, imports are £200m, exports are £150m – so there is a trade deficit of £50m.

*(c)* Imports £100m, exports £150m; trade surplus is £50m.

*(d)* At income £750m.

*(e)* In part *(b)*, we saw that this level of income entails a trade deficit of £50m. Such a deficit cannot be sustained in the long run, so fiscal policy to take the economy to full employment cannot be successful in the long run. Some commentators have regarded this constraint as the reason for Britain's slow rate of economic growth during the early post-war period.

**7** *(a)* $Y = \dfrac{I + G}{\{1 - c(1 - t)\}} = \dfrac{700}{0.28} = 2500.$

*(b)* $C = 0.8 \times 2500 \times 0.9 = 1800;$
tax revenue $= 0.1 \times 2500 = 250;$
government budget surplus $= t\,Y - G = 0.$

*(c)* Disposable income was $2500 \times 0.9 = 2250$, is now $2500 \times 0.75 = 1830$, and has been reduced by 420.

*(d)* Consumption falls by $0.8 \times 420 = 336$, but aggregate demand increases by $500 - 336 = 164.$

*(e)* $Y = 1200 / 0.4 = 3000.$

*(f)* Government budget surplus $= tY - G = 750 - 750 = 0.$

*(g)*  Multiplier = (change in *Y*) / (change in *G*) = 500 / 500. In this case the multiplier is unity.

**8**  *(a)*  *AB* is the aggregate demand schedule without foreign trade. Adding autonomous exports together with imports proportional to income moves the schedule to *CD*.

  *(b)*  *OG*.

  *(c)*  *OF*.

  *(d)*  *OE:* this corresponds to the point at which exports = imports. At this point, aggregate demand is the same on both *AB* and *CD*, as net exports are equal to zero.

  *(e)*  The multiplier is reduced by foreign trade through the effect of the marginal propensity to import (see Section 22-7 of the main text).

**9**  *(a)*  The national debt is the net accumulation of UK government deficits.

  *(b)*  Figure 22-2 is dominated by the substantial reduction in national debt (relative to GDP) between 1960 and 1973, suggesting that this was a period in which the PSNCR was under relative control and/or interest rates were comparatively low, enabling the stock of outstanding debt to be run down. The debt:GDP ratio then stabilized, falling again in the late 1980s when the government was running a budget surplus.

  *(c)*  It is sometimes argued that PSNCR must be kept low in order to keep the national debt under control However, it is clear that the debt:GDP ratio was at a relatively low level in the early 1990s, not only relative to the UK situation in the last 30 years, but also relative to other industrial economies (see Table 22-4 in the main text). An additional reason for monitoring the national debt carefully in the 1990s is that the debt:GDP ratio is a key element in the Maastricht criteria for entry into European monetary union.

**10**  *(a)*  It takes time to collect information about the economy and to realize that policy action is required.

  *(b)*  Having decided to take action, further time is needed to put changes in spending into practice: capital expenditure is inflexible, individual government departments will resist cuts in their own budgets.

  *(c)*  The multiplier is not an instantaneous process, but takes some time to work through the system – remember, the policy relies upon influencing the behaviour of agents such as households.

  *(d)*  There is likely to be uncertainty about how strong, reliable, and rapid the effects of the policy will be.

  *(e)*  By the time the policy has taken effect, the other elements of aggregate demand may be at different levels, affecting the equilibrium level of income.

  *(f)*  Our model is still rudimentary: there are many routes by which fiscal policy may have indirect effects upon other components of demand – especially investment.

  *(g)*  There may be other policy objectives, such as the control of monetary growth or inflation, which could be endangered by the effects of fiscal policy.

  *(h)*  Before we are induced to take action to combat unemployment, we need to be sure that there really is a problem – that the economy is not already at full employment.

These issues are discussed in Box 22-2 of the main text.

## True/False

1  False: more like one-fifth (see the introduction to Chapter 22 in the main text).

2  False: the reverse is true (see Section 22-2 of the main text).

3  True: although the proximity to full employment may be a relevant consideration.

4  True.

5  True.

6  False: it may be misleading (see Section 22-4 of the main text).

7  True.

8  True.

9  True: see Section 22-5 of the main text.

10  False: the ratio rose for many countries including the UK: see Table 22-4 in the main text.

11  False: exports are about 25 per cent of GDP, but net exports (the difference between exports and imports) were much smaller (see Section 22-7 of the main text).

12  False: there is the possibility of retaliation from competitors to consider.

## ECONOMICS IN THE NEWS

1  If the government runs a surplus, the public net cash requirement (or public sector net borrowing) will be negative, which implies that the stock of outstanding debt will fall. If you look back at Figure 22-2 you will be able to identify periods in which this happened.
2  If the Chancellor consistently adopts a pessimistic stance, and always expects the worse, there is the danger that the policy stance will be too cautious, which could mean a lower rate of economic growth, or a higher rate of unemployment, than could have been achieved.

## Questions for Thought

1  The introduction of government and foreign trade has the effect of reducing the multiplier. By comparing two alternative equilibrium positions, we neglect the process by which the new equilibrium is attained. This process may be spread over many time periods (see Section 21-6 of the main text). For hints on the inadequacy of the model so far, see the hints on question 3.
2  See Section 22-5 in the main text.
3  At this stage, the model is clearly much abstracted from reality. In particular, we have not considered the financial side of the economy; nor have we thought about what happens if prices are free to vary, or how the interest rate is determined. Neither have we explored how investment expenditure is decided. In addition, even a cursory look at the 'real' world suggests that the economy changes through time. All these issues are tackled in the following chapters.

# Chapter 23  Money and Modern Banking

## Important Concepts and Technical Terms

| | | | | | | | | | |
|---|---|---|---|---|---|---|---|---|---|
| 1 | (c) | 4 | (h) | 7 | (k) | 10 | (e) | 13 | (i) |
| 2 | (a) | 5 | (m) | 8 | (b) | 11 | (f) | 14 | (j) |
| 3 | (l) | 6 | (n) | 9 | (d) | 12 | (g) | | |

## Exercises

1  (a)  This exercise is intended to illustrate the inefficiency of the barter economy. It is possible in this case to arrange a sequence of transactions. For instance, Alice swaps with Henry; Daniel exchanges with Evelyn and then with Carol; Barry swaps with Gloria; Carol exchanges with Felix and then with Barry. The success of the sequence depends upon the ability of these people to agree fair quantities for exchanges as well as being able to sort out with whom to exchange – notice that poor Carol in our sequence holds in turn doughnuts, figs, and blackcurrant jam before she finally gets coconuts in the last round!
   (b)  Even in this simple world of only eight people with simple desires, the gains from there being a medium of exchange should be apparent – and notice that, by virtue of prices, the 'quantity' problem is also solved.
2  (a)  Gold is an example of commodity money – it is a substance with industrial uses which has at times been acceptable as a medium of exchange.
   (b)  A £1 coin is legal tender and token money – the value of the metal and cost of production is less than £1.
   (c)  Cigarettes have been used as a commodity money – for example, in prisoner-of-war camps during the Second World War (see Section 23-1 of the main text), but normally would be considered not-money.
   (d)  A cheque is an example of IOU money – and also token money.

(e) Petrol is normally not-money – but *The Times* on 11 December 1981 reported that parking fines in some towns in Argentina could be paid only in petrol, as inflation was eroding the value of money at such a rapid rate.

(f) The camera in part-exchange is not-money. It does not meet the requirement of being 'generally acceptable' and has value only in that particular transaction.

(g) A building society deposit is near money: it is readily converted into cash but cannot be used directly in payment.

(h) In general, these are considered not-money – but see the story of the singer Mademoiselle Zelie in Box 23-1 of the main text.

3   (a) Joe Public is now holding £20m instead of the desired £10m and will presumably deposit the extra £10m with the commercial bank.

(b) The bank is now holding £20m cash with £90m loans – and the cash ratio has increased to 20 / 110 = 18.2 per cent.

(c) The commercial bank will seek to make further loans to restore the desired 10 per cent cash ratio.

(d) Joe Public has now borrowed an extra £9m, so cash holdings have increased to £19m.

(e) The extra £9m eventually finds its way back into the bank.

(f) And the bank's cash ratio is back up to 20 / 119 = 16.8 per cent, so the bank again will try to make further loans.

(g) Equilibrium is restored in the condition shown in Table A23-1.

(h) Each time the bank makes further loans to Joe Public, money stock increases by the amount of the loans. The original increase of £10m leads to a £100m increase of money stock by the time the system settles down.

**Table A23-1   Commercial bank balance sheet (£m)**

| Commercial bank balance sheet (£m) | | | | | | |
|---|---|---|---|---|---|---|
| Liabilities | | Assets | | Cash ratio | Public cash holdings | Money stock |
| Deposits | 200 | Cash | 20 | | | |
| | | Loans | 180 | | | |
| | 200 | | 200 | 10% | 10 | 210 |

4   (a) is not a necessary characteristic. Once goldsmiths began to make loans to their customers, the 100 per cent backing of 'money' by gold deposits was weakened. When Britain left the Gold Standard, even legal tender ceased to be wholly backed by gold reserves. Characteristic (b) is also unnecessary: cheques are an accepted form of payment, but are not legal tender. Characteristics (c) and (d), however, are crucial. The 'medium of exchange' function is central to what we mean by money. Unless an asset has value in future transactions, it will not be acceptable as a medium of exchange.

5   (a) The money multiplier is $(cp + 1) / (cp + cb)$

where $cp$ = the proportion of deposits held by the public as cash.

$cb$ = the proportion of deposits held by the banks as cash.

This is set out in Box 23-4 in the main text.

Here, we have $( 0.25 + 1) / ( 0.25 + 0.05 )\} = \{1.25 / 0.3\} = 4.17$.

(b) M1= $\{(cp + 1) / (cp + cb)\} \times$ H= $4.17 \times 12 = 50.04$

(c) $1.25 / 0.29 = 4.31$.

(d) $4.31 \times 12 = 51.72$.

(e) $1.30 / 0.35 = 3.71$.

(f) $3.71 \times 12 = 44.52$.

*(g)* It is clear that both *cp* and *cb* influence the size of the money stock. The question is whether either of these ratios can be influenced by policy action. The alternative is to operate on the stock of high-powered money itself. The question of money stock policy is raised in Chapter 24.

**6** *(a)* £7000.

*(b)* £9000.

*(c)* In Chapter 24, we will see that the cash ratio is one possible tool that the monetary authorities could use to influence banks' behaviour, although it is not used in the UK of the early 1990s. In periods when regulations have been in force, banks have been observed to hold 'excess reserves'. This may be to avoid being forced to borrow at a penal rate if the cash ratio comes under pressure, or may perhaps be because the opportunity cost of holding excess reserves is low – for instance, where interest-bearing assets may be held as part of required liquid asset reserves.

**7** *(a).*

**8** The wide monetary base (M0) is defined as being notes and coin in circulation outside the Bank of England (29192) plus bankers' operational deposits with the Banking Department of the Bank of England (186);
M0 = 29 192 + 186 = £ 29 378m.
Since 1992, M2 has been defined as retail deposits and cash in M4: that is, cash in circulation (23 521) plus banks' retail deposits (409 345), plus building society retail shares and deposits (109 052);
M2 = 23 521 + 409 345 + 109 052 = £ 541 918m.
M4 is M2 + wholesale deposits: M4 =541 918 + 252 189= £794 107m.

**9** *(a)* Cash is the ultimately most liquid asset, but offers no return.

*(b)* Equities offer a return in the form of dividends but are not very liquid and highly risky – if the firm goes bankrupt, equities of that firm become worthless.

*(c)* Bonds are long-term financial assets offering a return (the coupon value) and the possibility of capital gains (or losses) if bond prices change. They are potentially liquid, but are affected by the uncertainty of future bond prices. Bonds are to be redeemed at a specific future date.

*(d)* Bills are short-term financial assets with less than one year to redemption. They are highly liquid and offer a reasonable return.

*(e)* See equities *(b)*.

*(f)* Perpetuities are bonds which are never repurchased by the original issuer. They are not very liquid.

For further discussion of these financial assets, see Box 23-3 of the main text.

## True/False

**1** True: see the introduction to Chapter 23 in the main text.

**2** True: see Section 23-1 of the main text.

**3** False: only notes and coins are legal tender – bank deposits are customary or IOU money. Shopkeepers are not legally obliged to accept a cheque.

**4** True: see Section 23-2 of the main text.

**5** True: the goldsmiths could create money only by holding reserves of less than 100 per cent.

**6** False: insurance companies, pension funds, and building societies are other examples of institutions which take in money in order to relend it (see Section 23-3 of the main text).

**7** True.

**8** False: in general, a higher return must be offered to compensate for loss of liquidity.

**9** True: see Section 23-4 of the main text.

**10** False: the monetary base also includes cash held by the banks (see Section 23-5 of the main text).

**11** False: examination of the money multiplier relationship suggests that the reverse is true.

**12** 'Trueish': it depends partly on why you want your money definition. If it is narrow money that you are trying to measure, you might not want to include building society deposits which are no more liquid than time deposits. Notice that building society deposits are included in the M2 and M4 definitions of money (see Section 23-6 of the main text).

## ECONOMICS IN THE NEWS

**1, 3** The key characteristics of money are wrapped up in its three functions – as medium of exchange, unit of account and store of value. As described in the passage, beenz may qualify – but the key is in its acceptability. This is where we might mention network externalities, in the sense that the more people and firms prepared to join the system, the more valuable it becomes.

**2** As much as anything, the effect may be seen in the velocity of circulation, as the ease of undertaking transactions is increased.

## Questions for Thought

**1** So far we have talked mainly about the supply of money. This question is asking you to think about the demand for money. This is an important issue which will be considered in the next chapter.

**2** How does the existence of credit cards affect the public's need to use cash? Suppose a significant number of motorists always buy petrol by credit card: what effect does this have on their need to hold cash? How does this affect the money multiplier – and hence money supply? There is some brief discussion of this topic in Section 23-5 of the main text.

# Chapter 24   Central Banking and the Monetary System

## Important Concepts and Technical Terms

| | | | | | | | | | |
|---|---|---|---|---|---|---|---|---|---|
| 1 | *(b)* | 4 | *(i)* | 7 | *(d)* | 10 | *(l)* | 13 | *(n)* |
| 2 | *(g)* | 5 | *(f)* | 8 | *(k)* | 11 | *(c)* | 14 | *(m)* |
| 3 | *(j)* | 6 | *(h)* | 9 | *(e)* | 12 | *(a)* | | |

## Exercises

**1**   See Table A24-1.

**Table A24-1   Balance sheets of the Bank of England, October 1999**

| Department | Assets | £ billion | Liabilities | £ billion |
|---|---|---|---|---|
| Issue | Government securities | 13.4 | Notes in circulation | 24.8 |
| | Other securities | 11.4 | | |
| | Issue Department assets | 24.8 | Issue Department liabilities | 24.8 |
| Banking | Government securities | 1.3 | Public deposits | 0.2 |
| | Advances | 26.1 | Bankers' deposits | 1.3 |
| | Other assets | 2.7 | Reserves and other accounts | 28.6 |
| | Banking Department assets | | Banking Department liabilities | |
| | | 30.1 | | 30.1 |

**2**   *(a)*   Recall that

$$M = \{ (cp + 1) / (cp + cb) \} \times H = 3.11 \times 12 = \text{£37.32m.}$$

    *(b)*   This has the effect of reducing the money multiplier from 3.11 to 2.8, so money supply falls to £33.6m.

    *(c)*   This has the same effect as *(b)* – money supply falls to £33.6m.

   (d)  This also has the same effect as *(b)* – money supply falls to £33.6m.

   (e)  Reducing $H$ by £1m reduces $M$ by the size of the money multiplier – i.e. by £3.11m, to £34.21m.

**3**  (a)  An increase in real income leads to an increase in the demand for real money balances through both transactions and precautionary motives.

   (b)  If this is interpreted as a decrease in uncertainty, then money demand will fall through the operation of the precautionary motive.

   (c)  Reduces real money demand, mainly through the asset motive.

   (d)  This is the reverse of *(c)*: nominal interest rates represent the opportunity cost of holding money.

   (e)  This will affect nominal money demand, but the demand for real money balances will be unaffected.

   (f)  If we consider broad money, this differential again represents the opportunity cost of holding money – so we expect a fall in real money demand.

   (g)  Increases real money demand through the precautionary motive.

   (h)  The effect depends upon how people react: if they do not change their spending patterns, then they may increase real money demand. However, they may choose to switch funds between money and bonds to earn a return on cash otherwise idle for part of the period, or they may choose to alter spending patterns by visiting the freezer food centre once a month.

   (i)  This item affects the supply of money: there may be an induced movement along the demand curve as interest rates change, but not a movement of the demand function. (This distinction between movements of and along a curve was first seen back in Chapter 3.)

**4**  (a)  $137.5 \times 100 / 139.7 = 98.4$.

   (b)  We see that real income fell during this period (but not by very much): this would tend to reduce the demand for real money balances (especially M1). However, nominal interest rates also fell, lowering the opportunity cost of holding money: this effect will tend to increase the demand for real money balances (especially £M3). Price changes should not affect real money demand, but no doubt would contribute to the substantial increases in demand for nominal money holdings.

   (c)  For real M1: $151.5 \times 100 / 139.7 = 108.4$.

       For real £M3: $178.0 \times 100 / 139.7 = 127.4$.

       These results are consistent with our observations, especially reflecting the changes in nominal interest rates – notice that, as predicted, holdings of real £M3 increased by more than those of real M1.

   (d)  The simple answer is that the authorities do not have precise control over prices: the available monetary instruments all affect nominal money supply – but it is real money supply that is relevant for influencing people's behaviour. The real problems are even more complex, of course, and the problems of trying to control a variable that cannot even be properly measured are immense. Developments in financial markets have added extra complications. Most obvious is the way that building societies have begun to offer baking services and also to become banks, making £M3 meaningless as a measure (as it excludes building society deposits. hence the replacement of £M3 by M4 as the measure of broad money stock in the UK.

**5**  (a)  With money demand at $LL_0$ and money supply $MS_0$, equilibrium is achieved with real money balances $OF$ and interest rate $OA$.

   (b)  The position of the $LL$ schedule depends primarily upon real income, an increase in which could explain a move from $LL_0$ to $LL_1$.

   (c)  With money demand at $LL_1$, but money supply at $MS_0$ and interest rate still at $OA$, there is clearly an excess demand for money of an amount $FG$.

   (d)  This is mirrored by an equal excess supply of bonds, in response to which the price of bonds will fall, in turn causing the rate of interest to rise. This process continues until equilibrium is reached.

   (e)  The new equilibrium is at interest rate $OC$, at which point real money demand is equal to money supply $OF$.

   (f)  The authorities can operate either upon the stock of high-powered money or upon the money multiplier, as we have seen. The former could be achieved by open market operations to sell bills or bonds to the public. The money multiplier may be operated on by influencing the proportion of deposits held by the banks as cash.

   (g)  Equilibrium at interest rate $OD$, real money balances $OE$.

6 The transactions demand for money (in nominal terms) is argued to depend upon nominal income; i.e. upon the price level and real income. Situations *(a) - (d)* would thus be expected to lead to an increase in transactions demand. Notice in *(b)* that the expectation of a price rise is sufficient to cause economic agents to alter their behaviour in anticipation. An increase in the rate of income tax *(e)* would reduce transactions demand. A fall in interest rates *(f)* would be expected to have a greater effect on the asset demand (and perhaps the precautionary demand) than on the transactions demand.

7 All of them.

8 Suppose that the money demand schedule is known to be given by *LL* in Figure A24-1 and that the authorities set *L0* as the target level for money stock. By fixing the rate of interest at *R0*, money supply can be allowed to self-adjust to the target level.

This technique relies on the stability of the *LL* curve – and upon the authorities having knowledge of it. If *LL* is neither known nor stable, the possibility of achieving targets by this route is remote. The method also requires that equilibrium is readily and quickly achieved.

9 In exercise 8, we saw how the authorities may set the interest rate at *R0* (in Figure A24-1), and allow money demand to be at *L0*. We might see the problem here as being the reverse: the authorities may set money supply at *L0* so that *R0* results from market equilibrium. However, two sorts of problem may arise. Firstly, there is the problem of achieving *L0* when the authorities do not have precise control of money supply. Secondly, there are still the problems of the stability of *LL*, as discussed in the answer to exercise 8.

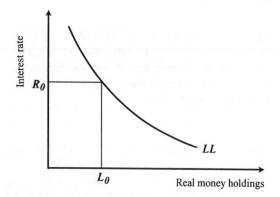

**Figure A24-1  Monetary control through the interest rate**

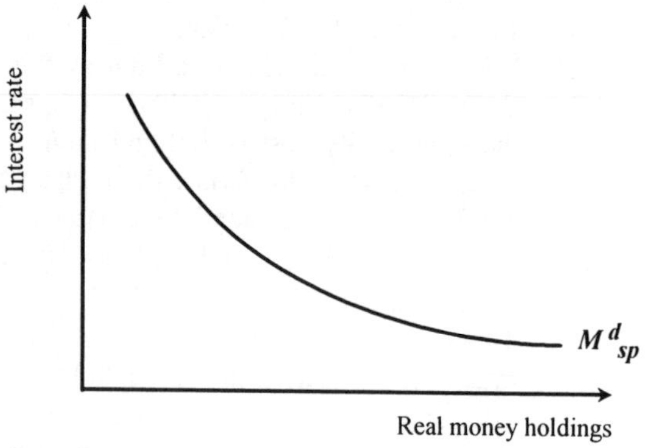

**Figure A24-2  The speculative demand for money**

## True/False

1 True: see Section 24-1 of the main text.

2 False: in order to reduce money supply, the Bank must induce the banks to hold larger cash reserves (see Section 24-2 of the main text).

3 True.

4 False of course: a reverse repo is a form of short-term borrowing. For instance, you might sell gilts to a bank, agreeing to repurchase at a specified price and date. See Box 24-1 in the main text.

5 True: see Box 24-1 in the main text.

6 False: for discussion of the Bank's role as lender of last resort, see Section 24-3 of the main text.

7 True: see Section 24-4 of the main text.

8 False: uncertainty provides the motivation for the precautionary demand for money.

9 False: the nominal interest rate better reflects the interest differential between holding money and bonds.

10 False: prices may vary in ways beyond the control of the Bank, so nominal money supply is more amenable to control (see Section 24-5 of the main text).

11 True.

12 True.

## ECONOMICS IN THE NEWS

1  The contingency for which the Bank was preparing was the possibility that individuals would demand more cash than normal, because of real or perceived panic about the banking system. If people were trying to celebrate (and thus needed money), but were reluctant to trust the banks to have got their technology sorted out, then there would be likely to be a big increase in the demand for cash. In the short run, the effects on money supply are a bit difficult to unravel, as people would be merely trading out of bank deposits into cash. However, as the system settled down again, there would have been an effective increase in the amount of notes in circulation. In order to analyse the full effects of this, we need to have a model in which the price level is explained within the system. We will see this soon, in Chapter 26. Another possibility is that the banks may have reacted to the additional liquidity by granting more loans. Given that they were not supposed to have opened the extra bundles of notes unless needed, this should not have happened.

2  If the notes could be gradually absorbed into the system, as new notes are normally used to replace old ones, then there would be no effect on money supply.

## Questions for Thought

1  (a) If you expect the rate of interest to rise, then you expect the price of bonds to fall – so you will hold all your wealth as money to avoid capital losses.

(b) If the rate of interest is high, and bond prices correspondingly low, then you would probably choose to put all your wealth into bonds to reap capital gains when bond prices rise. When the interest rate reaches $Rc$ (the 'critical rate'), you no longer expect bond prices to change and will be indifferent between money and bonds.

(c) This analysis appeared in Keynes's General Theory, which referred to it as the speculative demand for money. The aggregate relationship is shown in Figure A24-2 (opposite). The downward slope results from the assumption that different individuals have different expectations about $Rc$, but at some point the rate of interest becomes so low that everyone agrees that it can fall no further.

2  The fallacy in the question as it stands is that it assumes that monetary policy can only be conducted through the control of money supply. This chapter has been arguing that the way to deal with this is to target interest rates rather than money supply. This is a viable option, and money supply can be affected indirectly by this route.

## Chapter 25  Monetary and Fiscal Policy in a Closed Economy

### Important Concepts and Technical Terms

| 1 | (b) | 3 | (e) | 5 | (f) | 7 | (g) | 9 | (c) |
|---|-----|---|-----|---|-----|---|-----|---|-----|
| 2 | (a) | 4 | (h) | 6 | (i) | 8 | (d) | 10 | (j) |

### Exercises

1  (a) Although it seems that there is some association between the series, it is not easy to evaluate them by simple eye-balling. However, some features do stand out, especially the seemingly opposite movement of the two series after 1987, suggesting a negative correlation between these variables. The fall in savings up to about 1988 is associated with a boom in consumer spending which occurred at this time.

*(b)* See Figure A25-1.

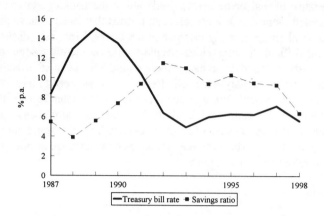

**Figure A25-1    Interest rates and the personal savings ratio in the UK**

*(c)* In the first few years of this period, these series seem to be negatively correlated – that is, they move in opposite directions. This may seem a little puzzling, as we have argued that savings may be expected to be high when interest rates are high. However, none of this evidence can really be said to prove anything. There are many other factors which affect people's consumption-saving decisions which have not been taken into account in this exploration of the two series. Nonetheless, this analysis has highlighted an economic feature of interest, which clearly bears further exploration.

2  *(a)* *OB*.

  *(b)* The area *ABC* reflects the fact that our individual must borrow in early life to maintain consumption above current income.

  *(c)* By borrowing at the market rate of interest.

  *(d)* This 'saving' is for two reasons – firstly, the individual must pay back the money borrowed in early life, together with the interest payments. Secondly, money must be set aside in order to maintain consumption after retirement.

  *(e)* *EFGH* represents dissaving.

  *(f)* By saving in middle age (see *d*).

  *(g)* An increase in initial wealth shifts up the permanent income line and increases consumption.

  *(h)* An increase in the interest rate reduces the present value of future income. The cost of borrowing in early life is increased. The permanent income level falls – and so will consumption. For more detailed discussion, see Section 25-1 of the main text.

3  The general pattern of the Figure indicates that investment tends to follow something of a cyclical pattern over time – you can see the way that the total amount of investment in real terms fluctuates as time goes by. For instance, notice the fall in investment expenditures in the early part of the 1980s, and the surge towards the end of that decade, only to be followed by another dramatic fall around 1990. Notice that these cyclical fluctuations affect some kinds of investment more than others. For example, investment in transport equipment seems much less subject to fluctuation than investment in other machinery. In case you are wondering, the thin black band at the top of the figure representing intangibles represents investment in such assets as computer software, mineral exploration and entertainment, literary or artistic originals. Clearly the computer software part of this has become increasingly important during the period shown.

4  *(a)* Projects *D* (return 20 per cent), *F* (16 per cent), and *B* (12 per cent) all offer returns superior to the market rate of interest and will be undertaken.

*(b)*  With the market interest rate at 13 per cent, project *B* would not be selected.  The firm could obtain a better return on the funds by lending at the market rate.  The market rate of interest represents the opportunity cost of investment.

*(c)*  We can construct the schedule by ranking the projects in order of their return and accumulating the amounts:

*(d)*

| Project | Return (% p.a.) | Cumulative investment demand (£) |
|---------|-----------------|----------------------------------|
| D | 20 | 5 000 |
| F | 16 | 15 000 |
| B | 12 | 21 000 |
| E | 10 | 24 000 |
| A | 6 | 28 000 |
| C | 2 | 32 000 |

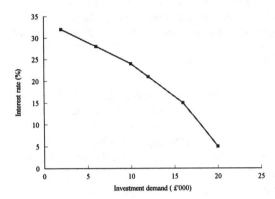

**Figure A25-2  Investment demand**

We can then produce the investment demand schedule (Figure A25-2).

*(d)*  An increase in business confidence will move the investment demand schedule outwards. The firm will uprate all its estimates of rates of return.

5  *(a)*  A fall in the rate of interest implies an increase in the price of bonds. If the price of bonds increases, people will choose to hold less bonds and more money, so there is an increase in money supply.

*(b)*  As the rate of interest falls, private consumption and investment tend to rise;

*(c)*  so aggregate demand rises, and

*(d)*  this brings about an increase in equilibrium output. This shows the initial phase of the transmission mechanism of monetary policy.

*(e)*  As equilibrium output rises, the transactions and precautionary demands for money increase.

*(f)*  The increase in the demand for money leads to an increase in equilibrium interest rates (through the influence of the bond market); this will moderate the original increase in aggregate demand through the effects of the rate of interest on consumption and investment.

*(g)*  The net effect is likely to be an increase in equilibrium output, unless neither consumption nor investment is sensitive to the rate of interest.

6  *(a)*  Reducing direct tax rates has an immediate effect in increasing disposable income, which leads to an increase in consumption expenditure and hence aggregate demand...

*(b)*  which leads to an increase in equilibrium output.

*(c)*  As income rises, there is an increase in transactions and precautionary demand for money, which,

*(d)*  given fixed money supply, leads to a fall in bond prices and an increase in interest rates.

(e) In turn, this leads to a fall in both investment and consumption;

(f) and there is a reduction in equilibrium output, owing to this 'crowding out' of private expenditure.

(g) Complete crowding out occurs when the demand for money is perfectly inelastic with respect to the interest rate: in this case the interest rate continues to rise until consumption and investment fall sufficiently to return aggregate demand to its initial level.

7   (a)   AB is the (downward-sloping) IS curve; CD is the (upward-sloping) LM curve.

    (b)

| Point | Money market | Goods market |
|-------|--------------|--------------|
| E | Excess supply | Equilibrium |
| F | Equilibrium | Excess supply |
| G | Excess demand | Equilibrium |
| H | Equilibrium | Equilibrium |
| J | Equilibrium | Excess demand |

Only at point H is there equilibrium in both markets.

    (c)   At J the money market is in equilibrium but there is excess demand for goods, tending to lead to an increase in output (and interest rates). A similar story could be told for each disequilibrium point – and under reasonable assumptions the economy can be seen to move towards equilibrium.

    (d)   (i)   Shifts IS to the right.

        (ii)   Shifts LM to the right.

        (iii)   Shifts IS to the left.

        (iv)   This reduces real money supply – and so shifts LM to the left.

        (v)   This may be expected to increase autonomous consumption, as the poor tend to have a higher average propensity to consume: IS shifts to the right.

        (vi)   A messy one – an increase in wealth may lead to higher consumption (IS shifts to the right) but also to an increase in the asset demand for money (LM shifts to the left).

8   (a)   Income $Y_1$, interest rate $R_1$.

    (b)   An increase in government expenditure (or cuts in taxation).

    (c)   Income increases from $Y_1$ to $Y_4$.

    (d)   Income $Y_3$, interest rate $R_2$ using LMb.

    (e)   Income $Y_2$, interest rate $R_3$ using LMa.

    (f)   With LMb (relatively elastic), crowding out is $Y_4 - Y_3$.

        With LMa (relatively inelastic), crowding out is $Y_4 - Y_2$.

    (g)   The sensitivity of money demand to the interest rate and to income.

    (h)   By financing spending through an expansion of money supply, shifting LM to intersect IS1 at income $Y_4$, interest rate $R_1$; this works all right in this fixed price world, but may have side-effects if prices are free to vary – as we shall see.

9   (a)   Income $Y_3$; interest rate $R_1$.

    (b)   A reduction in real money supply. The methods by which this may be achieved were discussed in Chapter 24.

    (c)   Income $Y_2$; interest rate $R_3$ using ISb.

    (d)   Income $Y_1$; interest rate $R_2$ using ISa.

    (e)   The degree to which private expenditure (investment and consumption) is sensitive to the rate of interest. The flatter is IS, the greater effect does monetary policy have on the level of income.

10   These arguments are fully explained in Box 25-1 in the main text.

11   (a)   We might convert the relationship into algebraic terms as:

        $C_t = \beta Y^p_t = 0.93\ Y^p_t$

        where $\beta$ = marginal propensity to consume out of permanent income and $Y^p_t$ = current estimate of permanent income, which we could write as: $Y^p_t = Y^p_{t-1} + j\ (Y_t - Y^p_{t-1})$, where j = the proportion of the change in disposable income expected to be permanent (here, 0.8).

        $C_t$ = current consumption.

    (b)   $Y^p_t = 15\,000 + 0.8\ (25\,000 - 15\,000) = £23\,000$.

*(c)*  The marginal propensity to consume out of current income *(Y_t)* is $\beta$ multiplied by j, i.e. $0.93 \times 0.8 = 0.74$.

*(d)*  The 'multiplier' is 1/(1 – the marginal propensity to spend on domestic output out of income).

Based on the marginal propensity to consume out of current income, we calculate the short-run multiplier as $1/(1 – 0.74) = 3.85$. However, in the long run (based on permanent income), we have $1/(1 - 0.93) = 14.28$. This seems to suggest that fiscal policy should be more effective in the long, rather than the short run. This runs against our normal expectation for this, but you should remember that we are still operating with a partial model. Once we have taken prices and exchange rates into account, the result will turn out to be very different. Notice that the multiplier here is telling us how far the *IS* curve shifts following a change in government expenditure. Under the assumptions of this question, full adjustment to changing income takes a number of periods to work through – hence the result.

## True/False

1   True: as specified in Friedman's permanent income hypothesis (see Section 25-1 of the main text).
2   False: if tax cuts are perceived to be temporary, consumption habits may not alter (see Box 25-1 in the main text).
3   False: business confidence, the cost of capital, and other factors affect the position of the investment demand schedule (see Section 25-2 of the main text). We will return to explore some further aspects of investment in Chapters 30 and 31.
4   False: a higher interest rate reduces the present value and leads to a fall in investment.
5   False: see Box 25-2 in the main text.
6   True: see Section 25-3 of the main text.
7   False: the multiplier is reduced, perhaps substantially (see Section 25-4 of the main text).
8   True: see Section 25-5 of the main text.
9   True: the price level affects real money supply.
10  False: monetary and fiscal policy have very different effects, especially in their influence on the composition of aggregate demand (see Section 25-6 of the main text).
11  True.
12  True: consideration of flexible prices, aggregate supply, and full employment are our next topics.

## ECONOMICS IN THE NEWS

1   The passage argues that strong consumer demand is related to wealth, income, and household borrowing. The implication of this in the context is that an increase in the rate of interest would be expected (and intended) to stem consumer demand. This chapter has discussed why this should be so. One prime reason is that an increase in the rate of interest raises the cost of household borrowing. If individuals face higher interest payments on existing debt, they have less income available for spending – and may be discouraged from undertaking further borrowing.
2   The rise in the cost of borrowing also affects firms, and may discourage investment, as some projects will no longer be economically viable at the new higher rate of interest. The passage also suggests that there may be an effect on confidence. This might lower firms' expectations about the future demand for their products – which may also discourage investment.
3   If Germans buy bonds, the funds may be channelled into productive investment, whereas higher house prices in the UK may be a less helpful result for the economy.

## Questions for Thought

1   (a)  Under the permanent income hypothesis, we would not expect consumers to change their behaviour in response to a transitory change. Thus, if faced with a temporary fall in income, we would expect them to try to maintain existing patterns of consumption. Of course, this may not always be possible. For example, they may find themselves to be liquidity-constrained: that is, they may be unable to borrow in

order to finance the level of consumption to which they are accustomed. Perhaps the bank does not accept their view that the reduction in income is only transitory.

In these circumstances, we find that consumption varies rather more with current income than would be predicted by the theory. Some empirical studies have found exactly this result.

(b) This is the Ricardian equivalence argument again. If consumers perceive the tax cuts to be transitory (in the sense that taxes will have to increase again at some time in the future so that the government can pay back the debt), then they will not respond to tax cuts by changing their consumption plans. Alternatively, they may perceive that it is only future generations that will have to pay back, or it may be that they were liquidity-constrained before the tax cuts. In these sorts of circumstances, consumption may react to tax cuts.

2   You may wish to look back at Chapter 13 of the main text as well as Section 25-2.

3   (a) The *IS* curve is derived by substituting for $T$ in the consumption equation and then for $C$ and $I$ in the equilibrium condition – i.e. we impose equilibrium.

$Y = A + c(Y - tY) - dR + B - iR + G.$

We can then collect terms in $Y$ and $R$ and rearrange the equation:

$$Y = \frac{A + B + G}{\{1 - c(1 - t)\}} - \frac{(d + i)}{\{1 - c(1 - t)\}} \times R.$$

The first term represents the autonomous element.

(b) Similar steps are taken for the money market equation:

$$R = \frac{N - \overline{M}}{m} + \frac{kP}{m} \times Y$$

(c) Plugging in the values of the parameters:

*IS*: Y = 4860 – 55.556 R.

*LM*: R = –100 + 0.025 Y.

These are plotted in Figure A25-3.

Equilibrium occurs with the rate of interest at 9 per cent, income at 4360.

(d)  C = 700 + 0.8 × (1 – 0.2) × 4360 – 5 × 9 = 3445.4.

I = 400 – 15 × 9 = 265

C + I + G = 3445.4 + 265 + 649.6 = 4360.

(e)  Md = 0.25 × 1 × 4360 + 200 – 10 × 9 = 1200.

(f)  T = 0.2 × 4360 = 872

G – T = 649.6 – 872 = –222.4

A surplus of 222.4.

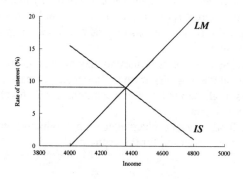

**Figure A25-3   *IS-LM* equilibrium**

## Chapter 26 Aggregate Supply, the Price Level, and the Speed of Adjustment

### Important Concepts and Technical Terms

| | | | | | | | | | |
|---|---|---|---|---|---|---|---|---|---|
| 1 | (m) | 4 | (h) | 7 | (f) | 10 | (j) | 13 | (e) |
| 2 | (k | 5 | (i) | 8 | (n) | 11 | (c) | 14 | (g) |
| 3 | (l) | 6 | (a) | 9 | (d) | 12 | (b) | | |

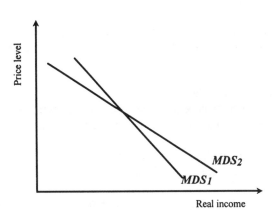

**Figure A26-1   The macroeconomic demand schedule and the real balance effect**

### Exercises

1  (a)  Income $OK$; interest rate $OD$; aggregate demand $OK$.

   (b)  $LMb$.

   (c)  Income $OJ$; interest rate $OF$; aggregate demand $OJ$.

   (d)  As price rises, the real value of money balances and other assets held by households is reduced. This has an effect on consumption and reduces aggregate demand, shifting $IS$ to $ISb$ and equilibrium income, interest rate, and aggregate demand respectively to $OH$, $OE$, and $OH$.

   (e)  A fall in price moves $LM$ from $LM0$ to $LMa$. In the absence of the real balance effect, equilibrium income and aggregate demand move to $OP$ and the rate of interest to $OB$. The real balance effect moves $IS$ from $IS0$ to $ISa$, so equilibrium income and aggregate demand are $OQ$ with interest rate $OC$.

   (f)  The position of the $LM$ schedule is partly determined by the size of real money supply. A change in price given fixed nominal money supply affects real money supply and thus moves the $LM$ schedule.

   (g)  In Figure A26-1 $MDS1$ shows the macroeconomic demand schedule without taking account of the real balance effect, which affects the slope, resulting in $MDS2$. The intersection of the two represents our original equilibrium point.

2  All the characteristics listed are features of the macroeconomic demand schedule – that's how we constructed it!

3  (a)  $OB$: where labour demand = job acceptances.

   (b)  Employment $OF$: registered unemployment $FJ$.

   (c)  The natural rate of unemployment is $FJ$ – there is no involuntary unemployment.

   (d)  Employment $OD$: this represents the number of people prepared to accept jobs at this real wage. Registered unemployment is $DH$. All those wishing to work at this real wage can obtain work – there is excess demand for labour – so there is no involuntary unemployment.

(e) With excess demand for labour, firms will be prepared to offer high wages to attract labour, so the market moves towards equilibrium.

(f) Employment *OE:* this represents labour demand at this real wage. Registered unemployment is *EK*, of which *EG* is voluntary, representing people who are willing to work but cannot find employment.

(g) Eventually – or instantly, in the classical model – wages will drift downwards, and the market moves towards equilibrium.

(h) In our static model, labour is the only variable input, so fixing employment implies the level of output/aggregate supply.

(i) If the labour market is always in equilibrium, the level of employment – and hence aggregate supply – will be stable.

4  (a) An increase in nominal money supply increases aggregate demand at each price, so the move must be from *MDSa* to *MDSb*.

(b) Output *OD*; price *OA*.

(c) Output *OD*; price *OB*; prices adjust instantaneously leaving output unaffected; money feeds only prices.

(d) A reduction in government spending is represented by a move from *MDSb* to *MDSa*.

(e) Price *OB*; output *OD*.

(f) Price *OA*; output *OD*.

(g) Price still at *OB,* output reduced to *OC.*

(h) *MDS* represents points at which planned spending equals actual output – to this extent the goods market is in equilibrium. However, this may not represent equilibrium from the producers' perspective: there is no implication that planned output is equal to actual output.

5  (a) This factor affects the workers' willingness to become unemployed and discourages adjustment.

(b) In the absence of a redundancy agreement, firms may be more willing to make adjustments to the size of workforce.

(c) This may encourage adjustment, as firms have less need to 'hoard' unskilled labour.

(d) This may discourage firms from adjusting employment and wage rates, as there is flexibility in labour input without needing to negotiate a new wage deal or indulge in hiring and firing. However, in the long run such adjustments may have to be made.

(e) This also discourages firms from making adjustments to employment and wages.

(f) If labour is scarce, firms may not be able to increase employment, and may be reluctant to lose workers. Workers may be more prepared to change jobs as they will perceive that it will not be difficult to find new jobs.

(g) Firms may wish to hold on to trained labour if demand falls temporarily. Workers may recognize that their skills are not readily transferred to other firms.

6  (a) Demand shock.

(b) Supply shock.

(c) Supply.

(d) Demand.

(e) Demand.

(f) Demand.

(g) Supply.

(h) Supply.

7  (a) An increase in supply, increasing potential output.

(b) An decrease in supply (see the discussion of an oil price increase in Section 26-8 of the main text).

(c) This increases autonomous investment demand, so represents an increase in demand.

(d) A (short-run) decrease in supply.

(e) A decrease in demand.

(f) Given the differing propensities to consume of the 'rich' and the 'poor', this leads to an increase in autonomous consumption and in aggregate demand.

(g) This represents a fall in labour supply at any given real wage, so there is a reduction in supply and potential output.

8  The only effect of the increase in aggregate demand would be on the price level, which affects only *(c)* and *(e).*

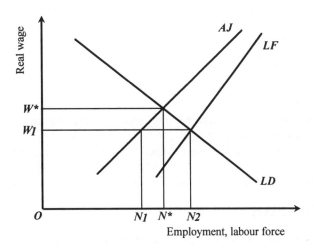

**Figure A26-2   Labour market adjustment**

**9**   All of them.

**10**   *(a)*   If the economy is in equilibrium, then it must be on the (long-run) aggregate supply curve *AS*; if we are to illustrate an increase in nominal money, *MDS* is to move to the right – so initially must be on *MDSa*. The initial position is thus at output *OG*, price *OA*.

   *(b)*   Given full wage and price flexibility the economy moves straight to output *OG*, price *OD*.

   *(c)*   The increase in nominal money supply moves the macroeconomic demand schedule from *MDSa* to *MDSb*; with sluggish adjustment, the economy moves to a position on the short-run aggregate supply curve *SASc* with output *OJ*, price *OB*. In the short run, this increase in output will be brought about through overtime working, etc., as firms cannot instantly adjust wages and employment.

   *(d)*   Firms find that there has been an increase in demand for their output and prices rise. In time, firms take on new workers, as adjusting employment is a more sensible long-run strategy than varying hours worked by the existing workforce. The *SAS* schedule begins to move – from *SASc* to *SASb* in the medium term, by which stage price has reached *OC* and output has fallen back to *OH*.

   *(e)*   Output *OG*, price *OD*.

   *(f)*   See Figure A26-2.

   The market starts in equilibrium with real wage *W\** and employment *N\**. As the price level rises, the real wage falls – say, to *W1* – at which point we have to think rather carefully about what is happening. Labour demand has increased to *N2* but job acceptances have fallen to *N1*. There is excess demand for labour, and if agents are always on the *AJ* function, employment falls at a time when output is rising. How do we explain this situation? It could be that in the short run workers prefer to hold on to their jobs rather than immediately incurring the costs of job search, perhaps because they realize that the real-wage reduction is temporary and are prepared to be 'off' the *AJ* schedule. In addition, firms may be prepared to offer lots of overtime, increasing output by this means rather than by increasing employment. As firms seek to adjust employment levels, wages will be bid up, carrying the economy back towards equilibrium – back at *W\*N\**.

   *(g)*   When wages need to fall we may expect resistance from workers and unions. When the adjustment is upwards, we may expect firms to be keen to adjust wages (there is excess demand for labour) and workers are unlikely to protest. We may thus imagine that the adjustment in this case may be more rapid.

   *(h)*   10 per cent (see Section 26-7 of the main text).

## True/False

**1**   True: see Section 26-1 of the main text.

**2**   True.

3   False: there will always be some unemployment even at full employment (see Section 26-2 of the main text). Unemployment is more carefully examined in Chapter 27.
4   Silly: money illusion is the confusion of real and nominal variables.
5   True: see Section 26-2 of the main text.
6   True: see Section 26-4 of the main text.
7   False: output is unaffected and only prices change.
8   True: see Section 26-5 of the main text.
9   False: firms are more likely to vary hours worked in the short run (see Section 26-6 of the main text).
10  True: see Section 26-7 of the main text.
11  False: a favourable supply shock leads to higher output, but lower price level (see Section 26-8 of the main text).
12  True: see Section 26-9 of the main text.

## ECONOMICS IN THE NEWS

1,2  The first passage asks whether monetary policy can be expected to cope with the problems facing the Japanese economy, at the heart of which seems to be the question of recession. Inflation has been low – or even negative, if we recognize changes in the quality of goods. Nominal demand for goods has been very sluggish. The normal hope for monetary policy would be that an increase in money supply would lead to lower interest rates, and thus stimulate aggregate demand in the economy, raising consumer demand and investment. The passage is pessimistic, however. It argues that interest rates are as low as they could possible be, and that efforts to expand the money supply would be ineffective because increasing bank reserves may not lead to a rise in lending. Technically, this suggests that Japan is in what is known as the 'liquidity trap'. This will be discussed from a theoretical stance in question 1 in Questions for Thought below.

The second passage switches attention to fiscal policy. It seems that between October and December of 1999, Japan decided that monetary policy was not the answer to the dilemma. The hope here is that an increase in spending will enable the economy to escape from the recession. In terms of our theoretical model, this would mean a rightwards shift of the *IS* schedule, and of the *MDS*.

### Questions for Thought

1   *(a)*  The story should be familiar by now: briefly, a reduction in money wages leads to a falling price level, an increase in real money supply, a fall in interest rates, and an expansion of consumption and investment – hence aggregate demand and output.

  *(b)*  The *LM* schedule of Figure 26-5 has a horizontal section. This results from the (Keynesian) speculative demand for money discussed in 'Questions for Thought' (1) of Chapter 24. $R_0$ represents an interest rate at which all agents expect a fall in bond prices and thus hold no bonds. It breaks the chain of part *(a)* because the interest rate cannot fall below $R_0$ and equilibrium income cannot increase beyond $Y_0$. The economy is stuck in what is often known as the liquidity trap.

  *(c)*  If the real balance effect is strong enough, then falling prices have the effect of increasing autonomous consumption, thus shifting the *IS* schedule. Examination of Figure 26-5 shows that, if *IS* moves to the right, the economy is able to escape from the liquidity trap.

  *(d)*  Fiscal policy would shift the *IS* schedule to the right, and be much more effective than monetary policy in this context.

2   *(c)*  If you do not recognize the jargon 'liquidity trap', refer back to the immediately preceding 'Questions for Thought', which talks you through the idea.

3   The analysis here parallels the discussion of a reduction in aggregate demand/nominal money supply (see Section 26-7 of the main text). Some transitional increase in unemployment may occur while the economy is adjusting towards equilibrium. There are still a number of themes to be further developed: in particular, we need to be able to analyse inflation – a situation of rising prices over time. We cannot easily do this with our static model. In order to analyse the UK economy fully, we also need to consider open economy effects. The following chapters explore these issues.

# Chapter 27  Unemployment

## Important Concepts and Technical Terms

| | | | | | | | |
|---|---|---|---|---|---|---|---|
| **1** | *(j)* | **4** | *(f)* | **7** | *(i)* | **10** | *(g)* |
| **2** | *(e)* | **5** | *(a)* | **8** | *(c)* | **11** | *(h)* |
| **3** | *(k)* | **6** | *(l)* | **9** | *(b)* | **12** | *(d)* |

## Exercises

1  *(a)*  Categories *(ii)*, *(iv)*, and *(vi)* joined the unemployed, a total of 2700.
Categories *(i)* and *(v)* left = 2600.
*(b)*  Categories *(vi)* and *(vii)* joined = 600.
Categories *(i)* and *(iii)* left = 700.
*(c)*  Categories *(ii)*, *(iii)*, and *(iv)* = 2300 left jobs; *(v)* and *(vii)* became employed = 2100; so the employed labour force fell by 200.
*(d)*  Labour force 26800, unemployed 3000. Although the employed labour force fell by 200, unemployment has risen by only 100.
*(e)*  $1.36 + 3.16 - 3.25 = 1.27$m.
The way the figures are compiled leaves a discrepancy between this and the actual figure of 1.29m.

2  *(a)*  This is structural unemployment. If textile workers are refusing jobs which do not match their acquired skills, then we regard them as voluntarily unemployed.
*(b)*  Frictional unemployment. Voluntary. Of course, there is a sense in which all unemployed (except school-leavers) are 'between jobs', but here we refer to those in the process of changing jobs, perhaps having left one job in the knowledge that they have a new job starting in the near future.
*(c)*  Usually regarded as part of frictional unemployment. This is a situation in which we may wish to remember that economists use words in a particular way. Some people in this group may want to work, but are incapable of work. As people, we may recognize these desires, but as economists we include them as part of voluntary unemployment – the wedge between *AJ* and *LF* in the diagrams.
*(d)*  Classical unemployment. As individuals, those suffering unemployment for this reason may see themselves as being involuntarily unemployed. However, we remember that they may be unemployed through the choices of their ex-colleagues – for instance, if real wages are sustained at a high level through union market power. In this sense, this unemployment is voluntary.
*(e)*  This is demand-deficient unemployment. Involuntary.

3  The regional variation in unemployment has not been discussed explicitly in this chapter, which is why this question carries a health warning. However, you should by now have had sufficient practice to be able to think through some of the main issues, using the techniques presented.
*(a)*  Comparing the columns, it is firstly apparent that some regions have maintained their relative positions. The South East, East Anglia, and East Midlands continue to enjoy lower unemployment rates than the national average, although the South East suffered a relative deterioration in 1996. On the other hand, the North, Yorkshire and Humberside, the North West, Wales, and Scotland continue to suffer more than most. The West Midlands fell dramatically down the rankings, starting below the national average and finishing above, in spite of a bit of a recovery after 1989. This in large measure may be attributed to the decline of manufacturing industry (especially motor vehicles) after 1974. The South West, on the other hand, improved its relative position. In general, the differentials seem less in 1996 than in 1974.
*(b)*  A fundamental issue is whether unemployment rates reflect the characteristics of the regions themselves or of the people who live there. If an area has a high proportion of young people, then we might expect high frictional unemployment, as such workers tend to switch between jobs more frequently. However, we are not presented with such information.

*Structural unemployment* may well contribute to our explanation, in the sense that different regions have differing employment structures. The immobility of labour between regions may create a mismatch between labour demand and supply. The decline of manufacturing in the West Midlands provides one instance of such unemployment. It has been noted that the recession of the early 1990s affected service sectors, and thus affected the differential between the South East and other regions.

*Classical unemployment* is less likely to vary between regions, but it is possible that national industry wage agreements may create wage scales which are locally inappropriate.

*Demand-deficient unemployment* may affect regions differently because of local product structure. In addition, regional disparities may be perpetuated by this route – if unemployment is high in a region, local demand will be low.

No doubt you have thought of many other factors.

4  (a)  Employment is 90 (thousand).
   (b)  At a real wage of $5, 129 register as being part of the labour force, so total unemployment is 129 – 90 = 39.
   (c)  From the table we see that 110 would be prepared to accept jobs at this real wage, so involuntary unemployment is 110 – 90 = 20 – the remainder is voluntary.
   (d)  Firms pay $5 per hour and workers receive $3.
   (e)  Employment is 90, given by labour demand at $5 per hour. As for unemployment, net real wages are $3, so the registered labour force is 115 and unemployment is 115 – 90 = 25. The labour market is in equilibrium, so there is no excess demand for labour – remember that the real wage paid by firms exceeds that received by workers. The workers receive $3 per hour, at which rate job acceptances amount to 90.
   (f)  All unemployment here is voluntary.
   (g)  Without tax, the equilibrium real wage is $4.
   (h)  Employment is 100, unemployment is 122 – 100 = 22. Unemployment has fallen by 3.
   (i)  With the labour market in equilibrium, all unemployment is voluntary.

If you found this difficult, you might find that it helps to draw a diagram using the figures of Table 27-2. There is a similar figure in Section 27-4 of the main text.

5  (a)  *LDb* must be the original labour demand schedule. The effect of the adverse supply shock will be to reduce the marginal product of labour and hence labour demand.
   (b)  Real wage *OB*, employment *OE*.
   (c)  *EG*.
   (d)  Employment falls to *OC*, unemployment rises to *CG*.
   (e)  Real wages *OA*, employment *OD*.
   (f)  *DF*.
   (g)  The natural rate has risen. As the real wage falls, the replacement ratio rises and affects the natural rate.

6  (a)  accounts for some of the increase in equilibrium unemployment, though less than is sometimes supposed.
   (b)  is partly a demand-side effect, which would contribute to demand-deficient unemployment, but not to the natural rate. However, there is also a terms of trade effect, which is claimed to have contributed significantly to the higher natural rate seen in the 1980s.
   (c)  is cited in Section 27-3 of the main text as an influence on the natural rate.
   (d)  is another demand-side effect.
   (e)  no doubt has contributed greatly to the rise in the natural rate, having generated structural unemployment through the skills mismatch effect.
   (f)  Changes in technology may have led to a fall in the demand for some types of labour – for instance, few clerks are required with computer-based filing systems. None the less, there is an increase in demand for computer operators... but again, there may be some structural unemployment.
   (g)  The participation rate of married women has increased in recent years – this may have added to the natural rate.
   (h)  These have made some contribution to the natural rate.

7  (a)  may cause immobility of labour and lead to distortions in resource allocation.

(b) may cause high levels of personal suffering but not have substantial effects. It would appear that in some countries where no unemployment benefits are paid, high unemployment is associated with poverty and high rates of criminal activity.

(c) may be politically difficult to enforce, and the effectiveness of incomes policy is in doubt. Incomes policy is discussed in Chapter 28.

(d) may affect demand-deficient unemployment but will affect the natural rate only if it has an effect on expectations of firms and thus encourages investment, or if marginal tax cuts have an effect on labour supply by improving the incentive to work.

(e) is potentially distortionary. It may prevent structural unemployment in the short run, but eventually the adjustment of employment structure will be necessary.

8 (a) A cut in the income tax rate would steepen the budget line.

  (b) *ACD*.

  (c) *D*: $I_2$ is the highest indifference curve that Jayne can choose. If she works, the best she can do is at *J* on $I_1$.

  (d) Income is *GD*; she does not work.

  (e) *K* on $I_3$; she works *EG* hours.

9 This exercise is based on the discussion of hysteresis in Box 27-3 of the main text. All of the arguments may be found there.

  (a) This is the discouraged-worker effect emphasized by Professor Richard Layard.

  (b) This argument has been studied by Professor Charlie Bean, but notice that it does not correspond directly to Figure 27-3: in this story, it is labour demand which remains to the left of its original position after the recession, and labour supply is not affected.

  (c) This explanation of hysteresis has been explored by Professor Chris Pissarides.

  (d) This explanation has been emphasized by writers in both Europe and the United States.

Notice that if hysteresis does occur, it has important implications for policy strategy on the demand-side as well as on the supply-side. Read Box 27-3 of the main text for more details.

10 (a) Real wage *OA*, employment *OD*, natural rate *DF*.

  (b) Labour demand *OC*, voluntary unemployment *EG*, involuntary *CE*.

  (c) With prices rigid, firms may well choose to reduce output – and hence employment – so that for a time they may be 'off' their *LD* schedule.

  (d) Voluntary unemployment *DF*, involuntary *CD*. In this situation, we have involuntary unemployment even though the real wage is at its equilibrium level!

  (e) The fall in employment reduces wage income and leads to a fall in demand for goods, confirming firms' beliefs that they cannot sell as much output as they would like!

Another way of viewing this story is that firms' pessimistic expectations actually shift the *LD* curve to the left, implying a new lower-wage equilibrium. Involuntary unemployment will arise because *OA* is now 'too high'.

## True/False

1 False: the monthly published series for claimant unemployment relate to those registered as unemployed, but this is almost certainly an underestimate of those who are actually unemployed.

2 True.

3 True: see Section 27-2 of the main text.

4 True.

5 False: this is the lump-of-labour fallacy, as explained in Box 27-1 in the main text.

6 False, although some economists would judge it to be closer than would others (see Section 27-3 of the main text).

7 False.

8 True: see Section 27-4 of the main text.

9 False: the reverse is true (see Section 27-5 of the main text).

10 True: see Section 27-6 of the main text.

11 False: for instance, some frictional unemployment may be necessary to allow reallocation of resources.

12 False: society may wish to take the social costs of unemployment into account.

## ECONOMICS IN THE NEWS 1

1   The obvious policy that captured the imagination of the headline writer was the dress code for unemployed people facing job interviews. However, more significant is likely to be the question of basic skills, especially in terms of literacy and numeracy. There are two issues highlighted in the passage. First, there is the question of how unemployed people can obtain jobs, especially when they have been unemployed long term or are from disadvantaged neighbourhoods or ethnic minorities. Second, there is the question of job retention, with the claim that 40 per cent of participants in the New Deal had failed to be placed into lasting jobs. Also mentioned in the passage is the withholding of benefit from those who refuse jobs offered to them.

2   As far as economic analysis is concerned, we might be doubtful about the claim that 'clothes maketh the man', but if smart clothes enable people to gain employment that they are capable of retaining, then this improves the flexibility and effectiveness of the labour market. Improving a worker's basic skills improves his or her marginal productivity, and should help with the attractiveness to the employer. Withholding benefit is a supply-side measure that should encourage more people to accept jobs, thus shifting the $AJ$ schedule to the right.

## ECONOMICS IN THE NEWS 2

1   An economist would want to think about unemployment in terms of people wishing to work at the going wage, but unable to find a job. Notice that the 'at the going wage' part of this definition causes difficulty in measurement terms. We wish to measure unemployment because it is indicative of disequilibrium in the labour market, and thus potentially indicative of market failure. We may also be concerned if the natural rate becomes so high that the economy is producing so far below capacity that society is incurring a welfare loss. Such market failures may justify some form of state intervention, although this is highly contentious in this context.

2   Neither of the measures correspond very closely to the theoretical ideal. In particular, it is difficult to identify those people who are only prepared to work at a relatively high wage. However, the ILO version is probably closer to what we would like, as it explicitly refers to people who are actively seeking work. This is now the accepted measure of unemployment.

3   As far as the claimant count is concerned, we would probably want to include people who were actively seeking work but who were for some reason ineligible for unemployment benefit. The claimant count does have the advantage of being very quick to count, whereas the ILO definition requires a survey, and is thus more expensive to produce. Over recent years, the differences have been relatively small (see the *Economic Review Data Supplement*, September 1997), but this is no guarantee that they will continue to be close in the future.

## Questions for Thought

1   Supply-side factors are vital in deciding whether there are grounds for believing that the natural rate has increased in the UK in recent years, and it is to these that your thoughts should turn (see also Section 27-3 in the main text).

2   One of the reasons that unemployment has tended to be relatively low in Japan, as compared with other industrialized economies, is the existence of this type of implicit agreement between firms. From economic theory's point of view, we would expect such agreements to work against the efficiency of the labour market, as potentially this could restrict the ability of firms to make desirable adjustments to their workforce. For instance, it might be difficult for a firm in a declining sector to move to a more appropriate scale of activity. It might also make workers less likely to search for new jobs and occupations. Notice that the agreements do not apply to women.

3   You might like to discuss this with your fellow students. If you look back to the analysis that you went through in Exercise 10, you may get some hints.

# Chapter 28  Inflation

## Important Concepts and Technical Terms

| | | | | | | | | | |
|---|---|---|---|---|---|---|---|---|---|
| 1 | *(l)* | 4 | *(a)* | 7 | *(m)* | 10 | *(b)* | 13 | *(n)* |
| 2 | *(f)* | 5 | *(k)* | 8 | *(d)* | 11 | *(g)* | 14 | *(e)* |
| 3 | *(i)* | 6 | *(c)* | 9 | *(h)* | 12 | *(j)* | | |

## Exercises

1   *(a)*   10 per cent: the same percentage as nominal money stock. This follows from the assumption of the Quantity Theory that the velocity of circulation is constant.

     *(b)*   In the short run, producers react to the increase in demand by increasing output. The price level may also begin to rise – but the main effect is on output. (Recall Section 26-7 of the main text.) The nominal interest rate falls to induce people to hold a larger quantity of real money balances.

     *(c)*   As adjustment takes place, the level of real output falls back to its original equilibrium level and prices rise. In the eventual equilibrium, the price level will have risen by the full extent of the original increase in money stock, but real output will be unchanged and interest rates will have gradually climbed back to their original level.

     *(d)*   Using the analysis of Chapter 26, we may argue that the cost increase is passed on as a price increase, reducing real money supply, raising interest rates, and reducing aggregate demand. Sluggish wages lead to unemployment.

     *(e)*   A government worried about unemployment may be tempted to accommodate the price rise by allowing an increase in nominal money.

     *(f)*   If the supply shock reduces long-run potential output, then the economy will eventually settle at this lower output level, which may entail higher unemployment. The more the authorities have tried to maintain output and employment by printing money, the higher the eventual price level – but output will still tend to its equilibrium level.

     *(g)*   A government concerned about inflation may refuse to accommodate the price rise, preferring to see unemployment rise in the short run.

     *(h)*   In the eventual equilibrium, real output will be at its potential level, but prices will be less high than in *(f)*.

2   *(a)*   10 per cent.

     *(b)*   Given $MV = PY$, we calculate that in year 1, $P = MV/Y = 8000 / 4000 = 2$. In year 2, $P = 2.16$(ish). So the inflation rate was about 8 per cent.

     *(c)*   The real interest rate is approximately the difference between the nominal interest rate and the inflation rate. Here, $9 - 8 = 1$ per cent.

     *(d)*   Given that the money market is in equilibrium, then from $MV = PY$, $M/P = Y/V$.
Year 1: $4000 / 4 = 1000$
Year 2: $4065 / 4 = 1016.25$.

3   This exercise closely follows the example pursued in Section 28-5 of the main text.

     *(a)*   Gross earnings are 3 per cent of £5000 = £150.

     *(b)*   30 per cent of £150 = £45.

     *(c)*   Net savings are £105; the rate of return is $(105 / 5000) \times 100 = 2.1$ per cent. In the absence of inflation, nominal and real rates of return are the same.

     *(d)*   Gross earnings are 13 per cent of £5000 = £650. Tax is 30 per cent of £650 = £195.

     *(e)*   Net earnings are £455. Nominal rate of return is $(455 / 5000) \times 100 = 9.1$ per cent. Real rate of return is $9.1 - 10 = -0.9$ per cent.

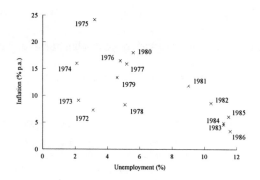

**Figure A28-1   Inflation and unemployment in the UK, 1972–86**

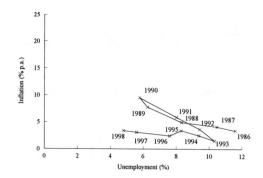

**Figure A28-2   Inflation and unemployment in the UK, 1986–98**

4   (a)  See Figure A28-1.

   (b)  There is little evidence of a stable relationship between inflation and unemployment. The points from 1980 onwards are perhaps not far from the 'classic' picture in shape, but are nowhere near the original position as established by Phillips. The years 1974 and 1975 fit no particular pattern. Between 1976 and 1979, unemployment varied little but there were substantial changes in inflation. We might perhaps speculate that under some policy conditions a short-run trade-off will emerge but that some policy stances may shift the position of the trade-off relationship. For instance, it could be that the Social Contract incomes policy enabled inflation to be reduced in 1977 and 1978 without a significant rise in unemployment.

   (c)  The authorities in 1974–75 followed an accommodating monetary policy. The result was that unemployment did not rise immediately, but the economy experienced high inflation. In 1980–84, no such accommodation ensued and inflation was reduced – but at the cost of rising unemployment. The remaining question is whether the adjustment of expectations will move the Phillips curve back to a lower inflation-unemployment combination or whether there has been an increase in the natural rate.

   These data were purposely out of date, but showing an interesting period in recent economic history. In case you wondered what has happened since, Figure A28-2 brings the story up to 1998. We have joined up the data points in this graph to make it easier to see what has been going on. This more recent experience seems closer to the 'classic' shape of the Phillips curve – but still a long way from the Phillips original. For more discussion, see Peter Smith's article 'The case of the vanishing Phillips curve', in *Economic Review*, 17(4), April 2000.

5   (a)  *SRPC0* is the zero-inflation Phillips curve, so the natural rate of unemployment is *OC* where *SRPC0* cuts the horizontal axis.

   (b)  *OC* is the natural rate, and the rate of inflation which will be stable at *OC* with *SRPC1* is *OA*.

   (c)  Initially unemployment falls to *OB*, inflation rises to *OA*.

   (d)  This position is untenable because *SRPC0* is valid for zero expected inflation. Once workers realize that prices are rising at the rate *OA*, they will adjust expectations and *SRPC* will move.

   (e)  Given answer *(b)*, the economy ends up back at unemployment *OC* but with inflation *OA*.

   (f)  A determined government would carry the economy to *D* in the short run.

   (g)  As expectations adjust, the short-run Phillips curve moves back down and unemployment falls back to the natural rate *OC* with zero inflation.

   (h)  The attainment of equilibrium requires that expectations adjust before the government loses its nerve at the sight of all that unemployment.

   (i)  It is possible that incomes policy may speed up the adjustment process by affecting expectations, and that unemployment need not rise so high or for so long.

6   Factors *(a)*, *(d)*, and *(f)* stem from the demand side, whereas factors *(b)*, *(c)*, and *(e)* affect the supply side. Item *(d)* may be debatable, in the sense that, whereas aggregate demand may be increased, future wage negotiations may be at lower levels if take-home pay has been improved. Some economists have argued that item *(e)* is an unlikely initial cause of inflation, as unions react to past events but do not initiate autonomous wage increases.

7  *(c)* and *(d)*.

8  *(d)*.

9  *(a)* is a real cost of inflation, but if inflation is anticipated it can be offset by the adjustment of tax thresholds.

  *(b)* is also a real cost, which can be minimized by indexation or by building in anticipated inflation.

  *(c)* is mere illusion, as it ignores changes in money income.

  *(d)* are real costs which are present whether or not inflation is anticipated.

  *(e)* is a real cost of inflation at an unpredictable rate; it is the effects of inflation on uncertainty and business confidence which have made inflation public enemy number one.

  *(f)* is an illusion: the cost is not a cost of inflation but the inevitable response to the adverse supply shock.

10  *(a)* Incomes policy can stem inflation only temporarily if other policy instruments are not used consistently and responsibly. At times in the past, incomes policy has been used against a backdrop of monetary expansion and thus had no chance of success. However, there could be a role for it if used in harness with other policies.

  *(b)* A problem in the past has been that governments have tried to achieve too much through a single policy.

  *(c)* Layard has argued that a permanent policy is needed; others have suggested that a policy known to be both temporary and consistent with other policies has a better chance of success.

  *(d)* If applied too rigorously, incomes policy could prevent desirable relative price changes.

  *(e)* Another Layard suggestion is that policies should be sure to offer proper incentives to both sides in the wage bargaining process.

## True/False

1  True: see the introduction to Chapter 28 of the main text.

2  True: in the sense that sustained inflation must always be accompanied by monetary expansion in excess of output growth. The direction of causality is not always clear (see Section 28-1 of the main text).

3  False: this is correct only when real money demand is constant.

4  True: see Section 28-2 of the main text.

5  True.

6  False: printing money is not the only way of financing a budget deficit (see Section 28-3 of the main text).

7  True: see Box 28-1 of the main text.

8  False: recent experience suggests that the Phillips curve cannot be exploited for policy purposes (see Section 28-4 of the main text). This may be a manifestation of Goodhart's law, which we encountered in Chapter 24.

9  True: see Section 28-5 of the main text.

10  False: the shoe-leather and menu costs remain; other costs result if institutions do not fully adapt.

11  True: see Section 28-6 of the main text.

12  False: in the long run, a tolerant attitude may lead to high rates of inflation with the consequent high menu and shoe-leather costs.

## ECONOMICS IN THE NEWS 1

1  Monetary policy is not a precise science. The complexity of the economy makes it difficult to assess the effects of an interest rate change. The chain of transmission entails a number of different links in a chain, and the sensitivity of economic agents to the change is hard to predict. The whole business is made more difficult because the sensitivity of agents to changes may be different at different times, depending upon conditions in the UK economy and abroad. The full article by Ben Martin from which this brief extract was taken is worth reading, as it contains more detail about the transmission mechanism of monetary policy. there is also a longer version of the article in the *Bank of England Quarterly Bulletin*, May 1999

2  The key issue here is the credibility of monetary policy. The Bank of England has a specific brief to hit the inflation target, and is required to pursue that target. If the policy were being run by the Treasury, then there could be a temptation to allow other concerns to influence the full-hearted commitment to the inflation target. The importance of credibility is that it will affect people's expectations of future inflation, which may in turn effect their decisions.

## ECONOMICS IN THE NEWS 2

1   The passage points to bias caused by the inability to take proper account of quality changes and new products, and (more esoterically) the fact that the CPI in the USA is not really a cost of living index. Notice that the passage also argues that the bias may be less significant in the UK than it had been claimed for the USA. One reason for this is that the UK's RPI weights are changed at the beginning of each calendar year. This helps to overcome the problems described when consumers change their pattern of consumption in response to relative price changes. Part of the argument here is one of whether we should use a base-weighted index which compares the cost of a specific bundle of goods at different points in time, and a current-weighted index that compares the cost of today's chosen bundle with the how much that bundle would have cost at some earlier date. The implicit deflator of consumers' expenditure is just such a current-weighted index (Paasche). The RPI is closer to a base-weighted index (Laspeyres), but complicated by the regular weight change. If you are feeling adventurous, you might look back to exercise 8 of Chapter 6, where we looked at the compensating and equivalent income variation methods of looking at the results a price change. If you think about it you will seen that there is a parallel to be drawn here.

2   Our intuition might suggest that the way we measure something is irrelevant except in affecting our perceptions of reality. Changing a measurement cannot affect what is happening out there in the real world. Calling inflation 2 per cent instead of 3 per cent does not have any effect on what has *actually* happened to prices. However, real effects may arise if tax thresholds, pension levels or wage negotiations are based upon the announced figures.

## Questions for Thought

1   There is no definitive answer to this question, which takes us into the realm of normative economics. We may regard both unemployment and inflation as being economic 'bads'. To a certain degree, it is a question of judgement as to which inflicts most harm on society. Recent governments have argued that the control of inflation is an essential prerequisite to tackling unemployment via economic growth. Other commentators have argued that the rise in unemployment since the late 1970s was too high a price to pay for lower inflation. The debate continues.

2   In the long run, velocity is likely to be determined by factors affecting the efficiency with which transactions may be carried out and will reflect real money demand. (What happens to velocity in a hyperinflation?) In the short run, velocity may at times reflect disequilibrium in the money market. For instance, in the mid-1970s velocity fell dramatically at a time when the authorities pursued an 'easy' money policy and there was perhaps excess supply of money. This was followed in the late 1970s by a period of higher-than-normal velocity. This was at a time when output was growing but Healey was beginning to restrict money growth. Since 1979, as inflation fell more rapidly than the rate of monetary growth, velocity fell again. Velocity may thus be a signal of conditions in the money market in the short run. Velocity is discussed in Box 28-1 of the main text.

3   See Section 28-5 of the main text.

4   (a)   *OF.*

   (b)   The real rate *(OA)* plus the inflation rate *(AB): OB.*

   (c)   *OC.*

   (d)   The real revenue from the inflation tax is given by the product of real money demand and the inflation rate, as explained in Box 28-2 in the main text. It is thus represented in the figure by the area *ABED.*

   (e)   In moving from 'G' to 'E', there is a deadweight loss given by the triangle *DEG.* This reflects the fact that at a higher rate of inflation, agents are forgoing some of the benefits from using real money balances: the convenience of having cash available, etc.

   (f)   As the economy approaches hyperinflation, people economize more and more in their holdings of real money, and the revenue from the inflation tax diminishes. This analysis does not seem to have deterred some countries (especially in Latin America) from attempting to finance their deficits in this way.

# Chapter 29  Open Economy Macroeconomics

## Important Concepts and Technical Terms

| | | | | | | | |
|---|---|---|---|---|---|---|---|
| 1 | (j) | 5 | (h) | 9 | (e) | 13 | (i) |
| 2 | (k) | 6 | (f) | 10 | (o) | 14 | (b) |
| 3 | (n) | 7 | (g) | 11 | (m) | 15 | (l) |
| 4 | (a) | 8 | (c) | 12 | (d) | | |

## Exercises

1  (a) Exports – imports = 164 132 – 184 897 = –20 765.
   (b) The invisible items here comprise services, net investment income, and transfers. (You might like to know that the most important items in services were sea transport, civil aviation, travel, and financial/other services. The item 'net investment income' includes interest, profits and dividends.) The invisible balance is 60 070 – 47 817 + 15 174 – 6526 = 20 901.
   (c) The visible and invisible balances combine to form the current account balance:
       i.e. –20 765 + 20 901 = +136.
   (d) The overall balance of payments must always be zero (given that official transactions are incorporated into the capital account); this is the sum of the current, capital and financial account balances and net errors and omissions: 136 + 421 – 9025 + 8468 = 0.

2  (a) The DD schedule shows the demand for pounds by US residents wishing to buy British goods and assets. The SS schedule shows the supply of pounds from UK residents buying US goods and assets.
   (b) OB is the equilibrium exchange rate with no government intervention. The balance of payments is zero at this point.
   (c) At OA there is an excess demand for pounds (the distance DG) which must be supplied by the Bank of England in exchange for additions to its foreign exchange reserves. The balance of payments is in surplus here.
   (d) At OC there is a balance of payments deficit of an amount EH; the Bank of England must purchase the excess supply of pounds, depleting its foreign exchange reserves in the process.
   (e) In the long run, the balance of payments deficit cannot be sustained, as foreign exchange reserves are finite. To maintain OC as the exchange rate, the authorities must influence DD and SS such that OC is the equilibrium. Experience suggests that promotion of British goods in the USA is unlikely to do much for DD, so perhaps it is more likely that the authorities will discourage imports, perhaps by a contractionary policy. Direct import controls may be tempting but may provoke retaliation from trading partners. We saw similar arguments back in Chapter 22 (see exercise 6(e) of that chapter).

3  See Table A29-1. For more detail, see Section 29-4 of the main text

### Table A29-1   Shocks and balances

| Nature of shock | Internal Boom | Slump | External Current account balance Deficit | Surplus |
|---|---|---|---|---|
| Reduction in autonomous consumption | | ✓ | | ✓ |
| Increase in real exchange rate | | ✓ | ✓ | |
| Tighter monetary and fiscal policy | | ✓ | | ✓ |
| Increase in world income | ✓ | | | ✓ |
| Increase in consumption with easier monetary and fiscal policy | ✓ | | ✓ | |

**4** *(a)* See Table A29-2.

**Table A29-2 Prices and the exchange rate**

|  | US$/£ exchange rate | UK price index | USA price index | Real exchange rate | 'PPP' exchange rate |
|---|---|---|---|---|---|
| 1985 | 1.30 | 75.0 | 82.4 | 1.18 | 1.30 |
| 1986 | 1.47 | 77.5 | 83.9 | 1.36 | 1.28 |
| 1987 | 1.64 | 80.7 | 87.1 | 1.52 | 1.28 |
| 1988 | 1.78 | 84.7 | 90.5 | 1.67 | 1.26 |
| 1989 | 1.64 | 91.3 | 94.9 | 1.58 | 1.23 |
| 1990 | 1.79 | 100.0 | 100.0 | 1.79 | 1.18 |
| 1991 | 1.77 | 105.9 | 104.2 | 1.80 | 1.16 |
| 1992 | 1.77 | 109.8 | 107.4 | 1.81 | 1.16 |
| 1993 | 1.50 | 111.5 | 110.6 | 1.51 | 1.17 |
| 1994 | 1.53 | 114.3 | 113.4 | 1.54 | 1.17 |
| 1995 | 1.58 | 118.2 | 116.6 | 1.60 | 1.17 |
| 1996 | 1.56 | 121.1 | 120.1 | 1.57 | 1.17 |
| 1997 | 1.64 | 124.9 | 122.9 | 1.67 | 1.16 |
| 1998 | 1.66 | 129.1 | 124.8 | 1.72 | 1.14 |

*(b)* See Figure A29-1.
*(c)* Most noticeable is the rise in the real exchange rate in the early part of this period. The divergence between the nominal and real exchange rates represents differences in the inflation rates of the two countries. Notice the sharp fall in the $/£ rate in 1993, following the UK's abrupt departure from the Exchange Rate Mechanism of the European Union. Remember that a rise in the real exchange rate implies a loss of competitiveness of British goods.
*(d)* See Table A29-2.

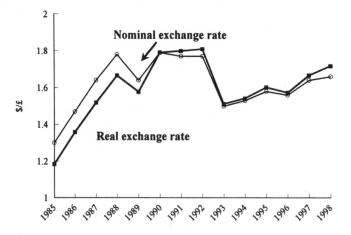

**Figure A29-1 Nominal and real exchange rates**

**5** *(a)* Competitiveness is improved: domestically produced goods become relatively cheap in both internal and external markets.
*(b)* Purchasers take time to adjust to new prices and may have existing contractual commitments; suppliers need time to adjust production levels.
*(c)* The elasticities of demand for imports and exports (the Marshall–Lerner condition), which determine the revenue response to the price changes.

(d) Eventually output will return to the full-employment level: competitiveness is eroded by increases in domestic prices and wages.

(e) A fiscal contraction could alleviate the pressure on aggregate demand.

(f) No: in the long run the supply side of the economy adjusts to the increase in import prices.

(g) The most obvious circumstance is if initially the exchange rate were being held above its equilibrium level, resulting in balance of payments deficits.

6 (a) In a closed economy, both monetary and fiscal policy may have short-run effects. In the long run, real output returns to its 'natural' level, but its composition may be affected by crowding out following fiscal action.

(b) Monetary policy is totally ineffective domestically in this situation, with the authorities committed to maintaining the exchange rate. Fiscal policy has a relatively powerful effect in the short run.

(c) The effectiveness of fiscal policy is much reduced here by the rapid adjustment of interest rates, but monetary policy is rendered more effective.

(d) If capital is not perfectly mobile, interest rates will be slower to adjust, so the crowding-out effect of fiscal policy is retarded: fiscal policy may have short-run effects. Monetary policy is somewhat diluted by the same argument.

7 In all the cases, if the funds are invested in Britain, £112 is the end year result. If funds are invested in the USA there are $170 to be loaned at the current exchange rate. Now read on.

(a) The key missing element is the end-of-year exchange rate, which we need to convert our dollars back into sterling.

(b) Return in $ is 170 × 1.09 = 185.3. Converting to £ at the expected exchange rate yields 185.3/1.5 = £123.5. The depreciation more than compensates for the interest rate differential: you lend in the USA.

(c) 185.3/1.65 is approximately £112. You will be indifferent as to where you lend.

(d) 170 × 1.08 = 183.6; 183.6/1.65 = £111: you invest in Britain.

(e) The expected exchange rate depends upon how you view the current rate as compared with the long-run equilibrium rate. Such expectations could be very volatile, varying with your perception of factors affecting the economy. It matters because there are enormous quantities of internationally footloose funds in search of the best return.

8 If you have any difficulty with these, work out the effect on demand/supply of pounds and thus on the equilibrium exchange rate, perhaps with the help of a diagram.

(a) Sterling appreciates.

(b) Sterling depreciates.

(c) Sterling depreciates.

(d) Sterling appreciates.

(e) Sterling appreciates.

(f) An increase in US interest rates induces capital flows from UK to USA, so there is a depreciation of sterling.

9 All but (e) and (g).

10 (a) 20 per cent.

(b) The real exchange rate will be unchanged in the long run, but the nominal rate will need to fall by 20 per cent to maintain the real rate, given the price change.

(c) A fall.

(d) In Figure A29-2 (overleaf), $e_1$ shows the original equilibrium nominal exchange rate. At time t the shock occurs, domestic interest rates fall, and the nominal exchange rate must fall to prevent capital outflows and to maintain equilibrium in the exchange market. The nominal exchange rate overshoots its new equilibrium value ($e_2$), falling initially to $e_3$ and then gradually adjusting as domestic prices adjust. The path thus involves a jump from $A$ to $B$ at the time of the shock and then adjustment to $C$.

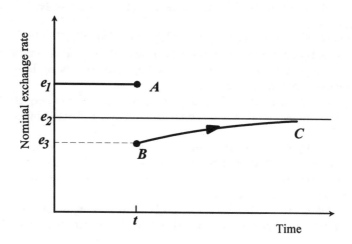

**Figure A29-2    Exchange rate overshooting**

## True/False

1    False: the dollar rate is important, but is not the only relevant rate (see Section 29-1 of the main text).
2    False: there is no guarantee that the chosen rate will turn out to be the equilibrium rate.
3    False: sale and purchase of services and other invisibles belong to the current account (see Section 29-2 of the main text).
4    True.
5    False: we cannot assume *ceteris paribus* here – competitiveness also depends on relative inflation rates (see Section 29-3 of the main text).
6    True: see Section 29-5 of the main text.
7    True: external shocks are more easily accommodated than domestic ones.
8    True: see Section 29-6 of the main text.
9    True: see Section 29-7 of the main text.
10   False: it may deviate in the short run.
11   False: this seems to imply that the government can independently choose both exchange rate and money supply, which is not the case (see Section 29-8 of the main text).
12   True: see Section 29-9 of the main text.

## ECONOMICS IN THE NEWS

This passage is to remind you that macroeconomic policy has effects at the micro level, in the sense that if the authorities maintain the exchange rate at a relatively high level, this will have an effect on the competitiveness of individual firms. Chapter 29 in the main text talks about how equilibrium will be reached.

## Questions for Thought

1    It must be remembered that any rapid depreciation of sterling tends to put upward pressure on prices in the short run. Import prices rise, increasing the demand for domestic substitutes for imported goods. We also expect the demand for exports to increase as competitiveness improves. This, of course, sounds like good news, but if domestic supply is relatively inelastic in the short run, there will inevitably be upward pressure on prices. In other words, if the government is intent on curbing inflation, it may be reluctant to allow the exchange rate to fall rapidly. Of course, once the exchange rate becomes the object of policy action, the government relinquishes independent control of the money supply.

**2** *(a)* An increase in the money supply shifts the *LM* curve to the right, as in Figure A29-3. In the short run, the economy moves to *R1*, *Y1*: income rises, and the interest rate falls. In this position, imports have risen with the increase in income, and capital inflows have diminished with the fall in interest rates. There is thus a balance of payments deficit, and pressure on the exchange rate. In order to maintain the exchange rate, the monetary authorities must buy excess sterling; domestic money supply falls, and the *LM* curve shifts back.

*(b)* An increase in government expenditure shifts the *IS* curve, as in Figure A29-4. The short-run response is to take the economy to *R1*, *Y1*, with a higher level of income and interest rate. The balance of payments is now in surplus, and the monetary authorities are again forced to intervene, this time by selling sterling. Domestic money supply thus increases, and the *LM* curve shifts to the right. Effectively, monetary policy is being forced to reinforce fiscal policy in this situation by the commitment to maintaining the exchange rate. The economy ends up at *R2*, *Y2*, and fiscal policy is seen to be highly effective. Of course, this is largely illusory: in the long run, there will be wage and price adjustment that will move the *LM* curve back to the left. In the long run, the economy returns to the natural rate.

We would like to have gone on to ask you about the effects of fiscal and monetary policy under a floating exchange rate regime. However, this would be ambitious for an exercise of this sort. Remember that the positions of both *IS* and *BP* are likely to depend upon the exchange rate. Thus any policy which alters the exchange rate induces movements in almost everything on the diagram. Feel free to experiment with this, but if you do, we suggest that you draw the diagrams fairly large, as they get a bit congested

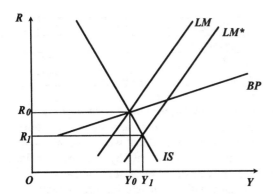

**Figure A29-3   An increase in money supply**

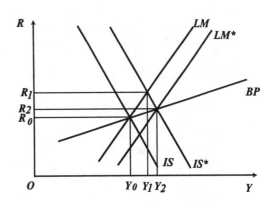

**Figure A29-4    The effects of fiscal policy**

# Chapter 30   Economic Growth

## Important Concepts and Technical Terms

| 1 | *(l)* | 4 | *(i)* | 7 | *(f)* | 10 | *(b)* | 13 | *(k)* |
|---|-------|---|-------|---|-------|----|-------|----|-------|
| 2 | *(j)* | 5 | *(a)* | 8 | *(e)* | 11 | *(m)* | 14 | *(g)* |
| 3 | *(h)* | 6 | *(n)* | 9 | *(d)* | 12 | *(c)* |    |       |

## Exercises

**1** Items *(d)* and *(f)* describe an increase in potential output, and this is what we intend by talking about 'economic growth'. The other items all represent once-for-all changes in output, but not sustained growth.

**2** *(a)* Technical progress: but possibly measured in practice as an increase in capital input, the cost of improvement being registered as investment.

*(b)* Technical progress and/or an increase in capital.

*(c)* An increase in the utilization of labour – but will not be measured as such.

*(d)* This represents an increase in human capital – an improvement in the quality of the labour input.

*(e)* Human capital again – but unmeasured.

*(f)* As with *(b)*, this is a combination of technical progress and an increase in capital input.

Much of the genuine technical progress is embodied either in capital input *((a), (b), (f))* or in labour *((d), (e))*. The extent to which technical progress is properly measured depends to a great extent on how carefully inputs are measured, and clearly the 'residual method' of calculation will be at best imprecise. Notice that item *(c)*, which has nothing to do with technical progress, may well be measured as such.

3   *(a)* Renewable.

   *(b)* Depletable.

   *(c)* Renewable.

   *(d)* Depletable.

   *(e)* Renewable – but with long gestation lags.

   *(f)* We don't usually think of rain as a resource, but the terrible drought in Ethiopia in the mid-1980s and the associated famine remind us of the fragility of the ecological balance. It is said that over-enthusiastic tree-felling had dire effects upon rainfall.

4   *(a)* See Table A30-1.

**Table 30-1   Average annual growth rates (%)**

|         | GNP     | GDP   | GDP  | Output per person-hour in manufacturing | | |
|---------|---------|-------|------|---------|-------|------|
|         | Germany | Italy | UK   | Germany | Italy | UK   |
| 1974–79 | 3.42    | 2.40  | 2.40 | 2.07    | 4.62  | 1.26 |
| 1979–83 | –0.05   | 0.62  | 0.62 | 3.65    | 1.56  | 3.47 |

*(b)* There are a number of criticisms that could be levelled. In particular, we would want to check whether the years chosen correspond to similar points of the business cycle. If not, there may be considerable distortion. If you were to look up our source for the data, you would find that we had simply taken the earliest and latest years in the table, together with one in the middle. Only by extreme coincidence would this be a sensible procedure! For the UK, at least, it seems unlikely that a comparison of 1979 and 1983 would be appropriate. Placing GDP side by side with manufacturing productivity is also unhelpful. The improvement in UK 'productivity' is more likely a result of falling employment than of rising output. For reasons mentioned elsewhere, GDP may be an inaccurate measure of economic growth and welfare.

5   All the items mentioned have been invoked as potential contributors to the slowdown. Inflation is said to have increased uncertainty and thus affected investment, and in addition to have wrought havoc with taxation systems and necessitated anti-inflation policies which have slowed growth. Increasing international competition has reduced profit margins and reduced investment. It has also been suggested that increased under-reporting of transactions has affected measured output. The oil price shock cannot be excluded, having (it is said) diverted resources to R&D and caused premature scrapping of capital equipment. Increased preferences for leisure and against pollution as society moves beyond the industrial age have also received mention. It has also been argued that the revival of economies following the Second World War allowed rapid expansion based on new technology – and that the 1970s represented the return to normal growth rates. We leave you to filter these ideas for yourself, to discover which you think are most reasonable.

6   A policy for growth is one which enables sustained long-run growth of potential output, not mere once-for-all increases. Items *(a), (c), (d),* and *(f)* would thus be appropriate, but not *(b)* or *(e)*.

7   *(a)* $n$.

   *(b)* If capital per worker is low, and the growth rate below the steady-state level, it will also be the case that savings per worker (and hence investment) will be seen to be higher than is needed to maintain that

level of capital per worker. Capital deepening will therefore take place in the short run until the economy returns to the steady state.

*(c)* Not a lot: it just means that the steady-state growth rate is now $n + t$.

*(d)* The convergence hypothesis suggests that poorer countries will be able to take advantage of developments in technology from richer countries, and thus begin to catch up in terms of growth rates.

*(e)* Lack of necessary human capital or other complementary inputs may impede the progress of poor countries, as may an inappropriate political, social or economic environment.

*(f)* If a firm benefits from capital accumulation in other firms, or from the existence of human capital, then the overall growth rate should increase.

*(g)* The nature of beneficial externalities is such that free market forces will result in less production than is socially beneficial. Thus, for example, there may be inadequate human capital formation unless the government intervenes to correct the market failure.

8   *(a)* $n1k$.

*(b)* $H$, where $sy = n1k$.

*(c)* Capital per worker is $OG$, and output per worker is $OB$.

*(d)* The rate of growth of labour, $n1$.

*(e)* With a growth rate of labour $n2$, the steady state is at $E$. Growth of output is more rapid ($n2 > n1$), but more capital accumulation is needed for capital widening, and output per worker is lower in the new steady state.

*(f)* Higher savings may allow higher capital and output per worker, but the long-run growth path is still constrained by labour force growth in the neo-classical growth model.

9   From points $C, D, E$, the economy will converge on $k2$. At $E$, savings and investment are insufficient to maintain the capital:labour ratio, and the economy shrinks. From any point between $k1$ and $k2$, capital-deepening takes place, and the economy moves towards $k2$ – however close to $k1$ we start. Below $k1$, savings and investment are again insufficient to maintain the capital:labour ratio, and the economy shrinks. Countries in this region are stick in a low-level equilibrium trap from which they cannot escape because they cannot generate a surplus for savings and investment. Notice that if an economy happens to *start* at $k1$, it could in principle remain there. However, this is a highly unstable position, as any move away from this point in either direction, and the economy will start to converge The problem for a number of less-developed countries is in getting to the right of $k1$. For some more details, see Box 30-2 in the main text.

# True/False

1   False: in some countries (e.g. Brazil) there may be great inequality of income distribution (see Section 30-1 of the main text).

2   True.

3   False: part of investment is for replacement of existing capital (see Section 30-2 of the main text).

4   True: see Section 30-3 of the main text.

5   False: this rather Malthusian argument ignores the potential for productivity changes (see Section 30-4 of the main text).

6   True: see Section 30-7 of the main text.

7   True: see Section 30-4 of the main text.

8   False: capital deepening increases capital per worker; it is capital widening that is needed to extend the capital stock as the labour force grows.

9   False: in neoclassical growth theory, higher savings may yield a once-for-all increase in real output, but will not affect long-run growth: see Section 30-4 of the main text.

10   False: unfortunately we cannot rely on convergence taking place in reality. Some countries are more able than others to take advantage of capital accumulation and technical progress (see Section 30-6 of the main text).

11   True: this is at the heart of the theory of endogenous growth: see Section 30-7 of the main text.

12 True: see Box 30-3 in the main text, and an article by Peter Smith ('Worlds apart – how the Four Tigers have leapt forward') in the *Economic Review,* February 1997.

# ECONOMICS IN THE NEWS

1  The reference to intellectual property reflects the importance of human resources in the growth of the Asian economies since the mid-1960s. It has been widely argued that the presence of a well-disciplined and skilled labour force has been a significant factor in enabling Asian economies to make use of technology developed elsewhere. In other words, convergence has been greatly assisted by the existence of human capital. This is in contrast to many countries elsewhere in the world, especially in sub-Saharan Africa. The passage argues that this will be equally, if not more important in the future, as technology becomes even more critical in the information economy of the future.

2  Commentators on the Asian economies have often argued that it is significant that the most successful economies have been concentrated in the Asian region. Sometimes, this has been ascribed to the cultural values that these societies have in common. In particular, it has been argued that a willingness of the population to place their trust in the government has contributed to rapid growth, by enabling a rapid restructuring of economies. Another view of this is that there may be externalities at work – that when one economy in a region begins to grow rapidly, other nearby countries will be drawn in to share that success. This is discussed in Section 30-7 of the main text.

3  The Asian crisis that interrupted the success story of the Asian Tigers in 1997 revealed some flaws in their financial systems. In particular, it has been argued that there had been inadequate financial regulation, so that funds were not always being channelled into productive uses, but into projects such as real estate that were not directly contributing to growth. Once this became apparent, there were large outflows of foreign capital as investors tried to protect their positions. This underlines the importance of sound market environments to enable sustainable growth to take place. Other commentators have argued that if the success of these economies was based on sound economic fundamentals, then rapid growth would reassert itself once the crisis had blown over.

## Questions for Thought

1  *Some hints:* What happens to price as a resource becomes more scarce? How does this affect incentives? On the matter of a renewable resource, think about short-run/long-run and private/social costs aspects.

2  The convergence hypothesis argues that poor countries are likely to be able to grow at a rate above the average, whereas rich countries will grow more slowly. Thus in the long run growth rates will converge. The data of Table 30-2 does not seem to lend a great deal of support to this argument. During the 1980s, many of the world's low-income countries suffered negative growth rates, rather than showing any signs of catch-up. There are, of course, exceptions to this: in the table Singapore, Korea, Thailand and China all grew at more than satisfactory rates. The final columns of the table hint at the importance of physical and human capital in the growth process. It could be argued that the slipstreaming effect (whereby poor countries may be able to benefit from technology developed in the richer countries) is not accessible to very low-income countries, which have low levels of human capital, or perhaps inappropriate economic, social, cultural or political environments (see Box 30-3 in the main text for some further data). Note that the measurement of GDP *per capita* in PPP\$ attempts to correct the GNP measure for distortions in official exchange rates.

3  The role of the government in promoting economic growth must flow from the theoretical arguments. If the steady-state growth path depends only on labour force growth, then the government's role may be extremely limited. However, if there are significant capital externalities, or other forms of market failure, then intervention may be justified, perhaps in subsidization of human capital formation, physical capital accumulation or research and development.

# Chapter 31 The Business Cycle

## Important Concepts and Technical Terms

| | | | | | | | |
|---|---|---|---|---|---|---|---|
| 1 | *(e)* | 4 | *(f)* | 7 | *(c)* | 10 | *(h)* |
| 2 | *(d)* | 5 | *(a)* | 8 | *(i)* | 11 | *(g)* |
| 3 | *(b)* | 6 | *(j)* | 9 | *(l)* | 12 | *(k)* |

## Exercises

1  *A* is the slump phase, being the trough of the cycle;
   *B*: recovery;
   *C*: boom;
   *D*: boom – the peak of the cycle;
   *E*: recession;
   *F*: slump – the trough again.
   The horizontal distance from *A* to *F* represents the (trough to trough) length of the cycle.

2  All of them, to some degree, although *(b)* is of course crucial in the investment decision. Indeed, we might argue that the other factors listed all have some influence on the way in which firms will perceive *(b)*. Some also affect the cost of borrowing: for instance, it may be less costly to finance investment from past profits than by borrowing in the market. However, ultimately, it is firms' expectations about the future which will be most important. The multiplier-accelerator model shows that if firms form expectations with reference to past output growth (factor *(e)*), then cycles in activity may be generated (see Section 31-2 in the main text for more detailed discussion).

3  See Table A31-1. With $v = 0.2$, the economy converges quite rapidly on the new equilibrium, but with $v = 0.8$, the adjustment path is cyclical and takes a lot longer. Other values of $v$ and $c$ can induce explosive cycles which never allow the economy to reach the new equilibrium.

**Table A31-1   A multiplier-accelerator model**

| Time period | $v = 0.2$ | | | $v = 0.8$ | | |
|---|---|---|---|---|---|---|
| | C | I | Y | C | I | Y |
| 0 | 30 | 30 | 60 | 30 | 30 | 60 |
| 1 | 30 | 40 | 70 | 30 | 40 | 70 |
| 2 | 35 | 42 | 77 | 35 | 48 | 83 |
| 3 | 38.5 | 41.4 | 79.9 | 41.5 | 50.4 | 91.9 |
| 4 | 39.95 | 40.58 | 80.53 | 45.95 | 47.12 | 93.07 |
| 5 | 40.26 | 40.13 | 80.39 | 46.54 | 40.94 | 87.48 |
| 6 | 40.20 | 39.97 | 80.17 | 43.74 | 35.52 | 79.26 |

4  *(a)*  The choice point would be at the tangency of $U_0$ and the *PPF*, at point *A* in Figure A31-1 overleaf. Notice that we are assuming here that the 'price line' would have the appropriate slope to encourage this choice.

   *(b)*  The effect would be to move out the *PPF*, as shown in Figure A31-1.

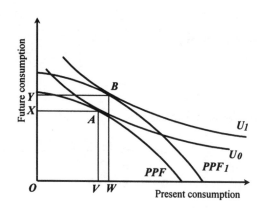

**Figure A31-1    A temporary shock**

*(c)* Present consumption moves from *OV* to *OW*, as the choice point moves from *A* to *B*: in other words, given these curves the increase in production possibilities has very little effect on present consumption.

*(d)* However, future consumption increases substantially from *OX* to *OY*. Essentially, what is happening is that the society is devoting more resources to investment in the present, in order to consume more in the future.

*(e)* In the long run, this increase in investment is likely to shift the *PPF* even further, by expanding the production possibilities of the society.

*(f)* This reaction by society to the change in production possibilities occurs because the indifference curves between present and future consumption are relatively 'flat', reflecting a preference for future, rather than present consumption. Had these curves been relatively much more steep, such that the tangency point came further to the right, then preferences would have much more biased towards present consumption. In these circumstances, the reaction to the change in the *PPF* would have been much more rapid, in the sense that more resources would have been devoted to present consumption; the long-run effects would then be less marked.

*(g)* The analysis above suggests that temporary shocks may have persistent effects through time. If successive shocks move the *PPF* in different directions, then cycles may result from this persistence.

5    *(a):* may help to explain persistence, in the sense that if people are subject to diminishing marginal utility of income, they may not feel the need to increase present consumption. However, if people show a strong preference for consumption in the present *(b)*, then the case for persistence is much weakened. Factor *(c)* affects the shape of the *PPF* between present and future consumption. If there are many opportunities which allow present resources to be translated into future consumption opportunities, then this will tend to add to persistence. If the motivation to leave bequests is strong, then again there is a sense in which this implies a preference for future rather than present consumption – so persistence may occur. Ricardian equivalence (encountered in Chapter 25) seems at first to be out of place in the present discussion. However, if the 'shock' that jolts the economy is the result of a government intervention that people believe to be temporary, then they will act accordingly. Tax cuts intended to affect present consumption may not have that effect, but lead to an increase in savings.

6    This exercise is like a parable of the 1980s. In the boom of the mid-1980s, consumers borrowed heavily, and savings fell. This was noticeable not only in the UK, but also in other industrial economies such as the USA and Japan. Household indebtedness rose, and asset prices fell. It is argued that recovery from the recession was delayed as consumers tried to remedy their debt positions (see Section 31-5 of the main text).

7    All of them.

8    The detailed year-to-year variations in growth rates do not suggest that all three economies follow precisely the same pattern throughout the period. The UK and USA both hit recession in 1991, but Spain was later (1993). The dip in the UK growth rate in 1998 was not mirrored in the other two countries. A longer time span is needed to search for commonalities between countries. See also Figure 31-3 in the main text, which shows common cycles in the EU, the USA, and Japan using quarterly data, which show rather more

variation than the annual averages shown in Figure A20-2 in this volume. Figure 31-4 in the main text focuses on business cycles in countries within the EU.

## True/False

1 Trueish – so long as we can afford to take a long-run view. Very often, the short-run problems are more obvious.
2 False: there may be an association between the two, but for an explanation we need to understand why demand may fluctuate (see Section 31-1 of the main text).
3 False: it is always tempting to want to blame the politicians for everything, but the 'political business cycle' does not provide a full explanation of cyclical fluctuations in economic behaviour.
4 False: see Section 31-2 of the main text.
5 True.
6 False: the hypothesis that the economy always moves rapidly to equilibrium does not prevent us from having a theory which says that potential output itself may be subject to fluctuations.
7 False: this is not what is observed in practice. See the discussion of the 'real wage puzzle' in Box 31-1 of the main text.
8 True: see Section 31-3 of the main text.
9 False: the opposite is the case: see Section 31-3 of the main text.
10 True: see Section 31-4 of the main text.
11 Trueish: this was a factor (see Section 31-5 in the main text), but probably not the only one. It is worth noting that parallel arguments have been advanced to explain the problems faced by low-income countries following heavy borrowing in international markets in the late 1970s. We will get to this in Chapter 36.

## ECONOMICS IN THE NEWS

1 Inventory cycles are discussed in section 31-2 of the main text. In recent years, the use of production techniques such as Supply Chain Management and Just-In-Time have changed the way in which firms view inventories. For instance, instead of holding large stocks of component parts in a factory, a firm may order them 'just-in-time' to feed into the production line. This makes for increased flexibility in the production process, so that if there is a reduction in demand, firms are more flexible in responding. This is just one way in which supply has become more elastic – more able to change in response to demand or price movements. The passage argues that this also has implications for inflation
2 The argument on inflation is that cycles can be exaggerated – or even initiated – by government reactions to inflation. Responding too quickly to an increase in the inflation rate by stemming aggregate demand may deepen a recession. This temptation is removed when inflation is low

## Questions for Thought

1 Hysteresis (introduced in Chapter 27) is another story about the way in which temporary shocks may have persistent effects.
2 (a) OA – the natural rate.
  (b) I3.
  (c) An expansion of aggregate demand could exploit the short-run Phillips trade-off and take the economy to point B on I4.
  (d) Back to the natural rate at D.
  (e) I2: worse than originally because inflation is higher.
  (f) Sliding 'up' SPC1 does not produce much gain and cannot be sustained anyway – better to contract aggregate demand and move to point F (making people worse off), recognizing that as expectations adjust, the economy returns to A – hopefully in time to slide back up to B as the next election comes round!
  (g) The Thatcher and Major administrations' unswerving commitment to the long run could not have countenanced such a procedure – indeed, the very existence of the short-run trade-off has been questioned.

# Chapter 32   Macroeconomics: Where Do We Stand?

## Important Concepts and Technical Terms

| | | | | | | | |
|---|---|---|---|---|---|---|---|
| 1 | *(i)* | 4 | *(h)* | 7 | *(g)* | 10 | *(k)* |
| 2 | *(j)* | 5 | *(d)* | 8 | *(a)* | 11 | *(e)* |
| 3 | *(f)* | 6 | *(b)* | 9 | *(c)* | 12 | *(l)* |

## Exercises

1   All of them: see Section 32-1 in the main text.

2   *(a)* Gradualist monetarist.
   *(b)* Extreme Keynesian.
   *(c)* New Classical.
   *(d)* Moderate Keynesian.
   *(e)* Extreme Keynesian.
   *(f)* Rational expectations are not uniquely identified with a single school. It is an essential assumption of the New Classical macroeconomics, but there are also devotees in the Gradualist monetarist and Moderate Keynesian groups.

3   *(a)* We cannot of course supply you with an answer to this: apart from anything else, we don't know when you are reading it!
   *(b)* Most people asked for a casual guess about inflation will think back to what inflation has been in the last year – perhaps with an adjustment for current conditions or recent TV reports. The dominance of past experience in this process suggests extrapolative expectations.
   *(c)* We always take more care when it matters! Whether people research sufficiently thoroughly to justify the rational expectations hypothesis is, however, more contentious.

4   *(a)* Real wage *OB*, unemployment *EG* – the natural rate.
   *(b)* Given real wage inflexibility, the real wage could remain at *OB* and unemployment would rise to *CG*.
   *(c)* In the 'medium' term, the market could still be at real wage *OB*, unemployment *CG*; but in the long run, adjustment would take the real wage to *OA* and unemployment to *DF*. The two groups would differ in their definitions of 'medium' and 'long' term, with the Gradualist expecting the long run to be closer.
   *(d)* The New Classicals would expect rapid adjustment to the new equilibrium with real wage *OA*, unemployment at the new natural rate *DF*.
   *(e)* The Extreme Keynesians would want demand management to combat the unemployment, which they view as being due to deficient demand. The Moderate Keynesians would perhaps want to allow some demand management to alleviate the short-run problem, or incomes policy to speed the adjustment – together with some long-run supply-side policies also. The Gradualists would probably want to ride out the short-run crisis and concentrate on long-run supply-side policies. The New Classicals would not recognize the short-run problem, but *might* wish to try to reduce the natural rate of unemployment.
   *(f)* Under hysteresis, the temporary fall in *LD* could lead to a permanent shift in *AJ*, and a new long-run equilibrium with a lower employment level. See exercise 9 of Chapter 27.

5   *(a)* Gradualist.
   *(b)* New Classical.
   *(c)* Extreme Keynesian.
   *(d)* Moderate Keynesian.
   *(e)* Moderate Keynesian.

6   *(d)*, *(b)*, *(a)*, *(c)*.
   The foreign exchange market clears very rapidly indeed – at least, under floating exchange rates. The money market is hardly less quick. The goods market is more sluggish for a number of reasons – remember the

oligopoly models of Chapter 10? There are also the menu costs of changing prices. The labour market is likely to be the slowest. For more detail, see Box 32-1 of the main text.

7   *(a)* Equilibrium would be at the intersection of *LM0* and *IS* in Figure A32-1, with rate of interest *OB* and real output *OC*. The important thing to notice about this diagram is the relative slope of *IS* and *LM* curves. In particular, the *IS* curve has been drawn to be almost vertical. This reflects the assumption of the Extreme Keynesians that investment will be highly insensitive to the rate of interest when the economy is in deep recession.

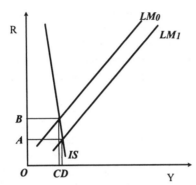

**Figure A32-1   *IS-LM* in recession: an extreme Keynesian view**

   *(b)* If prices were to be flexible downwards, then we would look for a rightward shift of the *LM* curve, because a fall in the price level would imply an increase in real money supply. Thus *LM* might be seen to move from *LM0* to *LM1*. However, given the steepness of the *IS* curve, this shift has little effect on output, which increases only slightly from *OC* to *OD*. Meanwhile, a substantial fall in the rate of interest (from *OB* to *OA*) is needed in order to restore equilibrium.

   *(c)* A monetary expansion would have just the same effect as in *(b)*, and is ineffectual in this situation.

   *(d)* A fiscal expansion that shifted the *IS* curve to the right would have a far greater impact, and help to pull the economy out of recession: if you are prepared to accept the Extreme Keynesian argument on which this diagram is based.

   *(e)* A major difference would be in the relative slopes of *IS* and *LM* in the figure. Under New Classical or Gradualist monetarist views, the *LM* curve would be much steeper – if not vertical – and the *IS* curve would be much flatter, reflecting the view that investment (and consumption) would be much more sensitive to changes in the rate of interest. Sketch such a diagram for yourself, and see the effect of these alternative assumptions.

8   You may find that your views do not place you firmly in any one school. This is not surprising, as there are considerable grey areas between our snapshots – which is why we refer to it as a spectrum.

## True/False

1   False: there are some positive issues which would command general agreement, but there are others where a variety of opinion exists (see Section 32-1 of the main text).

2   False: the statement presumes that demand deficiency is the only cause of unemployment. Some economists would attribute much of the rise to an increase in the natural rate.

3   True: see Section 32-2 of the main text.

4   True.

5   False: they would argue that output and employment may change in the short run but will gradually readjust to full employment. It is prices that are affected in the long run (see Section 32-3 of the main text).

6   True.

7   False: they would recognize the potential importance of supply-side policies in the long-run while wishing to carry out stabilization in the short run (see Section 32-4 of the main text).

8   True.

**9** True: see Section 32-5 of the main text.
**10** False: see Section 32-6 of the main text.

## ECONOMICS IN THE NEWS

**1** The debate in the passage rests in part on whether it was the 1970s and 1980s that were special cases, or whether it was the 1950s and 1960s. Certainly it seems that Keynesian demand management was effective during the earlier of these periods, at least with the benefit of hindsight. Notice that the global economic environment ahs changed substantially in the post-war period, as has our perception of macroeconomic policy. Another significant difference between the 1950s/60s and the 1970s/80s was the exchange rate regime (which we will explore in Chapter 34). This may be significant, because the effectiveness of monetary and fiscal policy can be seen to be influenced by whether or not the government is following an exchange rate target.

**2** What Deanne Julius was arguing in the article was that we must be careful in trying to use the past to predict the future. However, as economists we believe that there are some fundamental economic relationships that remain valid even in a changing economic world. This makes us aware of the possibility that parameters may change as conditions change. Economics can also help to identify changing relationships, and allow us to make sense of them. What all this suggests is that economics is vital in enabling us to gain better understanding of the economic world about us, and that only with the help of economic analysis can we hope to anticipate future changes in the macroeconomy.

## Questions for Thought

**1** This proposition rests on the belief that the economy will stabilize itself within a reasonable time span if left alone. In addition, it may be argued that misguided or mistimed policy action may have a destabilizing effect.

**2** The debate about 'rules versus discretion' has been a long-lasting one. The discussion of the problems of fine-tuning (Chapter 22) is worth reviewing, as it highlights some of the problems of discretionary policy. Friedman and other Gradualists are heavily committed to the idea of pre-set rules.

**3** No comment.

## Chapter 33   International Trade and Commercial Policy

### Important Concepts and Technical Terms

| | | | | | | | |
|---|---|---|---|---|---|---|---|
| 1 | *(b)* | 4 | *(f)* | 7 | *(i)* | 10 | *(g)* |
| 2 | *(e)* | 5 | *(a)* | 8 | *(d)* | 11 | *(h)* |
| 3 | *(k)* | 6 | *(l)* | 9 | *(c)* | 12 | *(j)* |

### Exercises

**1** *(a)* In general, goods in the last two categories tend to require relatively capital-intensive production techniques – which explains why countries like Ethiopia and the Côte-d'Ivoire have a low concentration of exports in these commodities. 'Other primary commodities' comprises mainly agricultural produce. The importance of oil to Saudi Arabia stands out. Trinidad's exports are also dominated by oil and pitch. The North Sea oil effect is apparent for the UK. The relatively labour-intensive nature of the Hong Kong economy can also be seen – together with its relative lack of natural resources. It turns out that Hong Kong and Singapore are both rather special cases when it comes to exports. This is discussed further in Chapter 36.

*(b)* In recent years the categories 'other primary commodities' and 'textiles and clothing' have been declining in relative importance while the other categories have been on the increase. The change in 'fuels' has been due in part to the oil price changes, but engineering and road vehicles have become increasingly important without such help from prices. If these trends continue, we would expect prospects to be good for Japan, Germany, and the UK, but poor for Ethiopia and the Côte d'Ivoire. However,...

*(c)* ...it is dangerous to read too much into these figures. In particular, the commodity groups are broad in coverage. No doubt there are some goods within 'other manufacturing' or 'other primary commodities' whose prospects are markedly different from the norm. We would thus need more detailed information about the commodities exported by each country. In addition, we are given only percentage shares, which do not provide clues to the importance of exports to each country. For instance, merchandise exports for Ethiopia comprised only 3.5 per cent of GDP in 1993, compared with 22.0 per cent in the UK. (In Singapore the figure was about 134 per cent – but that is another story!)

**2** *(a)* Anywaria has the absolute advantage, having lower unit labour requirements for each good.

*(b)* The opportunity cost of a unit of bicycle output is 2 units of boots in Anywaria and 3 units in Someland. The opportunity cost of a unit of boots output is 1/2 a unit of bicycles in Anywaria and 1/3 of a unit in Someland.

*(c)* Anywaria has the comparative advantage in bicycles, having the lower opportunity cost.

*(d)* See Table A33-1.

*(e)* See Table A33-2.

**Table A33-1**
**Production of bicycles and boots, no trade case**

|  | Anywaria | Someland | 'World' output |
|---|---|---|---|
| Bicycles | 100 | 50 | 150 |
| Boots | 200 | 150 | 350 |

**Table A33-2**
**Production of bicycles and boots**

|  | Anywaria | Someland | 'World' output |
|---|---|---|---|
| Bicycles | 150 | – | 150 |
| Boots | 100 | 300 | 400 |

World output of bicycles has been maintained at the no-trade level, but it has proved possible to increase the output of boots from 350 to 400 units. How these gains are distributed between the two economies is of course a separate issue. Indeed, the very feasibility of trade may depend on the exchange rate if the two countries do not share a common currency (see exercise 3).

*(f)* In Figure A33-1, *PPFA* and *PPFS* represent the production possibility frontiers for Anywaria and Someland, respectively. The key element which reveals the potential gains from trade is the difference in the slope of the two curves, reflecting the difference in opportunity costs.

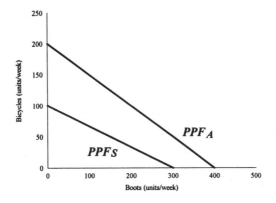

**Figure A33-1   Production possibilities for Anywaria and Someland**

3  (a)  Unit labour costs:
        Bicycles: A$300 in Anywaria, S$540 in Someland.
        Boots: A$150 in Anywaria, S$180 in Someland.
    (b)

|          | Anywaria | Someland |
|----------|----------|----------|
| Bicycles | 540      | 540      |
| Boots    | 270      | 180      |

    (c)

|          | Anywaria | Someland |
|----------|----------|----------|
| Bicycles | 360      | 540      |
| Boots    | 180      | 180      |

    (d) Trade will take place only at exchange rates between the values analysed in parts *(b)* and *(c)*, as one-way trade is not viable. With an exchange rate above A$1.8 = S$1, there would be no demand for Anywaria produce; below A$1.2, there is no demand for Somelandish output.
    (e) The equilibrium exchange rate will depend upon the size of demand for the goods in the two economies (see Section 33-2 of the main text).

4  *(a)*, *(b)*, and *(d)* encourage intra-industry trade, but *(c)*, *(e)*, and *(f)* work against it.

5  *(c)* is a first-best argument; *(b)*, *(d)*, and *(f)* are second-best arguments – in each case there are preferable and more direct methods of achieving the desired object; *(e)* is at best a second-best argument and may join *(a)* as a non-argument.

6  All of the factors mentioned are likely to ensue as a result of the imposition of tariffs. The question that remains is whether the effects will be adverse or not. In some cases, the answer is clear: tariffs impose resource and other costs on society and there is a deadweight loss arising from items *(b)* and *(e)*. Factor *(d)* is also part of this: society will be worse off because it is not making the best of its existing pattern of comparative advantage. If there is retaliation in export markets *(a)*, then this exacerbates the situation, in particular wiping out any gains that might have accrued from reducing import penetration *(f)*, which in any case is obtained at the cost of domestic inefficiency in production. The fact that imposing a tariff generates revenue for the authorities is a rather different argument. The proportion of government revenue that comes from taxes on international trade in the advanced industrial economies is very small. However, for a number of less developed countries who find raising tax revenue to be a difficult problem, tariffs are an attractive proposition, as they are easier to administer than some other forms of tax. Certainly, the potential loss of tariff revenue is a considerable stumbling block for some countries when they begin to consider trade liberalization.

7  (a) Price *OB* (= world price), imports *FP* (the excess of domestic demand over domestic supply at this price).
    (b) Price *OC*, imports *JM*.
    (c) *EG*.
    (d) *BCML*.
    (e) Tariff revenue *HJML*, rents *BCJF*.
    (f) *FHJ* remains: this is the extra that society spends by producing cars domestically rather than importing them at the world price.
    (g) *LMP*.
    (h) *FHJ+LMP*.

8  (a) Price *OA*, exports *GJ*.
    (b) Price *OB*, exports *EM*.
    (c) *HK*.
    (d) *CF*.

*(e)* *DEG.*

*(f)* *JLM.*

*(g)* It is sometimes argued that economic growth can take place only if accompanied by an expansion of aggregate demand. If the authorities perceive the domestic market to be too limited, they may wish to encourage exports – but notice that part of the increase achieved is at the expense of domestic consumption.

*(h)* A production subsidy would keep the domestic price at *OA*; the social cost would then be *JLM* rather than *JLM* + *DEG* (see Section 33-8 of the main text).

**9** *(a)* *DM.*

*(b)* *OB.*

*(c)* Domestic production increases from *OC* to *OE*, but consumption falls from *OL* to *OH*.

*(d)* If this diagram had been describing a tariff, this area would have represented tariff revenue. With a quota, this revenue accrues either to foreign suppliers or to domestic importers.

*(e)* *DFG* + *JKM* + the proportion of *FGJK* accruing to foreign suppliers.

*(f)* The principal gainers from this sort of policy are the producers: the domestic producers who expand output in response to the higher price they receive, earning extra rents. Foreign producers also gain in the form of rents. You might be interested to know that export licences in Hong Kong in connection with this sort of 'Voluntary Export Restraint' (VER) policy have been tradable, and it has been estimated by the World Bank that rents from VERs on clothing alone comprised 1.4 per cent of Hong Kong's GDP in 1982–83! The losers? Society as a whole in the importing country, especially consumers, who must pay a higher price and lose consumer surplus.

**10** *(a)* With wodgets being priced at the world price of £3, domestic producers supply $1000 \times p = 3000$ wodgets. However, demand is $10000 - (1000 \times 3) = 7000$. Imports will thus be $7000 - 3000 = 4000$.

*(b)* We already calculated domestic supply at 3000 wodgets.

*(c)* With a £2 tariff, the domestic price is £5, at which producers will supply 5000 wodgets.

*(d)* At the higher domestic price, demand falls to 5000 wodgets. Domestic producers now supply the entire domestic market, imports are zero ... and the government thus gets no revenue at all.

*(e)* The loss of consumer surplus is the area of the triangle with 'height' £2 and 'base' 2000 units of wodgets – i.e. the loss is £2000. As it happens, in this particular instance the production inefficiency triangle is the same size. This need not be the case – it depends on the elasticities of demand and supply. If you find all this difficult to envisage, try sketching the diagram.

## True/False

**1** True: see Section 33-1 of the main text.

**2** True: see Table 33-5 in the main text – but this would not be typical of less developed countries in other parts of the world.

**3** False: it is necessary for one country to have an absolute advantage in the production of at least one commodity, but it is not sufficient – comparative advantage is also important (see Section 33-2 of the main text).

**4** True.

**5** True.

**6** False: see Section 33-3 of the main text.

**7** False: comparative advantage ensures that potentially everyone may be better off but cannot guarantee that they will actually be so (see Section 33-4 of the main text).

**8** False: see Section 33-5 of the main text.

**9** True.

**10** False: it is a common argument but not a powerful one, and has often been misused (see Section 33-6 of the main text).

**11** True: see Section 33-7 of the main text.

**12** True: this is very common (see Section 33-8 of the main text).

## ECONOMICS IN THE NEWS

1    One of the key phrases in the passage is the reference to Germany as '...one of the world's most costly and organized labour markets...'. One might think that there is a danger that German workers will price themselves out of employment, but how real is that? After all, if productivity is higher in Germany, or if the workers are more highly skilled, or better disciplined, then this will clearly affect the viability of German manufacturing. If the labour market can be flexible, and if the economy can adapt to the changing pattern of international comparative advantage, then why should there be a problem?

2    For China, the picture may be very different. The suggestion in the passage is that labour in China is very cheap, but less skilled than in Germany. The tactic may thus be to look for improvements in human capital.

## Questions for Thought

1    Comparative advantage arguments indicate that there are gains to be made from free trade. However, Portugal may perceive that within the context of the EU, they have a comparative advantage in textiles, so stand to gain from facing free trade *within* Europe with the bonus of being protected from competition from outside. We would expect Europe as a whole to suffer from increasing protectionism, having to buy from the relatively high-cost Portuguese producers (high-cost relative to the rest of the world, that is).

2   *(a)*  The choice point is at *G*; production and consumption are *OF* units of good *X* and *OB* units of good *Y*. We saw how this point is reached in Chapter 19.

     *(b)*  If the world price ratio is equal to the domestic ratio, then country *A* holds no comparative advantage in the production of either good and there is no incentive for trade to take place.

     *(c)*  With the world price ratio at *RS*, a unit of good *X* exchanges for more units of good *Y* in the world market than at home, implying that country *A* has a comparative advantage in the production of good *X*.

     *(d)*  Country *A* can now produce at point *J*, making *OH* units of *X* and *OA* of *Y*. By trading at the world price ratio, country *A* can consume at point *E*, consuming *OD* of *X* and *OC* of *Y*. In the process, the economy moves to a higher indifference curve.

     *(e)*  Country *A* exports *DH* units of *X* and imports *AC* of *Y*.

     *(f)*  *OM* represents the terms of trade when the countries are at point *W*. This can be seen to be the equilibrium terms of trade – the point where the offer curves intersect represents the point at which the offers made by the two countries are consistent.

## Chapter 34   The International Monetary System

## Important Concepts and Technical Terms

| | | | | | | | |
|---|---|---|---|---|---|---|---|
| 1 | *(c)* | 4 | *(g)* | 7 | *(j)* | 10 | *(i)* |
| 2 | *(a)* | 5 | *(h)* | 8 | *(f)* | 11 | *(b)* |
| 3 | *(k)* | 6 | *(l)* | 9 | *(d)* | 12 | *(e)* |

## Exercises

1  *(a)*  Managed float.

    *(b)*  Gold standard.

    *(c)*  Adjustable peg.

    *(d)*  Adjustable peg (or conceivably a managed float in which the authorities have been holding up the exchange rate for an extended period).

*(e)* Clean float.

*(f)* Gold standard.

*(g)* Managed float.

*(h)* Clean or managed float: in either case, the nominal exchange rate tends to follow the PPP path in the long run.

**2** *(a)* 20.67 / 4.25 = 4.86.

*(b)* 20 ounces.

*(c)* £85 converts to $510, which buys 24.67 ounces of gold.

*(d)* 24.67 ounces of gold is worth £104.85 at the UK price – it would then pay to repeat the exercise, selling gold in Britain, converting to dollars, and buying gold in the US.

*(e)* Such a rate could hold only in the very short run because of the potential return from the sort of transactions already examined.

*(f)* With the exchange rate below the gold parity rate, the reverse set of transactions becomes profitable, selling gold in the USA and buying gold in the UK.

*(g)* *OB:* the equilibrium rate.

*(h)* *OC* is the rate at which everyone wants to convert into dollars, so demand for pounds falls to zero.

*(i)* Between *OA* and *OC* it is possible for the exchange rate to be out of equilibrium without all agents indulging in gold and currency transactions. This band arises because there are transaction costs – either brokerage or transport. It costs to ship gold about the world.

**3** *(a)* Exports fall and the balance of payments moves into deficit.

*(b)* Aggregate demand falls and so too will output and employment if wages and prices are slow to adjust.

*(c)* As we have seen, the exchange rate can never move far away from the gold parity rate. The balance of payments deficit must be matched by a fall in the UK gold reserves.

*(d)* Domestic money supply must fall to preserve 100 per cent gold backing. This tends to push up interest rates, further depressing aggregate demand.

*(e)* Eventually wages and prices must adjust, and this will lead to an improvement in British competitiveness. This continues until internal and external balance are restored.

*(f)* Adjustment in the US mirrors that in the UK – the balance of payments moves into surplus, aggregate demand increases, gold reserves and money supply rise, wages and prices are pushed up, competitiveness falls as internal and external balance are restored.

**4** *(a)* The restrictive monetary policy leads to high interest rates and to an appreciation of *A*'s exchange rate.

*(b)* Competitiveness declines, deepening the transitional fall in output and employment.

*(c)* As competitiveness in *A* declines, so it rises in *B* and *C*, as their exchange rates have depreciated. There is thus some upward pressure on prices.

*(d)* *B*'s exchange rate now appreciates.

*(e)* *A*'s exchange rate now falls relative to *B* and *C*, threatening upward pressure on prices.

*(f)* If all three countries were to co-ordinate their policies, the see-saw effect on exchange rates would be avoided and there would be much more stability. There would be less speculative movement in financial capital. In this more stable environment, it may well be that the transitional cost of anti-inflation policy would be less strong and less long lasting.

**5** *(c)* and *(f)* were features of the dollar standard, but none of the other items mentioned.

**6** Only *(a)* and *(b)* are valid under a clean float.

**7** *(c)* is a feature only of a clean float.

**8** *(a)* Arguably, the Bretton Woods system broke down because it could not cope with nominal and real strains. It has been argued that whereas flexible exchange rates did manage to cope reasonably well with the oil-price shocks, a fixed rate scheme would have been too rigid to enable economies to ride the storm. Thus, in terms of robustness in the face of shocks, the evidence probably favours a flexible system.

*(b)* As far as stability is concerned, the evidence is mixed. We could argue that only the fixed rate system offers fundamental stability, in the sense that future nominal exchange rates are known to participants in international trade. On the other hand, under a flexible rate regime, there is potential volatility. This argument is less strong than it seems at first, for a number of reasons. First, fixed rate regimes force any instability in markets to be accommodated elsewhere in the system: in other words, stability of the

nominal exchange rate is not the only dimension of stability. Second, it is real exchange rates that are crucial in determining competitiveness, not just the nominal rates. Thirdly, we might argue that the instability caused by exchange rate realignments in a fixed rate system are more destabilizing than the regular small movements under a floating rate system.

*(c)* Independence may not always be a good thing. One of the most powerful arguments in favour of a fixed exchange rate system is that it enforces financial discipline upon countries, and encourages policy co-ordination.

*(d)* To the extent that governments introduce protectionist measures in an attempt to bolster inappropriate exchange rates, we may view fixed rate regimes as having undesirable effects. However, many commentators might argue that governments can always find misguided policies to adopt, and that the exchange rate regime in operation will have little influence.

## True/False

1   False: governments bent the rules at times (see Section 34-2 of the main text).
2   True: see Box 34-1 of the main text.
3   True: see Section 34-3 of the main text.
4   False: speculators were well aware that a country experiencing balance of payments deficits was liable to devalue – and could take appropriate action in anticipation.
5   False: experience suggests that exchange rates can be sufficiently flexible to maintain PPP even in extreme conditions (see Section 34-4 of the main text).
6   True.
7   Not proved: see Section 34-6 of the main text.
8   Also not proved: tariffs were substantially dismantled through GATT under the adjustable peg. In the recession of the early 1980s there were moves towards protectionism under the managed float.
9   True: see Section 34-7 of the main text.
10  True: but only for those members of the EMS who were also participating in the ERM.
11  True: see Box 34-4 in the main text.

## ECONOMICS IN THE NEWS

1   The system is described in Section 34-5 of the main text: there is some further discussion in the above passage. It is essentially a form of commitment to a fixed exchange rate. If the central bank want to expand domestic money supply, they can only do so by expanding their reserves of foreign currency in line with the printing of domestic money. In the case of Hong Kong, such a system has been operating since the early 1980s, with the HK$ fixed in value against the US$.
2   Given such a system, adjustment to an external shock must come through an adjustment in the real economy. Thus the comment in the passage that Hong Kong has endured its worst recession in 40 years in the wake of the Asian financial crisis.
3   There is no definitive answer to this question, but we hope you enjoy debating it with your fellow students.

## Questions for Thought

1   This issue lies at the heart of the 'fixed v. floating' debate – can policy harmonization be achieved without the discipline of a fixed exchange rate regime?
2   These headings are used in the examination of fixed versus floating exchange rates in Section 34-5 of the main text. Some salient points are mentioned below.
    *(a)* Flexible rates are probably better at coping with real shocks. Flexible rates also cope with nominal shocks, but a fixed rate system may discourage the occurrence of such shocks (see *(b)*).

*(b)* Fixed rate systems force financial discipline upon countries, which must adopt domestic policies that keep their inflation rates in line with world rates. The discipline is lacking with a floating exchange rate, which is able to cope with variations in inflation rates between countries.

*(c)* Fixed rate systems by definition offer stability of exchange rates (except, of course, at the time of a devaluation), whereas under a flexible regime there may be day-to-day variability. Defenders of flexible rates point out that the volatility may find alternative expression in interest rates or tax rates.

*(d)* It is by no means clear whether protectionism is more likely under fixed or under floating exchange rates.

As far as assessing the UK's experience is concerned, we leave you to review the available evidence.

## Chapter 35   European Integration

## Important Concepts, Technical Terms and Initials

| | | | | | | | |
|---|---|---|---|---|---|---|---|
| 1 | *(h)* | 4 | *(a)* | 7 | *(k)* | 10 | *(g)* |
| 2 | *(c)* | 5 | *(e)* | 8 | *(j)* | 11 | *(l)* |
| 3 | *(i)* | 6 | *(b)* | 9 | *(f)* | 12 | *(d)* |

## Exercises

1 *(a)* This was certainly a key part of the 1992 reforms – indeed, many EU members had dismantled all controls much earlier.

   *(b)* This was also part of the reforms.

   *(c)* The harmonization of tax rates was seen as a desirable aspect of a single European market, but politically tricky to achieve. The 1992 reforms thus made provision for progress towards harmonization of tax rates.

   *(d)* This was part of the reforms, but some non-tariff barriers are subtle in nature, so enforcement could be a problem in some cases.

   *(e)* This is the wording used in the EC 'Directives' on trade and competition policies setting out the objectives for 1992.

   *(f)* This also is part of the reforms.

   *(g)* This was not part of the 1992 reforms.

2 Option *(d)* describes a tariff; all the other items are non-tariff barriers which have been used.

3 *(a)* The gradual depletion of the reserves of North Sea oil dilutes this argument.

   *(b)* This argument disappears as other EU members dismantle controls on capital movements.

   *(c)* The proportion of UK trade with other EU members has increased substantially since Britain's entry into the Community, so this argument becomes less powerful with time.

   *(d)* Look at what happened to the inflation rate in 1989/90.

   *(e)* It is argued that monetary policy is required as a short-term weapon against inflation to avoid the use of fiscal policy for this purpose. There is no definitive answer to whether this is a valid argument – it depends upon your evaluation of the consequences of fiscal management.

   *(f)* Time inevitably must dilute this argument.

4 Items *(a)*, *(c)*, *(d)*, and *(e)* are necessary characteristics of a monetary union; the others may be.

5 *(a)* Competitiveness will fall.

   *(b)* The loss in competitiveness will presumably lead to a reduction in the demand for exported goods.

   *(c)* Both output and employment are likely to be reduced.

(d) Adjustment will rely on the gradual restoration of competitiveness through changes in relative wage and price levels. Of course, this may take some time, and during the interim period the economy is likely to suffer from unemployment.

(e) The danger of adopting fiscal management is that it could lead to an increase in the inflation rate; this is what the Delors proposals were intended to avoid. A key question to consider is whether there are alternative ways of achieving the same objective.

(f) In the United States, an example of a monetary union, if one state suffers a temporary recession, the federal fiscal system will provide some automatic stabilization. See Section 35-5 of the main text for the full story.

6  (a) This is one of the benefits from the 1992 reforms.

(b) This was also part of the 1992 reforms: the hope was that transaction costs would be reduced by this move.

(c) The abolition of non-tariff barriers to trade (part of 1992) opened domestic industry up to intensified competition. Although this might be seen as a cost in the short run if it causes unemployment, the long-run effect should be beneficial.

(d) Monetary union will bring this loss of sovereignty, but hopefully the benefits of the union will be adequate compensation.

(e) A benefit of 1992.

(f) A benefit of 1992, although the extent to which labour mobility will be enhanced remains to be seen.

(g) This has been happening over the years in any case.

(h) Exchange rate certainty would come with monetary union – at least internally, rates would be fixed – but 1992 was also a step in this direction.

(i) An expected benefit of 1992.

(j) Monetary union is one way of establishing this, but not necessarily the only way.

(k) This is one possible result of a monetary union – see exercise 5.

(l) The establishment of a common currency is one way in which a monetary union could have the effect of reducing transaction costs, but notice that in principle it is possible to have a monetary union operating without a common currency.

(m) Both 1992 and European Monetary Union may be regarded as moves towards European integration – whether this is politically acceptable is to some extent a separate issue.

7  (a) A rate of interest as low as $r_1$ would be required if an income level of $Y_0$ were to be realised with the IS curve at $IS_A$.

(b) With the ECB committed to maintaining price stability via the interest rate, it is highly unlikely that the interest rate would be permitted to fall as far as $r_1$. Given that the country is said to be a small country within Euroland, its influence within the Union will be limited, and the country is not able to have a different interest rate from other countries within the system. So, this cannot be a solution. The only exception might be if all countries in the Union were also experiencing severe recession, so that the problem was seen to be a general one.

(c) In principle, the government could try to shift the position of the IS curve by use of fiscal policy, but this may be outlawed within the terms of the Union.

(d) It is still possible that the economy will get to $Y_0$, but it may take some time. If the economy is in recession but other countries are not, then it is likely that in time wages and prices will adjust, so that competitiveness begins to be restored. As this happened, imports into our country would fall, and exports would be stimulated. These effects would shift the IS curve to the right. Hopefully this would eventually take the country back to $IS_B$ and thus to $Y_0$. This is discussed in Section 35-5 of the main text.

8  See Section 35-4 of the main text for a more thorough discussion of these three alternatives. Of course, by the time you read this, events may be overtaking this question. You might then like to consider whether the best option has been selected!

9  (a) In the absence of the profit motive, a planner responsible for an industry will probably be concerned to demonstrate his or her skills by producing as much output as possible by whatever means necessary. This is a recipe for waste, and there is no guarantee that the output will actually be useful or appropriate. Output may at times be overstated for effect.

(b) Prices will be centrally fixed, but not necessarily with relative scarcity in mind. In many cases, prices will tend to be held at artificially low levels to create the impression that inflation is not a problem in the economy.

(c) This is straightforward: defence and industry will take highest priority, as consumers can wait – and queue.

(d) With prices held at artificially low levels, and consumers queuing for goods, there is of course a state of excess demand in the market.

(e) Incentives for managers are poor in the absence of proper signals to which they can react in their output decisions. Workers have little incentive to work hard, as they cannot obtain consumer goods in any case. This may perhaps exaggerate a little ... but perhaps not.

(f) If prices are to begin to reflect relative scarcity, they will naturally have to rise towards the equilibrium market levels...

(g) ...but this need not mean inflation. A once-for-all upwards adjustment in the price level is not the same as a persistent rise in the general level of prices, which is how we define inflation.

(h) The key is to have a firm and credible macroeconomic strategy that can avoid the spectre of hyperinflation, even at the cost of some short-term unemployment. See Section 35-6 of the main text for a fuller discussion.

(i) No comment.

## True/False

1  True: see Section 35-1 of the main text.
2  True.
3  Not quite accurate: the EU of 1993 had a population larger than either the United States or Japan.
4  False: tariffs were already outlawed before 1992.
5  Hopefully false: it is possible that such merger and takeover activity represents companies' attempts to restructure so as to be in a better position to exploit economies of scale and comparative advantage in the enlarged single market. Much will depend upon the strength and wisdom of European merger policy in the transition period and beyond.
6  True: see Section 35-4 of the main text.
7  False: Stage 3 involving EMU would only have begun in 1997 if a majority of the EU had been ready and willing to go at that time – which of course they were not! As you will be aware, 11 countries went ahead with the single currency in 1999.
8  True: see Section 35-5 of the main text.
9  False: the EU Structural Funds programme is not sufficient to fulfil that role.
10  True: see Section 35-5 of the main text.
11  True: see Section 35-6 of the main text. The plight of less developed countries is discussed in Chapter 36.
12  True, but Western governments have taken steps to reduce the burdens, for example by the establishment of the European Bank for Reconstruction and Development to finance market-oriented reforms.

## ECONOMICS IN THE NEWS 1

1  A number of factors may have influenced Japanese firms in choosing to locate in the UK. The skills of the labour force may have been a contributory factor, at least compared with some other parts of the world. The labour market in the UK is seen as reasonably flexible. Language considerations may also be relevant. If Japanese businessmen are experienced in dealing with companies in the USA, then being able to work in English rather than German or Portuguese may be a factor. However, of crucial importance is the wish to gain access to the European market.

2  It is this desire to tap the European market which is likely to be critical in forming Toyota's views about the single currency. The transactions costs of producing in Britain for export into Europe may be significantly different when comparing a Britain within rather than outside of the single currency area.

## ECONOMICS IN THE NEWS 2

1  The passage refers to the supply-side benefits that are likely to flow from membership of Euroland. It is no straightforward matter to evaluate how substantial these effects are likely to be. Table 35-3 in the main text highlights some of the potential gains from the Single Market measures. Arguably, the gains from membership of a single currency area may be more substantial, but much depends upon the degree of integration of the UK economy with the rest of Europe. Table 35-4 in the main text shows the extent to which the UK has become more dependent upon Europe in terms of its trade pattern, which has been transformed since 1972.

2  Again, it is difficult to evaluate this in practice. The past links of the ECB with the Bundesbank may suggest that the ECB will be pretty rigorous, but the Bank of England has also shown itself to be strongly committed to controlling inflation.

3  In recent years, the business cycle seems to have followed a rather different pattern from that in the rest of Europe, as was discussed in Section 35-4 of the main text. If this were to persist into the future, then there would be an argument in favour of retaining some independence to deal with the stabilization problem. Supporters of Euroland might argue that the differences might be ironed out in time, such that member countries would become so integrated that their pattern of business cycles would be harmonized.

4  This is clearly quite a close call, requiring a balancing of costs and benefits that cannot be precisely measured. We leave you to make up your own minds, and again hope that you enjoy debating this with your fellow students.

The full article by James Forder in the *Economic Review* is worth reading. It analyses these issues in more depth, albeit from the author's individual viewpoint. This in turn is based on James Forder and Christopher Huhne, *Both Sides of the Coin*, Profile Books, 1999.

## Questions for Thought

1  Some of the background to German attitudes may be found in Box 35-1 of the main text. The German concern with keeping inflation strictly under control has had a number of effects on the process of transition towards monetary union within the EU, as laid down in the Maastricht Treaty. Germany has also been influential in the operations of the ERM, where at times the German reluctance to cut interest rates has had widespread repercussions.

2  Some commentators have argued that the UK's entry into the ERM was delayed far too long, and that entry was at an inappropriate exchange rate against the DM, which was always going to be impossible to sustain. Speculative pressure then brought the premature exit. It is difficult to see successful transition towards EMU if the UK cannot survive within the ERM, but it could be that entering at an appropriate exchange rate would help. These issues remain contentious, however, and you are encouraged to read the relevant sections in Chapter 35 of the main text, and to come to your own conclusions about re-entry. The UK's exclusion from the ERM has already affected the chance of joining EMU, as one of the Maastricht criteria states that members should have been a member of the ERM without re-alignment for a period of two years.

3  Both discontent and envy probably had some part to play in the pressure for reform.

4  We recommend that you re-read Section 35-5 of the main text, which sets out the key characteristics of an optimal currency area. As you do so, think about the extent to which Euroland meets these conditions, and the extent to which the UK would share those characteristics. This will influence your views about whether Britain should enter Euroland.

# Chapter 36    Problems of Developing Countries

## Important Concepts and Technical Terms

| 1 | (d) | 4 | (i) | 7 | (f) | 10 | (a) |
|---|-----|---|-----|---|-----|----|-----|
| 2 | (c) | 5 | (k) | 8 | (h) | 11 | (g) |
| 3 | (e) | 6 | (l) | 9 | (b) | 12 | (j) |

## Exercises

1  See Table A36-1.

**Table A36-1    GNP per capita (US$ 1998), various countries**

| | |
|---|---|
| Low-income economies | |
| G  Burundi | 140 |
| C  Nepal | 210 |
| Lower middle-income countries | |
| E  Philippines | 1050 |
| A  Thailand | 2200 |
| Upper middle-income economies | |
| F  Mexico | 3970 |
| B  Argentina | 8970 |
| High-income economies | |
| H  United Kingdom | 21400 |
| D  United States | 29340 |

Normally, we would include as LDCs all low-income and middle-income countries.  Hopefully, this exercise will have illustrated the wide range of conditions represented under this definition.  It is easy to lose sight of this when we treat them together.  For more discussion along these lines, see Peter Smith 'Can we measure economic development?', *Economic Review*, February 1993.

2  (a)  Equilibrium price would have been $40 per unit and the buffer stock must buy up 75 (thousand) units to maintain price at $70.

(b)  Equilibrium price would have been $80 per unit.  The buffer stock sells 25 (thousand) units to maintain price.  The buffer stock now holds 50 (thousand) units.

(c)  The net additions to the buffer stock in the five years are 0, +50, +25, −50, +100.  Cumulative quantities held: 50, 100, 125, 75, 175.  The total cost of operating the buffer stock over the seven years amounts to $175000 \times 70 = \$12.25$ million – plus the costs of warehousing and storage.

(d)  Average supply over the period was 400 (thousand) units per annum; a price of $60 per unit would have kept the stock stable.  If the buffer stock continues to maintain the price at too high a level, stocks must build up in the long run, tying up precious resources.

3  (a)  With demand *DD1*, equilibrium price is *OA*, revenue is the area *OAKF*.

(b)  With *DD2*, equilibrium is *OC*, revenue is *OCMH*.

(c)  Quantity *OG*, revenue *OBLG*.

(d)  Buffer stock buys *EG*, revenue *OBLG*.

(e)  Buffer stock sells *GJ*, revenue *OBLG*.

4  See Table A36-2 overleaf.

The absolute difference between the two countries continues to widen, even though the low-income country is growing at a higher annual percentage rate.

**Table A36-2   Relative growth in low- and high-income countries**

| Period | GNP per capita Low-income country | GNP per capita High-income country | Absolute difference in GNP per capita |
|---|---|---|---|
| Initial | 380.0 | 8460.0 | 8080.0 |
| 1 | 391.0 | 8595.4 | 8204.3 |
| 2 | 402.4 | 8732.9 | 8330.5 |
| 3 | 414.0 | 8872.6 | 8458.6 |
| 4 | 426.0 | 9014.6 | 8588.5 |
| 5 | 438.4 | 9158.8 | 8720.4 |

5   The NICs included in the list are:
D   Singapore
F   Hong Kong
H   Republic of Korea
On the basis of these figures, country C (Sri Lanka) also seems to be following this path. Brazil (Country A) seemed at one point in time to be developing rapidly, but its success was gained before the 1980s. Brazil was adversely affected during the 1980s by debt and by inflation, while the East Asian NICs continued to prosper, although even they ran into occasional problems, most notably in he financial crisis of 1997. The other countries are Côte d'Ivoire (B), Uruguay (E), Jamaica (G), and Chile (I).

6   (a), (b), (c) and (f).

7   (a)   Clearly, comparative advantage will not lie with hi-tech manufacturing industries. More sensible might be labour-intensive activities, in particular primary production – either agriculture or mineral extraction.

   (b)   A problem with specializing in primary production is that there has been an historical tendency for the terms of trade to move against primary products, and for prices of such commodities to be highly volatile, as a result of fluctuations in either supply or demand.

   (c)   The 'infant industry' argument in favour of imposing tariffs has always been a tempting one: an LDC might hope that by imposing a tariff it would be possible to nurture new industries which would eventually be able to compete in world markets, after an initial period in which the country would save on imports. A problem has always been that the industry becomes over-protected, and never grows up. Import substitution tends to engender an inward-looking attitude on the part of domestic producers.

   (d)   Export promotion forces an outward-looking attitude on domestic producers. It has proved very successful for the NICs, but there is some doubt about whether the same route could be followed by all LDCs, especially given the increasingly protectionist attitude adopted by the industrial countries since the recession of the early 1980s.

8   (a)   It might be nice to imagine that donors act purely out of humanitarian motives, but realistically this seems unlikely. In 1997, only four countries in OECD (Norway, The Netherlands, Denmark and Sweden) reached the UN target for aid as a percentage of GNP, agreed back in the 1970s. Countries like the UK and the United States were giving a much smaller proportion in 1997 than in 1965. It seems more likely that donors are partly if not mainly motivated by self-interest.

   (b)   Many political motivations exist: donors may wish to preserve the ideology in which they believe, or to strengthen their own position in a region of the world. The changes in the geographical pattern of US aid flows in the postwar period are revealing.

   (c)   Much of aid is 'tied' aid. For instance, bilateral aid between countries may be based on an agreement that the recipient will purchase goods from the donor in the future, sometimes at prices above the competitive world prices for similar goods. Indeed, there is evidence that some countries regard aid as being part of trade policy.

(d) Political stability is important for development – and even more important for the government in power! There have been times when aid has been used to bolster the position of the government in power. At times this has involved the use of aid for 'prestige' projects, which may improve the image of recipient or donor but do little to promote development.

(e) The economic reasons for acceptance of aid by a poor country hardly need stating, but one potential problem is that the recipient country may find itself in a position of dependency. For instance, it might be that aid lowers the domestic incentives for saving, or even production, such that the LDC cannot break out of its reliance on other countries.

(f) It has often been argued that allowing LDCs to trade on fair terms with the rest of the world would have more beneficial effects than the simple granting of aid. This may be seen in particular in terms of the incentives for the LDC economy.

9 All of them. Item *(c)* is worth special mention: the increasing importance of bank loans relative to official aid is a significant feature of the international debt crisis.

10 In fact, the two countries are Sri Lanka (country A), and Cameroon (country B). In spite of its seemingly inferior development performance on every criterion in the table, Cameroon had a GNP per capita which is more than double that of Sri Lanka ($960 as compared with $470). This reinforces the view that GNP per capita may not always be a good indicator of the level of living achieved by the citizens of a country.

## True/False

1 True: see Section 36-1 of the main text.
2 True: see Section 36-2 of the main text.
3 Sometimes true: it takes time to develop work practices and the acceptance of factory working.
4 False: there are many problems with a heavy reliance on primary products (see Section 36-3 of the main text).
5 False: if demand and supply are relatively elastic, then price movements will tend to be small, even in the face of large demand or supply shocks. Draw a diagram to check it out.
6 False: this is too static a picture, which presumes that the pattern of comparative advantage cannot be changed over time (see Section 36-4 of the main text).
7 True.
8 True: see Section 36-5 of the main text.
9 A bit contentious: some LDCs have claimed that structural adjustment programmes have been too stringent, whereas some economists argue that there are times when it is necessary to dispense unpleasant medicine.
10 True: see Section 36-6 of the main text. Although true, however, it is also extremely unlikely.
11 True and false: more aid is necessary but not sufficient. Freer trade is also important.

## ECONOMICS IN THE NEWS

Having got this far, you should be able to cope with this evaluation without help from us!

## Questions for Thought

1 From the discussion of this chapter, it seems unlikely that LDCs can develop without the help (or at least the co-operation) of the rich countries. More difficult is the question of the form in which that help should come – aid, direct investment by multinationals, or freer trade? The focus of the second part of the question is on the consequences of default on international debt, which is often discussed mainly in terms of the effect on the international financial system.

2 In exploring this issue, you will need to draw upon material from a number of different parts of your economics course. For example, one of the arguments behind the insistence that countries follow structural

adjustment before qualifying for debt relief is based upon moral hazard. Countries may allow debt to build up in order to have it forgiven. Many commentators argued that this argument had been over-stated, and that six years was a long time to have to prove commitment. Others suggested that there were other ways of seeking to ensure that debt relief was channelled into appropriate policies. For example, in Uganda (the first country to qualify for relief under the HIPC initiative), funds were set aside for expenditure on primary education.

3   As you think about this question, you will need to think back through the whole of the book. You will need to consider the causes of market failure, and whether there are forms of market failure which may affect LDCs in particular. Some discussion of this will be found in Chapter 30, where we talked about the 'convergence hypothesis', and why it might not always work. You will also need to consider the various ways in which the policies adopted by industrial economies may affect LDCs. This will include consideration of trade policy (protectionism, etc). The pattern of the business cycle and the effects of interest rate policies may also be seen to impinge upon LDCs.

4   The distinction between normative and positive economics was made in the first chapter of the book, and it seems appropriate that we should return to it right at the end. In assessing the economic performance of different economies, and in particular in looking at the problems of LDCs, it is very easy to become emotional, and to allow value judgements to cloud our view of the economic issues. Being aware of this may serve to minimize its effect.